ROUTLEDGE LIBRARY EDITIONS:
PRISON AND PRISONERS

I0028234

Volume 8

ALBANY:
BIRTH OF A PRISON –
END OF AN ERA

ALBANY:
BIRTH OF A PRISON –
END OF AN ERA

ROY D. KING
AND
KENNETH W. ELLIOTT

Routledge
Taylor & Francis Group

LONDON AND NEW YORK

First published in 1977 by Routledge & Kegan Paul Ltd

This edition first published in 2024
by Routledge
4 Park Square, Milton Park, Abingdon, Oxon OX14 4RN

and by Routledge
605 Third Avenue, New York, NY 10158

Routledge is an imprint of the Taylor & Francis Group, an informa business

British Library Cataloguing in Publication Data
A catalogue record for this book is available from the British Library

ISBN: 978-1-032-55549-2 (Set)
ISBN: 978-1-032-56258-2 (Volume 8) (hbk)
ISBN: 978-1-032-56266-7 (Volume 8) (pbk)
ISBN: 978-1-003-43471-9 (Volume 8) (ebk)

DOI: 10.4324/9781003434719

Publisher's Note
The publisher has gone to great lengths to ensure the quality of this reprint but points out that some imperfections in the original copies may be apparent.

Disclaimer
The publisher has made every effort to trace copyright holders and would welcome correspondence from those they have been unable to trace.

Albany: birth of a prison – end of an era

Roy D. King
Department of Sociology and Social Administration
University of Southampton

and

Kenneth W. Elliott
Centre for Social Work and Applied Social Studies
University of Leeds

Routledge & Kegan Paul
London, Henley and Boston

First published in 1977
by Routledge & Kegan Paul Ltd
39 Store Street,
London WC1E 7DD,
Broadway House,
Newtown Road,
Henley-on-Thames,
Oxon RG9 1EN and
9 Park Street,
Boston, Mass. 02108, USA
Set in 10 on 12 Times 327
and printed in Great Britain by
Lowe & Brydone Ltd.

British Library Cataloguing in Publication Data

King, Roy David

Albany: birth of a prison, end of an era
(International library of social policy)
1. Albany Prison – History
I. Title   II. Elliott, Kenneth W.   III. Series
365' 9422'82   HV9648.A/   77-30157

ISBN 0 7100 8727 6

Contents

Preface   ix

Part I   Introduction to the study   1

1 Background and overview   3
   The old order changes   4
   Chronological overview   23

2 Doing research in prison   33
   Types of research role   36
   Conduct of the research at Albany   51
   Writing the report   63

Part II   Birth of a prison   65

3 A caravan in a meadow   67
   Planning and design of Albany   70
   Humane treatment and prison management   75
   Commissioning the prison   90

4 The emergent blue print   96
   The new management   97
   Social training   106
   Industrial training   113
   Security   119

5 The category-C regime   122
   Prisoners and staff in Albany   124
   The daily routine   128
   The state of social order   137

Part III   **The rise and rise of Albany fences**   147

     6   Consolidation, consistency and new priorities   149
         A new style of government   149
         The demise of social training   157
         Upgrading the security   167
         Industrial production   173

     7   The standard category-A regime   186
         The research programme   186
         The prisoner population and sample   193
         The staffing establishment and sample   199
         The regime   204

     8   Doing time in Albany Prison   226
         On doing time   226
         An evaluation of Albany   231
         Making out and getting by:
             strategies of prisoner response   235
         Making out and getting by:
             strategies of staff response   261
         Reactions to change   273

     9   The electronic coffin   281
         The events   282
         Interpretation   305

Part IV **Conclusions**   329

    10   The end of an era   331
         Research in prison   331
         Sociology of the prison   332
         Re-writing Prison Rule 1   335
         Prison administration   340
         The future of the dispersal policy   344

         Postscript   355

         Bibliography   360

         Index   365

Illustrations

between pages 114 and 115

1 Birth of a prison: site work in March 1965
  (Hawkins of Gosport)
2 Pedestrian entrance to Albany and new-style façade
  (Central Office of Information)
3 Architect's model of main prison complex
  (Hawkins of Gosport)
4 Simplified plan of main prison complex
5 Dining room (Syndication International Ltd)
6 Association room (Syndication International Ltd)
7 Tailoring shop (Syndication International Ltd)
8 Lord Stonham in a typical Albany cell
  (Syndication International Ltd)
9 Vehicular entrance to the prison
  (Syndication International Ltd)
10 Use of the A-hall Tannoy (Paterson's of Ryde)
11 Hall staircase and landing before installation of
  electronic locking (Paterson's of Ryde)
12 Hall staircase and landing after installation of
  electronic locking (Paterson's of Ryde)
13 Category-B security fences
14 New woodmill and carpentry shop (Central Office of
  Information)
15 Prison officers and dogs assemble during a security alert
  (Roger M. Smith of Cowes)
16 Prison yard after the 1972 August Bank Holiday
  search and lock-in (*The Times*)
17 Parkhurst prisoners demonstrating against Albany
  conditions, August 1972 (Roger M. Smith of Cowes)
18 Wives of prison officers demonstrating outside
  Albany in October 1973 (London Express News
  and Feature Services)
19 A fire alert at Albany in 1973 (Roger M. Smith of Cowes)
20 The security fence becomes a gunited wall (Jonathan Bayer)

Tables

7.1 Percentage age distribution of the sample
and Albany population: May 1969   195
7.2 Percentage distribution by marital status:
sample and population   196
7.3 Percentage distribution by current offence:
sample and population   197
7.4 Length of sentence: sample and population   197
7.5 Age in relation to length of current
sentence   198
7.6 Time served and time left to earliest date
of release   199
7.7 Discipline staff May 1968 and May 1969   199
7.8 Percentage age distribution of Albany
uniformed staff sample   201
7.9 Military service of uniformed staff in Albany   203
7.10 Contacts with specialist staff since reception
and during two months preceding interview   214
7.11 Staff-prisoner contact scores by halls   220
7.12 Frequency and quality of observed staff-
prisoner contacts during association   221
8.1 Evaluation of Albany: prisoners and
uniformed staff   233
8.2 Modes of adaptation by prisoner sample   258
8.3 Modes of adaptation by uniformed staff sample   273
9.1 Percentage distribution by current offence:
1969 and 1971   311
9.2 Percentage distribution by time left to
serve until EDR: 1969 and 1971   312

Preface

There can be few prisons in any country that have seen so many far-reaching changes in so short a space of time as Her Majesty's Prison Albany on the Isle of Wight. Planned and built as a medium-security establishment, it was intended to replace Dartmoor – a worthy enough aim that was defeated, like so many others, by the growth in the prison population. Even before Albany opened, its future became inextricably bound up with the controversy over the plans for a maximum-security unit in Britain's first attempt to concentrate long-term, high-security-risk prisoners. The top-security prison, at first anonymous, was to be built on the Albany barracks site; later as Vectis, and then as Alvington on a site to the north-west of Albany; but it was never built. When finally it was decided to disperse top-security prisoners instead of concentrating them in Alvington, Albany became a part substitute for it. At the opening ceremony in April 1967 Albany was hailed as a 'breakthrough', a 'new concept in prison accommodation', in which a number of enlightened experiments and innovations were to be introduced to provide a more 'dynamic and personal training' for recidivists. The atmosphere was understandably charged with expectation, and there was much in the programme that could be held to justify the hopes which were held out. But just five and a half years later, after an increasingly stormy series of incidents culminating in an alleged mass escape attempt and a riot, it had become known as the 'jail of fear' in which 'mafia groups' were said to 'terrorize' staff and prisoners alike.

It was tempting, of course, to write a sensational account of a notorious prison. We have tried to resist that temptation. Instead we have attempted to document and analyse some of the changes which happened at Albany in those five and a half years, and as far as possible to account for them. It is inevitably an incomplete account, but it is an account from which we think many lessons can be drawn, both for social research and for social policy in regard to prisons.

Most conspicuous among the changes at Albany, if only because they marked relatively sudden discontinuities in the ongoing social process, were the changes of governor: four governors in a little over six years. We were invited by the first of them, Mr Albert (David) Gould, to study the working of Albany in its initial period of settling down and to play an active role in advising on its development. For a variety of reasons, which we discuss in chapter 2, we did not adopt the kind of consultancy role that was envisaged; and we are only too conscious that we did not fulfil David Gould's original expectations. Instead we took advantage of what was at that time a unique opportunity and privilege: simply to observe a new prison over a sustained period with virtually unlimited access to staff, prisoners and documents throughout. Nevertheless David Gould continued to give us encouragement to complete our study, even after he had left the institution. And, true to his philosophy, he never tried to extricate us from the state of 'therapeutic anxiety' in which we frequently found ourselves.

We began work in Albany in May 1968. It might be thought that a research team directed by a member of the Parole Board for England and Wales, and headed in the field by a former police officer, would have difficulties in speaking to both sides of the moral divide in prisons. In fact we enjoyed an ease of contact and access, without of course using keys, that can rarely have been found in other institutional studies, and perhaps could only have been achieved in an institution such as Albany at that particular stage of its history. It would be arrogant to claim that we got to know the prison better than those who worked and lived there, even though we were frequently told that was the case by our respondents. There was much that we did not see, and we made no attempt to seek out and dwell on scandal. But we did get to know the prison in considerable depth and we saw its faults as well as its virtues. We think we were able to establish working relationships which were very nearly as satisfactory and satisfying to staff and prisoners as they were to ourselves. One measure of this is that in 1968, when we embarked on a more formal programme of interviewing, all of the 94 staff and 69 of the 72 prisoners approached participated fully. Another, more rewarding, measure is that some of the relationships built up at that time between members of the research team and staff and prisoners have been sustained over several years since the fieldwork was carried out.

Within three months of our entrance to Albany, the governor

was promoted and replaced by Captain Brian Howden, who not only willingly accepted the existence of an ongoing research project within his prison, but readily granted all of our frequent and enormously burdensome requests – even those that we made after we had officially left the prison. We stayed at Albany, off and on, for a total of fifteen months during his term of office and it is that period, therefore, that we know best. In September 1969 we left Albany to embark on a comparative study of prison regimes for which the work at Albany was to serve as a valuable pilot. But we were fortunate in being able to maintain contact with the prison on a more or less regular basis long after that. Again it is a reflection of the strength of the relationships established that whenever any member of the team returned to the prison he was welcomed back in spite of what must have seemed the inordinate length of time before any of our 'results' materialized.

We first began to write up our Albany experience in the summer of 1971; but by that time it was clear that Albany had become a very different establishment from that we had first entered three years earlier. It had begun to receive top-security prisoners in October 1970, and already a number of incidents of arson and indiscipline had been reported in the Press. Moreover, for the second time in its short history, Albany's governor was moved on and Brian Howden was replaced by Mr Gifford Footer in May 1971. In July that year we initiated new contacts with the prison, which were maintained on a reduced and intermittent basis through 1972. It is a testament both to the change in attitudes towards research within the prison service in general, and to the open-mindedness of the late Mr Footer that one of us (KWE) was allowed to return to the prison so long after our original programme had been completed, and at a time when Albany was becoming the focus of adverse publicity. It was not possible to make any systematic study of the prison in its new circumstances and we did not try to. We were given access to files and documents, however; and at the end of this period we were able to conduct a few interviews using the same schedules that we employed in 1969. In the light of our earlier experience we discussed the changes that had taken place with both staff and prisoners. Our comments on this phase of Albany's existence should thus be seen as a necessary rounding out of a process that had begun much earlier. During our writing up we learned that Mr Footer had died in post, shortly before his tour of duty was due to end. He was replaced by Mr Tom Carnegie.

In writing up such a study as this, when a single institution is the subject of a detailed investigation over a long period, the usual guarantees of anonymity count for little. We have not mentioned anybody other than the governors by their own names, and we have protected uniformed officers and prisoners by providing false names and occasionally by changing minor identifying details. However, in discussing particular decisions or issues it is difficult to avoid the influence of personalities, and no amount of disguise could prevent the identification of the holders of key posts. In the course of our research therefore we gave the following undertakings: that we would show a pre-publication draft to the governor or his nominated representative; to the local branch committee of the POA; to representative prisoners, who could be selected or elected in whatever way seemed appropriate at the time; and to anybody else from the prison who could make a reasonable case for seeing it. We offered to discuss any points which were raised, and to make necessary amendments only if we could be convinced that what we had said was inaccurate or misleading, or potentially damaging to any identifiable individual who was not prepared to take that risk. We assured our respondents, who were sometimes fearful of Home Office interference, that we would take the same approach to any points raised by the Prison Department or by the Home Office Research Unit. We reiterated that the ultimate responsibility for publication must be ours.

It remains for us to pay our debts to those people and institutions who, in one way or another, not only made this research possible but also made it a most enjoyable and rewarding experience. First we must thank our colleagues at the University of Southampton, John Smith and John Martin, who lent support, encouragement and advice whenever it was needed. We cannot adequately do justice to the contribution of Robin Williams and Rodney Morgan, who shared with us the whole experience of the research virtually from its inception. They did not share in the writing because they moved on to the Universities of Durham and Bath and to other things. But the merits of our work owe as much to them as to us.

It would be invidious for us to attempt to single out the names of persons who were involved in the study. It must be clear from our report that we enjoyed more willing co-operation from our respondents than researchers have any right to expect. To officials at Prison Department and members of the Home Office Research Unit, to the successive governors of Albany, to the members of the central management team, to the uniformed officers and their representatives on the POA, to the non-uniformed staff, and to the prisoners, all of whom helped us so much in so many ways, we therefore say a collective thank you, and express the hope that our, and their, efforts will be thought to have been worth while.

Roy King would particularly like to thank the Ford Foundation for the award of a Fellowship which enabled him to spend a year commuting between the Law School and the Sociology Department at Yale. Discussions there with Al Reiss, Stanton Wheeler, Franklin Zimring and Dan Freed were never less than stimulating, and each of them may recognize some of the points we discussed in this book. Rotha Lane in the Sociology Department at Yale bore the burden of typing the first draft with great good humour. Several people read the whole or parts of that draft. First there were those to whom we gave the undertakings mentioned above, and whose reactions we discuss in a brief postscript. Second, there were official representatives of the Home Office, including the Research Unit. Finally, John Martin and Terence Morris provided specially helpful comments and criticisms, many of which have led to revisions and improvements in the structure of the text. We alone are responsible for the faults which remain, but we are grateful to all those who took so much time and trouble to read and comment on our work. We also thank our editor, Peter Hopkins, for his patience and forbearance during the long interval which separated the first and final drafts while we absorbed the reactions of friends and colleagues.

When the Department of Sociology at Southampton reappraised secretarial duties so that the typing of manuscripts for books was assigned the lowliest priority, Amy Elliott stepped into the breach to type the final draft. In doing so she set a standard for speed and accuracy that must be the dream of all authors and subeditors. To Amy and Janet, as well as to Simon and Matthew who did not even exist when this work began, we owe special thanks: they all contributed to its completion. During the correction of proofs we learned, with great sadness, of the death of Brian Howden.

December 1976   R.D.K. Southampton
                                            K.W.E. Leeds

Part I

Introduction to the study

1 Background and overview

In this monograph we tell the story of Her Majesty's Prison Albany on the Isle of Wight. The account begins in April 1967 when Albany was formally opened with a blaze of publicity by the late Lord Stonham. It was a semi-secure prison for difficult but not dangerous recidivists, and was described by its first governor as being about as safe as a caravan in a meadow. It was a training prison intended to provide training of a dynamic and personal kind, and its methods were widely reported to be revolutionary. It was a showpiece prison, much displayed and much visited. Fittingly the relationships between staff and prisoners were generally recognized as about the best to be found in any English prison for adult males. The account ends just six and a half years later at the end of 1973. By then the prison had changed out of all recognition. Through a massive programme of strengthening and up-grading it had become one of the most secure prisons in the land, and it accommodated many prisoners who were regarded as among the most dangerous in the system. The training programme had collapsed to such a degree that one member of the management team could describe the institution as little more than an electronic coffin. Co-operative relationships had been undermined by intimidation among the prisoners and disputes among the staff. As incident succeeded incident, so the tension mounted and confrontations were the order of the day. For prisoners no less than staff, to use the headlines of the Press, the famous prison of the future had become the notorious jail of fear.

It is a dramatic and tragic story of the decline in social order of one prison, which in one way or another directly affected several hundreds of participants. But it is also much more than that. The beginning and the end of our account are arbitrary cutting points, set by the limits of our fieldwork and the exigencies of preparing a report. In reality the story begins much earlier and has no definitive end. Albany still exists, and no doubt by the time this is read it will again be a different prison. We hope that nothing we say here will make it more difficult for today's staff and prisoners, or tomorrow's staff and prisoners, to find ways of coping with the difficult situation they inherit. But most of the events we describe in this volume, or events very like them, have occurred in other prisons also, and the ramifications of the policy decisions that led to them have been experienced throughout the prison system of England and Wales. What happened at Albany in these traumatic years points up what has happened in the prison system as a whole. There are lessons to be learned from the scars and the bruises. We hope that in the analysis provided in this book we shall have something of interest to say to many people: to prison officials and to prisoners, to criminologists and other scholars interested in the sociology of the prison and the experience of imprisonment, to those responsible for the making of penal policy and anyone concerned that what is done in their name is both rational and humane, and to all those members of the public who are curious to know what goes on behind the headlines and behind prison walls.

In this opening chapter we try to set out some of the changes in prison policy which gave birth to Albany and which later shaped its growth. And since the story is a complex one we provide a chronological overview of events which may serve as a reference point for the account which follows.

The old order changes
The years since the Second World War have been momentous ones for the prison service. For fifty years it had tried to implement the proposals of the Gladstone Committee of 1895 that 'prison discipline and treatment should be more effectually designed to maintain, stimulate or awaken the higher sensibilities of prisoners, to develop their moral instincts, to train them in orderly and industrial habits, and whenever possible to turn them out of prison better men and women physically and morally than when they came in' (c.7702, 1895, para. 25). It tried to do so within a framework of institutions designed and built before the advent of the Prison Commission in 1877, and on which Sir Edmund Du Cane, the first chairman, had imposed a centralized uniform pattern of management and a brutalizing and punitive regime (Cross, 1971). Scant progress was made under Du Cane's successor, Ruggles-Brise, whose efforts were directed at holding 'the balance between what is necessary as punishment . . . and what can be conceded, consistently with this, in the way of humanizing and reforming influences' (Prison Commission, 1912, p. 27). This

was followed by nearly a quarter of a century under the influence of Paterson, the first commissioner to be appointed from outside the prison service or the Home Office. A missionary zealot, he provided that special blend of compassion and arrogance so long the hallmark of English public service. Though never the chairman, he brought many fine phrases and some real changes in an attempt to reconcile his paradox of training people for freedom in conditions of captivity (Cross, 1971). But by the early post-war years there was still no very clear conception of the end state towards which the service was moving, no detailed specification as to how the Gladstone ideals would or could be achieved. In a service peopled at the top by gentlemen and amateurs the best that had been done was to incorporate the heady statement that 'The purpose of training and treatment of convicted prisoners shall be to establish in them the will to lead a good and useful life on discharge, and to fit them to do so' as Rule 6 of the Prison Rules (S.I. 1949, 1073). That statement was only slightly modified upon promotion to Rule 1 in 1964, and still governs current prison practice (S.I. 1964, 388).

Without well-defined objectives or ways of knowing whether they had been accomplished there was nevertheless a well-meaning and paternalistic commitment on the part of the commissioners to a process of liberalization and reform. While some of the ideas may have seemed adventurous to a public conditioned to believe in the danger in their midst, the resulting measures were usually well within conservative limits of good order and discipline. There appears to have been little expectation of, and perhaps no real pressure for, major capital expenditure to carry through radical changes to the system. Meanwhile in the prisons, so long as there was no scandal, the governors administered their establishments with something like the authority of eighteenth-century naval captains and with much the same procedures. However, they navigated not with charts and compass, but in response to local currents and more distant groundswells and the occasional directive from the flagship.

With the growth in crime figures after the war and the consequent pressures on the prisons the service grew from 40 establishments in 1946 to 73 in 1958. Most notable among the developments of this period was the bringing into service of nearly a dozen military camps as open prisons, following the successful pre-war establishment of open borstals and the building of New

Hall Camp in 1936. Tentative steps were taken in the classification of prisoners and the diversification of prisons. This was partly in response to the search for a more scientific basis for dealing with offenders, and partly to take account of the new schemes of preventive detention and corrective training introduced under the Criminal Justice Act, 1948. Preventive detention and corrective training were soon to prove abortive as ways of dealing with persistent offenders, but the principle of differentiated prison regimes was established. Educational facilities were provided in all prisons. Psychiatry and psychology were applied to the problems of diagnosis and treatment. More systematic attention was given to rehabilitation and aftercare. All of which sounds fine in the language of annual reports, although in reality, as anyone acquainted with the system knows, these schemes amounted to little enough. Gradually, however, it was realized that a more comprehensive approach was required, in which the success of the system in reaching its declared objectives should be assessed, and the ideas and resources of the service reappraised, preparatory to further advance. This view was reinforced by the renewed growth in the numbers of crimes known to the police from the mid 1950s.

The first fruit of that reappraisal was the white paper, *Penal Practice in a Changing Society* (Cmnd 645, 1959), generally attributed to Sir Lionel Fox, who had been chairman of the Prison Commission since 1942. In one sense, *Penal Practice* represented a watershed in British penal thinking. For the first time it placed the major emphasis on the need for research into the causes of crime, and for a professional and external examination of the effectiveness of the various forms of treatment. It looked forward to the foundation of the Institute of Criminology at Cambridge and it provided the mandate for the opening up of prisons to social research. It also called for a more fundamental review of penal philosophy and the practice of punishment: a review which was finally started, though never completed, by the Royal Commission on the Penal System 1964-6, after a further white paper, *The War Against Crime* (Cmnd 2296, 1966) had renewed the request. But in other respects *Penal Practice* firmly maintained its links with the past. Its call for professionalism was limited to the field of research and to the processes of diagnosis, classification and treatment of offenders. In this it represented the final attempt to get to grips with the aspirations of the Gladstone Committee. And the expressed hope that prisoners would co-operate 'willingly in their training' (para. 95), given the right 'team spirit' (para. 97) and 'training in case work' (para. 99) among the staff, was reminiscent of much that Paterson had said about borstals before the war.

The most important contribution of the white paper, however, was the building programme which it ushered in. Pride of place went to the new psychiatric prison at Grendon Underwood, in which a psychotherapeutic regime was to be established for suitably identified cases. As well as more open prisons Fox called for several new closed prisons to provide about 1,800 places where recidivists with medium-length sentences would receive the kind of training which could not be provided in the overcrowded local prisons. And to aid in the process of selection and classification he advocated the setting up of sufficient remand and diagnostic centres to accommodate all adult untried prisoners and all convicted prisoners who required observation before being classified. Such a programme, he hoped, would enable the local prisons to be re-built and to assume a training function for shorter-sentence prisoners. In his desire for a system based on careful observation, accurate diagnosis and classification, and appropriate training, Fox had been influenced by the 1951 UN-WHO seminar on the micro-psychological and social examination of offenders (Klare, 1964); and there is little doubt that *Penal Practice* represents the most optimistic official expectations of applying positive science in penology.

Little came of Fox's plans for the diagnostic and observation centres (only Risley was built), and nothing of those to re-build the local prisons. But the new closed prisons appeared in quick succession. Everthorpe had already been completed by the time the white paper was published. It had been greeted with a storm of architectural criticism (Fairweather, 1961) for retaining in its cavernous halls the least useful features of nineteenth-century design. After Everthorpe a new design team was set up with a brief to break down the old structure of the landing and the wing found in radial-style prisons, in a way that would allow a different pattern of staff-prisoner relationships to develop. The new blue print, with a series of linked but separate halls each of which was divided into smaller units, was first tried out at Blundeston in 1963, to be followed, with modifications, at Stoke Heath (1964), Gartree (1966), Albany (1967) and Coldingley (1969). Some of the new features were incorporated at Hindley, which was already under construction and was completed in 1961 (Peterson, 1961a). But

Hindley, like Everthorpe and Stoke Heath, was immediately appropriated for use as a borstal.

Whether or not the new design could be regarded as 'a realization in modern terms of the requirements of treatment in secure conditions', as the new chairman of the commissioners claimed (Peterson, 1961b), two features of the thinking behind it deserve special mention because one was soon to be abandoned and the other was to become a matter of dispute. First, the main security was to be in the buildings themselves and not in the perimeter: there were to be no high walls, only modest fences (Peterson, 1961a). Second, security should not be 'excessive having regard to the purpose for which the establishment is intended' (Peterson, 1961a). In passing we may note that experience at Albany and elsewhere has shown that to break down the structure of the landing and the wing so that the whole prison can no longer be kept under surveillance by one officer standing at the centre creates serious problems for supervision, in spite of the apparent attention given to this by the design team (Peterson, 1961a).

It is of considerable importance, in the light of subsequent events, that among the priorities of the future building programme announced in the white paper was a high-security prison for dangerous prisoners serving long sentences, and a commitment to the complete re-building of Dartmoor, which was approaching the end of its serviceable life (para. 91).

But in retrospect, and perhaps to a few observers at the time, the truly remarkable thing about *Penal Practice in a Changing Society* was that it expected that its aims could be achieved by new building and staff training, and without major overhaul of the creaking administrative structure and unwieldy procedures which had grown up over three quarters of a century. Its concern for science and professionalism was directed solely to understanding the causes of crime and finding better ways of treating it, not at all with the management of the prison system itself and the control of the establishments which make it up.

All this was to change dramatically in the 1960s and the early 1970s. Two concepts came to dominate the service: perimeter security and modern management. It would be to misunderstand the nature of the service to suppose that the dilemma of training for freedom in conditions of captivity had been either resolved or abandoned. But until the old Prison Commission was merged into the Home Office as the Prison Department in 1963 it seemed that the service had progressed towards its own conception of treatment and training by trying to pretend that captivity was not there, or at least that the outdated conditions of captivity with which the service was saddled were an unfortunate hindrance to more high-minded pursuits. After a brief transitional period such a stance became increasingly untenable. By 1968 it had become clear that captivity was a central and problematic task in itself, requiring strategic planning and rational management. If anything else could be accomplished in the way of treatment and training, well and good; and what might be accomplished within the new emphasis, or so it seemed, was a semblance of real economic activity.

In not much more than half a decade the prison system underwent a process of evolution that at times bordered on mutation. In security and control, men with keys performing ill-defined roles were replaced by a combination of men, dogs and electronics in an explicit pursuit of perimeter defence, internal control and supervision hitherto unknown in the UK. In communication, the era of the quill pen and the field telephone gave way to the UHF radio and the teleprinter. In industry, the avowed acceptance of the goal of efficiency yielded workstudy, incentive earnings schemes, a specially designed industrial prison and, eventually, the claim that prison industries were running at a profit (though it has to be remembered that few prisoners yet earn more than one pound a week). And in central and local administration, management by fiat was subjected to protracted and painful review, from which has emerged something like management by objectives accompanied for the first time by a small measure of decentralization and a streamlined headquarters organization.

Apart from considerations of policy, three cataclysmic series of events in English criminal and penal history forced the changes and then set seal to them. First, there emerged a new class, or classes, of long-sentence prisoners. They ranged from sophisticated and large-scale thieves, through violent and ruthless underworld gang members and racketeers, to a variety of amateur and professional spies; and later, as the impact of the abolition of the death penalty was realized, they included a group of child- and police-murderers for whom the life sentence might have to mean just that. Whether any of these prisoners really represented a new class of criminal is not at issue: the point is that they were almost universally regarded as such and were sentenced accordingly.

Second, it became evident that the prison system was hopelessly ill-equipped to deal with or even contain such prisoners, as some of them quickly escaped or were 'sprung' with a panache that overshadowed even their original crimes. Last, but by no means least, the prison population continued its generally upward post-war trend. In spite of temporary abatements in the early 1950s, the early 1960s and again in 1968, an unprecedented leap of more than 4,000 extra prisoners between 1969 and 1970 could only reinforce the need for rational planning and for greater co-ordination within what seemed to be an ever-growing system.

Although the real pressures for change came from outside the service, some developments in the system were already emerging either as a result of the same process of reappraisal that produced *Penal Practice* or as a direct response to the changing circumstances. As early as 1961 a special unit was set up at Durham Prison to deal with recalcitrant prisoners and escapers; and, as we have mentioned, a security prison for long-term prisoners was in the future programme of the 1959 white paper. By the beginning of 1966 special wings were set up at Leicester and Parkhurst to hold high-risk long-sentence prisoners, and the Durham unit assumed a similar function. Prison Department officials made visits to maximum security prisons in the USA, West Germany and Sweden, and our own top-security prison planned for the Isle of Wight was in the design stage. The works directorate was said to be testing electronic and televisual devices. A series of reports from the Advisory Council on the employment of prisoners culminated in 1964 with a demand for sweeping changes in the organization of prison industries, which was accepted by successive governments. In 1964 also the seeds of a regional structure were planted in the new Prison Department with the establishment of a northern office in Manchester; and a management studies unit at the staff college introduced management courses for staff. By July 1966 a joint Home Office and Treasury working party on organization and methods had reported on the scope for management services in prisons. But these developments were piecemeal and, while often imaginative, were pursued with little or no confidence. Such changes as were made were not systematically followed up, and they had scarcely any impact on the system as a whole.

The single event which was responsible for the belated wrenching of the prison system into the second half of the twentieth century, the catalyst that produced the reaction required for accelerating change, was the escape of George Blake from Wormwood Scrubs on the evening of Saturday, 22 October 1966. Two days later Earl Mountbatten of Burma was appointed by Roy Jenkins, the Home Secretary, to enquire into this and other escapes and to make recommendations for the improvement of prison security. Just how far – and how fast – the process would have gone without the benefit of a public inquiry we shall never know. But the evidence presented by Mountbatten in his report of December 1966 (Cmnd 3175) suggests that progress to that date had been slow.

Scandals occur in the best-regulated of institutions; and the history of prisons, mental hospitals and similar establishments in western society has been punctuated by exposures, inquiries and attempts to reform, only for the cycle to repeat itself. But though it was couched in restrained terms and was careful to avoid apportioning blame, there can scarcely ever have been such a devastating critique of the effectiveness of a system in respect of its most essential function as that contained in the Mountbatten report. The evidence adduced by Mountbatten, the central findings and recommendations are well known: that there was no really secure prison in the country (para. 14); that prisoners should be classified into four categories, A, B, C, and D in descending order of their security risk, and sent to prisons suitable for their containment (para. 217); that to this end the new maximum-security prison planned for the Isle of Wight, for which he suggested the name Vectis, should be built with all possible speed and with even stronger perimeter defences, to house category-A prisoners (paras 212, 215); that a second such prison should be built in due course if required (para. 214); and that up-to-date security aids including dogs should be deployed, and staff trained in their use (paras 232, 295).

What may be worth recording here, in support of the argument that the report accelerated change, are Mountbatten's comments on related matters and especially on the administration at head-quarters and local levels. Concerned at the need for inspection of prisons, he noted that 'instructions from Head Office are issued without sufficient regard to the manner in which governors are expected to implement them and without sufficient steps being taken to check that the instructions are being effectively carried out in practice'; and 'governors are too inclined to pass on instructions from the Head Office to their subordinate staff without ensuring that the machinery for carrying them out exists' (para. 241). Later he frankly comments that the 'Head Office has clearly to some extent lost touch with the establishments under its control' and that 'the present structure does not enable the Department to do much to resolve the difficulty' (para. 244). Mountbatten had seen the joint Treasury and Home Office O and M report on the scope for management services in prisons, with whose analysis of the old-fashioned administrative arrangements inside prisons he substantially agreed. He also knew that the Prison Department was calling in expert advice (in the form of management consultants) to make proposals for putting right the defects. But he none the less went out of his way to recommend 'not only that the existing studies should be prosecuted vigorously but that their progress should be regularly reviewed at the highest level, and that as soon as a broad outline of recommendations is completed a definitive time table for the introduction of improvements should be laid down and steps taken to see that it is adhered to' (para. 256) – which is presumably a measure of his fear that reports, once completed, all too easily only gather dust. He exerted much the same kind of pressure, for presumably much the same kind of reason, about staffing. Noting that work was being carried out within the Home Office to assess the staff complement required for various kinds of establishment, he recommended that 'the study should be pursued vigorously, and that a decision should be taken *now* to fix "realistic" establishments for all institutions and for the Prison Service as a whole' (para. 219, emphasis supplied). As if it did not have enough to contend with, the Prison Department was soon on the receiving end of a major review by the House of Commons Estimates Committee, whose eleventh report was presented in July 1967. The committee endorsed Mountbatten's criticism of the relations between headquarters and the prisons, and called for a job evaluation of the governor grade and the speeding up of the process of regionalization.

Almost since the Mountbatten report was issued, and certainly since the effects of the Prison Department review of security arrangements were first felt, it has been fashionable (for nearly everybody except the Prison Officers' Association) to criticize it on the grounds, either that the inquiry and the recommendations provided a panic response to a panic situation, or that the Admiral of the Fleet had no qualifications for the job, or that the recommendations set the service back a decade or more in the process of liberalizing the prisons (Fowler, 1967; I. Taylor, 1968; S. Cohen and L. Taylor, 1972; I. Taylor *et al.*, 1975; Klare, 1975). In our view none of these criticisms is well founded. While it is true, as both Mountbatten and the Prison Department pointed out, that the number of escapes had not risen bearing in mind the increases in prison population, the quality of escapes had changed. Since the escape of Blake (serving 42 years) followed the escape of the train robbers, Wilson (serving 30 years) in 1964 and Biggs (30 years) in 1965, as well as a number of dramatic incidents in 1966, it could be argued that the enquiry was long overdue. That there was also urgency was evidenced by the fact that Blake escaped before the new precautions, devised after an escape by six prisoners from the same hall four months earlier, could be put into effect; that Frank Mitchell absconded from the honour party at Dartmoor during the course of the Mountbatten investigation; and that a flurry of escapes accompanied the publication of the report just before Christmas 1966. As to the second criticism, it is difficult to know what qualifications, in a technical sense, would have been appropriate for the job; certainly there is nothing in the analysis by Mountbatten of the essential problem of keeping prisoners in prison to show that he had in any sense misunderstood his brief. No one reading the report could fail to recognize the obvious defects in the security arrangements which he pointed out, or that his recommendations would substantially solve the security problem. Finally, there are several reasons for thinking that the judgment that Mountbatten had set the service back was unfair; and these deserve some discussion.

First, Mountbatten made it clear, both at the time and later, that he was aware of this danger and that he did not want it to happen: 'I consider that the modern policy of humane, liberal treatment aimed at rehabilitating prisoners rather than merely exacting punishment is right, and that escapes should be prevented by far better perimeter security' (para. 14); 'Nothing which I say subsequently in my Report is intended to suggest a reversal of the trend towards treatment in open conditions. On the contrary . . . many more prisoners now in closed conditions could be transferred to open conditions without danger' (para. 208); 'there is clearly room within the prison system for outside working parties with varying degrees of supervision' (para. 195); 'hostels within prison walls should not be closed before alternative premises can be found' (para. 304); and in an interview following his famous address at York in 1971 Mountbatten is quoted as saying, 'the last thing I wanted to do was to reduce rehabilitation projects in prisons', and 'the sooner it is publicly acknowledged that security measures should not be allowed to interfere with the progress of rehabilitation planning, the better it will be for the prison population, on both sides of the bars' (Mountbatten, 1972).

Second, most of the recommendations which Mountbatten made, including the most important one for a maximum-security prison which was never in fact implemented, were very broadly in line with existing policy, as both he and the Prison Department took care to point out. What Mountbatten did was to try to accelerate the implementation of that policy and to ensure that it was pursued with a vigour, determination and professionalism that had not been customary in the past. Perhaps it is not surprising that the Prison Department, so lately under public scrutiny and attacked not just for its security defects but for its out-of-date administrative structure, should have adopted a 'no risk' policy immediately. And it is perhaps equally unsurprising that Prison Department, caught on the horns of a dilemma with the demands of the Press on the one hand and reformers on the other, tried very hard to face both ways at once, as the following contradictory statements in successive annual reports show.

> Preoccupation with these urgent and far-reaching measures inevitably had a profound effect on the working of prison service establishments. Staff who had long been encouraged to develop treatment relationships towards prisoners had little time left for this important work after discharging tasks arising from the need to concentrate on security. There was some curtailment of prisoners' activities, a reduction in the number of outside working parties and of educational classes. Hostels at Cardiff, Chelmsford and Wandsworth were closed (Cmnd 3774, 1968, p. 5).

> When the position was reviewed in Autumn 1968 it was found that in the great majority of prisons the educational and other facilities had either been unaffected by the actions following the Mountbatten Report or had since been restored to normal. The small number of prisons which had not been able to resume all their former activities, for example outside activities, were still able to pursue a satisfactory programme (Cmnd 4186, 1969, p.5).

Whatever the truth of these matters, it was clearly the view of Mountbatten at the time of his York speech that his report had been made the pretext for security precautions which would have been unnecessary had the main recommendation of his inquiry, the building of Vectis by June 1969, been implemented. He was thus giving confirmation to views widely canvassed at that time that many prisoners were now housed in conditions far more secure than they required – in effect, that the principle that security should not be 'excessive having regard to the purpose for which the establishment is intended' had been neglected. In 1966 he had described the conditions in the temporary wings as such that 'no country with a record of civilized behaviour ought to tolerate any longer than is absolutely essential as a stop-gap measure' (para. 212). There is no doubting his disillusion, five years later, when he remarked: 'Unfortunately the rejection of my advice has proved that nothing is as permanent as the temporary' (Mountbatten, 1972).

Third, it should not be forgotten that Mountbatten was also largely responsible for pushing through the long-overdue improvements in the career structure for prison officers (paras 224-30), although here too he was to receive further support from the Estimates Committee. Or that among other things he came down firmly against the arming (para. 214), in favour of more frequent and more regular home leave (para. 324), and urged the consideration of 24-hour family contacts for prisoners whose leave would present a threat to security (para. 325).

The main reason why the security wings, in spite of all the adverse publicity they had received since their inception, had remained in existence for so long – the wing at Durham was closed in August 1971, while Chelmsford, which had not opened until late in 1968, was closed in February 1972, by which time it was said there were only some 20 prisoners in the special wings at Parkhurst and Leicester (Cmnd 5037, 1972, para. 151) – was because of a radical change of policy in respect of category-A prisoners. Only two months after the presentation of the Mountbatten report the Home Secretary invited the Advisory Council on the Penal System to consider the regime for long-term prisoners in conditions of maximum security, and a sub-committee was appointed under Professor Radzinowicz for this purpose. The sub-committee could hardly consider the regime for long-term prisoners without considering the environment within which it was to be provided, so the whole question of the new maximum-security prison, now renamed Alvington by the Home Office, was re-opened. The main recommendations of the sub-committee are again well known: that there needed to be an increase in the 'co-efficient of security' in closed prisons (Advisory Council, 1968, para. 45); that category-A prisoners should not be concentrated in a single maximum-security prison but be dispersed among (para. 62), and from time to time transferred between (para. 154), a number of secure prisons; that there should be a liberal regime within a secure perimeter (para. 48), which would include observation towers (para. 53) manned by armed officers (para. 61); and that there should be the possibility of moving recalcitrant prisoners into specially constructed segration units within each prison (para. 164). They were endorsed with the exception of the one relating to firearms, on which the sub-committee was in any case divided, by the Advisory Council and substantially accepted by a new Home Secretary, James Callaghan. Even so, the Council admitted that the dispersal policy would result in a marginally lower degree of security and that some members of the Council were 'not entirely convinced that some form of concentration might not be the right solution' (p. v).

The new policy was generally welcomed by the Press and informed opinion, especially once it became clear that guards would not be armed, although ironically, on the very day the report was published, the prisoners in the Durham special wing went on hunger strike. *The Times*, in an editorial on 3 April 1968, thought it was worth gambling on the dispersal proposals as the more constructive choice over concentration, and Klare (1968) substantially agreed with that view. Morris (1968) balanced the arguments in favour of concentration, but felt that if the Prison Department studied the details of the Radzinowicz report trouble might yet be avoided in the prisons. Hall Williams (1970) simply took the view that time alone would tell which report was right. In recent years, and especially since the emergence of such organizations as Radical Alternatives to Prison and Protection of the Rights of Prisoners and the prison disturbances of 1971 and 1972, some writers such as Thomas (1972, 1974) have added their voices to that of the POA, which opposed the dispersal policy from the outset (Castell, 1968).

We shall frequently have to refer to the effects of the dispersal policy in the course of our analysis of the situation at Albany; and we may as well say here that we think that the evidence presented in this monograph points to the conclusion that the policy has been both needlessly disruptive and excessively traumatic for staff and prisoners, and so far at least largely ineffective. We shall return to the matter of staff in our final chapter. But since such a radical departure from the central conclusion of Mountbatten was advocated by the Radzinowicz sub-committee, with such far-reaching consequences as a result, it is worth drawing attention to some of the consequences of the two reports here.

Two of the most obvious differences between the Mountbatten report and the Radzinowicz report were the scope of the inquiries and the speed with which they were carried out. Earl Mountbatten was appointed on 24 October 1966; he and his assessors visited some 17 establishments in this country and took oral and written evidence from a formidable range of interested parties and organizations. The report was published within 59 days. The admittedly part-time Radzinowicz sub-committee met for the first time on 13 March 1967, nearly a month after the matter was referred to the Advisory Council. They visited only six prisons and one special hospital in this country, although a large part of the inquiry involved visiting several institutions in Denmark, Sweden, West Germany, France and the United States of America. They took evidence from an equally formidable, but much more broadly-based, body of witnesses, and four small research projects were commissioned at very short notice. In spite of the concern to present a report as soon as possible, publication did not take place until more than a year later in April 1968, although the chairman of the sub-committee had written to the Home Office in September 1967 strongly advising against the Alvington concept.

Of course the inquiries were directed to rather different problems in rather different circumstances. But it is difficult to escape the conclusion that the Mountbatten report is the more satisfactory document. The Mountbatten report provided a single-minded and straightforward analysis of an essentially simple logistic problem based on direct experience of the situation which existed. It presented clearly documented evidence about the matters under review and produced unambiguous and uncompromising answers at a practical level. And, considering the short period of time involved, it made some unusually perceptive assessments of the kinds of change in staffing and administration that would be required to support those solutions and to improve

the service generally. The Radzinowicz report, by contrast, at
once sought a more sophisticated and multi-faceted approach to a
philosophical problem which was deliberately framed in a much
broader perspective. It tried to give answers about the kind of
prison system that we ought to have for long-term offenders. It
found that as far as this country was concerned there was no
evidence which really had any bearing on the matters in hand, and
apart from a useful review of escapes and the prisoners currently
assigned to category A, undertaken for the committee, no evidence was presented. Not surprisingly it was tempted to turn to
evidence from abroad, largely American, and it was on the basis
of this that the committee chose to reject the concentration
philosophy. Unfortunately there was really no basis for comparing
the American experience with the English situation, and the
committee certainly made no attempt to do so. Instead a series of
largely hypothetical arguments and conjectures, many of which
contained inherent confusions, were presented. To be fair, the
committee was aware of, and even drew attention to, many of
them.

Perhaps we should illustrate these remarks. The committee
argued that a prisoner sent to the maximum-security prison would
be publicly labelled as the most incorrigible, and that therefore it
would be illogical to move him until it was felt that security
precautions could be reduced for him. This would result in an
excessively custodial, repressive and potentially explosive environment (para. 35). However, the committee pointed out that a 'high
proportion' of their witnesses felt that a small number of dangerous and difficult prisoners dispersed in a prison would mean
increasing restrictions for all prisoners to prevent the escape of a
few, and that the influence of that group by intimidation and
manipulation could produce an atmosphere of ill-will that could
permeate the whole prison (para. 39). There seems no obvious
way of choosing between these evils; but the committee made the
choice apparently on evidence about the 'sociology of the prison
community', which was said to be 'subtle' (para. 41). Presumably
it was too subtle to be disclosed in their report, for it received no
real discussion. What they quoted instead was the American
decision to close Alcatraz, and the assertion that to send the most
recalcitrant prisoners to a small maximum-security prison and to
leave them there would only increase the numbers of incorrigible
prisoners. We cannot see how such a policy could conceivably

increase the numbers of incorrigible prisoners elsewhere in the system, though this is stated as though it were a self-evident truth. But in any case, in the same paragraph, the committee notes that a prisoner's response may change at different stages of sentence; and in paragraph 28 that the concepts of 'maximum-security' and 'dangerous' prisoners are likely to be shifting ones. So it is difficult to see why they should assume that allocation to a small maximum-security prison should be such a permanent affair, when they do not make this assumption for the removal to a segregration unit under the dispersal system (para. 163). Certainly Mountbatten had not seen the allocation as permanent (Cmnd 3175, para. 218).

It was partly because the committee saw the concepts of dangerous or maximum-security prisoners as shifting ones, that they felt that it would be difficult to assign with any accuracy the appropriate prisoners to the right prison. They foresaw either that some who needed high security might be assigned to lower-security establishments and escape, thus producing a new outcry (para. 37), or that officials making the classification would play safe and greatly expand the maximum-security classification to include prisoners who were not really dangerous (para. 30) – which was something of an each-way bet, to say the least. Of course, the first possibility may occur under any system which attempts to divide prisoners among institutions of differing security standards, including the dispersal system. And the second possibility is in fact more likely to occur under the dispersal arrangements since, with several highly secure prisons, the scope for increasing the numbers of persons defined as requiring maximum security is very much greater, and because the real difference between the top category of security and the one next below it is considerably reduced. But perhaps one of the most obvious areas of apparent contradiction was the need to resort to segregation units within each dispersal prison as a means of dealing with the hard core of recalcitrant prisoners. The committee was at pains to point out that these were to be used not to separate the high security risks but to forestall trouble; but it is difficult to resist applying the committee's own arguments against concentration to the segregation units, as the committee knew it would be (para. 167).

One of the advantages of dispersal was said to be the possibility of transfer, either as part of deliberate policy or simply for a change of scene, from one dispersal prison to another. It has to be admitted that for prisoners serving very long sentences this could be an advantage. But there is no reason why there could not be considerable variation from unit to unit even within a single prison, and since the original proposals envisaged a second prison which the Home Secretary was, in February 1967, prepared to build if necessary, some transfer between prisons would eventually have been possible.

Given the fine balance of argument, it is a wonder that the committee felt able to choose to depart from what had so recently become the established policy, and to which the logic of events had for some years past been pointing. It is entirely possible that the major consideration was not that of the regime for long-term prisoners, but cost. Certainly the Radzinowicz sub-committee thought that their proposals would be cheaper than to build Alvington. Indeed, unless there were financial reservations it is hard to understand why the plans for Alvington had not gone further by the time that Radzinowicz first wrote to the Home Secretary foreshadowing the outcome of his inquiry. There were clearly no difficulties about the site; and as early as December 1965 Frank Soskice, the then Home Secretary, had pressed the Ministry of Works to proceed with all speed on the new maximum-security prison after he had deemed it necessary to call in military assistance to guard the train robbers in Durham Prison. If costs were the deciding factor it is hoped that these were carefully calculated to take account not only of the artificial reduction in capital costs per head which is achieved by dividing the costs of physical security among prisoners who do not need it, but also the extra staffing required for the greater number of dispersal establishments. And in that connection it should be noted that twice as many dispersal prisons have been brought into operation as were envisaged by the Advisory Council.

The main effect of the acceptance of the bulk of the Advisory Council recommendations was to widen the impact of the security measures originated by Mountbatten. That was scarcely surprising since, by implication, the Advisory Council is to be understood as turning Mountbatten's tactical response into a general strategy (para. 46). While it is not entirely clear why the committee should regard a 'tactical response' as reducing respect, and a 'general strategy' as enhancing respect for the custodial function of prisons (para. 38), there can be little doubt that the recommendations led to the raising of the coefficient of security in all the closed prisons of the country. And that meant perimeter security, thus reversing the principle on which the post-war building programme had been based. Alvington was first postponed and finally abandoned. Initially Gartree, Hull and Parkhurst were designated as dispersal prisons and were brought into use in 1969. These were followed by Albany in 1970 and Long Lartin in 1973, and still others are planned for the future. While some category-A prisoners without serious records could be sent either to Wakefield or Wormwood Scrubs, the remainder stayed in the special wings. The programme of increasing security beyond the levels originally planned continues unabated today (Cmnd 6523, 1976, para. 114).

But if the Radzinowicz report resulted in a major departure from the concentration policy, in other respects it greatly reinforced the pressures exerted first by Mountbatten and subsequently by the Estimates Committee for changes in management structure. Although the Advisory Council did not address this problem directly, the need to implement the policy once accepted, and to devise a strategy for accommodating category-A prisoners as and when security precautions reached the appropriate standard, inevitably demanded greater co-ordination in planning, and in turn greater sophistication in the management of the system as a whole. Moreover, the Radzinowicz sub-committee paid considerable attention to prison industries, expressing disappointment at the apparent lack of progess in certain areas (para. 105), and reiterating the demand for an eight-hour day, five-day week for prisoners (para. 107) in a reduced range of jobs (para. 108). The Estimates Committee had earlier provided a long-overdue reminder of the need to find ways of showing more accurately the financial state of prison industries. In fact things were already moving in this direction and a 'guiding group' for the new industrial regime at Coldingley (which was opened in May 1969) was by then in existence. With this experience, and mounting pressures from the Advisory Council and elsewhere, it was becoming apparent that prison industries were a major part of prison planning. Perhaps prison industry, if not other forms of training, was compatible with captivity in conditions of maximum security and at least its results could be measured. Certainly it came to be realized that the same kinds of skill required to run prison industries efficiently were just as essential for running the prisons themselves.

In 1968 a management review team was set up, comprising

representatives of the Treasury and the Home Office organization and methods branch and a firm of industrial management consultants. The review was planned in several stages and was required to look initially at two problems; headquarters organization and regionalization. The following year, just ten years after *Penal Practice in a Changing Society,* a new white paper, *People in Prison* (Cmnd 4214, 1969), set forth the new strategy for the prison system; and the annual report for 1969 was able to present the results of the first two stages of the management review. Under the new headquarters structure the position of the Inspector General, introduced as part of the implementation of the Mountbatten proposals, was limited to inspectorial duties and divorced from the executive functions of the department. Three broad 'controllerates' were devised to deal respectively with planning and development, tactical management, and the operations of establishments, each under a controller responsible to the Director General of the service. Regional offices were established in the Midlands, the south-west and the south-east, in addition to the northern office, with responsibilities for the general supervision of the establishments within each region, and with 'telex' communication to headquarters (Cmnd 4486, 1970, chapter 1). In 1971 a new review team was established to implement the third stage of the management review, the examination of the role of each institution within the system, a process apparently completed in 1974 (Cmnd 6148, 1975, para. 29).

The changes that were introduced as a result of the pressures from within and without the service have by no means operated universally across the system. The application of incentive earnings schemes in prison industries, for example, had progressed somewhat unevenly until in 1971 some 1,600 prisoners out of the 15,500 then employed in workshops were covered by these arrangements, and about 800 prisoners were expected to be added each year (Cmnd 5037, 1972, para. 201). The manpower control teams set up to examine the staff complement of different prison service grades had completed their work by 1974, but with no published indication of the results (Cmnd 6148, 1975, para. 27). The protracted negotiations over the introduction of a five-day week for prison officers, which had been agreed policy for many years and which had seen several experimental schemes, was completed in 1972 (Cmnd 5375, 1973, para. 23). One can find many examples of old attitudes in the newest establishments, and one can find old institutions where the new ideas have hardly penetrated at all. The traditions of any service die hard, of course, and the scope for modernization, especially (but not only) in the local prisons, which still hold the majority of prisoners, was and is daunting. But change breeds change; and no one could deny the extent of the changes which have taken place nor the momentum for further developments, for good or ill, which has been built up. The rapid rise of the prison population to unprecedented heights in the 1970s, while it may make the effect of the changes seem small, can only serve in the long run to strengthen the need for the planning and modern management techniques which will increasingly characterize the prison system in the new era.

To study HM Prison Albany is to see all these changes in microcosm. Born out of its time, Albany was caught between the optimism of Paterson and Fox and the preventive rigour of Mountbatten and Radzinowicz. Not surprisingly it had a traumatic childhood.

Chronological overview

The build-up: 1961 to 1966

1961
The first public mention of what was to become Albany Prison occurred in February 1961 with the publication of the Civil Estimates for 1961-2 (HMSO, 104, 1961), in which a provisional figure of £1 million was earmarked for the sixth secure prison of the post-war building programme. No site was fixed and no sketch plans had yet been made. In May the architects gave a qualified approval to a site at Albany barracks, and this location was announced in August (Cmnd 1467, 1961). It was clear that building costs would be higher than first thought because of the steep fall of the land (1:20), the heavily sulphate clay subsoil, and the expense of transporting men and materials from the mainland. The planning brief indicated a prison to Blundeston standards of accommodation and security, to house 480 long-term recidivists, and which would enable the Prison Commission to give up Dartmoor.

1962
In January the planning of Albany first became linked with the embryo of the new maximum-security establishment. Commission

files were minuted with 'the need to provide a small, entirely separate prison for between 30 and 60 inmates somewhere in this area'. By March the Ministry of Public Building and Works was invited to explore the possibility of building a specially secure block to the west or south of the main block on the Albany site. The new block was intended to house 'lifers' who had not received a release date and who might expect to spend many years, perhaps a lifetime, in prison.

1963

The Estimates for 1963-4 (HMSO, 125, 1963) showed a new figure for building Albany of just over £2 million. They also showed the only Treasury-approved estimate we have been able to discover for the special security block, of £270,000. Later that year, when the Prison Commission was dissolved, the design of the security block was referred to a working party of the new Prison Department and little more was heard of it for two years. In November, after some pruning of the specification, a building tender for Albany was accepted – of £1,650,000, excluding establishment charges and subject to limited cost variation.

1964

Site work began at Albany with an expected completion date in October 1966.

1965

By November an outline brief had been developed for the maximum-security block to hold 80 prisoners in conditions of security 'as complete as can be contrived'. Apart from floodlighting, televisual and electronic aids yet to be decided, the main security was to be in an uninterrupted reinforced concrete wall, thirty feet high with an inward and outward overhang, surrounded by dead ground planted with concrete anti-tank blocks and further enclosed by a chain link fence. Entrance to the main prison was to be by underground tunnel. Internally there were to be 'humane standards of accommodation both in space and amenities'; these included large cells with adjoining toilet facilities, accommodation for conjugal visits, and a heated indoor swimming pool. In mid-December, Sir Frank Soskice, who had earlier been persuaded to call in troops to guard the train robbers in Durham Prison, wrote to the Minister of Public Buildings and Works in an effort to expedite the planning and building. A week later officials of the two departments met to agree procedures, in the course of which the plans for conjugal visits were dropped and the swimming pool was held over for review.

1966
Following a review of security after the escape of Wilson and Biggs, the first serious doubts about the safety of the new buildings at Albany, Coldingley and Long Lartin were raised in July. Plans were made to strengthen the grilles covering windows and skylights, and at a site visit it was revealed that the vehicle access gate at Albany also constituted a possible weakness. A provisional programme for opening Albany was agreed, with the first prisoners expected on 17 April 1967.

On 22 October George Blake escaped from Wormwood Scrubs; and two days later Roy Jenkins appointed Earl Mountbatten to conduct an inquiry.

At the beginning of December David Gould, the governor-designate for Albany and then still in post at Dover Borstal, attended his first meeting on the co-ordination of arrangements for opening the prison. He was told that Albany would be used for 'difficult recidivists', and that, until improvements to the perimeter security (which would take about nine months to complete) were made, great care would be needed in the selection of inmates.

Just before Christmas the Mountbatten report was published, with its proposal for Vectis to be completed by June 1969. Mountbatten had visited Albany on 7 December and was critical not only of the inadequate security but also of the failure to provide for effective night sanitation. Less than two weeks later the works directorate were asked to make 'such alterations to the living accommodation as would provide access to WCs at night by similar [electronic] means to that planned for Long Lartin'.

The David Gould regime: January 1967 to June 1968

1967
January. In mid-January the governor and a skeleton staff took possession of the Albany site and the central management group that was to administer the prison was formed.

February. Roy Jenkins asked the Advisory Council on the Penal System to consider the regime for long-term prisoners detained in conditions of maximum security, and the Radzinowicz sub-committee was appointed. Later that month, in the light of the

firm decision to designate Albany eventually as a category-B
prison, it was decided that Albany should have a new perimeter
fence seventeen feet high, to replace the original one which was
only twelve feet high.

April. Albany was officially opened by Lord Stonham on 20
April, one week later than originally planned. The event was
surrounded by favourable publicity in the local and national press
(*The Times,* 21 April). Considerable attention was given to the
experimental use of a two-shift system of industrial work for
prisoners, and Lord Stonham looked forward to the time when
prisoners on incentive earnings would receive wages comparable
to those in outside industry. Lord Stonham also expressed the
hope that the maximum-security block, now re-named Alvington
after local objections had ruled out the use of Vectis, would be
completed in 1970. By the end of the month the still incomplete
Albany Prison received its first prisoners: 11 from Parkhurst and
30 from Wandsworth.

July. The publication of the eleventh report of the Estimates
Committee brought strong criticism of the procedure whereby an
estimate had been approved for Albany before sketch plans had
been made or a site selected (HMSO 599, paras 149-50). The
committee had visited Albany a month earlier and were impressed
by the evidence of the governor in which he spoke of his plans for
the prison and of his hope that they would be monitored by
research (pp. 405-18).

August. Work began on erecting the category-B security fence
around a prison, as yet less than half filled with category-C
prisoners. Thus began an escalating programme of upgrading the
security at Albany which continued for many years.

September. On 23 September the Home Office received a letter
from Professor Radzinowicz foreshadowing the findings of his
committee's report. He wrote that 'the concept and design [of
Alvington] is wrong' and that it was 'regarded by the Americans as
retrograde'. The proposed completion date for Alvington had
already been moved back to 1971, but a week later the Alvington
file was minuted to the effect that there would be a pause in
planning pending a review by the prisons board.

October. Work commenced on converting A hall to the ELSA
system of electronic locking and unlocking, complete with a small
control room, that would permit prisoners to visit the toilet
recesses at night. After many delays, and some changing of minds,

it was decided to extend the experiment to all five halls and to transfer the control function to the new security control room when that was built. In the course of this it was found necessary to re-wire the original A hall installation to a higher standard, and the whole process was not completed until April 1973. Because prisoners had to be moved out of each hall as the wiring was installed, one or other of the halls was out of use for a period of five and a half years.

November. In spite of many teething troubles Albany attracted very favourable publicity, culminating in a glowing report under the headline *Albany – Revelation of the Revolutionary* (IOW *County Press,* 11 November), which was reprinted in the *Prison Service Journal.*

1968

February. Given the hesitation in the Home Office over Alvington, the Ministry of Works decided to take no further action until instructed to do so. Later that month, James Callaghan, the new Home Secretary, gave the first indication that a policy of dispersal might be an alternative to concentration, but he said that Alvington had been deferred rather than abandoned *(Evening Standard,* 20 February).

April. On 3 April the report of the Radzinowicz sub-committee was published. Like Mountbatten and the Estimates Committee, the sub-committee visited Albany to take evidence. The report raised the possibility of using Albany as one of three or four prisons for dispersal purposes (para. 63). Significantly, it was claimed that the two-shift system of work for prisoners, as used at Albany and Gartree, was unsuitable for long-term prisons (para. 110).

May. The research team began work in Albany.

June. At the beginning of the month the electronic locking system in A hall was opened to the press. Again widespread and favourable publicity resulted.

On 14 June David Gould left the prison to take up an appointment as assistant director on the headquarters staff.

The Brian Howden regime: July 1968 to May 1971

July. Captain R. A. B. Howden took up appointment as governor of Albany on 8 July.

On 25 July, in answer to a Parliamentary question, Callaghan announced that he had accepted the Radzinowicz recommendation for dispersal, and that the Alvington project had been abandoned (Hansard, vol. 769, col. *170).* Albany had already begun to prepare for the contingency that it might become a dispersal prison, though at this time it contained only category-C prisoners and was still only designated officially to become a category-B prison. The new perimeter fence had not yet been completed.

October. In answer to a further Parliamentary question on 24 October, Callaghan announced that Albany had been earmarked as a dispersal prison and was expected to receive category-A prisoners in December 1969 (Hansard, vol. 770, cols *333-4).* But that decision had been common knowledge in Albany ever since the governor had been invited to attend a working party on the dispersal of category-A prisoners two months earlier. In those two months it had become clear that Albany was to have a second security fence seventeen feet high, a new control room, a segregation unit, and a team of dogs and handlers as part of the new security arrangements. And these were just part of the many alterations to strengthen the prison that were to come. By the beginning of October it was known that the system of two-shift working at Albany was to be phased out.

November. Six dogs and their handlers began duties in Albany.

1969

January. The first security fence was completed. Almost immediately work began on the second security fence, some twenty feet inside the first; and the original fence together with its modest wooden screening was removed. This and many other security projects continued throughout the year.

February. The two-shift working scheme was abandoned and single-shift working introduced as part of the standard category-A regime, although as yet only a few category-B prisoners had been received on an experimental basis.

March. The prison officially assumed category-B status and the numbers of category-B prisoners in the population began steadily to increase.

September. The research team withdrew from the prison, having completed the main body of fieldwork. Thereafter contact was maintained on an informal basis until the middle of 1971, when a new entry to the prison was negotiated. Visits were made on a periodic basis from then until the end of 1972.

October. On 24 October the Parkhurst Prison riot, sparked off by a new Home Office requirement that only 'approved' persons could visit category-A prisoners held in the special wings, was heard in Albany. Some Albany officers were drafted into Parkhurst to help to quell the riot, and some Parkhurst prisoners were later transferred to Albany to await trial. The scene was being set for cracks in staff-prisoner relationships to appear in Albany.

1970

September. After many delays, which had put back the date of arrival of top-security prisoners, the segregation unit was finished. The second fence had already been completed, as had the installation of television cameras, high-mast lighting, geophonic alarms, the building of the control room and the strengthening of the gate house. The segregation unit provided the fail-safe which finally transformed Albany from a category-C prison to a category-A dispersal prison.

October. The first category-A prisoners arrived on 26 October, and every effort was made to implement both the spirit and letter of the dispersal policy. A few days later another enthusiastic article on the work of prison officers at Albany was published in a local newspaper *(The News,* 30 October). The article was notable for remarks attributed to the POA representative. After noting the dangers of working in the newest maximum-security prison he concluded that nevertheless relationships between staff and prisoners were friendlier than at any other prison where he had served.

December. Shortly before Christmas the first incidents of arson were revealed, and the numbers of prisoners seeking removal from association under Rule 43 because they were afraid of intimidation began to rise.

1971

March. Minor incidents continued in the prison, and the number of prisoners seeking protection under Rule 43 had doubled compared with October 1970.

April. On 19 April Brian Howden left Albany to take up an appointment at headquarters. He left behind some notes on Albany for his successor in which he predicted a 'definite bid for power' by some prisoners.

The Gifford Footer regime: May 1971 to November 1973

May. On 4 May 1971 Gifford Footer took over as governor of Albany. In the period before his arrival there had been an attempt to deal with 'subversive' prisoners by withdrawing them from association under Rule 43 and locating them in the segregation unit. Nine such prisoners were already in the segregation unit when the new governor took office. Later that month the Albany POA representative complained to the annual conference of the frequency with which alarms were raised in Albany and the constant need to search cells for firebombs. He argued that unless something was done about subversive prisoners someone would get hurt.

June. A letter was smuggled out of Albany to the National Council for Civil Liberties alleging that about a fifth of the long-term prisoners were held in solitary confinement. A Home Office spokesman played down the allegations, but they had been close enough to the truth – except that by the time the letter was published the governor had succeeded in transferring 'subversives' back to their own halls.

September. After a number of incidents in which prisoners had been intimidated into refusing food, two notorious prisoners were removed, struggling, to the segregation unit on 7 September. The next day disturbances in the segregation unit resulted in more serious injuries to several staff and one prisoner. The *Daily Telegraph* headlined the story 'Kray gang men in prison battle' (8 September) and the next day the *Daily Mail* reported that 'Mafia gang blamed for jail violence' (9 September). The prison was locked up for two days, two prisoners lost remission, and several were transferred to other prisons. One prisoner was charged with making false allegations that he had been assaulted by several officers; and relationships in the prison had reached a new low.

1972

January to April. Through the early months of 1972 there were many more or less serious incidents of intimidation and confrontation, especially in the dining halls.

May. Preservation of the Rights of Prisoners (PROP) was unveiled as a pressure group composed mainly of ex-prisoners and academics dedicated to radical penal reform. The POA, at its annual conference, expressed concern at the agitation carried out by PROP in several prisons.

June. A new kind of incident occurred at Albany on 2 June, when more than 100 prisoners staged a demonstration in sympathy with PROP by staying in their cells for 24 hours.

July. Disturbances in the dining halls continued.

August. Albany prisoners gave 100 per cent support to the PROP call for a national prisoner strike on 4 August. It passed off peacefully and with apparent good humour. When the Home Office agreed to talk to PROP about specific complaints, Albany officers led the POA towards a new mood of militancy. On 5 August the governor started his annual leave. When he returned he faced a confrontation with staff, who threatened to work to rule unless firm action was taken against subversive prisoners. The troubles were soon picked up by the Press and the story of one Albany officer was published by the *Daily Express* under the headline: 'Locked in with the prison Mafia'. Two officials from the POA national executive visited Albany to mediate between the local branch and the governor. After they left the governor was advised that, in view of the discovery of some escape equipment, a complete security search was required. The search began on Friday 25 August and continued throughout the weekend. Prisoners locked in their cells at first thought that staff were working to rule, and then felt they were being needlessly provoked. On Saturday night prisoners rioted in their cells and continued on and off for two more days and nights, causing extensive damage. 'Siege at the jail of fear' was the headline in the *Daily Mirror* for 28 August, and Albany had become the most notorious prison in the country.

September. E hall had to be pressed into service as an emergency extension to the segregation unit as 158 prisoners were adjudicated on 654 charges arising out of the riot. The Home Secretary, Robert Carr, announced a review of the dispersal policy and of the methods available for dealing with troublemakers, as a result of which the POA temporarily called off their threats to work to rule. But it was several weeks before Albany began to function again with prisoners out of their cells, and then only on a restricted regime. The use of the dining halls was abandoned in favour of meals in cells.

November. Fifteen prisoners who had been held continuously in the segregation unit since the riot barricaded themselves in and broke down the partition walls between cells.

December. By the end of the year there were only 12 prisoners still held in the segregation unit on Rule 43, and E hall had been handed over to workmen for re-wiring.

1973

April. Albany had not returned to a normal routine but the prison was quieter, and when the re-wiring of E hall was completed, all five halls became operational for the first time.

May. As a result of his review of policy Robert Carr announced that the number of dispersal prisons was to be increased from six to nine, that segregation units and perimeters were to be strengthened, that limits would be imposed on the numbers allowed to associate at meals, work and recreation, and that 'control units' would be introduced for troublemakers (Hansard, vol. 856, cols *215-16*, 11 May).

June. In Albany, as in other dispersal prisons, the effects of the review were soon felt. Work was to begin on reinforcing the partition walls in the segregation unit, while the perimeter fence was to be solidified into a wall through a process of guniting. The completion of E hall permitted the separation of prisoners in a way that substantially undermined the original concept of dispersal but which effectively produced the limits on association required by the review.

July. A prisoner burned to death in Albany after setting fire to his cell.

The POA, in dispute about manning levels and overtime duties, called for a ban on excess overtime throughout August.

August. The staff ban led to further restrictions in the regime at a time when the prison inspectorate was calling for a restoration of the normal working week for prisoners and a return to communal dining in Albany. Prisoners saw the restrictions as a provocation, and officers responded to complaints by renewing their demands for isolating the subversives. At the end of the month an officer was taken hostage at knife point by a prisoner demanding to see his wife – and the tension mounted. The situation was safely resolved, but other incidents followed.

October. The wives of prison officers picketed the prison calling on the governor to take firm action against troublemakers.

November. On 9 November, at the height of the latest confrontation and seven weeks before he was due for transfer to Risley remand centre, Gifford Footer died.

2 Doing research in prison

It is seldom easy to do social research, and it is usually much harder than many researchers suggest. It has become increasingly fashionable to lay bare the mystique, and rightly so. Research objectives are not often clear in advance. Almost any investigation requires the sometimes extensive co-operation – or at least response – of other people if it is to be carried out at all effectively. Even if that is forthcoming, the reliability and validity of the data can scarcely be guaranteed by any of the available techniques of study and instruments of research. The activities of the researcher, his judgment and discretion are always more problematic and usually more consequential than they seem. And the publication of the 'results', still more than the conduct of the research itself, raises fundamental problems of ethics and responsibility. Perhaps few contexts can provide such a bewildering complexity of considerations for the research worker to take into account as the legally and morally divided world of the prison.

Much, of course, depends on what one wants to do. But anyone who wishes to do more than count heads or make pencil and paper tests of abilities, attitudes or opinions with a captive population in a kind of human laboratory will have to establish, and live, a role which is acceptable both to himself and his respondents. He will certainly find that he provokes anxiety in those he researches and that no less will he have his own anxieties aroused. Terence Morris, reflecting on the experience of his research at Pentonville, likened the situation of the research worker in the early stages of a project to 'a man taking a moonlight walk through a minefield: he may reach his objectives unscathed, but he may on the other hand take a step which will produce disastrous results' (Morris, 1967, p. 147). Morris's simile graphically portrays the sense of uncertainty that is likely to be felt by the researcher. But in some ways it is also an unfortunate comparison and possibly revealing of the methodological problems involved in the Pentonville study. Unfortunate, in that it suggests a military confrontation between the researcher and the researched. Revealing, in that the role of the 'man' in the minefield is not specified; since he is not said to be a soldier, he may conceivably be a spy, though surely not just an innocent abroad. Revealing too, in that the outcome for the intruder is seen as a chance matter beyond his control, whereas the invaded are seen as having had sufficient advance warning to have prepared a well-organized, if somewhat inflexible, defence.

No one, of course, would wish to be judged on a figure of speech, and to be fair, much also depends on just when, in the history of research and of society, one carries out the study. For not only do we learn from the experiences of others, we also respond to the intellectual and moral climate of the day both in what we seek to do and in how we go about it. There have been many studies carried out *in* prisons, though few studies *of* prisons. Several fine American and Scandinavian accounts have appeared in the literature (see, for example, Clemmer, 1940; Sykes, 1958; Wheeler, 1958; Mathiesen, 1965; Street *et al.,* 1966; and Irwin, 1970; as well as the papers in Cressey, 1961; Cloward *et al.,* 1960; and Christie, 1968). But for our knowledge of the English system, and the social structure and culture of particular prisons, we have had to choose between the 'official' accounts by successive prison commissioners or the memoirs of prison governors and chaplains on the one hand and the steady stream of accounts by prisoners, or more usually ex-prisoners, on the other. These have tended to become either curiosities or classics; and among the more recent examples of the latter Frank Norman's *Bang to Rights* (1958) and Tony Parker's *The Frying Pan* (1970) stand out for their refreshing economy as well as their remarkable capacity to convey something of the inner life of the prison. They also reveal something of the changes and similarities, both in prisons and the outlook of prisoners, over the period. With the exception of Tony Parker, however, who has over the years brought his listener's ear to a state of perfect pitch, none of these writers has been an outsider who has had to pay attention to the establishment of a viable research role. At the time we began our research at Albany, the only modern and avowedly sociological study of an English prison which had been published was the Morrises' account of Pentonville (Morris *et al.,* 1963). Since we began, two further social-psychological studies have appeared, though they could scarcely be more different in approach: the first of Bristol Prison by Emery (1970), and the second of the special security wing at Durham by Cohen and Taylor (1972). Before our own writing was completed the report on the research at Dover borstal by Bottoms and McClintock (1973) had been published. Although this is not strictly a prison study we have taken the opportunity to discuss points of similarity and difference with our own research here, not least because the governor of Dover borstal through most of that study and the governor of Albany at the beginning of this were one and the same man, Mr A. (David) Gould. Other studies are now in progress, so a review of the conduct of research in prison may be timely.

The Morrises' work in Pentonville was carried out, at their own request but with the encouragement of the Prison Commission and financed by Home Office grant, from 1958 to 1960 and was published in 1963. In their monograph, and subsequently, they devoted some attention to the role adopted by the research workers, and indicated the lessons for future research which were to be drawn from their work. They also gave, albeit in a rather sketchy fashion, some indication of what the research workers did. Emery's study was also conducted between 1958 and 1960, although publication did not take place until a decade later. The research was done as a result of a request from the Prison Commission to the Tavistock Institute of Human Relations, and it was concerned to evaluate the applicability of what used to be called the 'Norwich system' of greater association and closer staff-prisoner relationships in a medium-sized local prison. Although Emery was careful to secure an understanding that he would be concerned with the interests of prisoners as well as staff, he does not explain how that concern was communicated and carried through. Some indication of his research role can be gleaned, however, from the methodological notes which are contained in an appendix and which deal mainly with matters of sampling and the conduct of interviews. Quite apart from the fact that security wings did not then exist, the work of Cohen and Taylor could scarcely have been contemplated at the time of the earlier studies. Their research 'emerged' out of the sociology classes they were giving in E Wing at the invitation of Durham University extra-mural department in 1967. It was developed as a 'mutual collaborative research project' on the part of themselves and their 'students', continued for about four years, and was published with commendable speed in 1972. The work was done without special funding and, initially at least, without the knowledge of the Home Office, who were subsequently said to have rejected both their 'ideas for research' and their 'applications for research facilities'. The authors discuss their own role at some length, and explicitly locate themselves as being 'on the side of' the prisoners with whom they collaborated. The study by Bottoms and McClintock evidently arose out of the complementarity of ideas and interests held by the principal investigator and the then governor of Dover borstal, which became apparent in the course of seminar discussions at the Institute of Criminology. It was carried out between 1963 and 1969 with Home Office funding, and published in 1973. The authors give a concise account of their methods and sources in the text and appendices and also discuss the role of the research workers. From the outset the research involved the close collaboration of research workers and institutional personnel 'in a common endeavour to improve the effectiveness of penal institutions'.

These four studies thus cover a wide and interesting range of possible approaches: independent (Morris), officially-sponsored (Emery), mutual prisoner and research interest (Cohen and Taylor), and mutual staff and research interest (Bottoms and McClintock); and each raises its own problems. In the section which follows we explore some of the implications of the research roles adopted in them.

Types of research role

The Morrises were pioneers of research into the working of prisons in the United Kingdom, and we have benefited immeasurably both from their experience and their mistakes. Because the issues which it raises are so fundamental for any future research, the conduct of their work deserves the most careful and critical analysis. Terence and Pauline Morris were sensitive to the possible impact of research upon the researched: so much so that at the beginning of their study one of them visited Trenton, New Jersey, among other things to gauge staff reactions to the publication of Sykes's *The Society of Captives* (Morris, 1967). Surprisingly, it was found that the American research had had little effect on the staff at Trenton. This was certainly not the case with the work at Pentonville, the publication of which was accompanied by widespread Press publicity and followed by a storm of protest and critical comment in the *Prison Officers' Magazine*. Moreover, because of the high degree of geographical mobility that characterizes the English prison system, several members of staff and even one or two prisoners at Albany during our research had been at Pentonville in 1958-60, and many more had worked with or knew someone who had been there. While most prisoners at Albany expressed little interest in the Pentonville study one way or another, many officers who had no connection with the London prison were prepared to see the study as typifying 'research', and by implication as having been about themselves by virtue of their common membership in the prison service. We mention this because it adds a new, and possibly taxing, dimension to the already complex considerations to be taken into account by research workers in establishing a research role: that of representing, or at least of being expected to represent, 'research' and 'research workers' in some more general sense. Just as we had to cope with the legacies of the Pentonville study, so some future research workers will have to contend with the aftermath of our own; and the burden will surely grow as research multiplies within the system. We hope we have not contributed unduly to the problems of others in attempting to solve our own.

Even after an interval of several years *Pentonville* was one of the most heated subjects that enlivened almost all of our early meetings in Albany – at least those with staff. What emerged from repeated public and private discussions was that officers felt a sense of disillusion or even betrayal at the disjunction between the conduct of the research and its publication. Some of those who had been at Pentonville looked back on their experiences during the fieldwork with something like affection and certainly with a reasonable appreciation of the research activity; and they swapped stories with us rather like soldiers discussing old campaigns. By contrast the publication was seen as a stab in the back, and the assurances which were said to have been given in the course of collecting the data were re-interpreted as a kind of anaesthetic. Though the passing of time had dulled the edge of what many saw as the Morrises' knife, recollection of the operation could still produce a sharp twinge from a raw nerve. It is worth considering how this situation came about. There seem to us to be two main reasons: lack of communication, and the ambiguity, even misleading nature, of the research role which was adopted.

We began by noting the military metaphor chosen by Morris (1967) and there can be little doubt that he saw the confrontation as between the researcher on the one hand and the uniformed staff, who had set the minefield, on the other. Now it is hardly surprising that any body of men who suddenly find researchers in their midst virtually unannounced, which is more or less what happened at Pentonville, should feel threatened. One can imagine the reaction, for example, of the academic community – faculty, that is, not students – to a similar intrusion. The Morrises were aware of this difficulty, and noted that whereas in their pilot study at Maidstone they had been able to address a meeting of staff and prisoners with the governor in the chair, this was not possible at Pentonville where 'an order was merely read out to the staff on the Centre, and prisoners were not given any information whatever' (Morris *et al.*, 1963, p. 9). At the time the authors noted that this led to endless questions about the nature of the research, although it is interesting that in the recommendations to future researchers in their appendix they do not return to the question of introducing a research project into a prison. Four years later, however, at the European Conference of Directors of Criminological Institutes, Terence Morris recalled the lack of an introductory meeting and said that 'a number of minor problems arose in consequence' (Morris, 1967, p. 151). It is not entirely clear what he had in mind when referring to 'minor' problems. Perhaps time had dimmed the memory, because in the appendix to *Pentonville* reference was made to a number of what we would regard as major problems, including staff 'deliberately spreading falsehoods around the prison about what the research workers were alleged to have said or done in order to destroy the basis of rapport with prisoners' (Morris *et al.*, 1963, pp. 324-5), and which were there attributed to the suspiciousness or hostility of the staff. In any case, by 1967, Morris reflected that 'It may be of some advantage for the researcher to make a deliberate attempt to disseminate information about the study at an early stage to both the staff and prisoners through more formal channels of communication', which was advice from which we were to take considerable profit.

Reading between the lines of *Pentonville* it is clear that there was as much suspicion of the staff by the research workers as there was suspicion of the research workers by the staff. Certainly better communication at the outset would have done a great deal to reduce the tension and anxieties felt by both sides. Given the way the research had to be introduced, it is scarcely surprising that the researchers felt exposed in a minefield; and once they were in it was already too late. With more careful preparation and co-operation from the authorities they might have taken a path which was more of their own choosing, and perhaps even have avoided the minefield altogether. But this was the lesser of *Pentonville's* problems; and is likely to be the lesser of any research project's problems. The real question is: why were they in the arena in the first place? The day is fortunately gone, or going, when (more and better) communication was seen as the convenient cure-all for social ills, and especially the ills of complex organizations. The problem is not just communication but what is communicated.

No one who has carried out research in institutions can have avoided the situation of salesman. If the researcher is to sell his goods at all then he needs to provide a clear specification of what those goods are and why they are needed. Just as a good salesman needs to have a single-minded belief in the utility of the product and the virtues of the business of selling, so the researcher needs to demonstrate that the research will have the effects claimed for it and that the activities of the researchers are intelligibly geared to bringing about those effects. The dilemma of the researcher as salesman, especially in exploratory studies, is that he must only offer goods that he will be able to deliver, but that he has to offer them for sale before they are in production. If repeat sales are to be made, the closer the correspondence between the goods and their specification the better. Of course the product of social research, the role of research workers in producing it, and the relationships between researchers and researched, are all more complex than our analogy suggests; but it is none the less instructive in analysing some of the difficulties which arose during, and as a result of, the Pentonville research. In our view these difficulties may be accounted for by the vagueness of the definition of the research task, the unrealistic – though at that time unexceptionable – conception of the role of researchers, and the consequent ambiguities in relating the latter to the former.

The Morrises appear to have said rather little about what they were selling. Their basic answer to the query 'what is it all about?' was 'an independent study of the prison to see how it worked, so that we might be able to assist those responsible for making changes' (Morris *et al.*, 1963, p. 9). This statement, or something like it, was given to both staff and prisoners. It is vague, and because of its open-ended reference to making unspecified changes, is likely to be perceived differently by different groups. In the circumstances we discuss below prisoners would probably regard any changes as being for the better while staff would regard most changes as being 'reforms' which might threaten to make their jobs more difficult. Of course the aims of any pioneering study are likely to be blurred at the edges, but even in the most tentative exploration there seems no reason why the basic descriptive intent should not be openly declared at the outset. And where early ideas are too vague to warrant elaboration there seems everything to be gained from an acknowledgment that certain options are being held open and can be discussed as the research progresses. It should be no surprise that the vaguer the specification the more open it becomes to interpretation.

The conception of the research role adopted at Pentonville, and incidentally the researchers' view of respondents, is encapsulated in a single sentence: 'To gain the co-operation of both groups and at the same time avoid identification with the interests of either was often difficult; fortunately the more perceptive prisoners and officers understood something of the problem' (Morris *et al.*, 1963, pp. 7-8). Such a definition of the scientific role would not have attracted widespread comment from sociologists at that time. The task set was indeed a difficult one. Whether it was also a reasonable one in terms of the burden on the researchers, or an understandable one from the point of view of the researched is another matter. But it is almost certainly a measure of the authors' struggle to maintain the ideal-typical role of the researcher as then conceived, that throughout the book those staff and prisoners who understood 'the problem' (presumably those who co-operated) are cast as perceptive; whereas those who did not co-operate are cast as not having understood it because they were unintelligent, or else they are seen as gratuitously malicious, or even hostile because they had something to hide. A few examples will illustrate: 'Officers by and large felt threatened by the research, specially those with limited educational attainment' (p. 9); 'the concept of social research was wholly alien to them. . . . There was, in consequence, a disappointingly high refusal rate among the sample of officers selected for interview; some staff members were quite deliberately unco-operative' (p. 324); 'those who were most hostile were often those who had most reason to feel guilty about their treatment of prisoners' (p. 327 – although from a footnote on the same page it seems that this last refers only to one officer in spite of what is said in the text). Doubtless some members of staff *were* unco-operative. What is surprising is that no consideration seems to have been given to the possibility that the unco-operative responses were based on a realistic appreciation of the ambiguities in the research role and its tenuous connections to the threatening research goals. Instead the Morrises seemed tacitly to assume that staff really *ought* to have co-operated, regardless of their own interests, because the research was a valid scientific activity with which no good citizen could reasonably quarrel.

The central problem in the research role, of course, concerned the identifications and interests of the research workers. The basic difficulties are admitted, but they are none the less assumed to be difficulties which the competent research worker, or the trained social worker, can resolve within himself. The Morrises presented themselves as not being committed to either side; nor were they committed to the study of a particular problem. If anything, the aims of the research were presented as being somewhat management-oriented ('so that we might be able to assist those responsible for making changes'); and their very presence in the institution suggested a degree of official support. In spite of the fact that the Morrises gave great stress in their recommendations to future researchers to the need to establish a role which was independent of the prison, it seems that this was not such a severe problem for them. It is not clear how they dealt with such matters as Home Office financing of the project as distinct from their own salaries, and the prisoners' fears that they would be prevented from seeing the adjudication of visiting magistrates (p. 9) – a fear which turned out to be justified (pp. 323-4) – nor for that matter with prisoners' beliefs that there was 'big money in it' for the research workers (p. 325). But on reading the book one is left with the impression that the researchers were reasonably successful in establishing their independence, by pointing out that they worked for the university and were not on the Home Office payroll, by not using keys and so on, so that prisoners, after a time, came to accept them. Indeed, it is clear that they were so successful in establishing their independence that their real difficulties were in securing the co-operation of the staff.

The fundamental issue at Pentonville, then, is whether there was any justification for the fact that 'the bulk of the staff came to the conclusion that research, like reform, is basically prisoner-oriented' (p. 327). The Morrises maintained that there was not; that such a view arose because the staff 'had little capacity for conceptualizing research as an independent activity' (p. 327); that they, the Morrises, were merely objective observers, who were not to be identified with either side. In his subsequent paper to the European Conference, Terence Morris put it as follows: 'The social scientist, both before he begins his work and throughout its course, normally must constantly reassure the prison official and the administrator that his approach is entirely objective. In writing his report, he must make it clear that whatever facts he may comment upon are not to be regarded as forming a criticism or indictment of the administration, but have been selected merely for their sociological relevance' (Morris, 1967, p. 129). It is our belief that such a position involves an academic notion of objectivity, and a social work notion of neutrality, which are curiously divorced from reality. For the salesman selling his research it involves offering goods which are not only difficult to deliver, but may not be available at all. And most of the staff reactions reported in *Pentonville,* in our view, can be interpreted as an entirely understandable and rational appreciation of that fact.

Morris (1967) went on to outline the difficulty and the solution as he saw it: 'The difficulty is that many research workers are themselves personally committed to a "reformist" viewpoint, a fact which is often widely known in the prison. It is therefore of great importance that researchers suppress any subjective reactions that might be engendered by their own observations' (p. 129). The assumption that this problem has to be dealt with by suppression rather than by acknowledgment and discussion points both to the extraordinary power of the approved model of scientific research and to the weakness of the method, that is soon likely to be spotted by respondents. The salesman who suppresses private reservations about his product is not likely to be trusted, certainly not for a second time. No more is the researcher. It is clear that the suppression was not entirely successful at Pentonville. The Morrises, in *Pentonville,* do not for the most part declare their subjective views, although their place in the British reformist criminological tradition is tacitly implied throughout. The one instance where their private views are declared is in relation to the two executions which were carried out in Pentonville during 1959, and it was known in the prison that the research workers were opposed to capital punishment. They note that 'Prisoners by and large became more co-operative in consequence of the strain and stress of events', although some officers, we are told, 'took advantage' (which is a curious choice of words to convey a difference of opinion) of the research workers' views and became 'unambiguously hostile' (p. 10). It would seem that this alone would give some justification for the belief that the research was 'prisoner-oriented'.

But even more revealing is the comment in the later paper about the reasons for securing co-operation and the purposes of research: 'Any project that does not gain the full co-operation of the custodial staff is bound to run into difficulties at an early stage, for not only is their co-operation vital to ensure that the researcher has access to all parts of the prison – they possess the keys – but it is important that rumours about the research are not spread to inmates *from* the staff, which would damage rapport with the inmates' (Morris, 1967, p. 148, emphasis in original). If staff co-operation is dismissed as merely facilitative, while the researcher gets on with his real business through rapport with prisoners, it is small wonder that officers who were perceptive enough to detect this would become hostile and would regard the research as being neither in their own interests nor concerned with their own problems. In spite of this, the Morrises attempt to maintain not only their belief in their own objectivity, but also the fiction that such objectivity should not be regarded as criticism. In our view it is unrealistic to expect that remarks of the kind we have quoted (and there are many other examples), even if 'selected merely for their sociological relevance', will not also be viewed by those on the receiving end as criticism. Yet the Morrises expected just that: 'To make matters worse, prison officers are very sensitive to what *they* understand as criticism' (Morris *et al.*, 1963, p. 324, emphasis added). It is as though the Morrises see the researcher as a kind of social worker in the middle of a family breakdown who listens carefully to both sides without making moral judgments and whose recommendations are purely neutral and in the best interests of all. In fact, social workers have increasing difficulty in sustaining such a role in the face of a perplexed and sceptical clientele; and we should not be surprised that research workers face similar problems.

In sum it seems to us that the difficulties at Pentonville arose because the researchers invited their respondents to collude in a mystically defined research role which not only could not be sustained in practice but did not really represent what the researchers were actually doing. They might have been overcome had the researchers confessed their interests and identifications, presented a clearly defined research problem, and invited co-operation in solving it.

The study by Emery had little to say about the role of the research worker or about lessons for future research; those by Cohen and Taylor, and Bottoms and McClintock had rather more. But each, in their different ways, was less ambiguous in what they had to say than the Morrises and we therefore need spend less time on them here.

Emery's study of Bristol Prison was essentially a before and after comparison of changes in the regime, in which the investigator acted in some measure as a consultant. The author gave a 'clear, unambiguous guarantee that neither praise nor blame would be attributed to identifiable individuals, whether staff or inmates', and in his report tried 'to concentrate on the bare bones of oft-repeated behaviours that might tell a general story' (Emery, 1970, p. xv). Even officially commissioned research, contrary to many current and facile beliefs, is not guaranteed the support of the staff; and relations in the prison were said to be 'so sensitive' that it was not possible to introduce research assistants. Neverthe-less staff were said to have co-operated once they were convinced that the 'research aims were concerned with their welfare as well as that of the inmates' (p. xv) and prisoners 'were – with few exceptions – co-operative . . . within a relation in which any question of personal gain or loss was rigorously excluded' (p. xvi). No further details are given about how the research was received, although it seems likely that the aims were sufficiently clear-cut that they could be explained without too much difficulty. In the methodological appendix, however, Emery reveals that he antici-pated difficulties with prisoners, which suggests that his concern with their interests was not very direct: 'It seemed very likely that inmates would not tell the truth about matters concerning their own criminality and fairly likely that they would be so biased in their view of the official prison world as to be misleading. Several counter-measures were decided upon and followed in each inmate interview' (p. 106). Although these measures were straightforward enough, no similar doubts appear to have been entertained in respect of the responses of staff and certainly no counter-measures to deal with them are reported. It is notable that the proposals for the Bristol research included the working through of the final report with the governor and his working party, and that in keeping with the policy of the Tavistock Institute no results would be published 'without these being first cleared with the Commissioners' (p. 101). We do not wish to suggest in any way that undue influence was brought to bear on the research, or that the data should be questioned on those or other grounds. It is even perhaps necessary today to reassert that this is a perfectly viable form of research. Our point is simply that the role of the research worker here was fairly explicitly management-oriented, that no attempt was made to conceal that, and that Emery's concern that the interests of both staff and inmates would be considered really amounts to no more than an assurance that the researcher would in all conscience be sympathetically concerned with the welfare of both groups as he saw it.

The study by Cohen and Taylor of Durham Prison was born in a different period and in very different circumstances. It is, so far as we know, unique in that it is the only study which could in a real sense be said to have been commissioned by prisoners. And although it is a good deal less ambiguous because of that, it none the less raises fundamental issues which, in our view, it needlessly oversimplifies.

Cohen and Taylor's research grew out of a 'general criticism of traditional prison studies' – which was voiced both by prisoners and themselves in the course of their sociology classes in E wing – that 'many such studies failed to do justice to the full psychological effects of imprisonment' (Cohen and Taylor, 1972, p. 32). The authors make it clear that the idea of the research project was discussed with prisoners, in terms of the main interests of the men who would be involved: that it was, in effect, a 'mutual' research project. With refreshing candour, Cohen and Taylor review their own ideological positions, and make no pretence at having played the roles of detached seekers after information. Following Becker's (1967) discussion of research sympathies in the study of deviant groups, they note that their own commitment was as much to the men and the relationships they formed with them as to any research endeavour as such. They adopted, in Matza's (1969) phrase, 'the appreciative stance', involving an attempt to empathize with their subjects while keeping in mind the dangers of sentimentality and romanticism. Though they 'would have liked to have known how [staff] viewed the situation' they doubted 'whether it is possible to see both sides at the same time' (pp. 182-3).

Now there is no reason at all why research should not be carried out from such a perspective; indeed, it can reveal a great deal about the experiences of prisoners which is neglected in other studies, as Cohen and Taylor have ably shown. But, speaking strictly of the problem of the role of a research worker in prison, it seems a pity that Cohen and Taylor should appear to make such a virtue of what was manifestly also a necessity. Since in their own words they 'started without a problem' (p. 32) and were presumably constrained by what could be done within the framework of extra-mural classes and without more general access (the situation about wider access is not clear from their report), there was little else they could do but explore the world of those closest to them. And given that their work was thus commissioned by prisoners, it was perhaps inevitable, whatever the inclinations of the researchers might have been, that this should be explored from their point of view. To the extent that the extra-mural classes presented the researchers with an opportunity to do what they already wished to do, of course, it would no longer be possible for them to say that they began without a problem. And it should be remembered, as far as lessons for the role of research workers is concerned, that such an opportunity will not be likely to occur again. In any case, given the circumstances in which the research was born and carried out, and the eventual nature of its emergent problem, it would clearly have been impossible for *those researchers* to examine seriously and convey the views of the staff.

Whether it is possible for *any* researchers to see both sides at the same time remains to be seen. Certainly we did not achieve it, at least not in equal measure and not on all issues; nor did we always try to achieve it. But it is important not to fall into the trap of seeing side-taking in simple monolithic terms. There are some issues which are of more interest and importance to one side than the other, and even some issues for which the sides are somewhat obscurely drawn. Generally, when the issues are clear-cut it is fairly obvious what each side thinks and feels about them. In such circumstances one may wonder whether the kinds of identification and commitment which Cohen and Taylor discuss are in fact prerequisites for the kind of appreciation which they sought to achieve. Indeed, as the authors readily admit, the identification was by no means complete. We assume that Cohen and Taylor would agree that prison staff, no less than prisoners, do not always correspond to their stereotypes, and that each side is, on occasion, capable of taking the side of the other. What is possible for the participants should not be beyond the capabilities of the sociologist, whatever his ideological position may be. Conceivably the professed identification of Cohen and Taylor with the prisoners may be just as difficult to understand as the professed detachment of the Morrises from any interest group, no matter how genuinely each position may be held.

Cohen and Taylor's insistence that they began without a problem is clearly related to their attempt to dispose of what they term the 'chronological lie' of 'aims, methods, presentation of results and finally the discussions or conclusion' which they take to be 'at the heart of most research' (p. 32). We would agree with much of their criticism, though, to be fair, the 'lie' is usually at the heart of research *reports* rather than the research itself, a fact which says more about the culture of academia than it does about the business of doing research. We also agree with much of their criticism of one such study contained in their appendix, although it was a bit gratuitous to provide a rather incomplete critique of the methods of their colleagues in the psychology department at Durham without also providing more detail on their own methods of research, which are only sketchily reported. There also seem to be some rather simplistic statements about the implications of Home Office funding. Perhaps all this was inevitable given the nature of the book they chose to write, in which prisoner approval of the product is seen as a demonstration of its validity. But on reading the book one cannot help wondering whether their determination to separate themselves from the existing research tradition blinded them to the nature of their own 'research methods'. They went in as teachers, a role they evidently perform well and which is also their profession. The methods they rightly reject as being inappropriate and irrelevant were by no means the only ones available; but the methods which they adopted have a remarkable resemblance to those employed by the teacher who has embarked on a rewarding relationship with his students: unstructured group interviews (non-directive seminars); men's writing (essays); literary identification (encouragement of self-expression); and correcting the writing up of the research (positive feedback and evaluation of the course). Having said all this, it is a pity that the work will not now be followed up (Cohen and Taylor, 1975). It may or may not become a manual for psychological survival in extreme situations, but it does breathe common humanity into the process of research, and adds to our understanding of the situation of the long-term prisoner.

The study by Bottoms and McClintock is, in one sense at least, the polar opposite of the Cohen and Taylor research, for the commitment of the former to the aims of progressive prison management is as clearly proclaimed as that of the latter to the interests of long-term prisoners. Thus Bottoms and McClintock list three main aims of their work: (a) through diagnosis of the problems requiring individualized treatment to develop classifications of prisoners that would be 'generally useful in penal practice'; (b) to study the process of modifying the regime at Dover borstal in an attempt to develop 'a more effective system' of dealing with such problems; and (c) to assess the impact of the regime and its effectiveness in 'preventing further criminal behaviour' (Bottoms and McClintock, 1973, p. 3).

It is worth emphasizing that the identification of Bottoms and McClintock was with the top management and treatment personnel within the institution they studied, rather than with the staff generally or with officials at headquarters. It was intended that the 'maximum amount of co-operation' would take place between 'the treatment personnel and the research workers' in an action research project (p. 143). The co-operation between the two groups was evidently extensive and occurred 'in the creation of, and in operating, the modified training regime, in developing in-service training as well as in collecting the data required primarily for research purposes' (p. 389). And it was hoped that the results 'would be of value to those directly responsible for dealing with the penal problem' (p. 413). Given such local support, the entry to the institution for Bottoms and McClintock and their associates was evidently much smoother than that of the Morrises, or even of Emery with his sponsorship from headquarters. And to the extent that the research workers made it clear to staff and inmates within the institution that these were their intentions it is probably the case that their research role was more readily understandable to all parties – if not necessarily equally acceptable – than in any of the other studies reviewed here.

However, Bottoms and McClintock say very little about what they actually said to staff and prisoners, and what they do tell us suggests that they blurred the apparent clarity of their research role. It is almost as though the authors, anxious at the degree of naked involvement with managerial aims, were tempted to strive for a clothing of scientific respectability which they expected to find in the same kind of detachment and neutrality pursued by the Morrises. Thus they point out that although their aim was to 'study the situation in order to bring about changes in a defined direction . . . the research workers always presented themselves to staff and inmates as having a separate identity, but with emphasis on staff collaboration' (p. 6). Moreover, 'in two particular contacts with inmates' an assurance was given that nothing would be communicated to the staff, and it was said to be 'tacitly accepted' that the same would apply for minor breaches of the regulations observed by the researchers (p. 6). The authors assure us that 'the position of *relative* independence was for the most part understood and accepted by the offenders' and that the action research design should not be taken to imply an absence of independent observation and assessment (p. 6, emphasis in original).

The meaning of these assurances is not altogether clear because the authors do not further discuss their relationship with inmates and non-treatment personnel in any detail. Nor do they elaborate on the concept of relative independence of observation and assessment. Instead they refer the reader, via an unhelpful footnote, to the discussion by Max Weber (1904) of the 'various issues involved' (p. 434). It is a pity these issues are not discussed directly because the Dover researchers appear to have had no difficulty in getting inmates to respond to their social attitude tests or pre-discharge interviews. Yet in the questions asked of inmates, for example about their expectations of future 'constructive leisure activities' (p. 226), the authors do not always exhibit a sensitive attunement to the aspirations of borstal boys. And at one point in the report the authors had cause to suspect 'some lack of frankness in the interview situation' (p. 242). We do not wish to make too much of this point, for we should stress that an action project with an explicit managerial orientation is a perfectly viable form of research activity, and we doubt that the Dover researchers ever strayed far from this central commitment in their approach to inmates. Certainly they were aware of the limitations imposed by their identification with treatment staff and were careful always to qualify statements about matters which could not be handled easily from such a stance; for example, in their discussion of involvement in the inmate subculture (p. 160). However, we do wonder whether inmates might have responded more readily to researchers who presented themselves as single-minded in their pursuit of treatment aims than to researchers who confused the matter by making additional claims to objectivity and relative independence. In the circumstances it seems likely that the best interpretation of the authors' 'relative independence', or what Radzinowicz in his foreword refers to as dedication to 'detachment even when most involved', is that the researchers accepted the perspective of the governor and treatment staff but were determined to subject what those persons said or thought they did to a sceptical, systematic and rational appraisal.

Leaving aside the difficulties with inmates as respondents, it is clear that this particular research model brought its own problems at many other levels. It is well reported in the literature that there is often a basic split between treatment personnel and other staff, particularly uniformed officer grades, in penal institutions. Such a split is almost certainly less marked in borstals than in other kinds of institution, although it is clear that the researchers were aware of problems that might arise in this direction because of their identification with treatment objectives. Indeed, the difficulties were frankly acknowledged, and the authors discuss the gradual process of building up confidence and understanding without glossing over 'periods of intense hostility and outright discord' that had to be worked through before 'a sense of partnership was developed' (p. 388). But although Bottoms and McClintock discuss the institutional staff in terms rather more sympathetic than those employed by the Morrises, one cannot escape the feeling that the process of identification had gone deeper than the researchers knew, and that often they saw staff as persons to be won over, rather than as the bearers of valid views in their own right. Nowhere is this more clear than in their discussion of the complex role of the governor, where difficulties were curiously attributed to 'a *misunderstanding* of the personality of the governor on the part of many of the staff, both officers and housemasters' (p. 173, emphasis added).

Finally, one might note that the joint sponsorship of the project by institutional staff and the researchers seems to have raised issues both at headquarters in the Home Office and at the Institute of Criminology, which produced unsatisfactory compromises about the appropriate amount of resources to be allocated to research of this kind. And it is clear from the discussions in the text, as well as the valuable appendices contributed by the principal investigator and the governor, that the collaboration was not an easy process. Both treatment staff and research staff were inclined to be more ambitious in their plans than either time, resources or the contemporary level of skills warranted, and the sharing of a common perspective was clearly no guarantee of immunity from many genuine clashes of interest.

We have stressed throughout this review that each of the approaches described above is, in its own way, a viable form of research activity bringing with it its own problems. Our own approach was based on our belief that the most understandable role for a researcher to play involves a commitment not to management, or prisoners, or scientific objectivity or social work neutrality, but to the specific nature of his own research problem. The social researcher is, after all, something of a boffin, and most people in a sophisticated society can readily appreciate his obsessions. Outside of that the researcher is, whether he likes it or not, a citizen with all the fads, foibles, problems and interests to be encountered in others of that breed. We tried to explain that with as much honesty as we could muster. No doubt we did not entirely succeed, and others will be more aware of the problems of our approach than we ourselves. But having discussed four studies, critically and at some length, it is time to report in detail on our own role at Albany, and the way in which we attempted to carry it through.

Conduct of the research at Albany

There were no official plans for research at Albany; and the present study had its genesis in a request early in 1967 by the first governor to Professor John Martin at the University of Southampton, that he consider the possibility that some research might be carried out by the Department of Sociology and Social Administration when the prison opened. At that time what David Gould had in mind was not dissimilar from the collaborative project he had so recently left at Dover borstal. He envisaged an ongoing programme of monitoring, and eventual evaluation, of the experimental schemes to be introduced at Albany. He hoped the researchers would be able to feed back information into management meetings, where problems would be identified and remedies suggested – which, if implemented, would in turn be monitored and evaluated. He was particularly anxious that the research should examine the problems associated with setting up a new prison, although the possibility of a longer-term relationship between the prison and the university for research and training purposes was also discussed.

Following the initial enquiry, one of us (RDK), who had just been appointed to the Department at Southampton but who was then still working at the Institute of Education in London, was invited to put forward proposals for research at Albany. Since he would not be able to take up post until October 1967, six months after the opening of Albany, and since it was expected that several months would elapse before permission and funding for any study would be forthcoming, the possibility of centring a research project on the opening of a new prison receded. In his preliminary response to the invitation, therefore, a number of alternatives were discussed: conscious of the limitations of organizational case studies, and wary of the difficulties of research in which the researcher is placed in a consultancy role, he favoured a comparative study – perhaps involving all the prisons on the Isle of Wight, including Alvington if and when it was built – of closely specified problems in which Albany might be used as a sympathetic testing ground. If at least some of the problems which were specified were also of interest to persons at Albany, then this might go some way towards meeting the request of the governor, but without committing the research workers to a managerial role.

A seminar was held in the Department of Sociology at which the governor discussed his ideas for the development of the prison. He made it clear that the prison would be very receptive to any research so long as some practical relevance could be seen and an outcome could be envisaged. From his point of view and that of his staff, and conceivably of the prisoners also, the more immediate the outcome the better, though speed was not now seen as essential. This was followed by a visit to Albany by Professor Martin in which he discussed the possibility of a research project with two groups of staff. It was, by all accounts, a lively occasion. Then, in June 1967, Professor Martin was invited to join the Board of Visitors at Albany. In deciding to accept the appointment he also agreed to restrict his involvement in any research that might materialize to a purely advisory capacity, and executive control and responsibility was vested in one of the present writers. After consultation with the proposed research director and the governor, Professor Martin drew up a memorandum which clearly specified the principles which would be observed in any conceivable situation where his role as a member of the Board of Visitors and his role as advisor to the research might be perceived by anyone to be in conflict. We mention this procedure here, even though it occurred almost a year before the research actually began, not only because the principles then enunciated were followed throughout, but also because the procedure, though it was never needed in such an elaborate form, illustrates the spirit in which all future questions of role ambiguity were to be dealt with.

Formal research proposals were put to the Home Office Research Unit in September 1967; they were amended in January 1968 and approved. Given the experimental regime to be introduced at Albany, and the presumed policy of the Prison Department to provide a variety of different regimes in its training establishments (a policy which was later declared in the White Paper, *People in Prison),* it was decided that the study should be concerned with exploring the nature of prison regimes and finding ways for systematically comparing them. The proposals were submitted under the title *Prison Regimes Project* with the following aims:

i. To describe, and to develop reliable measures of, the nature of the regimes provided in different prisons.
ii. To describe, and develop reliable measures of, some of the organizational influences on, and principles underlying, different types of prison regime.
iii. To attempt to relate the prison experiences of particular prisoners to the treatment plans envisaged by the prison authorities.

It was proposed that initially the research be carried out in two stages, each lasting approximately eighteen months: the first an exploratory study in Albany, and the second a comparative study in four or more prisons. It was suggested that the development of adequate ways for measuring and comparing regimes was a necessary step for any assessment of whether prisons really did offer varied training programmes to meet the presumed needs of prisoners, as well as for any future evaluation of their effectiveness, however that might be judged.

These proposals had only just been submitted to the Research Unit when their proposer was invited to join the Parole Board for England and Wales as one of the criminologist members specified under the Criminal Justice Act, 1967. Once again it seemed possible that problems of role conflict might occur. After consultation, however, it was agreed that both prisoners and staff would understand the problem of fulfilling multiple roles in a complex society, providing these were honestly declared and openly discussed. Again a set of procedures was devised in order to specify the limits of each role and to obviate any possible conflict between them. Accordingly the Home Secretary and Lord Hunt, then Chairman of the Board, were asked to release the research worker from the responsibility of considering any cases which came from Albany or any other prisons in which he conducted research during his term of office. This release was readily granted and communicated both to the members of the Parole Board and eventually to the staff and prisoners at Albany (and later at other prisons). Although letters to members of the Board from prisoners or their families urging special consideration of their cases are by no means uncommon, in no case was the research worker approached, either in person or in writing, by a prisoner involved in the project about his own case. Occasionally members of the Board would seek 'inside information' from the research worker about an Albany case, but this was always tactfully refused with a reminder about the procedures which had been agreed. In the event the main effect of membership of the Parole Board was to reduce the amount of time that one of the present writers could spend in the prison and to shift the burden of day-to-day responsibility for the fieldwork to the other.

The research began in May 1968. In addition to ourselves the research team included Robin Williams and he was joined six months later by Rodney Morgan. From the outset we decided on three principles to govern the conduct of the research and the role of the research workers in relation to the people who would become involved in the project; these, in varying degrees, contrast with the four studies discussed earlier. First, that our prime interest and identification was with our research, which in general terms at least was clearly defined; and that any problems of conducting that research and using any of the methods we proposed to employ would be fully discussed with respondents. We are convinced that the fact that we did have a clear research problem to which we were committed contributed greatly to the acceptance of the research team by staff and prisoners with so little reservation. Our role was acceptable precisely because we knew what we wanted to do and were able and prepared to tell our respondents about it. Second, that any relevant interests of any of the research workers would be matter-of-factly declared, and the implications of these for the research, and for anyone involved in that research, would be discussed with whosoever wished to discuss them. Third, that anyone who wished not to participate need not do so, but that we would give no assurances that we did not feel that we could reasonably back up in the event in an effort to persuade people to co-operate.

Building on the experience of the Morrises at Pentonville, we decided to make a concerted attempt to disseminate information about the research as widely and as quickly as possible. At a preliminary meeting with the governor, which was held at the university, it was agreed that the most effective way of introducing the research would be to hold a series of meetings, first with staff and subsequently with prisoners, and that as far as possible the existing administrative structure of meetings and committees should be used as a way of organizing the introductory discussions. A brief written statement about the research by the research team would also be distributed by the governor to heads of departments. In order to have a clear channel for dealing with any problems which might occur in the course of the research it was agreed that the principal psychologist should act as liaison officer between the research team and the prison.

Between 9 May and 1 June 1968 a series of meetings was arranged with representative groups of staff and prisoners. Nine meetings were held with staff groups as follows: central management staff (1), principal officers (1), perimeter defence staff (2), administrative and clerical staff (1), hall officers (2), Prison Officers' Association representatives (1), industrial and trade staff (1). Four meetings were held with prisoners, one in each of the halls then occupied.

At the first meeting the governor opened the proceedings and then found an excuse to leave the meeting. At subsequent meetings the research team was usually introduced by an assistant governor or by one of the chief officers. Some meetings, including all those with prisoners, were introduced by the research workers themselves. At each meeting the research director gave an outline of the aims of the project, and asked his colleagues to indicate the nature of the work they would actually be doing in the prison. The meeting was then invited to criticize or comment on what we proposed to do, or else to give their views on research in prisons. The discussions ranged widely over many matters, although the amount of talk and the points raised varied somewhat from meeting to meeting. Nearly always the staff raised questions about Pentonville, and a discussion of those provided a convenient sounding board for dealing with research problems generally. In the course of this discussion the research workers gave biographical details and indicated the nature of any interests which they had and which could conceivably be seen as relevant to the research. It may be helpful if the main questions that were asked by staff and prisoners and the answers we gave are summarized here.

'What is it all about?' This question was asked in one form or another at every meeting. We answered that we were interested in what was meant by people when they spoke of 'a prison regime', and that especially we wanted to find out just what was meant when one regime was said to be different from another. *How* was it different? And *how much* was it different? If it was different for staff was it also different for prisoners? And did it matter if it was? To answer these questions, we explained, we would need to talk to as many staff and prisoners as possible to seek their views; to attend meetings and committees to find out why some things were done and not others; to be around the prison to see what did happen and to discuss what we saw with staff and prisoners; and finally to try to find ways by which we could express what was happening in quantitative terms. We usually went into whatever detail was required about the theory and problems of social measurement and its uses and limitations.

'Why Albany: it is changing so fast that you will be out of date before you finish, and anyway it is not a typical prison?' We discussed the difficulties of choosing a research location. We pointed out that we had been invited by the governor rather than the other way around; but that this did not mean that we were there to serve the governor, merely that he was willing to have us in his prison whereas other governors might not be. We also argued since Albany was a prison which was devoting a good deal of thought to the nature of its regime, this was a good place to start. Its changes would present a challenge. But we would also be very interested in the whole question of how changes came about, and we would follow changes through wherever they took us, in case they proved to be of importance that we could not see in advance. The typicality of Albany or otherwise did not matter greatly to us, we said, because we would go on to study other prisons, including some more traditional ones, in due course.

When prisoners asked this question it was often accompanied by the assertion that we had been sent to see a 'showplace' and that the wool would be pulled over our eyes by the staff. We replied that their remarks were already providing an antidote, should it be needed, to what the staff told us and we thanked them for alerting us to Albany's show-piece status. When we said we were interested in comparing it with other prisons, a lively discussion of 'prisons we have known' usually followed.

'What is in it for us?' To which we honestly answered probably very little, or possibly nothing at all. We pointed out that we had no power to introduce any changes, nor did we seek any such power. Although we were interested in, and concerned about, the direction of penal policy we did not propose to make any recommendations about changes in Albany, certainly not until some time after the research team had left Albany, when we would eventually write up our experiences. On the other hand we did hope that our research would be concerned with some things which would be of very close interest to both staff and prisoners. We recognized that staff and prisoners would have different views on many, though by no means all, matters relating to imprisonment, and that we might find ourselves sometimes in agreement with one group, sometimes with the other, and sometimes with neither. We had no special claim that what we would say would constitute the 'real' truth, though we promised that what we said would be based on a careful weighing of the evidence as we saw it. We thought that whatever influence we had would be long-term and cumulative and would depend, among other things, on how others weighed our evidence and conclusions. In the long run we hoped that our research might contribute to an improvement in the dignity and quality of life in prisons, which we regarded as necessary evils. In the meantime we hoped that both staff and prisoners would find some interest in the work we were doing and in taking part in the research.

'What is in it for you, then?' Some staff and some prisoners were surprised to find that our motives for doing research were so mundane, and so complex. We pointed out that 'research' as such posed intellectual problems that interested us, that we had to earn a living within a career structure which placed a high regard on accomplished research; that we hoped to write some articles and possibly a book that would possibly be to our advantage, although we did not realistically expect to make very much money out of it.

Apart from this we had to admit that prisoners, prison staff and what went on in prisons all had some interest in a prurient society and that we were not immune from those interests. We each of us probably had more private reasons which they would probably learn as they got to know us in the course of the research. We admitted that our interest was likely to be very intrusive, and, so far as we could while continuing to intrude we apologized for that.

A great many questions were raised about practical issues and we made it clear, again following the Pentonville experience, that we did not wish to have keys. Some staff were surprised by this self-imposed restriction, but they fairly readily accepted our reasoning that we did not wish to be seen as members of staff. One or two officers pointed out that we were probably already contaminated by our connection with staff as far as prisoners were concerned. This was before any meetings had been held with prisoners, and we agreed that this was a possibility. Several members of staff even gave consideration as to how we could free ourselves from this contamination when we approached prisoners. We said that there was no technique for doing this: that in the long run we would have to be judged on the way we behaved towards both sides, and we were sure that was how we would be judged once staff and prisoners got to know us. We had every intention of being there for a long time to establish our credibility.

'What will you actually be doing?' We said that we could not be entirely sure of all that we would want to do in advance. We would certainly start by talking informally to as many staff and prisoners as we could and who were prepared to talk to us. While some staff had clearly been instructed to attend our meetings, we stressed that no one need talk to us if he did not want to, although we would probably ask twice before accepting 'No' for an answer. We would attend meetings of all kinds, including adjudications, and we also hoped to have access to documents in the prison and at headquarters which would throw light on the research problems we had already outlined. We would spend a large part of our time simply being around the prison, the workshops and so on at all times of the day and night, weekdays and weekends, with the intention of seeing all aspects of the prison. Eventually we would almost certainly want to speak to staff and prisoners in a more formal way, to ask detailed questions about the regime and related matters, although again no one need participate who did not want to. If anyone, staff or prisoners, had any queries at any time about what we were doing or why, we urged them to ask us; and if necessary meetings could be arranged to discuss any controversial aspects of the fieldwork. We also offered to show examples of questionnaires and interview schedules to a representative group of staff and prisoners before we used them; and from time to time in the course of the research we did just that.

The question 'What will you do if . . .?' was asked either directly or by implication by both prisoners and staff seeking our reaction to ill-treatment, bribery and corruption, escape plans, contraband, baroning, protection and other breaches of the discipline code and prison rules, should any of them come to our knowledge. And it was the most difficult question we had to answer. We said that we were aware of the proper channels for dealing with such matters, but that we felt unable to give unequivocal guarantees either that we would use them or that we would not. We pointed out that our area of central interest did not involve the most sensitive areas directly, that most of our information would probably be comparatively innocuous, and that we did not intend deliberately to search out scandal. We regarded it as inevitable, however, that if we spent a long time in the prison some less innocuous matters would come to our attention. We thought that almost everything that we learned indirectly, as a result of just being there, would be dealt with in confidence – as would, of course, everything that we solicited in the course of our enquiries. But we did not think we could extend the umbrella of privilege indefinitely. It was pointless to talk in terms of hypothetical situations, we argued; much would depend on the circumstances in which were told or came to learn of the matter in question; and in the last analysis we would have to act as individuals. We thought that both staff and prisoners would quickly establish how far we could be trusted by our demeanour and behaviour in prison; it was that on which we would prefer to be judged – just as anyone else in prison or in life is judged – rather than on any assurances we might give before we started. In the event we did learn of several matters that we felt could not and should not be revealed, though we have not felt unduly constrained by the confidences entrusted to us. For the most part we were simply able to decide that such matters were not relevant to the subject of this book, and at no time did we feel the need to resort to the official channels.

'In that case, what will you publish?' We said that we had come neither to whitewash the prison, nor to lift the lid off. But that we would have to feel free to publish whatever had a bearing on our research at Albany. We were happy to guarantee that nothing an individual prisoner, or member of the uniformed staff below the rank of chief officer, said in response to our questions would in any way be used against him. And we would strive to preserve anonymity as far as possible. But we could not guarantee not to be critical, and in the case of some higher level staff we did not see how anonymity could be maintained. We were anxious not to make criticisms which could be interpreted as simply scoring points. We would try not to publish anything that we could not back up with evidence. But we thought it inevitable that there would be critical remarks about organization, treatment and so on, as well as perhaps a certain amount of praise. In view of this we gave an undertaking to show a pre-publication draft to the governor or his nominated representative; to the local branch of the POA; to a group of prisoners who could be selected or elected in any way that seemed appropriate at the time (bearing in mind that most of those we would get to know would no longer be in Albany at the time of publication); and to anybody else from the prison who could make a reasonable case for seeing it. We offered to discuss any points which were raised, and to make necessary amendments only if we could be convinced that what we had said was inaccurate, or misleading, or potentially damaging to any identifiable individual who was not prepared to take that risk. Staff, no less than prisoners, were sometimes fearful of Home Office interference. We assured them that we would take the same approach to any points raised by the Prison Department or by the Home Office Research Unit. We reiterated that the ultimate responsibility for publication must be ours. We report briefly on our attempts to carry out these undertakings in a postscript.

We hope we have not conveyed the impression that these meetings were an unqualified success as a means of communicating the nature of the research. They were not. It seems likely that we tried to communicate too much in too short a space of time, and that we probably held more meetings than were necessary merely to effect an introduction. But the meetings developed a momentum of their own and certainly nothing was lost by the element of overkill involved. What the meetings did do was to give us an opportunity to make a fairly clear declaration of intent and to get to know many people quickly. They also gave staff and prisoners an opportunity to express their views and grievances and to form their own impressions of us long before we made any real demands of them. In a few cases, after an initial exchange of views, we could only agree to differ, though to the best of our knowledge there was never any attempt to undermine anything that we subsequently tried to do. For ourselves, and most of our respondents, the meetings provided a point of reference to which we could, and did, return as we subsequently made our way around the prison; and a point of departure from which further contacts could easily be developed.

One of the difficulties involved in arranging the introductory meetings with staff and prisoners was that, whereas it was fairly simple to follow the administrative structure in talking to staff, and to arrange *ad hoc* meetings with those who could not readily be incorporated in that way, there was no obvious procedure to be followed for approaching prisoners. Prisoner committees we thought would provide too small a group for our purposes, and we had no way of knowing, in advance, how such committees were viewed by other prisoners. We wanted to organize open meetings, but we wanted to organize them in such a way that the invitation obviously came from us and not from the staff. Moreover, we did not wish to have a delay between issuing the invitation and holding the meetings, because we did not want prisoners to be wondering what it was all about except in a situation where we could attempt to answer their questions. We were opposed to the idea of trying to communicate anything about the research in writing, because the use of circulars and notices are typically the ways in which official matters are communicated. They can too easily be misunderstood; and they provided no possibility of two-way communication.

Unable to think of a suitable avenue for approaching prisoners, we delayed direct contact with them until after the staff meetings had been completed. We had some difficulty, moreover, in persuading staff not to call all the prisoners together on our behalf and tell them what the research was about. Eventually the following procedure was adopted. On the first available Saturday after the staff meetings we arrived early in the prison. At breakfast time, when all the prisoners were in their dining halls, we went from hall to hall, and after a word from the officer on duty that we wanted to speak to them, we made a simple announcement as to who we were, and invited them to meetings to be held in each hall later that morning. About a third of the prisoners present subsequently came to the meetings.

Our initial contact with prisoners was not entirely satisfactory, although we have not been able to think of practical ways in which it could have been more effectively accomplished. As we have mentioned, one or two officers thought we had compromised ourselves as far as prisoners were concerned by talking at such length to staff first. We do not think that was true, at least not for the majority of prisoners, whose fears were directed much more to the possibility of Home Office censorship than that we would become mouthpieces for the staff. It might well have been better if the prisoner meetings could have taken place at the same time as the staff meetings; but we were very conscious of the lessons of Pentonville and we feared that too early an approach to prisoners would have jeopardized our relations with staff. We certainly would not recommend that anyone attempt to make mealtime announcements in prisons unless they have lustier lungs, and a more theatrical presence, than either of us. Even so the meetings with prisoners reasonably fulfilled our requirements, and those who attended seemed reasonably prepared to take us as they found us in the course of the research. That they were willing to reserve judgment in this way was as much as we could have hoped for.

We give further consideration to the methods of research and the activities of the research workers at appropriate points in the text. Suffice it to say here that we had access to all documents in the prison except confidential medical records and those specifically relating to security. We attended all meetings in the prison at least once, with the exception of security meetings, and many meetings we attended on a regular weekly basis as observers. When we did not attend meetings we often had access to the minutes, so that we were able to keep abreast of events. We were able to sit in on all boards and committees as well as applications and adjudications both by the governor and by the Board of Visitors, and at various times we carried out systematic observations of all these proceedings. We were allowed to talk to any prisoner and any member of staff who was prepared to talk to us, as often and for as long as we liked. We were allowed to visit the prison at any time, could talk to prisoners in their cells, and had access to all parts of the prison without supervision, except the control room and the punishment block, where staff were always present. At Prison Department we were given permission to look at a number of files relating to Albany, and we were also lent copies of many internal reports and other relevant official documents.

On the whole prisoners and staff accepted our focus on the research problems we had set, and gave every co-operation in the many demands that we made. When finally we embarked on a formal programme of interviewing with a sample of 72 prisoners and 95 staff, all of the latter and all but three of the former agreed to participate. One of us, once, had a cell door slammed in his face, accompanied by threats of physical violence; once, after we had unwisely intruded even more than usual by sitting in the visiting room during visits, a prisoner complained about us to the editor of the prison magazine; and once when we attempted some systematic time-sampled observations of association activities we provoked some unusual, and amusing, behaviour on the part of prisoners and staff who colluded at our expense. But these incidents represented the more extreme forms of what might be called the normal friction of research, and all were satisfactorily contained within the framework of procedures we had agreed with our respondents. More usually, whenever we set foot in the prison we became involved in chatting with staff or prisoners at such length that careful timetabling became necessary to ensure the completion of the programme. The varied outlooks, backgrounds and ages of the members of the research team meant that most people in Albany could find one of us with whom they could relate, and we soon acquired more or less affectionate nicknames. That some of the most useful data emerged from discussions between prisoners and an inquisitive ex-policeman whom they referred to as the 'guv-geezer' or 'the prof' suggests something of the success with which relationships were established.

Writing the report
Most of the material contained in this report, broadly that reported in chapters 4 to 8 inclusive, was collected in accordance with the above procedures during fieldwork in Albany between May 1968 and September 1969. In preparing this volume for publication, and in order to give a more complete account of the prison, we have added material relating to the periods before and after our fieldwork, in a way which was not originally envisaged.

Although we arrived in the prison too late to study at first hand the opening of the establishment, we have examined the detailed notes kept by key participants and discussed them with their authors. We have also perused contemporary records in the prison as well as official files kept at the headquarters of Prison Department. These materials form the basis of chapter 3. After September 1969 we maintained informal contacts with the prison which enabled us to keep abreast of developments. In the middle of 1971, after the first troubles had occurred, we re-negotiated entry to the prison and brief visits were made periodically until the end of 1972. Thereafter an informal contact was once again maintained. Although the research activity in these later visits was necessarily less systematic and extensive than formerly, it was possible to resume the research role as outlined in this chapter. In particular it was possible to examine the minutes of various meetings, the annual reports of the governor and a number of crucial documents, such as the records of adjudications and punishments, which enabled us to check on many newspaper stories. These materials form the basis of chapter 9. Throughout the book we have discussed our findings in the context of emerging prison policy.

Part II

Birth of a prison

3   A caravan in a meadow

When Lord Stonham opened Albany Prison at Newport in the Isle of Wight on the third Thursday in April 1967, more than a hundred dignitaries were invited to the ceremony. Then, and at the earlier Press conference, he conveyed a sense of the growing challenge facing the prison service and of the hopes for meeting it that were vested in Albany and other new prisons like it. 'Albany', he said, 'is going to be a prison where dynamic and personal training will be given to some of the medium-sentence men now held under the unavoidably restrictive regimes imposed by the gross overcrowding in London prisons.' But he warned that the prison service still had to work out 'the interdependence of constructive prison training and rehabilitative treatment, while maintaining the standards of security for which the Governor of the island, Earl Mountbatten, designed the blue print'. It was the intention of the Prison Department, Lord Stonham disclosed, to bring up the standards of perimeter security at Albany to the level regarded as appropriate for prisoners in category B, those for whom the very highest conditions of security were not necessary, but for whom escape must be made very difficult. Because of overcrowding elsewhere in the system, however, it was not possible to wait for the completion of this work before bringing Albany into use. Accordingly the Prison Department proposed sending selected men in category C – prisoners who could not be trusted in open conditions but who did not have the ability or resources to make a determined escape attempt – to Albany as an interim measure until the security was improved. With these announcements Lord Stonham not only revealed the extent to which the new prisons designed in the previous decade had fallen short of the current requirements for security, but he also articulated the central problem which was to bedevil Albany for the next three and a half years: how to live with one class of prisoner while preparing for the reception of another.

Even so, as Lord Stonham noted, security was not just a question of floodlights, bolts and bars; and he drew attention to paragraph 322 of the Mountbatten report which best gave expression to the hopes of Albany Prison: 'the nature of the prison regime itself can also contribute greatly to the reduction of the kind of tensions that turn prisoners' minds towards escape'. The corner-stone of the regime at Albany was to be a two-shift system of industrial work, based at first on tailoring and other 'needle trades' and later also on carpentry, which would provide not only the prospect of profit through the more intensive use of machines, but also higher wages for prisoners and the opportunity to earn a respectable livelihood on release. Lord Stonham looked forward to the possibility of wages comparable to those in outside industry 'at some future date', but in any case expressed the hope that 'if we teach prisoners nothing else we shall teach them that work is a privilege, not a curse'. The two-shift system would also provide prisoners, when not working, with an opportunity to take advantage of educational and recreational facilities, and give specialist staff access to prisoners which would not involve the interruptions that hindered the workshop routine in other prisons.

In his speech Lord Stonham made no mention of the closing of Dartmoor, which Albany had been intended to replace. By the time that Albany was opened it had become clear that no serious consideration could be given to the closing down of any Prison Department establishment, no matter how antiquated, with the pressure on prison accommodation which then existed. But he did announce that the design for Mountbatten's maximum-security prison, now to be called Alvington after the local council had objected to the suggested name of Vectis, was being revised. It would be built to accommodate 120 prisoners instead of the 80 for which it had first been planned, and he thought that it would be completed by 1970. Even as he spoke, the Radzinowicz sub-committee that was eventually to dispose of the Alvington concept had been deliberating for nearly six weeks on the regime for long-term prisoners.

The opening ceremony was widely reported in the Press, and Albany evidently created a very favourable impression. The report in the *Isle of Wight County Press* for 22 April 1967, for example, conveyed the enthusiasm of prison staff as well as that of reporters, as the following extracts show.

A new concept in prison accommodation, far removed from the soulless environment which, inevitably, still exists in many penal establishments, was revealed when Albany Prison was opened.

The layout, evolved for ease of supervision and control, is an object lesson in good communication.

The old-fashioned barred window has given way to reinforced frames designed in mullion fashion and adorned by curtains.

The cell will be used . . . mainly as a bedroom only – because of the longer (more civilised) working hours and the varied association activities occupying more of a prisoner's day.

The pleasant dining rooms, where meals are to be served in cafeteria fashion, are grouped together with a connecting central kitchen.

The splendid facilities, recognising the dignity of the individual, as well as the need to reform and rehabilitate, were described by one of the prison officers as a breakthrough.

A tour of Albany Prison was a revelation of enlightened thinking – welcomed both by the prison officers (who volunteered to come here) and in due course, no doubt, by the prisoners, the first of whom are due to arrive next week.

If these remarks seem unquestioning and uninformed, they none the less faithfully represent the way in which Albany was received by the media in its early days. If anyone present in Albany five years later had occasion to read them they would surely have seemed a cruel parody. Even at the time the realities behind the scenes belied the public image.

In the governor's first annual report, David Gould acknowledged the sense of 'confidence and hope' experienced by persons who visited Albany. But he was aware that the occasional visitor was too easily beguiled, by the evident contrast between the old and the new, into believing that what was new must necessarily be the embodiment of reform and rehabilitation espoused in Lord Stonham's rhetoric at the opening ceremony. With heavy irony David Gould began his report by saying: 'In a new prison one may hope to find the most clear expression of the best and most up-to-date thinking about prisoners and prison management. The potentials for safe custody and humane treatment can surely nowhere else be so well provided: nor the staff so carefully selected, briefed and prepared.' Such was certainly not the case at Albany. In fact the departmental thinking on prison management and the methods of humane treatment was so confused that what was about to be introduced into Albany as official policy was already emerging as unworkable in the eyes of a Home Office organization and methods review team. All too little attention was given to the selection, briefing and preparation of the staff for their allotted tasks. The changes in the intended use of the prison meant that the very structure of the buildings was unsuited to its purpose, and the question of safe custody was to become a permanent bad joke.

In this chapter we describe the planning and design of Albany, the hurried process by which the buildings were brought into commission, and the thinking, as we understand it, about prison management and the treatment of prisoners that influenced what was to take place in them.

Planning and design of Albany
The planning of Albany had an unhappy history. When approval was given in the estimates for 1961-2 for the spending of £1 million on the building of the sixth secure prison in the post-war building programme, no site had been fixed and no sketch plans had been drawn up. This fact was to become the subject of much criticism in the report of the Estimates Committee in 1967, for, once a site had been found and the plans put out to tender, it was clear that the costs would be nearly double the original figure. Work began on building the prison at Albany barracks in 1964; and the sloping nature of the site, with a fall of one foot in every twenty, and the heavily sulphate clay subsoil were to cause many problems of drainage and subsidence even after the contractors handed over the prison. From as early as 1962 it was proposed to use part of the Albany site for a small maximum-security block for lifers, and it was this plan that was subsequently developed by Earl Mountbatten. But such a unit was always conceived as a separate establishment from Albany, whose own security was planned on a much more modest scale and on altogether different principles.

In its essential design features, if not in detailed layout, Albany followed the Blundeston prototype as this had been modified by a development group of architects and prison administrators which had been charged with making improvements to prison design. It was thus planned as a series of five blocks or halls, four storeys high and each of cruciform shape. The radial design of the traditional prison with wings converging on a central hub was rejected in favour of separate halls linked by a continuous corridor. Rejected also were the cavernous central spaces extending from the ground to the roof in each wing, which were achieved by locating all the cells around the sides with access provided by spiral staircases and narrow landings on each level. Instead solid floors were to be provided between each level, and the cells or rooms grouped around central staircases on a pattern to be found on many university campuses. Security, according to the philosophy outlined by Peterson (1961a) was designed into the buildings themselves rather than into the perimeter defences which, for most of their length, were to consist of a chain link fence some twelve feet high, topped by barbed wire coils and screened in parts by close wooden boarding. And that in fact is how it was built.

One of the features of the Albany design, in common with that for other new prisons, was that the administration block was separated from the main prison complex and situated, together with the gatehouse and visiting accommodation, as a kind of frontispiece facing the road. In this way it formed part of the perimeter and it was hoped that the depressing effect created by the blank walls of nineteen-century prisons could be avoided (Peterson, 1961a). This device also aided security, because visitors had no need to enter the main prison and prisoners normally had no access to the administrative offices. The front elevation of the prison was further enhanced by a brick wall, which extended for some distance in a zig-zag design and was screened partly by trees, before giving way to the chain link fencing at the sides and back. As the *County Press* reporter commented 'every effort had been made in the design of the building nearest to public view, to avoid the traditional prison appearance'.

Inside the perimeter and behind the main administration building was the main prison complex. The five halls, lettered A to E, each contained 96 cells, thus providing accommodation for a total of 480 prisoners. The cells were grouped into 'nests' of eight, with such nests in three of the four arms of the cross on each of four floors. A typical cell was 8 feet 3 inches long, 7 feet 1½ inches wide and 7 feet 6 inches high, with the walls finished in a mottled rendering and the cement floor covered with linoleum. It contained the following basic furniture: a bed, a built-in chest of drawers with work top, a chair, a pin board, a coathanger and a rug. A large window with mullioned bars provided plenty of light. There was, of course, no sanitation in any of the cells; wash basins, baths, showers, urinals and WCs were situated in the fourth arm of the cross.

The halls formed part of a larger prison complex and they were separated internally from the remaining, predominantly single-storey, structure by steel gates. Access to the halls was provided through lobbies off the central corridor block which linked all the halls. On one side of the corridor block, and adjacent to the lobby for each hall were the hall offices, quiet rooms and association rooms. On the other side of the corridor were the education office, a number of small classrooms and hobbies rooms, a library, canteen and various offices and stores. Church of England and Catholic chapels were situated at the south-eastern end of the corridor, while at the north-western end, opposite D and E wings, a large projection contained the hospital and sick bay, five separate dining halls served by a central kitchen, and accommodation for the separate confinement of prisoners for punishment or other purposes. The punishment area, known as Y hall, contained twenty cells, which were rather larger than those in the halls, and two special cells as well as a separate exercise yard. Another projection from the central corridor, opposite A hall, provided the main entrance to the complex and contained reception accommodation on the ground floor and a large gymnasium-cum-theatre-cum-assembly hall on the upper floor.

Not all of Albany Prison was new. A number of substantial buildings left over from the army barracks remained, mostly on the western side of the site; these were converted for workshop and other uses. One such building, Albany House, was situated outside the perimeter and was taken over as the prison officers' mess. One new workshop was provided for the tailoring industry. The spacious grounds provided ample room for recreation and sports activities to the east and west of the main complex; both these areas were considered as sites for the original maximum-security block and Mountbatten's Vectis.

Long before Albany opened, and even before the Mountbatten inquiry was launched, Albany's security arrangements were in question. In July 1966, in the course of the Prison Department's own review of security, some discussion occurred about the need to improve the grilles, windows and skylights planned for all the new prisons. A site visit to Albany at the end of that month revealed that the rear of the covered vehicle entrance, next to the gatehouse, gave direct access to the main prison compound and thus constituted a possible security risk. As a result it was proposed to develop a secure vehicle compound inside the prison, surrounded by a chain link fence to prevent access to the main prison complex. When Mountbatten visited the site in December 1966 he too was critical of the mild steel bars at the windows, and of the insecure gatehouse and vehicle access, as well as the low security fence. He also noted that in some places the decorative wall bars provided a virtually continuous ladder to the prison roof. Mountbatten expressed disappointment at the failure to do away with 'slopping out' in a new prison, and within two weeks of the publication of his report the works department was asked to consider making electronic provision for the prisoners to have access to the sanitary facilities at night. By February 1967, in the light of the firm decision to designate Albany as a category-B prison, it was decided to erect a new security fence 17 feet high to replace the modest original. None of these modifications, which were, of course, to be but the first instalment of a massive programme of strengthening, had been carried out by the time of the opening ceremony. Indeed, parts of the basic structure were still at that time incomplete. When the gates of Albany were closed behind its first group of prisoners, the prison was, as the governor picturesquely described it, about 'as secure as a caravan in a meadow'.

Several modifications were to begin soon after the prisoners arrived. The category-B security fence began slowly to circle the prison at the beginning of August 1967. Two months after that work commenced in A hall on the installation of wiring for the experimental ELSA (electronic locking sanitary arrangements) system. Under this system prisoners could use an intercom device to request access to the toilets, and the cell doors were operated electronically by a single officer situated in a small control room. It had been hoped originally that it would be possible to install the wiring one floor at a time without emptying an entire hall, thus enabling Albany to make a greater contribution to the relief of population pressure in the prison system. But it soon became apparent that such partial arrangements would be inadequate to protect the security of the equipment and the circuitry, and so A-hall prisoners were transferred to E-hall, which was brought into temporary use for the first time. Eventually, after many delays and some changing of minds, it was decided to extend the system to all the halls and to transfer the function of the small A-hall control room to a new security control room when that was built. This transfer to the centralized automatic control system (CACS) involved the rewiring of A-hall to higher standards and was not finally completed until the end of 1971. Through all that time Albany thus had only four of its five halls operational. The electronic locking systems, introduced to effect night sanitation, came to have security implications also. If prisoners were to be allowed out of cells, one at a time and unsupervised, it was necessary to ensure that they had access only to the toilet recess. Accordingly the central stairwells were enclosed and internal gates were similarly fitted with electronic locks.

It was not just the security of the prison that caused problems. Even before the prisoners arrived the governor and skeleton staff had recognized that it would be difficult to supervise the halls, and virtually impossible to maintain a complete surveillance while prisoners were unlocked. Unless undue restrictions were placed on physical movements during association periods an improbable number of staff would be required to supervise the cells and toilet recesses on each of four levels as well as the association and quiet rooms on the ground floor. Once the first prisoners had arrived it was clear that movement from five separate halls, down a single central corridor, to five separate dining halls would again be almost unsupervisable unless severe limits on timing and use were introduced.

Many other design defects soon came to light. The accommodation for welfare staff was inadequate and too far away from their centre of operations. After vacating their allotted share of the administration block they moved to one of the old buildings on the site where there was more room, though they were still too far away from the main complex. The space allocated for church services was too large bearing in mind the demand, while the provision for educational activities was too small. The hobbies rooms were thoughtlessly built without running water to help clearing up afterwards. And as if this wasn't enough many of the buildings, including staff quarters, and their equipment did not work. The cryptic comments in the governor's annual report tell the story of these imperfections, and of their dangers and discomforts for those who had to use them, much more forcefully than we could:

> Fittings suddenly falling from position, e.g. kitchen cupboards and Venetian blinds causing grievous bodily harm; and continuing to happen after given warning. An attached back porch and water closet subsiding. Flooding: we have been built on clay; and all round the mis-appropriation (should it be called theft?) of top soil and destruction of trees forces us to live in semi-swamp conditions. The omission of hand rails on stair ways. The expectation that water will flow up-hill to reach drains, even in bathrooms. The expectation that hot air will not rise and flow out of unclosable ventilators. The lack of protection against snow, so that the regulating office and the main prison corridor were at one time inches deep in snow. The flooding of an expensive gymnasium after a few hours of frost. The explosion of a baker's oven, mercifully in the middle of the night. A grille falling on the man who unlocked it . . .

No doubt all new institutions have their teething troubles, though the number of defects at Albany, of which the governor's list was just a sample, was unusually large. What was truly remarkable, however, in view of the incomplete state in which the prison was delivered up and the many proposed modifications, not to mention the repairs which became necessary, was that no provision had been made for the works department, and temporary accommodation had to be found for them.

Humane treatment and prison management
If the 'potentials for safe custody' in this newest of prisons were not all that they appeared to be, what of 'the most up-to-date thinking about prisoners and prison management' referred to in David Gould's ironic opening paragraph?

We indicated in chapter 1 some of the forces which were to produce such rapid and radical changes in official thinking about prisoners and prison management. Most of these forces had emerged, or were evidently emerging, by the time that Albany opened. But they came too late to have any major effect on the overall planning of the Albany programme and its implementation. Though these forces must have served to heighten the anxieties of the chief participants there, Albany, like Gartree and

Blundeston before it, was conceived within the general philosophical framework of *Penal Practice in a Changing Society* and born
out of the ramshackle and amateur organizational apparatus that
had been bequeathed by the Prison Commission. Both the
philosophical framework and the organizational apparatus were
under challenge, and even in process of modification. But the
evidence from Albany suggests the process had not gone far.
Dissatisfaction with the existing specification of goals and roles
had not yet produced the realization that the specification of new
ones was a full-time job; and though the need for managerial
innovation was recognized, the need to provide the professional
resources and training to achieve it was not.

Two themes came to dominate the governor and his senior staff
at Albany. The first was the attempt to devise and create a regime
which would provide opportunities for prisoners to restructure
their attitudes and behaviour. The second was the struggle to
evolve a flexible, participative but viable, management structure
which moved away from the centralized, militaristic model of the
traditional prison. The first statement of the Albany programme
that we have been able to find appeared in the form of a staff
circular issued by the governor on 23 May 1967, the text of which is
given below.

Albany Prison

Aims

The prison shares with all prisons the objectives of humane
custody and behaviour changing from criminal to non-criminal.

Method

The prison has two basic items in its programme.

1   Industry i.e. needle trades, and woodwork and certain other
    domestic tasks necessary to run and maintain the prison. A
    shift system is to be established.
2   Social Training, i.e.
    (a) involving the prisoner with the staff in running the
        prison.
    (b) giving the prisoner opportunities to talk with staff both
        in groups and especially individually.

(c) letting the prisoner take as many decisions for himself as possible.

(d) using careful reports on the prisoner's response to make reports to parole boards, hostel boards, and working out boards.

Management

The management of the prison is in the hands of the governor. He has various staff of several grades working with him. The management will be shared with staff to the level of their capacity. The governor must help the staff to know what they are responsible for, and to understand what they are doing and why. He must help them to know what sorts of decisions they may make and what not.

Development

The new prison has to progress by trial and error. It becomes what the staff, the prisoners, the various departments of Head Office, the government and the people collectively want it to be. This can be, because of conflicting interests, a hopeless muddle. The staff, led by the governor, must work out methods of work to achieve specific ends. They must consult prisoners but not be put off by them. Sound ideas put forward by prisoners should be respected, and used if they take us towards our ends. Development will be by taking decisions about methods of operation following discussions with the personnel concerned. A final method of operation is unlikely ever to be reached. Changes should follow from experience and insight gained as we work together.

Staff participation

It is important that staff should feel and know that their participation is necessary and wanted. There is no magic formula for running our prison. We must all intelligently work out the best way to do our tasks, and to collaborate with others. It is hard but interesting work. Ideas do not come only from the governor or from Head Office. It is the governor's pleasure to harvest ideas from anywhere, and to consult staff both formally and informally whenever he can. The detailed arrangements, at this stage, may change but they are being set out for all to see in subsequent papers.

A. Gould
Governor
23.5.67

This rather rudimentary statement has been quoted in full for several reasons. It provides, of course, a dramatic declaration of intent on the part of the governor as to the way in which he proposed to run his prison. And in a real sense it constitutes the scratch line, as it were, from which all subsequent developments took their departure. As such it is useful to have it as a yardstick now against which these developments may later be judged. But it is also remarkable for its very primitiveness and for the fact that it was a month after the first prisoners had arrived in Albany before the governor was in a position to issue such a statement. The incompleteness of this initial statement, however, was entirely understandable. No English prison in modern times had, to our knowledge at least, ever specified a programme more precisely. And it is clear that there were no more clearly worked-through ideas available at headquarters.

So far as we were able to ascertain, from our discussions with senior management at Albany and from our examination of headquarters files, there was no systematic documentation of the aims of Albany Prison or of the methods to be used in implementing them. No ongoing committee or policy group appears to have been charged with specifying the detailed programme or for thinking through the consequences of its implementation. This is not to say, of course, that the statement prepared by the governor was the idiosyncratic response of one man produced in isolation from the general thinking of Prison Department. There were, presumably, some *ad hoc* meetings at which the outlines of the Albany programme were worked out; and there is evidence, both from his talk at a seminar held in the University of Southampton in March 1967, and from his writings, that the governor was charged by headquarters with finding ways of clothing the *haute couture* concept of 'social training' in a more substantial workaday garb.

It is probably true to say that, in so far as any serious attention had been given by prison administrators and prison reformers to the aims and methods of imprisonment over the years, more thought was given to the methods than to the aims. The tendency, until recently at least, had been to ignore the less fashionable notions of deterrence and safe custody, which were viewed as rather routine matters, the unfortunate setting within which the higher-order objectives of reform and rehabilitation ought to be pursued. Without specifying too closely just what 'reform' or 'rehabilitation' meant, efforts were geared towards devising more effective methods of 'treatment' on the one hand, and to classifying prisoners according to their supposed 'needs' on the other. By 1967 the importance of security in its own right had once again been brought to the forefront of penal philosophy; and the governor of Albany suffered from no illusions about this. He was well aware, as all prison governors must be aware, that the first duty of any prison is to contain its prisoners; he was all too conscious of the precarious defences of Albany and the public concern that would be expressed at the first escape; and he was always ready to remind the more enthusiastic members of staff or visitors that 'there is nothing any prison can do for a man who has already gone over the wall'. By 1967, too, the need to specify what was meant by reform and rehabilitation was also being felt. Some dissatisfaction with the vagueness of Rule 1 of the Prison Rules – 'The purpose of the training and treatment of convicted prisoners shall be to encourage and assist them to lead a good and useful life' – was being expressed; but it was by no means clear what should be put in its place. Since the alternative formulation of purposes put forward by the governor in his circular – 'humane custody and behaviour changing from criminal to non-criminal' – purports to relate to other prisons besides Albany, it may reflect the then thinking within the Department. It is notably more ambitious and more precise than Rule 1 and for that reason more vulnerable. But the difficulties experienced in finding adequate words to express the purposes of 'prison treatment' were not so easily solved, for in the declaration of aims in the 1969 white paper, *People in Prison*, alongside the most explicit statements about humane but secure custody, there is a return to the wording of Rule 1, and even to the venerable words of the Gladstone Committee, to convey the meaning of such terms as 'reformation', 're-education', 'treatment', 'training' and 'rehabilitation'. Had the governor of Albany prepared his statement of aims with the benefit of his Albany experiences behind him, no doubt it would have been expressed more cautiously in terms of the more limited and more realistic objectives which came to be set in the course of his term of office.

Official thinking on the methods to be used in Albany appears to have been equally vague. The 'trawl' notice sent out by the Home Office to recruit staff, for example, simply stated that the new prison would provide for the south-east the same sort of regime as Gartree provided for the Midlands. It would thus require 'the maximum involvement of staff' in the training programme for prisoners which would be organized around a two-shift system of industrial work. The involvement of staff in the training of prisoners was not a new idea. Peterson (1962), then chairman of the Prison Commission, had already spoken of the need for a new role for the prison officer; and in 1963 the POA had passed a resolution calling for a more satisfying job specification. A joint working party, set up to consider the role of the prison officer under the auspices of the Whitley Council, has issued periodic reports on the matter ever since. But it is still hard to know just what, in behavioural terms, 'involvement' really means, and how it is related to the objectives of treatment and training. In the circumstances the limited specification offered by the governor undoubtedly represented an advance. The thinking behind the two-shift system of work seems to have had two ends in view. On the one hand more time would be created for staff to pursue their 'involving' activities with prisoners, whatever they might be. On the other the more intensive use of resources might contribute to the economically efficient industries beloved by some penal reformers and aspired to in the reports of the Advisory Council on the employment of prisoners (1961, 1964).

Although the concepts of social and industrial training were not new there was little enough experience in applying them systematically, and most traditional institutions paid little more than lip-service to them. The task of devising a management structure that would enable them to be implemented was, therefore, a matter of priority if any progress towards the ambitious goals was to be made. As we pointed out in chapter 1, by the time Albany was launched the administration of the prison system was under attack and changes in the style of prison management were very much under discussion in the Home Office. Two important reports by the organization and methods divisions of the Treasury and the Home Office had been produced. The first, on *The Scope for Management Services in Prisons,* was circulated within the Department in July 1966 and recommended that an attempt be made to 'devise different and more effective organization structures for different kinds of prison service establishment'. The second, entitled *Structure of Responsibilities in Training Prisons,* appeared six months later in January 1967. What surprised the authors of the later report was that so few differences in management structure could be found between prisons of supposedly different types. Though they pointed out the inappropriateness of existing arrangements for present-day needs, perhaps they had not fully realized that there had been few changes to that basic organizational plan for more than a hundred years. Thus the Pentonville staff list given by the Morrises (1963, p. 73) for 1959 was noticeably larger than the list cited by Mayhew and Binny (1862, p. 121) for 1856, but the growth had not produced real structural change. Apart from the addition of a deputy governor, the possible upgrading of the foreman of works to a senior foreman of works, and the disappearance of the schoolmaster, the only differences were either in numbers (an extra medical officer, for example, and more discipline staff in all grades), or in nomenclature, 'officers' having officially replaced 'warders' as long ago as 1919, though the age-old titles of 'steward', 'steward's clerk' and so on still remained.

Pentonville was not, of course, a training prison, and change came there even more slowly than elsewhere. But so long as the only objectives of the prison were to hold prisoners in custody and perhaps to give them some kind of occupation while they were there, then an organization structure in which a body of officers were responsible through their chief to the governor for security, good order and discipline, together with a chaplain and medical officer to look after the spiritual and physical well-being of the prisoners, a foreman of works to care for the fabric of the prison, and a steward to take charge of general administration, cash and accounts, employment and manufactures, victualling and stores, was all that was required. Towards the end of 1959, however, the belated arrival of its first welfare officer, then under the employ of the National Association of Discharged Prisoners Aid Societies (NADPAS), and in the early 1960s the arrival of its first assistant governor and the reappearance of the schoolmaster in the form of a tutor organizer, represented Pentonville's move towards rapprochement with the new demands of treatment, training and rehabilitation. Such changes had begun earlier in training prisons and gone further. Here and there since 1946 prison psychologists had been appointed, initially to help with court reports, diagnosis and allocation but subsequently concerned with therapeutic and advisory duties. Industrial managers, though that title had always been a misnomer for workshop managers or even foremen, were appointed as the commitment to prison employment increased. Welfare officers, brought in under the probation and after-care service from the beginning of 1966, were encouraged to undertake ongoing casework as well as routine reporting, liaison and other administrative duties. And all grades of discipline staff have been under increasing pressure to play a part in treatment and rehabilitation in addition to control and supervision. But these new categories of staff and accretions to old roles were introduced almost completely without regard to their place within the existing administrative structure and often without any clear idea as to what was the nature of their task. There was, moreover, no machinery for establishing just what tasks were being carried out, to what end and with what effect. It was as if headquarters operated under the delusion that the expression of good intentions, which appeared to be consistent with the new philosophies, was synonymous with their achievement. It was this kind of out-of-touchness, of course, that was to be criticized by Mountbatten and by the Estimates Committee.

It would be quite wrong to say that the changes that were introduced did not influence thinking or affect the existing structure. They did. And what they did was to introduce a substantial element of doubt: doubt as to the validity of simply locking and unlocking; doubt as to what should be done instead; doubt as to who should do it; and doubt as to what priority should be accorded to whatever it was that was going to be done. Doubts which could not be resolved by reference to the vague wording of Rule 1. What these changes also did was to raise expectations, realistic or not, on the part of prisoners about what could, might or ought to be done for them. In these circumstances it was left to the governors of institutions to resolve the doubts and to meet the expectations as best they could. We have remarked that the power of governors – and the machinery for exercising it – was not unlike that available to eighteenth-century naval captains. Formally there was little to prevent them from responding to the new pressures in whatever way they wished. In practice they were likely to be too stretched by the exigencies of the prison to be able to formulate a consistent policy in respect of any of them. And most appear to have been bound, however unwillingly, by the traditions of the service and the realities of the situation; these demanded supportive action for the discipline staff in the pursuit of order and control, and left supportive words for the rest. Administration was conducted largely without discussion through the issuance and acceptance of governors' orders, which could and did cover every aspect of institutional life, including any directives from headquarters. As Mountbatten noted, there was often no procedure for checking whether such directives were carried out. Often the nearest thing to a management meeting was what was known as the 'knitting circle', a daily meeting of the governor with the chief officer and other heads of department at which the mail was opened and the business of the day reported and discussed.

Many of the difficulties and conflicts which had grown up in the organization structure of prisons were well known to the participants as well as outside observers. The problem was how to solve them. Perhaps we should summarize the main issues as they probably appeared to most informed critics at the beginning of 1967, for it was with these that Albany had to come to terms.

First, though the governor's role was perhaps the most clearly understood in any prison it was structured in such a way that his capacities for fulfilling it adequately were severely strained. In addition to his legal duty to deal with prisoners on an individual basis as required, and his formal responsibility for a complex but essentially *ad hoc* structure of boards and committees within the prison, he was charged with the sometimes heavy burden of representing his prison to the public. But what took a disproportionate amount of his time and attention was the unco-ordinated work of the separate departments within the prison, especially as the heads of each of them often reported directly to the governor on their activities. As a result he could easily take on too much detailed responsibility for quite trivial matters, leaving him no time or opportunity to deal with affairs of greater moment. What was needed was some way of narrowing the governor's span of control, and regrouping the responsibilities of his subordinates.

Second, the position of the deputy governor was clear enough when he was deputizing for the governor, but much less clear when he was not. In terms of rank the deputy governor can be either a governor class III or an assistant governor class I, depending on the size and function of the prison. Sometimes the deputy might be given responsibility for fairly specific areas of activity – usually labour allocation or staff training, and sometimes both – but his place in the hierarchy and his role as co-ordinator varied from prison to prison and were seldom made plain. If he was reduced to the same status as other heads of service he could do nothing but add to the burden of the governor. If, on the other hand, everyone had to report to the governor through the deputy, then either the fate outlined for governors befell him instead, or else he became merely a post office, which solved nothing.

Third, and perhaps most difficult to resolve, was a series of dilemmas surrounding the positions of assistant governors and chief officers. The post of assistant governor class II in prisons appears to have been modelled on that of the housemaster in borstals; according to the recruiting literature he could expect either to be given responsibility for the oversight of a group of inmates or to be charged with the supervision and training of staff, or both, though 'his precise duties will vary with the approach to training of the particular establishment in which he is serving'. But the fact is that, given the existing management structure, difficulties were bound to ensue no matter in what way his role was cast. When not required to act up in the absence of his superiors, the AG occupied only an ambiguous place in the hierarchy. When the chain of command did not run directly from the governor to the chief, it went normally through the deputy and not through the AG at all. Indeed, the chief officer had by tradition occupied a position very close to the governor, especially on matters relating to good order, discipline and security. In some smaller prisons where there was no deputy the chief officer would formally be the second in command. At the same time, the AG was clearly a member of the governor grades, albeit an apprentice member, and he could reasonably expect to control his own establishment one day. If his line position were to be formalized it would almost certainly have to come immediately below the deputy, thus effectively demoting the chief officer. Add to this that AGs tended to be young and freshly trained whereas chief officers, because of the promotion structure, tended to be close to the end of their careers, and it is hardly surprising that the difficulties between them were often uneasily resolved into a relationship not unlike that between a subaltern and an RSM in the army.

If the AG was given a managerial role in respect of staff supervision and training, this too was likely to be at the expense of the chief officer, for these had traditionally been the concern of the chief officer, even though he usually delegated them to a principal officer. If the AG was given responsibility for a group of prisoners in a hall or wing, he by no means escaped problematic line relationships and he might find that he had problems with the specialist staff as well. On the one hand his wing or hall was staffed for him by the chief and the principal officer in charge of the staff detail, and though the hall staff could expect to take instructions from the AG they remained answerable to the chief. In so far as he discharged his duties in a narrowly managerial or supervisory way he might come into conflict with his hall or wing principal officer, who would expect to supervise the basic-grade officers and to have some say in the general routine. On the other hand, in so far as he interpreted his role in a casework or treatment sense in the borstal tradition, he was likely to overlap with the welfare officer, the psychologist and even the medical officer. To the extent that an attempt might also be made to widen the role of basic-grade officers into the casework and treatment areas, these problems, both with senior discipline staff and the specialist staff, could only be exacerbated.

Fourth, and possibly most importantly, were problems surrounding the general administration of the prison, especially those concerning the tangle of responsibilities for prison industries and the relationship between headquarters and local organization. Many of the problems centred on the role of the steward, which had itself developed from the role of the governor's clerk, and which by this time had been renamed administration officer. The responsibilities of the AO, who was normally an executive-class civil servant with no specialist training though often with long experience of the system, had grown considerably over the years until they occupied a complex, multi-functional department. The administration officer was typically in charge of at least four distinct functions: *(i)* authorizing expenditures and keeping accounts and records in respect of pay and personnel, stores and supplies, and controlling all cash transactions; *(ii)* providing general office services; *(iii)* maintaining information on the various legal and quasi-legal matters concerning prisoners and the courts, including up-dating of the records, i.e. the functions of what had come to be called in the mysterious terminology of the prison system 'the discipline office'; and *(iv)* managing prison industry. While the first two functions were what might have been expected for such an office and raised no particular difficulties except, perhaps, over what could properly be authorized at local level and what should be authorized at headquarters, the third and fourth functions raised many problems.

The difficulties arising from 'discipline office' matters were basically of two kinds: the efficiency of the work and the availability of the results. In a system that sets such store by the records and the files it was remarkable that the methods used in collecting, recording and storing data were several decades behind the times. Moreover, these records formed only part of the total record system in any prison and there was no effective means for integrating the parts. Thus information maintained in the discipline office about alterations to dates of release, appeal dates, prison transfers, parole eligibility and so on was vital to the planning of manpower needs in the workshops; but the industrial manager would also have to go to several other sources – labour allocation board, home leave board, hostel board, hall officers and so on – to keep up to date on internal changes of status and location, in order to plan effectively. Usually the industrial manager would not have too much difficulty in collecting the data, though the process might be time-consuming and cumbersome. But the same sort of information might, for reasons of geography or departmental protectiveness, be less accessible to, say, the welfare department or the psychology department for whose work it could be equally vital. There was clearly a need for a centralized, accessible system of record-keeping, perhaps using modern techniques of data retrieval, which could easily be updated and readily cross-referenced to departmental records. But the problems over the discipline office, though serious, paled into insignificance alongside the problems surrounding prison industries.

Prison industries had emerged but slowly, and the allocation of responsibilities for them had been unclear, contradictory and self-defeating. This reflected the successive philosophies used to justify prison industries, which had ranged from providing occupational therapy or simply occupation, through character training and vocational training, to the economic use of resources and the eventual promotion of the economic independence of prisoners. Traditionally the deputy governor would have final responsibility for allocating prisoners to labour, and thus for their wages. The industrial manager, usually a technical officer with some specialist industrial qualifications or experience, would be expected to supervise both the workshops and their instructors, some of the latter being civilians and some being prison officers. On these and other technical matters he would be responsible to his superiors in the department of industries and stores, both at headquarters and in the newly emerging regional structure. But he would also be expected to inspect the raw materials and to control the pace of work and the quality of the product, for which he would be responsible to the administration officer. Though the AO had nominal control over industries, he would typically have neither specialist knowledge nor managerial skills. Nor did he have real financial responsibility, since sales and contracts and therefore costing were dealt with at headquarters. More often than not the AO tended to limit his role to looking after the stocks of raw materials and finished goods and attending to the necessary paper work. One of the results of this ambiguous structure of local and central responsibilities was that no one could really say whether any particular industry was profitable or not; there was simply no machinery for gathering the information to make the calculations (Cooper and King, 1965). There was also plenty of scope for disagreement: between the industrial manager and the administration officer over technical and administrative matters; between the chief officer and the AO over the control of officer instructors; between the IM and the deputy governor over allocation of prisoners; and, of course, between the industrial staff at all levels and the treatment staff – welfare officers, psychologists, and assistant governors – over the removal of prisoners from the workshop and the priorities to be given to social and industrial training. Disputes had to be resolved by the governor, but since so much was out of his hands and in the control of headquarters it was not always possible to reach satisfactory solutions.

Line and staff problems of central-local relationships were by no means limited to the industrial sphere. Possibly the next most difficult area concerned the position of the foreman of works, whose activities were increasingly supervised by the directorate of works at headquarters and its regional office, though he remained responsible to the governor at local level. Finally there were various professional staff who were in varying degrees responsible to the governor for the services they provided, but who also had areas of independent jurisdiction, as well as professional superiors either at headquarters or outside the prison service entirely. Thus the medical officer, the chaplain and the psychologist all had superiors at headquarters to whom they could turn when delegated powers were insufficient, while the welfare officer could look to his principal probation officer, and the tutor organizer to the local education authority. Apart from the problem of balance between central supervision and local autonomy in these areas there was also a clear need to establish priorities, particularly as between industries and the various specialist services.

The report on the *Structure of Responsibilities in Training Prisons* made a start in addressing these and other organizational problems. It defined the three primary areas in which prison management operated as security, rehabilitative treatment, and the economic use of prisoners' time. While security was rightly deemed to be a factor in all establishments, rehabilitative treatment and the economic use of prisoners' time were seen as alternative emphases at opposite ends of a spectrum of possible regimes. The authors of the report suggested that whereas any economic activity of the kind that was likely ever to be practised in prisons would be suited to a relatively 'mechanistic' structure in which there was a clear hierarchy of vertical communication and control, rehabilitative treatment probably required a more 'organic' structure in which there was room for initiative and for information to flow in all directions (cf. Burns and Stalker, 1961). Accordingly they proposed model organization structures for two types of training prison. One of these, code-named 'Worksop', was to be a prison in which 'emphasis, even priority . . . is given to industry and where a more businesslike structure seems appropriate'. The other, code-named 'Folkestone', was to be a social training prison providing a regime 'where prison officers are directly involved in rehabilitative treatment and group therapy'. At 'Worksop' a written constitution would guarantee the economic priority and a new structure of responsibilities would ensure that it was carried out. The governor would retain overall responsibility for the establishment, but his deputy would be a suitably qualified business manager in charge of the industrial side of the prison. An assistant governor would fill the role of personnel manager, and specialist staff would effectively report to the governor through him. The personnel office would also combine the functions of the old discipline office and the chief officer's clerk, thus centralizing record-keeping and the allocation of staff. In effect the administration officer would be abolished and his duties redistributed. The residual functions of providing general office services, victualling and supplies, and so on, would be dealt with by an executive officer, also under the personnel manager. On the industrial side headquarters would be charged with financial accountability, but the business manager would have to be closely involved in all decisions taken. He would have the assistance of a workshops manager. The appropriate Mountbatten standards of security were assumed, and responsibility for external security and internal good order and discipline would fall to the chief officer. Since the regime would make no attempt to provide social training or treatment, and the inmates would be carefully selected so that they did not require such training, the discipline staff would be just that, concerned only with supervision and control.

At 'Folkestone' the structure of responsibilities conceived by the O and M study teams was rather more problematic. The main innovation proposed was a division among the uniformed staff with a separate corps of discipline officers concerned with external security, while the majority of officers would be concerned with social training and internal order (an idea, incidentally, which was later considered and rejected by the Radzinowicz sub-committee). Security would be the responsibility of a high-ranking discipline officer with direct access to the governor. But the chief officer and the deputy governor would be regarded as equal and interchangeable with a new title of social training officers. Each would be responsible for the training plans of half the prisoners to a training control group comprising themselves, the welfare officer, the tutor organizer and the medical officer, under the chairmanship of the governor. An executive officer would take over the discipline office function and serve as secretary to the group. Basic-grade staff would implement the training plans under the supervision of principal officers or assistant governors, who were again regarded as equal and interchangeable. The chief and the deputy would also be responsible for good order in their respective halves of the prison and subordinate staff would report to them on these matters. Industry would have to play some part at 'Folkestone' also, and this would remain the domain of the administration officer, assisted by a workshops manager.

It may be argued that the structure proposed for 'Folkestone' would have created as many problems as it solved, but something along the lines of the 'Worksop' proposal was eventually to be incorporated in the first industrial prison at Coldingley in 1969. What is interesting is that the authors of the report, with good reason, made no attempt to specify just what kinds of regime might fall into the intermediate ranges of the spectrum they delineated. Indeed, while it is possible to think of prisons organized on entirely different lines and serving quite different objectives, the only intermediary regimes which could at all be considered to be on the same general dimensions as those used in the 'Folkestone-Worksop' report would include some combination of 'social training' and 'industrial training'. And it was just that kind of combination that the authors, rightly in our view, identified as producing many of the role conflicts in prisons. It was one of the misfortunes of Albany that it was required, like Gartree before it, to make a further attempt to provide both social and industrial training at the very time that the emerging O and M advice was that each regime emphasis required a different organization structure. It is ironic, therefore, that Albany came close to solving some of the managerial problems that had been posed for it, and might have succeeded had it not been for the implementation of the dispersal policy.

Commissioning the prison
Given the extraordinary nature of the task allotted to Albany, one might have supposed that there was greater reason for the staff being 'carefully selected, briefed and prepared' than David Gould had suggested in his report. But the process of actually getting the Albany caravan on the road was carried out in such a cavalier fashion that it could scarcely have had a less propitious start.

The general procedures for opening Albany seem to have followed more or less closely the pattern described by Towndrow (1964) for the opening of Blundeston four years earlier. We have not been able to find any account of the opening of Gartree in 1966, though there is no reason to suppose that different procedures would have been adopted there. The arrangements for Albany were the responsibility of a rather loosely formed committee for the co-ordination of the opening of new establishments. This committee, as far as we have been able to ascertain, met infrequently, and, as its title suggests, its functions were limited to ensuring the co-ordination of dates for the arrival of staff, stores, and prisoners with the dates of the completion of prison buildings and staff quarters, and eventually with the convenience of the minister for the opening ceremony. The committee's functions ended with the opening of the establishment, although

Albany, unlike Blundeston before it, had the benefit of some help and guidance during the early days from two members of the management studies department of the staff college at Wakefield.

On 29 July 1966 the secretary to the committee visited the Albany site, in the company of the then governor and administration officer of Parkhurst Prison. Allowing time for the completion of the most essential buildings, and a delay factor of two or three weeks, it was thought that the governor, who had not yet been designated, his deputy, the chief officer and one principal officer, together with the administration officer and a skeleton support staff, could take up post, and their quarters, in the week beginning 17 January 1967. Stores and supplies would be introduced in the weeks immediately following that, while the assistant governors, principal officers and the cook and baker officer were not scheduled to arrive until the week beginning 6 March. The remaining staff would arrive between 2 March and 10 April, the later date being set for the opening ceremony. The first reception of prisoners was planned for the week commencing 17 April. The secretary's memorandum on his visit was distributed to some seventy-five people, none of whom were actually to serve at the prison. On 1 December 1966, a meeting was called at Prison Department to discuss arrangements for the opening. By this time at least three of the key posts at the prison had been designated: the governor, who attended the meeting, the chief officer and the foreman of works, who did not attend but who received copies of the minutes. The time-table suggested four months earlier by the secretary was agreed with one modification: at the request of David Gould the date for the arrival of the main body of staff was brought forward by one week to facilitate their introductory training. In the event the dates of the ministerial opening, and thus of the arrival of prisoners, were put back several days, so that the period with a full or nearly full complement of staff and before the arrival of prisoners was increased from the ten days or so that was originally planned to rather more than three weeks.

The time schedule for Albany was thus very similar to that at Blundeston: about four months between the designation of the governor and the opening; about two months between the arrival of the advance party and that of the main body of staff; and about ten days for the induction and training of staff before the arrival of prisoners. The completion of Blundeston was delayed for nearly three months by persistent bad weather, and during that period most staff remained at their posts in their old prisons. Perhaps the long delay at Blundeston had some advantage because, according to Towndrow (1964), 'the preparations [for the main party] had been thorough and fairly comprehensive' to such a degree that 'a picture of management as dependable, protective and almost omniscient seems to have developed'. Even so, problems arose, especially in the first three months: from the governor's own confessed inexperience; from the lack of preparedness and training of the staff to develop a regime with which they were only briefly acquainted; from the all too familiar task of completing buildings after the prisoners had arrived; and from the too rapid build-up of the population from 0 to 163 prisoners in eighteen days.

Much the same problems were voiced, though more graphically, by David Gould in his first annual report. When the advance party took up post in Albany on 16 January 1967 they found:

> no chairs, or desks, no telephones, no paper or pens, no teacups, just uncompleted work and mud. . . . Someone arrived with a bundle of files marked *For Albany Governor on Arrival*. There was nothing to wipe or scrape off the mud, no soap or towels, so we went home, to wade through more mud and sort out our furniture, and meet again the next day. We met, our domestic bases a little more secure, and resolved to lick this muddy bloody mess into passable working order in three months. The Central Management Meeting of the prison had held its first meeting and made its first decision.

The Albany induction and training programme for staff began on 10 April and finished on 19 April, though new members were still arriving in the prison throughout that period and several missed the programme altogether. Moreover, while Albany was perhaps quite well staffed compared with many prisons, there were a number of confusions about just what the eventual staff complement would be. Following the Mountbatten recommendations, the prison was intended to have 22 senior officers on its authorized strength. But they had still not been appointed by the end of 1967, and the prison, having sacrificed a number of principal officers in exchange for these newly-created posts, was noticeably short of experienced discipline staff. In May 1967 the chief officer, to whom responsibility for assessing staffing needs had been delegated, still did not know how many senior and how many principal officers would finally be available. And since one hall was to remain empty during the installation of electronic locking devices, and the intake of prisoners was slower than planned, so the prison only gradually reached a full staff strength. In October 1967 there were still 61 members of staff who had not yet arrived, though by that time all the quarters that had been provided had been taken anyway. As for the senior staff, only one assistant governor was in post before the induction scheme began; the second did not arrive until mid-June; a third was 'needed' but was never appointed. The principal psychologist took up his appointment on 4 April, about the same time as the tutor-organizer and the welfare officer. None of these members of staff had formed part of the advance party, although the principal psychologist had been available for occasional consultation. It was not until September 1967 that a senior welfare officer was appointed, and he was attached to all the island prisons. It was small wonder that new staff took some time to find their feet.

Albany fared rather better than Blundeston in relation to the build-up of prisoners, but only as a result of last-minute pressure to control the intake within more manageable proportions, given the need to improve the security of the prison. At the co-ordination meeting of 1 December 1966, when the director of prison administration first announced that Albany was to receive difficult recidivist prisoners, the agreed plan for receptions was as follows: 48 per week for the first four weeks, and thereafter 24 per week until the prison was full. In the event, the pace was much slower, averaging only 10 prisoners per week after the initial reception of 11 prisoners from Parkhurst and 30 from Wandsworth. It thus took Albany around three months to reach the total that Blundeston achieved in under three weeks. One factor in this change of policy was perhaps a visit by the governor to Gartree Prison in February. There he was told of the apparently disastrous results for good order and discipline of a headquarters demand that 100 prisoners be received immediately from Winson Green, where they had been reported as sleeping in classrooms because all the cells were full *(The Times,* 9 February 1967). Still, the early receptions from Parkhurst were difficult enough. And once again the problem of taking on both new staff and new prisoners without adequate preparation was expressed most eloquently by the governor.

> The Department's notion that at a new prison one first gets the
> staff, prepares them, then gets the prisoners, and proceeds is
> over-simple. One gets some of the staff, then some of the
> prisoners. Every influx is a dilution. The training and retraining
> gets out of step. Furthermore new duties are not taught in a
> fortnight, attitudes and behaviour take longer to grow and
> change. . . . The late arrival of senior staff is especially
> damaging. They more than any one else tend to be most in need
> of consultation and help into new roles.

But what seems truly perverse, rather than merely incompetent,
about the commissioning of Albany, is that during this initial
period the governor was required to spend three weeks on
detached duties at Camp Hill! Whether this was to enable an ex-
borstal man to 'gain experience' of prisons, or because his
presence in an empty prison was seen as 'wasteful' we do not
know. But, as the governor remarked: 'We think more planning is
required, not less, to open a new prison.'

We will be offering comments and recommendations on the
commissioning of new establishments in our concluding chapter.
But it is only fair to say here that some of the lessons of Albany,
together with the growing awareness of the need for rational
management which was emerging from internal reviews and
external pressures, may have already produced a change of policy
within Prison Department. Eighteen months before HMP Coldingley was opened in 1969 a guiding committee had been
established to oversee its general planning and development.
Following the 'Folkestone-Worksop' report it had been decided to
make Coldingley the prototype of the industrial prison, and there
was indeed a great deal of planning to do. The committee
appointed a project team to attend to the details for introducing
the industrial regime, and since the team included the nucleus of
what was to become the senior management of the prison they
were well motivated to do their task well. They began work more
than a year before the scheduled opening and were given
accommodation at headquarters until facilities became available in
the prison. The senior psychologist designate was appointed to the
team from the outset and given a special responsibility for devising
research to evaluate the Coldingley regime and to study the
implications of the new management structure for future develop-

ment. A professional management consultant was also invited to join the team to give advice. It would be foolish to pretend that all this resulted in the trouble-free commissioning of Coldingley. It did not. The decision to make Coldingley an industrial prison came late in the day and involved several modifications to the basic Blundeston design. So too did the decision to install electronic locking – as it had at Albany. But it did mean that some prior thought had been given to just what was going to be implemented, and that the project team had time to anticipate the problems that would arise even if they could not stave them off. No one, so far as we were aware, suggested that the governor designate should be detached for duties elsewhere during the run-up period. Indeed it was indicative of the change in thinking that he was encouraged to undergo further management training and to become a member of the British Institute of Management.

4   The emergent blue print

It is difficult to convey at all adequately the mixture of confidence and hope, frustration and disillusion that characterized the early days of Albany. The problems in the design and use of the buildings, the inherent confusions of the brief to pursue both social and industrial training in a single, hurriedly commissioned prison, and the lack of preparation of staff could hardly have formed a less solid foundation for future development. And yet the prison survived and did so with some style. A new participative management structure was forged out of the meagre, traditionally bounded resources, and an imaginative training programme was devised and pursued with great vigour. That the prison was finally unable to overcome the intrinsic difficulties which had surrounded its birth, especially when these were added to by the increasing demands of security that were placed upon it, was not the fault of any of those who were charged with attempting to make it all work. For by any standards the attempt was a remarkable one.

In a curious way the irritating teething troubles that beset Albany from the outset contributed to the solidarity and sense of purpose, and ultimately of achievement, among so many of the staff that was revealed to the Press and public under the David Gould regime. As we have already noted, the advance party, on seeing the site for the first time, resolved to 'lick this muddy, bloody mess into passable working order in three months'. That sense of creating something from scratch, in conditions of adversity, that characterizes all pioneers quickly spread throughout the prison as during the early months scores of new issues arose and were dealt with. Even the most dyed-in-the-wool traditionalist on the staff – and several among the prisoners – could not conceal some sense of pride, elitism or excitement at his association with what was perceived to be a show place and an important experimental endeavour. Unfortunately, Albany was not a genuinely experimental establishment. No official research was built in to evaluate the exercise, and the governor's hope that the university researchers would monitor the programme from the beginning was not fulfilled. Our own research began nearly thirteen months after the prison opened and just five weeks before the effective departure of the first governor on promotion. Nevertheless, from long and detailed discussions with the participants, and a close examination of the written records, as well as our own observations of the prison after we arrived, it has been possible to provide an account of the struggle to develop a new management structure, the pursuit of social and industrial training, and the maintenance of security under the David Gould regime.

The new management
The details of the management structure at Albany evidently evolved gradually, in response to new situations as they arose, and as experience of old situations crystallized. Such was the declared policy of the governor in his initial statement which we cited in chapter 3. But it was, perhaps, the only policy that could have been operated in the circumstances, given that some attempt was to be made to break away from the existing patterns. This is not to say that the departures that were made from tradition were as radical as either of the proposed structures in the 'Folkestone-Worksop' report. Nor that the situation was so fluid that no stable structure could be discerned. But rather that ideas had to be tested out within the limits of the available staff and against the background of what the governor referred to as the 'exigent day'. As far as staff were concerned, there was no careful recruitment of personnel to fill roles in a previously worked-out organizational chart or blue print. Instead staff were supplied in such grades and numbers as were traditionally provided in training prisons, and roles had to be specified in such ways as would make best use of their abilities and yet still form a viable working structure when fitted together as a whole. The problem of the exigent day was that the everyday task of keeping the prison going did not go away while the perfect blue print was being designed. Immediate situations required immediate decisions, often compromises, and each short-term expedient stood to become a precedent for longer-term solutions.

The task of devising the management structure began as soon as the advance party arrived in the prison in the second half of January 1967 to commence preparations for the opening. The advance party of 30 staff consisted of the governor, the deputy governor, the chief officer class I, one principal officer, five basic-grade officers, and a night patrol from the discipline staff; the administration officer with some of his supporting staff, including storemen; and the foreman of works and farm foreman with supporting tradesmen, stokers and so on. Just over one half of the remaining staff arrived, mostly in time for the induction and training programme, in March and April 1967; and this group included the first assistant governor, the first welfare officer, the principal psychologist, the tutor-organizer, the medical officer and the industrial manager. The rest, including the second AG, welfare officer and psychologist, were appointed to Albany after the opening. They came in dribs and drabs, at the rate of about seven or eight a month through 1967 and three or four a month during 1968. As each new senior member of staff arrived the governor tried to provide him with a minimum job specification over and above any obligations placed on him by statute, standing orders or circular instructions, making it clear that he would be happy to discuss possible revisions and improvements in the light of experience. As far as everyday management was concerned, the governor sought to encourage the participation of as many staff as possible, who were invited to discuss alternative ways of working and to reach agreement on the most appropriate methods. In short there was a determined effort to avoid management via the 'knitting circle' and governor's orders.

The main instrument of management at Albany came to be the central management meeting (CMM), which held its first rudimentary meeting amid the chaos of the unfinished site in January 1967. The meeting indeed had humble origins, and both its structure and functions were to change rapidly with the development of the prison. In any case it was led with different styles by successive governors; some of the later changes we discuss in subsequent chapters. But in the early days it appears to have been not unlike the meetings held at Blundeston (Towndrow, 1964), and to have suffered from the same general problem: the fact that no one, not even the governor, had any real experience of such circumstances. It began by meeting on a daily basis, and in the period before the prisoners arrived any member of the advance party could attend to discuss whatever topics arose in the day-to-day development of the prison. Its functions were nowhere spelled out and no minutes were kept. It is thus not clear to what extent it was intended at that time to be either a policy-making or a decision-taking body. Certainly decisions were dispensed, perhaps more often by the governor at the meeting than by the meeting itself. Certainly too, broad policy issues were discussed in relation to the function of the prison and the future management structure. But it seems that most of the business was directed either at keeping people in touch with the hundred and one practical details of opening up the prison, or at reassuring particular members of staff who had found themselves in an unfamiliar setting. It was, in short, a meeting of first and last resort, and a clumsy, unwieldy instrument of government.

During April 1967, however, an attempt was made to lay down the main lines of policy with regard to handling the arrival of the first prisoners, and when they did arrive the meeting moved into a different phase. The meeting was no longer regarded as open to all and was limited to 'senior staff'. It was now intended to establish whether or not action along the lines of the agreed policies was actually being taken, and staff were expected to report on the progress of their departments. Meetings were reduced in frequency, first to three meetings a week, and then to two. Apparently in consultation with the two members of the management studies department at the staff college, who had occasionally attended the CMM, it was decided that minutes should be kept. Though these changes gave the meeting a greater sense of purpose and an appearance of efficiency – to such a degree that the governor recorded his satisfaction that the meeting had become 'established' – it was soon clear that the meeting could not continue on this basis for long. For one thing, whatever the difficulties some staff may have had about being asked to participate in management, many had become used to the joint problem-solving approach which had been adopted in the original meetings, and they enjoyed the sense of solidarity and achievement that this had engendered. As the outlines of staff duties became clearer and confidence mounted, the meeting was used less and less as a means for seeking reassurance. But the tendency to want to get anything and everything reviewed by the meeting continued unabated and there was never a shortage of topics for discussion. With fewer meetings than before to get through the business, each session tended to become bogged down with trivial details; and the administrative arrangements for the meeting did little to ease that situation. The minutes were recorded longhand, in an exercise book, and were merely kept available for reference. For most meetings the agenda was either chalked on the blackboard at the start of the meeting or else given verbally. More often than not, therefore, much discussion occurred under 'any other business'.

Increasingly the governor recorded in his journal that he found it difficult to close down the meeting, and that more and more frequently he had to limit the discussion in an attempt to focus on what he considered to be the essentials. Not surprisingly, given the circumstances we have outlined, he provoked strong criticism about his handling of the meeting on these occasions. It was becoming apparent that there was a need to differentiate between matters which were proper subjects to be considered by central management and matters which should be dealt with at middle-management level. If this were to be done, more effective ways would have to be found for developing second-line management, especially in the halls; and staff would have to be trained to function effectively in their managerial roles. There was some support for this analysis from the management studies department at the staff college.

In July the CMM was again restructured and the membership was limited to the holders of thirteen named posts. The frequency of the meetings was reduced to once a week, in the hope that this would allow more time for senior staff to devote to their departments and to strengthen middle management. But perhaps more talk was generated than action at this time, partly because of the pressing need to attend to the demands of the security fence and related matters, and partly because too much formalization at this stage would not have suited the administrative style of the governor or his managerial objectives. A situation in which all the lines were clearly drawn could represent the same kind of security that was entailed in 'management by governor's orders', and would not encourage the self-examination that probably had to accompany any significant changes in roles. In any case the real problems were perceived to lie below the central management level; and the CMM continued for a further year without the benefit of circulated minutes and agenda, and without further clarification as to whether it was a decision-making body or merely a forum for general policy discussion. Meanwhile the arrival of the second AG had afforded an opportunity to reconsider and re-allocate managerial responsibilities. By October the senior AG, the chief officer I and the principal psychologist had been charged with undertaking a review of the management structure, and all the staff were invited to attempt a closer specification of their jobs and of their relationships to each other.

Up to this point it had been the intention to divide the prison into broad areas of responsibility and to delegate authority in such a way as to free the governor from the obsessive concern with the exigent day. As far as the division of responsibilities was concerned the two major areas, apart from security and general administration, were social training and industrial training. Since social training, whatever it might ultimately consist of, would have to be carried out by the basic-grade prison officers, it was hoped to have their activities in this area firmly represented at central management level by the chief officer. To identify him more clearly with this managerial function it was hoped that the chief would relinquish his uniform in favour of civilian clothes. In spite of some pressure this was never accomplished. Though he was a member of the CMM and undertook negotiations with headquarters about the staffing of the prison, the chief never did come out of uniform and he remained uneasy in the general managerial context. By the time the research team entered the prison it was clear that the future of Albany would prevent any further attempt to recast the role of the chief outside his traditional concern with security and discipline. On the industrial side it was hoped that the administration officer would participate in the management team in a role approaching that proposed for the business manager at 'Worksop', delegating his other functions to subordinate staff. This hope too went unfulfilled. While the administration officer did play a full part along with the industrial manager in the development of industries, his participation in the CMM was typically on a more generalized basis, and during the course of the research there was no evidence to suggest that any special priority was given to his function in respect of industries. The net effect of these frustrated ambitions was probably the widening of the role of the deputy governor and the restructuring of the relationship between the two chief officers class II and the two assistant governors.

The deputy governor was originally intended to be a 'spare' governor. He was, of course, required to deputize in the absence of the governor, but apart from a general requirement that he would help to 'train and encourage' other staff in the skills of management he had no special area of functional responsibility. Instead he was expected to absorb or head off many of the problems that would normally go to the governor. His main task was to 'trouble-shoot': if any 'area of inefficiency, friction or malfunctioning' was identified he was to devote all his resources to bring about improvements. He was a member of the CMM and directly responsible to the governor, but no other line relationships were delineated in his brief. It is not difficult to see how such a parallel role was essential at the beginning. But as it became clearer that the original expectations of the chief officer and the administration officer would not come to full fruition, the luxury of a spare governor could not be afforded, and the exigent day once more encroached on the governor's time. Though the job specification was not formally re-written until the deputy governor was promoted and replaced in February 1969, his role had altered significantly by that time. He retained the 'trouble-shooting' function; but he had also assumed the chairmanship of the local security committee on the one hand, which required close liaison with the chief officer and the security principal officer, and the traditional function of labour allocation and some supervision of the industries on the other. He was also increasingly involved in the development of second-line management, and he acquired numerous specific responsibilities which did not fit easily elsewhere.

At first there was only one assistant governor in the prison, who was expected to cover two broad areas of functioning. First, he was to be responsible for staff resources and staff training, liaising fully with the chief officer and the two chief officers class II as well as other management staff. Second, he was given responsibility for individualizing the social training programme for prisoners, and in this he was to work with the principal psychologist. The speculative nature of these assignments was indicated by the governor, for in the job specification he wrote: 'as to whether these two functions prove too much or alternatively not enough we can discuss as we go along'. It would have been surprising if these tasks did not prove more than enough for one man, and after the arrival of the second AG – and a good deal of discussion – the two functions were separated out. Thereafter the first AG became responsible for 'staff resources and training', and the second for 'social training of the prisoners'. A principal officer was assigned to assist in staff training, but, after due reflection on the original staff induction programme and some months of actually operating the prison, the staff training function was considered to be of such importance that it required still more resources. One of the chief officers II, whose own previous job specification had been somewhat vague, was therefore permanently assigned on virtually a full-time basis to work under the guidance of the assistant governor. The development of the second AG's responsibilities was to follow a similar pattern. After a period of working alone a successful case was made, in the course of the review of the management structure, for the appointment of a supporting principal officer to bridge what was seen as a developing gap between the staff resources side and the social training side. Eventually, and partly as a response to other problems that were emerging in hall management anyway, it was decided to restructure the work of the second chief officer II to allow him to work, permanently and more or less full-time, with the AG on the development of social training. One of the major tasks of the social training team was to integrate their programme with the industrial training. This involved what might be called the social organization, as distinct from the economic organization, of industry, and required close co-operation with the deputy governor.

Both the assistant governors and the chief officers had additional duties of a more traditional kind for which they were responsible in the usual way, but by May 1968 the most important and novel feature of the organization structure at Albany had become the central division of function between the two AGs and their relationship with the two chief officers II. It was, for example, very different either from the normal training prison arrangement whereby AGs might be responsible for hall management or a large group of inmates, or from the structure that had been envisaged for 'Folkestone' where the AGs were to be regarded as equal and interchangeable with principal officers carrying out the plans of a 'training control group'. Both assistant governors at Albany were members of the central management meeting and were responsible to the governor and to that meeting for the fulfilment of their appointed tasks. Though the chief officers II might report directly to the governor or the chief officer I on other matters, they stood in a subordinate and learning relationship to the AGs in respect of staff training and social training. Since these areas provided their major fields of activity they developed a real degree of involvement, and in the absence of his assistant governor each chief officer II would act up in much the same way as he would in the absence of the chief I. On the whole, the arrangement did avoid many of the problems usually to be found between the assistant governor and chief officer grades.

Somewhat outside the main lines of authority at Albany, but with representation at central management level, were the various specialist and professional departments.

The principal psychologist had been charged on arrival with a number of duties. Initially his main task was to set up an induction programme for prisoners and a system of allocating them to halls. In this process, which involved the development of an analytical case file for each prisoner, including a diagnosis and a set of recommendations for training, he was expected to liaise with the senior chief officer II who was then in charge of A hall from where the induction and allocation were carried out. He was also required to consult with the assistant governor in respect of the design and implementation of staff training programmes. The principal psychologist still retained these functions when the research team arrived, although the restructuring of responsibilities at chief officer level after the arrival of the second AG meant that they were carried out in a different organizational framework. As one of the members of the central management meeting who had been concerned in the management review, he had helped to bring that new framework into being; and as time went by he increasingly played a consultative role on organizational matters. He was, of course, called upon to deal with anything requiring his expertise in the assessment and handling of prisoners, and in this he was assisted by a second psychologist and eventually by a psychological tester.

Apart from the works department, which was represented at the CMM in the person of the foreman of works (and received some priority, given the incomplete state of the prison), the remaining specialist departments were only loosely integrated into the management structure or else were almost completely isolated. The welfare department consisted of two welfare officers under the supervision of a senior welfare officer who was responsible for co-ordinating the welfare services in all of the island prisons. When the CMM was reorganized in July 1967 much of the discussion was concerned with the problem of who should represent the welfare department at the meeting. It was resolved that only the senior welfare officer should be a member; but in the event, because of the part-time nature of his concern at Albany, he was rarely present. Although one of the welfare officers substituted in his absence, he could speak with little authority at central management level and the main contribution of the welfare staff was made in middle management. Late in 1968, when their numbers were increased and the senior welfare officer became a full-time Albany appointment, their voice was somewhat strengthened at the central management meeting.

The medical officer was required by statute to care for the mental and physical health of the prisoners; and in this he had the support of a dentist, an optician and a visiting psychotherapist. The sick-bay at Albany was an out-patient department of the Parkhurst Prison hospital and was staffed by two hospital officers and two prisoners, one of whom acted as orderly, the other as cleaner. Some 60 or so cases were dealt with there in an average week, and any prisoners requiring in-patient treatment were transferred to the Parkhurst hospital. The medical officer was also responsible for certifying the fitness for work of members of staff who had been sick, and in his capacity as Medical Officer of Health he could advise the governor if any action was needed to comply with health and hygiene requirements. Although he was a member of the central management meeting he rarely attended it, and never did so during the currency of the research.

Both the tutor-organizer and the prison chaplain were members of the central management meeting. Neither had any authoritative position in the prison hierarchy, and both sought to bring their services to the attention of often unwilling recipients in the course of the prisoners' non-work time. As a result of these difficulties they often presented a similar plea for support in their dealings with their central management colleagues. On the other hand, since both departments had something to offer during the long periods of the day when prisoners were not working a shift, there was a clear need to co-ordinate their activities as part of the social training programme. There might well have been some organizational advantage, therefore, in incorporating the educational service and the chaplaincy within a broad social training department, with the tutor-organizer and the chaplain formally responsible to the chief officer II and the assistant governor. Shortly after the first change of governor at Albany the structure of the CMM was again rationalized, this time into an eleven-man team. The medical officer, the chaplain and the tutor-organizer were dropped, and the industrial manager was brought in at the top level for the first time. This was to reflect, of course, the changing function of Albany within the prison system as a whole, a change which was to give it a new set of priorities.

As far as the devolution of decision-making was concerned, it was clear from the beginning that it was both necessary and desirable that the process should go down at least as far as principal officers. Necessary, because the size of the authorized establishment did not permit the use of assistant governors in their conventional role as hall managers; and if principal officers were not utilized in this way they would represent a greatly under-used resource, given their length of service and seniority. Desirable, because if principal officers could be involved in management it seemed more likely that they would become involved in social training as well. It was much less clear how this might be achieved, and what kind of mechanisms would be appropriate for integrating this level of management into the structure as a whole. As we have already indicated, the need for co-ordination at the middle-management level only emerged as the central management body became progressively bogged down in just those trivia the structure was intended to avoid. We will deal with the development of middle management in the course of our discussion of social and industrial training below.

Social training

The philosophy which emerged in the attempt to give substance to the concept of social training, and which was intended to inform the staff approach to prisoners at Albany, may best be expressed as the endeavour to create and use a state of what the governor called 'controlled and therapeutic anxiety'. His original statement of aims suggested that the goal was 'behaviour changing from criminal to non-criminal'. When a new document was prepared in the course of the review of management structure the senior assistant governor changed the emphasis from a future to a present orientation, and somewhat toned down the ambitious goals of the prison. He referred instead to the more immediate notion of changing behaviour from 'unacceptable to more acceptable'. But neither of these formulations really conveys what the prison was about, and both imply a more active and goal-directed role for the staff and a more passive role for the prisoners than was actually the case. Certainly the governor came to adopt the view that the prison could do no more than provoke, or perhaps nudge, the prisoner into such a state where he might wish to take stock of his situation and consider the consequences of his actions. To this end the formal provisions of the system – parole, home leave, hostel and working-out schemes, and so on – as well as the structure of the regime itself and any contacts with the outside world that it afforded, should be marshalled by the staff to provide, if not leverage *vis-à-vis* the prisoners, then at least some confrontation with the realities of the relationship between cause and effect within the penal system.

The fact that many of these situations were experienced with some anxiety by most prisoners was seen as an opportunity to be used: the prisoners were encouraged to resolve their anxiety by their own decision; and the temptation to reduce their anxiety by the staff's removing the decision or making it for them was, as far as possible, resisted. If the prisoner wished to make some change while he was in the prison, then the prison provided some facilities whereby that change might be accomplished or supported. The facilities, it is true, were comparatively meagre – it is characteristic of new as well as old prisons that the chapel is both more spacious and better designed for its purpose than the classrooms – and the governor was well aware of that. But what facilities there were would be put at the disposal of those who would use them, and some effort would be made to obtain those that were lacking.

The facts that when prisoners are anxious staff are also apt to get anxious, and that staff, no less than prisoners, have a vested interest in 'knowing where they stand in a quiet nick', were soon seen as problems, and probably always were. It was here where the need for the training of staff was most acutely recognized: not only were discipline staff expected to learn how to control the anxieties of prisoners, but they also had to deal with their own anxieties in a situation where they were required to exercise rather more discretion than they had been used to, and even to take decisions on behalf of management. How to teach them how to do it was another matter, and one that stretched the senior AG and his chief officer II throughout our acquaintanceship with the prison.

Some extracts from the governor's annual report after eight months of operation nicely illustrate the dilemmas involved in his attempt to foster social training.

> Prisoners are the greatest reactionaries and constantly force
> staff back to the habits of mind and conduct of the local prison.
> . . . Keeping the prisoner as contented as possible, which is
> what our population believes we should do, and what we also
> wish to do for the sake of a quiet life, is not the same thing as
> disturbing him to the point of changing his behaviour. When we
> do disturb him, he disturbs us and may complain. . . . The
> elaborate arrangements made for prisoners to make complaints
> are not matched by equally elaborate arrangements to get them
> to justify themselves and change their behaviour. Parole may be
> the beginning of such a movement . . . [but] the design of the
> prison is opposed to individual involvement: the lack of
> interview rooms and suitable space for paper work militates
> against it. . . . We found that many staff had not interviewed
> prisoners, or read records, or written up reports. Training to do
> these things cannot be accomplished on a short crash program-
> me. It must arise in work. . . . Being understanding of prisoners
> is tough work, a damn sight harder than banging 'em up. For
> hard work one needs training, support and rewards. At present
> we are finding training, support and rewards for televiewers,
> dog handlers, control panel watchers. So we should no doubt,
> but these jobs are not as demanding, as tiring, or as skilful, as
> living with prisoners especially when they are put into a state of
> therapeutic anxiety. The next major task of management must
> be the development of hall staffs to the point where hall
> management is thoughtful and brings most confrontation and
> interaction.

Wise and constructive hall management by discipline staff was
intended to provide the context for social training at Albany; and
social training was to be mediated through what came to be called
'the case-officer system'. What the social training was to consist of
was to be determined by the drawing up of training plans in the
course of the induction procedure.

When the prison opened, prisoners were received into A hall,
where they stayed for an induction phase lasting about three
weeks. The induction hall was at that time managed by the senior
chief officer II, who was assisted by two principal officers and a
number of basic-grade staff. The main functions of the induction
hall were to check that all receptions were suitable for category-C

conditions, to introduce the prisoners to the organization of the prison, and to prepare the 'Albany file' for each prisoner. This last task involved compiling a digest of the relevant information in the prisoner's official record, the F 1150, interviewing and preparing a report about each man, and writing out a provisional training plan based on an assessment of the prisoner's needs and the resources available. Training plans were drawn up under the general supervision of the principal psychologist, who had been instructed by the governor to distinguish as far as possible between what was 'merely desirable and what was practical'. There is little doubt that the Albany file represented a development of the 'Joca' file which had been in use at Dover borstal (see Bottoms and McClintock, 1973, pp. 132-9).

At the end of the induction period prisoners were allocated to labour – as the traditional prison language still has it – and also to the hall which was to be their more permanent placement. Some prisoners, mainly those employed on domestic tasks, were allocated to remain in the induction hall. Others were allocated to B hall, which was initially the only other accommodation available. C hall was opened at the end of July, and D hall soon afterwards, though spare capacity was maintained there for some time to allow movement of prisoners while faults in the sewerage and central heating systems were located and corrected. E hall was only brought into temporary use in October 1967 to accommo-date prisoners from A hall while the ELSA system was being installed.

B hall was under the management of two principal officers, assisted by basic-grade staff, who were known locally as 'case officers'. Each prisoner, including any who remained in A hall, was assigned to a particular case officer in his hall. The case officer was responsible for monitoring the progress of the training plans which had been devised for up to eight prisoners under his control. He was expected to discuss the plan with each prisoner, to tackle any problems as they arose, and to get to know the men sufficiently well to be able to report effectively at periodic internal reviews and at boards relating to such matters as home leave, hostel and outworking schemes and parole. It was at this level that the consequences of being placed in a state of therapeutic anxiety were to be picked up and worked out.

But difficulties arose early in the management of A and B halls, as well as in the lines of responsibility for the various aspects of the induction scheme; and it was soon apparent that changes would be necessary. In accordance with prison service traditions discipline staff were allocated to duties on a 'division' basis, with two divisions each nominally under the direction of a chief officer. It was thus necessary to assign two groups of staff to the halls to cover the working day, and differences in routine administration soon emerged between one division and another which prisoners were apt to resent. The problem of knowing just which officer was in charge of the hall was exacerbated by the need to take principal officers away from hall duties to serve as orderly officer, for example, or to supervise night staff. Moreover, the principal officers, themselves unused to the uncertainties of management, found the situation difficult to cope with and began to press for clear responsibilities and common ways of working. It was therefore decided that one PO should be appointed to take charge of each hall – though not for the induction unit until the build-up of the prison was complete. Both C and D halls were opened on this basis, and although E hall had no prisoners when the research team was there it too had its principal officer designate. It was hoped that eventually the hall POs would each have two senior officers to assist them when that grade was finally introduced. Meanwhile the more experienced basic-grade staff were assigned to the halls on a more permanent basis, to function rather like landing officers in other training prisons. Some of these staff would be promoted to senior officer grade in due course.

The situation in the induction unit was more complicated. One of the problems of A hall was that it had to provide both an induction programme for receptions and a training programme for prisoners permanently allocated to that hall. It was originally intended that the chief officer II should be responsible for general hall management only, but in practice he also assumed some responsibility for the induction process itself, and in the absence of clear managerial responsibilities in B hall he had tended to exercise a general oversight there as well. This produced a certain amount of overlap with the functions of the principal psychologist and the newly-appointed assistant governor in charge of social training. After consultation with the staff college representatives, the role of the chief officer II was limited to the general management of A hall, the allocation of prisoners to labour within the framework of the training plan, and making arrangements for the transfer of prisoners to other halls. The principal psychologist's responsibility for the diagnostic process, the development of training plans, and deciding the criteria for allocating prisoners to halls was re-affirmed. So too was the assistant governor's responsibility for supervising the implementation of training plans by the hall case officers. The anomalous use of the chief officer II as a hall manager was eventually resolved when the management structure was reviewed. By the time of the change-over to electronic locking he had relinquished his responsibility for A hall, which was taken over by a designated principal officer, and the chief II was working directly to the AG on the implementation of social training.

Although the revised structure did much to clarify the responsibility for hall management, it did nothing to ensure that it was carried out effectively. Principal officers had been placed in a position of some anxiety, subject to pressure from above and to hostility from below. The governor and senior management staff were determined that principal officers should learn to make wise decisions themselves, but the prisoners resented this delegation of authority and felt that their problems and complaints were dealt with at too low a level. Although the staff training discussions went some way towards relieving those anxieties, no permanent supervisory structure for monitoring progress was instituted until the principal officers' meeting became a regularized instrument of middle management in the autumn of 1968. Until that time, though the need for supervision and support of the principal officers was well recognized, meetings were held on an *ad hoc* basis, usually just after a problem had developed. Perhaps, with so much attention required for so many other aspects of the prison, there simply wasn't time to do more. But in these circumstances the development of hall management was an uphill task, and it is not surprising that meetings of the hall representative committees – to which both staff and prisoners were elected – were held on a rather similar basis.

Probably the biggest problems, in the induction scheme and the case-officer system no less than in hall management, were experienced in trying to train staff so that they *could* carry out their roles, and in trying to devise some machinery to ensure that they *did*. Though a good deal of effort was expended on both fronts – involving as it did much of the time and attention of both assistant governors and their respective chief officers – and some progress was undoubtedly made, the problems were never really solved.

When staff in the induction hall were required to make a digest of the existing F 1150s and to interview prisoners, it was for most of them their first experience of such matters. The F 1150 is not the best-designed of documents, and though it is frequently bulky the information it contains rarely penetrates the character of those it purports to characterize. In most prisons it is completed as part of a dull ritual on arrival, and then passed from board to board and department to department where more or less stereotyped reports are added according to the formulae adopted by different specialities. As a document for everyday use it leaves a great deal to be desired. The governor, the deputy, the principal psychologist and the assistant governor for staff training all spent some time with the chief officer, principal officers and basic grade staff discussing the shortcomings of the F 1150 and the need for practical ongoing documentation. For the most part staff were quick to show enthusiasm for interviewing prisoners, for distilling relevant information from the records and for attempting to distinguish fact from opinion, though their abilities in these respects varied quite widely. With some support and guidance, however, the Albany file was launched, ready to be passed on to the case officers who would be responsible for implementation.

The Albany file was rather less than a perfect instrument: some staff were more skilled than others at interviewing and more perceptive in making their analyses. And who, in any case, would say with any confidence just what was the right kind of information to be included? If nothing else it did, for a time at least, bring the induction staff who compiled it and the case officers who read it face to face with the anxiety-provoking situation of coming to grips with prisoners about their lives and crimes. But there is something about the nature of written records that tends to make the compilation an end in itself, and the task of actually using the files and implementing the plans, rudimentary though they often were, was something else again. In the long run the less the file was actually used, and the less the plans could actually be seen to be implemented, the more routine the record-keeping was bound to become.

Case officers had rather little training in the detailed business of being case officers. Though the working of the system was discussed in the staff induction programme, and case officers attended the various 'teach-ins' which were organized by the AG for staff resources about a wide variety of matters, the actual amount of attention that could be devoted to the problems of any individual case officer was quite small. And the number of staff to be trained, and the range and complexity of topics to be covered, were dauntingly large. The second assistant governor, in charge of social training, instituted periodic review boards under his chairmanship, which were designed to assess the response of prisoners to training and to review the validity of the existing training plans. The boards also served, less directly, as a means of assessing the quality of work of the case officers and as a medium for further training. But the boards proved to be very difficult to organize; and when they were held, initially at about six-weekly intervals, it was difficult to make more of them than a rather formal reporting occasion. There is no doubt that there was a lot of face-to-face interaction between staff and prisoners, and many opportunities for informal discussion. But using these contacts as a device towards behaviour changing, and recording the progress made, required skill and co-ordination and above all persistent effort to prevent backsliding. By 3 August 1967 the deputy governor, in one of his first essays at trouble-shooting, was able to mediate between those responsible for staff allocation and those in charge of social training, to ensure that case officers were available in the halls at the times when they were needed to interview prisoners and to prepare reports. But finding enough time to take case officers away from hall duties to attend review boards, without curtailing prisoner activities or even having to lock prisoners up, was more difficult. Though the necessity of review boards was affirmed at the central management meeting, they were rarely organized without cost.

There was also the vexed question of priorities. As the governor recorded in his journal as early as 13 May. 'We have received today two circulars offering rewards [allowances] for special duties; nothing for men who actually come face to face with prisoners. In a prison with a specific social training aim this is a disaster – the lowest rated job being the main job of the prison.' Social training, of course, was not to remain the main job, though it was then still too soon to have guessed that security and industrial work were to become the principal tasks of the prison.

Industrial training
For a prison in the vanguard of the movement to put prison industries on the most efficient basis, Albany got off to an

inauspicious start. Industrial training was to be based on workshop production in the needle trades and woodwork; and the workshops were to be organized on a two shift basis. There was to be no vocational training in the traditional sense, only training for the job in hand. The domestic and maintenance work-force, which in most prisons constitutes a sizeable and ill-equipped army that can always soak up any extra bodies who would otherwise remain unemployed, was in Albany to be kept to a minimum and to be provided with mechanized labour-saving devices wherever possible. But it was almost fifteen months before the carpentry industry even began, and the needle trades never did achieve fully operational status on a two-shift basis. By the time Albany came to the end of its first phase of development under David Gould – and in spite of quite prodigious efforts on the part of the Albany staff – the workshops employed only 56.8 per cent of the population; the remainder were employed, as they would be elsewhere in the time-honoured traditions of the system, on the various parties servicing the establishment, or not at all.

The thinking behind the choice of industries for Albany seems to have been as follows. The needle trades, though not beloved of either prisoners or prison reformers because of low pay, monotony, and the chauvinist associations with women's work, nevertheless represented a major undertaking on the part of the service as a whole. The reasons are obvious enough: the workshops can be operated at a high-density ratio of prisoners to space; the machinery required is simple, low-cost, easy to install and service; and there is a large potential market, especially in the public service sector, for mailbags, coin-bags, bandoliers, uniforms, overalls and other items of simple design. It was inevitable that Albany should share in that undertaking, and light textiles and tailoring were to provide its major source of employment. The carpentry trade, always a more popular proposition among prisoners and reformers alike for its higher pay, its perks and its more constructive and manly associations, was chosen for the subsidiary industry at Albany presumably because it could be more easily transported there than elsewhere from Parkhurst, whose own carpentry shops were to be closed. In fact, two of the shops at Parkhurst were to be pulled down to make way for a new security fence there; but since Parkhurst had an underemployment problem its low-density carpentry shops were to be replaced by the ubiquitous needle trades.

1 Birth of a prison: site work for a medium security prison at Albany in March 1965

2 above: Pedestrian entrance to Albany showing the new style prison
façade

3 above right: Architect's model of the main prison complex

4 below right: Simplified plan of main prison complex (not to scale)

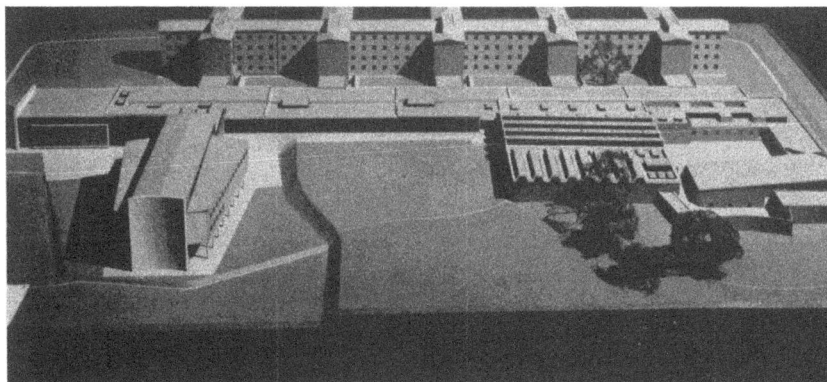

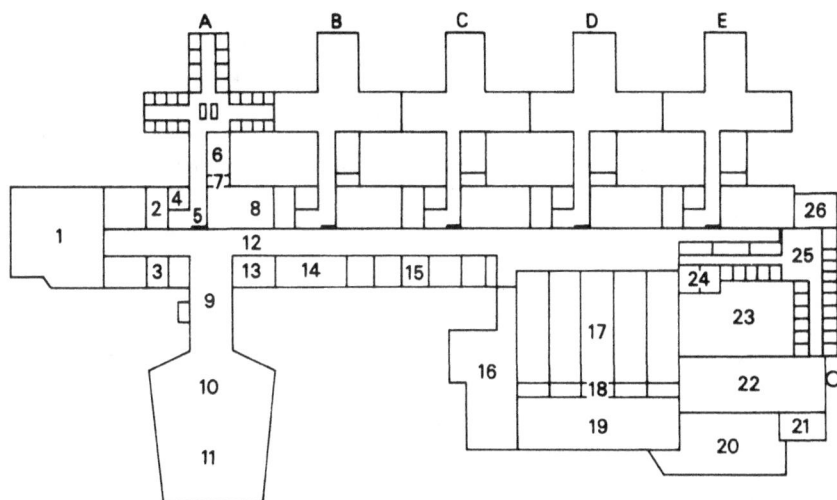

1 Chapels	14 Library
2 Quiet room	15 Hobbies and classrooms
3 Offices	16 Hospital
4 Hall manager's office	17 Dining halls
5 Lobby	18 Serveries
6 Ablutions	19 Kitchens
7 Hall office	20 Service yard
8 Association room	21 Sub station
9 Main entrance	22 Boiler house and fuel store
10 Reception below	23 Exercise yard for segregation unit
11 Assembly/gym above	24 Special cells
12 Central corridor	25 Segregation unit
13 Canteen	26 Adjudications room

5 One of the communal dining rooms. Not used for dining purposes since 1972 because of the difficulties in supervising movement to and from halls and the many demonstrations over food

6 One of the association rooms photographed before the arrival of the first prisoners

7 The tailoring shop. The first Albany workshop in which the incentive earnings scheme was applied, but never popular with prisoners

8 Albany's first 'prisoner'—Lord Stonham in a typical Albany cell during the formal opening of the prison in April 1967

9 Vehicular entrance to Albany photographed at the opening ceremony. Its direct access to the main prison was one of the first security weaknesses to be sealed by the provision of a fenced vehicle compound

10 Prison officer using the tannoy in A hall, introduced with the electronic locking system so that prisoners could contact the control room

11 Hall staircase and landing before the installation of the electronic locking system

12 Hall staircase and landing after the installation of the electronic locking system. Bandit-proof glass panels and gates limit access

13 above: The rise and rise of Albany fences. Category B security fences surround the prison during 1969

14 above right: New woodmill and carpentry shop built inside the security fence and opened in January 1971

15 below right: A security alert: prison officers and dogs assemble under the closed-circuit television camera outside the prison

16 Bedding and cell furnishings litter the prison yard during the 1972 August Bank Holiday search and lock-in

17 Prisoners on the roof of adjacent Parkhurst prison demonstrating against the conditions in Albany, August 1972

18 Wives of prison officers demonstrating outside Albany in October 1973 in an attempt to persuade the governor to take a tougher line with prisoners

19 A fire engine arrives at Albany during one of the many fire alerts in 1973

20 The security fence becomes a gunited wall. Closed-circuit television cameras outside the perimeter and high-mast flood lights inside the prison are clearly visible

The decision to operate the industries on a two-shift basis had, as Lord Stonham noted, two justifications. First, it would involve a more intensive use of machines and shops, thus enabling the prison to function reasonably efficiently with only half the workplaces that would be necessary on a single-shift system: with two shifts, each working approximately 30 hours a week, 100 workplaces could produce a total of 6,000 man-hours weekly, compared with 8,000 man-hours produced from 200 workplaces operated for 40 hours a week on a single shift. It was recognized that the two-shift system could not operate *as* efficiently as the single-shift in the prison context, unless Saturday working was considered, because the need to accommodate both shifts within the limited, even though expanded, daily unlock period inevitably resulted in a shorter working week for each prisoner. But it was thought that the saving in capital costs would go some way towards off-setting this, and that the resemblance to outside industry afforded by shift work provided an additional advantage. Secondly, the two-shift system offered a feasible way of reducing the traditional conflict between the needs of industry on the one hand and the needs of social training on the other. The social, medical, welfare, educational, spiritual or indeed any other needs of prisoners, in so far as they could be met at all within the prison setting, would be met while they were off duty and without interfering with production. Moreover, since half the prisoners would be at work, the pressure on domestic and recreational resources at any one time would also be halved, so that there was some hope that social training might be carried out with greater effect. The two-shift system, then, was the keystone which held the twin pillars of Albany's commitment together.

The reduced capital costs involved in a two-shift operation were not matched, of course, by reduced running costs. Extra staff would be needed not merely to cover the double shift in the workshops, but also the longer period of unlock in the halls, and staff would have to be organized on a shift system that was broadly congruent with the shifts worked by the prisoners. The ramifications of two-shift working at Gartree, the only other establishment to have tried out the system, had produced difficulties with the Prison Officers' Association, and the POA was not happy about its introduction at Albany. But whatever problems there may have been in this direction they were of a minor order when measured against the other troubles of establishing double-shift industries.

And in any case the POA and the Prison Department were soon to become absorbed in complex negotiations over functional group working schemes and a five-day week for prison officers.

It can rarely be an easy matter for an industrial firm to start up factory production from scratch. It is certain to be more difficult in a prison. And in a new prison, which only builds up its work-force gradually, there is clearly a problem of co-ordination if public money is not to be spent on resources before they are needed. But if the Albany experience means anything at all the lesson must be that in industry, as elsewhere, it is far better to have the resources available before the prisoners than the other way around.

Although since July 1966 the opening of the prison had been scheduled for April 1967, there seems never to have been any intention to start the industries before 12 June. The instructors, as supervisors and foremen in prison industries are known, were to be in post one week earlier than that. When 5 June arrived and the requisite number of instructors was not actually forthcoming, the prison was invited to recruit them from its own discipline staff! The governor made strong protestations to headquarters and regional office about the unreadiness of the industries and the almost complete lack of instructors; but it *was* only through recruitment from its own ranks that the Albany industry got under way at all. On 13 June the first workshop — the cutting shop — opened for one of its two shifts, employing 13 prisoners on 'an instructional basis'. One week later the light textile shop began its first tentative production on a contract for bib and brace overalls, again on one shift only. At least the two-shift system was operating, on a small scale, even if it did look curiously lop-sided: prisoners worked from 07.30 to 13.30 hours one week while the shops closed in the afternoon, and from 14.00 to 20.00 the next week while the shops closed in the morning. There were then just five instructors on the staff, mostly recruited from Albany, and so new to the work that they needed to be trained themselves before they could instruct the prisoners.

There could be no question of starting up the second shift in light textiles, or opening the tailor's shop until more instructors were available. It transpired that part of the difficulties in recruitment had come from aiming too high, and the unsuccessful advertisements for 'bespoke tailors' were replaced by advertisements for anyone with experience of 'factory mass-production'. Sufficient instructors had arrived by the end of August to begin the second shift in light textiles. It was decided that rather than start the second shift from scratch it would be better to split the first to provide a corps of experienced workers on each, in spite of the repercussions this would have in the halls. The tailoring shop finally began working, on one shift employing five men, on 11 September 1967. The shift gradually built up to full strength, though it was not until a year later that there were, at last, enough instructors to bring the second tailoring shift into operation. But by then the whole two-shift system was under critical review, and the second shift never did start.

Given the expressed aims of the establishment, it is hard to avoid the conclusion that headquarters were hopelessly unprepared for the opening of the Albany industries and were subsequently less than responsive to the realities of the situation. The only reference to industries in the co-ordination meetings on the opening of new establishments seems to have been an assertion that 'no difficulties were envisaged'. In the event, virtually all of the difficulties reported on two years earlier by one of the present writers in a study of the industries at Maidstone — a conventional, old-style training prison — were found in much the same form at Albany (Cooper and King, 1965). Foremost among those problems was the one that had always bedevilled British prisons: shortage of work. It arose first, in a minor way, over what work should be given to those prisoners confined to their cells. The directorate of industries and stores had suggested the old stand-by: mailbags. In view of Lord Stonham's express statement at the opening ceremony that there would be no mailbags in Albany this was vigorously opposed, and these prisoners were given the shoulder straps to fold for the overalls being made in the light textiles shop instead. But by August the problem had hit the workshops. The instructor in charge of the cutting shop informed the governor that all the overalls had been cut out and that he would soon have finished cutting the blouses which were to be made up in the tailoring shop when that opened. There was no work available after that, although headquarters had long been informed of the situation. Not only was there no work for the cutting shop, but the light textiles soon completed their overalls and the shop had to close down for three days.

The prison continued on a hand-to-mouth basis with workshops intermittently closing down after small orders were completed. The governor soon began to doubt whether there would ever be enough work to keep all the prisoners busy all the time. In discussion with the regional supervisor of industries he pointed out that 384 cells would soon be available, but that the occupants would remain idle unless someone came up with something soon. He stressed the need for getting carpentry under way as a matter of urgency. Some small orders just kept the prison going until the new year, when the first major long-run contract arrived. Ironically it plunged the whole prison into despondency. It was for six months' work on airmail bags, with the possibility of a further six months after that! The order had only been accepted to prevent the shop from closing, but most prisoners and staff regarded the nylon airmail bags as but one step removed from the 'heavy embroidery' of canvas. Fortunately the repeat order did not have to be taken up because of the proposed upgrading of the light textiles shop to tailoring status, and substantial orders for coinbags, bandoliers, mattress covers and overalls eventually followed.

The prison had to get along for more than a year with no alternative to the needle trades because of the absence of a carpentry shop; and when the carpentry industry was started, it was housed outside the security fence, in one of the former army buildings, which had taken some four months to rewire so that it could take the equipment. The need for a purpose-built workshop had long been conceded; and after some delays it had been promised for the end of 1968, in time for the arrival of category-B prisoners. It was eventually opened in December 1970, though it could not then be used for several weeks because the dust extracting system did not work. Much of the needle work too was carried out from shops housed in the original buildings left over from Albany barracks. Though the buildings were basically sound enough, they had been intended for use as stores, not workshops, and were too well ventilated, especially in winter. On occasion work had to be stopped because of the cold, and it was not until February 1969 that the problem was effectively solved.

It is clear that no special priority was given to Albany in getting the two-shift system operational, in spite of its apparent experimental status. The fact that it was made to work at all and that so many difficulties were overcome, or almost overcome, may be attributed to the extraordinary and strenuous efforts that were made by staff at local level. Two middle-management meetings, which met every two or three weeks, debated the issues, pondered the problems and strove for solutions. The progress meeting was intended to inaugurate and monitor any action needed to smooth the build-up of the prison as a whole, but since that function was largely discharged by the CMM it came to dwell almost exclusively on industrial matters. The development of industries meeting had been intended specifically to deal with the industrial sphere and especially the launching of the shift system. Both meetings were attended by much the same representatives from central management and the same senior industrial staff. Although junior members of staff, especially on the industrial side, were often present, they were less likely to be found at the progress meeting than at the industries meeting. Sometimes the meetings were attended by a representative from the regional office or from headquarters. In view of the overlap between the two meetings, the development of industries meeting was abandoned after about six months, although it was later reintroduced as a means of keeping junior industrial staff informed. From the voluminous minutes which were taken, read at each meeting, and filed — a procedure in marked contrast to the CMM — it was apparent first, that there was ample business to keep both meetings fully occupied; second, that the industrial manager came to occupy an increasingly important role in the prison; and third, that it would not be possible for instructors to make a systematic contribution to the Albany file, as had at one time been hoped. Nevertheless it was clear that the early progress and industries meetings discussed at some length how industry could be made an integral part of the total training structure through the operation of the two-shift system. And when that system subsequently came under threat many members of the staff were to exercise a great deal of ingenuity in trying to preserve at least some of its benefits.

Security
From the outset, although there was only a gradual build-up of selected category-C prisoners, the prison was inevitably preoccupied with the task of reaching the standards of security required for a class B prison. A principal officer was appointed as security officer (in accordance with paragraph 233 of the Mountbatten report) just before the first prisoners arrived, and was quickly dispatched to the newly-introduced course for security officers at Wakefield. Even before the opening ceremony a demonstration of

police-dog handling had been attended by representatives from the prison, although dogs were not introduced to Albany until a much later state in its development. Internal alarm systems were instituted, and links were forged with the local police and neighbouring prisons to ensure prompt action in the case of emergencies. The police were also brought in for discussions on the use of UHF radio equipment, and later for advice on the siting and security of the control room.

It was some while before televisual surveillance was introduced, together with high-mast lighting to floodlight the grounds at night; and in the early months of development the most noticeable addition to security was the building of the first security fence with its attendant geophonic alarms. As the work on the fence progressed, no one inside the prison could fail to sense the inexorable tightening of the net around Albany. Something of that sense was conveyed by the governor when he noted in his daily journal some five weeks after the work began: 'The great fence goes on surmounting the prison.' Here was the tangible expression of the priority to be given to security; that it was actually built around the people who were already there only reinforced its symbolic effect. But this was just a fraction of what was to come: even during the construction of the first security fence at Albany, the developments that were eventually to lead to the construction of a second were already falling into place.

Perimeter patrols were set up to man key observation points throughout the prison as soon as there were any prisoners to be observed. The staff were allocated to their perimeter duties, as they might be to any other duties, on a daily basis by the detail PO under the supervision of the chief I. Early in May the governor spent some time talking to the perimeter patrols. When he wrote up his journal that day he remarked how unpleasant and boring the perimeter duties were and he noted that the POA had asked that they should be paid at overtime rates. The security PO had day-to-day oversight of security matters and a direct line of communication wherever it was needed. He was assisted by a basic-grade discipline officer, who deputized for him in his absence. By October 1967 two issues had been brought to the attention of the security subcommittee and were then put before the central management meeting. One was whether the perimeter could best be secured by static or mobile patrols. The other was whether or not it was possible to create a special perimeter defence force who could be identified with their task on a more permanent basis. In spite of its soporific potential, static observation was the preferred solution to the first matter, supplemented by occasional and irregular mobile patrols. The inadequate heating in the sentry boxes, while it may have inhibited stupor, was to give some cause for concern as the winter progressed. But the obvious advantages to be gained from a permanent and separate perimeter force – ease of training a smaller group, increased specialization, and continuity of experience – none the less raised policy considerations, and guidance was sought from headquarters. The Radzinowicz subcommittee eventually advocated that a clear distinction be drawn between security duties and other duties, but was also to counsel against any split between a custodial staff and a treatment staff. In fact the logic of the situation demanded some degree of stability and it was decided to withdraw staff from the halls for periods of three months at a time to serve on the perimeter. This was to pave the way for much longer tours of security duties under the functional-group working scheme which was later introduced in exchange for the five-day week for prison officers. At the time the research began, when the prison was still category C and before the dogs were introduced, 12 basic-grade staff on each division were employed on perimeter defence under the supervision of a principal officer. Five officers manned the sentry boxes, with one on relief duties; two, drawn from a group of specially trained men, were in the control room, at that time still adjacent to A hall; and four officers controlled the gate house. All were in two-way radio contact. Between them they effectively maintained the distinction between freedom and captivity.

5   The category-C regime

In the present chapter we try to show how the prison actually worked under the influence of its first governor, and to characterize the state of social order in the prison, as we saw it, at the end of his regime in mid-1968. We should begin with a disclaimer. Only five weeks separated the arrival of the research team from the effective departure of David Gould, and during that time most of our attention was devoted either to organizing meetings to introduce the research or to finding our way around the prison. Although this involved us in talking to many staff and prisoners, both collectively and individually, on the basis of which our first impressions were formed, it is perhaps only fair to say that at the time we were much more under investigation by our subjects than vice versa. We did not develop close contacts in the halls and workshops until we established a continuous presence at the prison after the governor's promotion had been announced; and our second impressions, therefore, were doubtless already coloured by that announcement. Fortunately we were able to fill in some of the gaps in our factual knowledge from documentary sources and the recollections of staff and prisoners to whom we spoke subsequently, and this information has been incorporated into our description. But we have not called upon any of the systematic data which we collected a year later, when we asked staff and prisoners to make a retrospective evaluation of the major changes that had occurred in Albany, even though these would round out some of the views presented here. We report on that material in part three. For the present we prefer to let our first and second impressions, as we recorded them at the time, stand for what they are.

There was an air of considerable confidence in Albany when the research team arrived. Confidence born out of the successful struggle to get the prison operational and sustained by the very favourable publicity the prison had received throughout that process. A few months earlier the Isle of Wight *County Press,* under the headline *Albany – Revelation of The Revolutionary,* had published an extensive account of the aims and methods of the governor and his staff, together with photographs of the senior managers. The report was notable for the sympathetic way in which the aspirations of the staff were presented:

> We saw government by central management, in which every officer and department played a part – and a revolutionary system by which every prison officer was a 'case officer' devoted to the welfare of his charges throughout the period of their detention.

Nowhere in its 184 column-inches was there to be found any criticism, either expressed or implied, still less any indication of the problems that were to come. The reporter, like most visitors to Albany (and there were many), seems to have caught the obvious enthusiasm and essential optimism which was exhibited by so many of those involved in the venture. The article was later reprinted in the *Prison Service Journal,* thus establishing Albany's reputation as a show-piece within the system. Indeed everything about Albany made news: even the Christmas menu and the dedication of the chapels had been reported in the newspapers.

There was also an air of excitement about the prison. The installation of the ELSA system in A hall had just been completed, and we were encouraged to try it out. We duly 'banged ourselves up' and were released a few moments later at the touch of a button after we spoke to the control room over the intercom. The following month A hall was opened to journalists, who responded with approval. Thus the *County Press* reported on 29 June 1968:

> A revolutionary experiment, which might well serve as a pattern for the prison service as a whole, is taking place at Albany Prison. Upon reasonable request, cell doors are un-locked and relocked by remote control. Particularly valuable in respect of night sanitation – but with a much wider potential – this is an imaginative experiment, admirably combining the elements of enlightened thinking and advanced technology. It is yet another appreciation of the inmate; and for the prison officer the system saves time and tedium.

But though for the most part the staff remained outwardly confident and excited about what was happening in Albany, it soon became apparent that the process of defining roles and writing job specifications was by no means complete, and that some staff were less than clear about what they were doing and why they were doing it. Even so, in a situation in which the staff had started virtually from scratch and were given such scope for initiative, it speaks volumes for the persuasiveness of the governor and the subtlety of his government that such a cohesive and dynamic structure was created and operated more than passably effectively in his own image.

Prisoners and staff in Albany

Before discussing how the prison operated in practice, we should say something about the population in Albany at the beginning of the research and about the staff who guarded them and participated in their training.

As soon as practicable after our arrival in Albany we conducted a census of the prisoner population. Our task was very much simpler than the one which had confronted the Morrises ten years earlier at Pentonville, because the population was smaller and relatively static, and the records were more accessible and reasonably complete. We therefore extracted certain information from the records (F 1150) of all the prisoners who, according to the nominal roll, should have been in the prison on the chosen date: 1 May 1968. We stored the data on punched cards. By punching new cards for all receptions as they arrived and keeping a record of discharge dates, it was possible for us to reconstruct the population at any time during the research; we did so from time to time. On the first day in May 1968 there were 313 prisoners locked up in Albany, and two prisoners temporarily absent, one on home leave, the other in Parkhurst hospital. At that time Albany was still a category-C prison and prisoners had been carefully chosen bearing in mind its security weaknesses. According to the files, 224 prisoners were classified as category C. One had formerly been rated as a category-A prisoner and was still listed as such in his F 1150; although we were told that his security rating had long since been downgraded, we were not able to verify that. Six were classified as suitable for category-D conditions, and the remainder were unclassified, either because they were recent receptions whose security status had not been confirmed, or because the decision just had not been recorded.

In spite of its security rating Albany contained, for the most part, a young but very experienced and quite 'difficult' recidivist population from the outset. Just over half were 30 years or younger, but about two-thirds had six or more previous court appearances, and half had been in prison four or more times before. The overwhelming majority were currently imprisoned for offences in Class II, property offences with violence, or Class III, property offences without violence, with slightly more in the latter category than the former. They were often described by the staff as 'tearaways rather than real villains – yet', and this is perhaps reflected by the fact that two-thirds of them were serving comparatively short sentences of two years or less. About two-thirds had left school before the age of 16 years, and a quarter of those had completed their education at approved schools. Hardly anyone had not had some custodial experience at some time, and about half had graduated to prison through approved schools, detention centres and borstal institutions. Three-quarters of the population had been transferred to Albany from Wandsworth. About a fifth came from either Winchester or Canterbury local prisons and a few from Oxford, but nearly all of them identified themselves with London as their home base. Two-fifths had never married, and the remainder were almost equally divided between those who were still married or cohabiting and those who were no longer married or cohabiting for whatever reason.

Not all the prisoners at Albany followed this pattern, however. A sixth were over the age of 40 years. And there were some prisoners serving comparatively long terms, usually for the more serious Class II offences or for Class I offences against the person; an eighth had sentences of four or more years, and one prisoner was serving a life sentence. Among these long-term prisoners were nine of the original 11 prisoners from Parkhurst who, together with 30 from Wandsworth, were the first prisoners ever to be locked up in Albany. The problem of dealing with groups of prisoners who had different lengths of sentence, different criminological backgrounds and penological experiences, and different expectations of the prison – which was later to cause so many difficulties – was thus not a new one for Albany. But in 1967 and 1968 it was a problem on rather a small scale: a problem which could be resolved within the flexible Albany approach of the early days, often using the resources of the governor until more confident staff-prisoner relationships were established. By 1971 and 1972 the scale of the problem had grown out of all recognition as a result of the implementation of the dispersal policy.

Moreover, the resources for dealing with it had been diminished by the changes in regime and administration, some of them brought about in preparation for dispersal, which had occurred in the interval.

When the research team entered the prison the following authorized posts were filled by full-time personnel:

Discipline staff

Governor Class I	1
Assistant Governor Class I (Deputy Governor)	1
Assistant Governor Class II	2
Chief Officer I	1
Chief Officers II	2
Principal Officers	12
Basic-Grade Officers	109
Temporary Officers	6
Foreman of Works	1
Engineers II	3
Officer Trade Assistants	7
Officer Instructors	7
	152 152

Non-discipline staff

Professional grades	
Chaplain	1
Medical Officer	1
Principal Psychologist	1
Psychologist	1
Welfare Officers	2
Tutor-Organizer	1
	7 7

Technical grades		
Technical Officer II (Industrial Manager)	1	
Technical Officer II (Farm Foreman)	1	
Civilian Instructors	12	
Civilian Workmen	17	
	31	31

Administrative grades		
Higher Executive Officer (Admin. Officer)	1	
Executive Officers	2	
Clerical Officers	8	
Clerical Assistant	1	
Typists	4	
Storemen	4	
Cleaner	1	
	21	21
		211

In addition to these 211 full-time staff there were the following part-time employees: a senior welfare officer responsible for all the island prisons, five teachers, one chaplain, one visiting psychotherapist, one typist and one cleaner.

Of course the staff situation did not remain stable after the arrival of the research team. During the period covered by this monograph and by the time the fifth hall was brought into use, the strength had grown by about another 50 per cent. Most notable among the subsequent changes were the appointment of most of the 22 senior officers on the authorized establishment, and the addition of nearly a dozen dog-handlers.

Though we collected no information about the staff immediately, it was evident that a large number of the basic-grade discipline officers were young and in the probationary period of their service. We were later to learn that the great majority had less than five years' experience, and that 45 per cent had not served in any other prison apart from the institution where they had joined, and in which they had typically spent only weeks or months before attending the officer training school.

The discipline staff in Albany, as in most training prisons at that time, worked a twelve-day fortnight, which was intended to provide officers with one weekend off in every two. Basic-grade staff were divided into two broad divisions, and each division worked alternately on the early shift and on the late shift. During weekdays the early shift was from 06.15 to 13.00 hours, and at weekends from 08.00 to 13.00; the late shift was from 12.45 to 21.00 both during the week and at weekends. In his twelve-day 'charted period', therefore, each officer was nominally required to work six late shifts of $7\frac{1}{2}$ hours, five early shifts of 6 hours, and one early shift of 5 hours, making 80 hours in all. In practice, because of a shortfall in staff numbers and to cover periods of leave, sickness and detached duties, they were frequently 'called back' during off-duty periods to work overtime. Principal officers worked to one of three sets of duty hours, all of which spanned in varying degrees both the shifts worked by basic-grade staff. Special duty periods were worked out for certain posts – hospital officers, gate officers and so on – where unusually long hours might be necessary. And several posts – canteen, censor, searcher, reception and the like – which did not have to be covered in the early morning or in the evening were manned on a single 'main-shift' basis. The hours of workshop staff, of course, were tied to the length of the industrial shifts for prisoners, though slightly different arrangements applied to officer and civilian instructors. At night, when the prison was locked up and during which time even the admission of the governor would have to be justified, the prison was controlled by ten men under the charge of an experienced basic-grade officer. Of these, three were allocated to duties patrolling the halls and two manned the control room, one being concerned with the electronic locking system and one keeping contact with the other night staff by radio. Shortly after the research began the night staff in the control room was reduced to one man who fulfilled both functions.

The daily routine

Four halls were in operation at the commencement of the research, and each was under the management of a principal officer. A hall, complete with its new ELSA system, was virtually full, as were B and C halls. D hall was occupied to only about half its capacity, while E hall was once again empty, awaiting the next stage of electronic installation. Eight basic-grade staff from each division were assigned to duties in each of A, B and C halls, and five to D hall. None of the posts in the halls was regarded as fixed, and officers could be moved to other duties as needed by the detail principal officer to fill gaps elsewhere. In practice two officers in each hall were regarded as 'spares', and when it was necessary to move staff these were called on first: a serious attempt was thus made to leave other hall staff in post to carry out their case-officer functions.

Now that the prison had reached something like its maximum number of prisoners, the original A hall induction scheme was no longer in use. Instead new prisoners were allocated direct to vacancies in the halls, where a case officer opened the Albany file under the supervision of the principal psychologist and assistant governor. A hall was still used for housing prisoners employed on domestic and maintenance parties, and held no prisoners working the industrial shifts. This, coupled with the impact of the electronics, meant that the routine there was different from that in the other halls. The day began when A hall staff on the early shift would carry out a roll check immediately on arrival, while prisoners were still in cells. The hall was unlocked at 07.00 hours. Since prisoners could if they wished use the sanitary recesses at night the need for the ritual of 'slopping out' was greatly reduced, though here as in other halls the prisoners were provided with 'the very latest design in plastic pots', as the governor put it, and some prisoners preferred them. At 07.30 after washing, shaving and the initial taking of applications, the prisoners went to their dining hall for breakfast, returning half an hour later. Work began at 08.15. Because most prisoners were employed on main-shift parties and few would remain in the hall during the day, all but three officers left the hall with their parties and remained with them during the working day. The work parties returned at 11.50, and at noon the principal officer heard any applications that did not require the attention of the governor. At 12.15 the prisoners went to the dining hall for the midday meal, again returning after half an hour. Between 12.45 and 13.00 the two staff shifts overlapped and the hall was formally passed over from one to the other. At this time prisoners again went to work, returning at 16.45. Tea was taken in the dining hall between 16.55 and 17.30, and from 18.00 until 20.30 the prisoners could attend classes and other association activities. Prisoners collected supper from the dining hall at 20.30, and were locked in cells for the night at 20.45. A final roll check was then taken before the late staff went off duty.

The electronic locking and unlocking system was designed primarily to facilitate night sanitation; but it could also be used during the day, and it obviously served as a demonstration of the possibilities of electronic control as an alternative to the turnkey function for staff. For routine purposes cells could be unlocked, eight at a time, by the turn of a switch in the control room. At night, or for that matter at any time when the prison might be locked up, a prisoner could contact the control room by pressing a button in a small metal plate fitted flush to the cell wall. On receiving a reply from control the prisoner could state his request through an intercom grille. If the request was acceptable, and providing no one else on that landing was out of his cell at that time, the control room officer could, after warning the night patrol that a prisoner was to be let out, release the bolt on the cell door by activating an electrical impulse. The prisoner could then open his door and go outside to the recess. Once out of his cell the prisoner was confined to his landing, because the staircase was sealed off with bandit-proof glass and the doors to the stairs were time-locked. For the period that the cell was unlocked a light showed on the control panel and the night patrol remained alerted. When the prisoner returned to his cell, he closed the door and again contacted the control. The cell door was then locked again and the night patrol notified that all was clear. An intercom device was also fitted to each landing for the use of staff.

Two important by-products resulted from the introduction of the electronic locking system. First, the cells were fitted with light switches to facilitate use of the intercom, and thus prisoners could control their own lights-out time at night. Second, while the electronics were being fitted a Tannoy broadcasting system was also installed, whereby separate radio programmes could be relayed to each landing if required. Although all prisoners in Albany could have personal radios if they wished, providing they were not on punishment or on Rule 43 as a subversive, not everyone had them. The Tannoy was thus particularly welcome for late-night sporting broadcasts, which could not be made available in other halls where the communal radio was contained in the recreation rooms. Night lights in each cell could be operated by staff from the landings for inspection purposes without waking prisoners. But there were drawbacks also: most notably the loss of recreation space involved in modifying and closing in the stairwells to restrict movement at night.

The routines in B, C and D halls varied quite considerably on points of detailed procedure – for example, on the frequency and manner of inspections, or how disbursements were made from the 'common fund allocation' – but were broadly similar in outline and timetabling. Virtually all the prisoners in these halls worked the industrial shifts and, as part of a policy to maintain an even use of staff and facilities throughout the prison, each hall housed prisoners working on both shifts. For ease of administration prisoners working different shifts were located separately within each hall: those on one shift were situated on the ground floor and first landing, while those on the other were on the upper two landings. Any prisoners who were not working in the workshops were normally, though not always, located on the ground floor.

Here too the day began with a roll check while prisoners were still in cells. In B hall the early-rising cooks would already have been unlocked by the night staff, but there and elsewhere the first early shift workers were unlocked at 06.25. Their morning schedule was tightly organized, and geared entirely to work or preparing for work; all other activities for the early workers, including governor's applications, were left until the afternoon. Between 06.25 and 06.50, at which time they were taken to the dining halls for breakfast, they had to slop out, wash and shave. At 07.20 they returned from the dining halls, and then paraded for work at 07.25. At 07.30 they were expected to arrive in the shops, where they would work until 10.30; at this point they had tea and a sandwich brought over to the shops by discipline staff from the halls, who supervised the break. At 13.30 the early shift left the shops and at 13.35 were due in the dining halls for the midday meal. From there they returned to the halls at about 14.00. By this time, of course, the hall staff had changed their shift, so that a different set of officers was on duty in the afternoon. The afternoon was to be devoted to the various social training activities: applications were taken immediately after the return from the dining halls and heard at 15.00 by the principal officer. Case officers were expected to undertake case-work activities with the eight or so prisoners who had been assigned to them, and to keep the Albany files up to date. Prisoners were also available for interviews with the welfare officers and the psychologists and could attend any treatment activities or educational classes which might be offered. It was usually possible for them to spend up to an hour on the sports field for outside activities. And prisoners who were not involved in any of these activities could associate freely in the halls or spend time in their cells if they chose. Prisoners on association could avail themselves of hot water to make tea or coffee with supplies bought in the canteen. Purchases from the canteen could be made at this time on the appropriate day for each hall. By 17.15 the activities had ceased and early-shift workers went for tea to the dining halls. They returned at 17.45 and from 18.00 until 20.30 they were again free to associate in the halls, either to watch television or to take part in other recreational activities, or they could go to evening educational classes. At 20.30 they went to collect supper, and they were locked in cells at 20.45. After a final roll check the staff went off duty.

Those who were on early shift one week would be on the late shift the following week. The late workers were unlocked at 07.00, and they could slop out, wash and shave at a more leisurely pace between then and 07.45. During this time they handed in any applications that they might wish to make. At 07.45 they went for breakfast, returning at 08.15. From then on they were in association, although social training activities for the late workers did not begin until 09.15. Between that time and 12.15 they were available for visits to the welfare and psychology departments, educational classes, and so on. Again it was usually possible to fit in an hour on the sports field, weather permitting, and each hall had a day scheduled for canteen purchases during this period. Applications were heard by the principal officer at noon. After a roll check at 12.30 the late workers went to the dining halls, returning just over half an hour later. They could then take their exercise period if it had not been possible to have outdoor activities, and they were taken to the workshops at 13.55. The afternoon work shift lasted from 14.00 until 20.00, with a break in mid-afternoon for tea and sandwiches. When the late workers returned from the shops, therefore, they had to go almost immediately to collect their supper before being locked up at 20.45 for the night. On 17 June 1968, shortly after our arrival, the afternoon shift was shortened to five hours, with prisoners returning to the halls at 19.00, leaving somewhat longer for association before lockup.

From time to time throughout the day hall discipline officers might be expected to relieve other staff on fixed duties during meal breaks and so on. And various routine inspections were also carried out: the staff from A hall, which was unlocked later than the others, began their day by searching the workshops; in all halls locks, bolts and bars were routinely examined after the staff returned from breakfast; routine cell searching took place during the evening association period.

At weekends no workshops were in operation, and only a few prisoners – required to run the kitchens, the officers' mess and so on – were working. The prisoners were unlocked at 08.10; and after breakfast on Saturdays they were expected to clean their cells and the hall ready for a principal officer's inspection at 10.30. Thereafter prisoners were on association for the rest of the day, and were usually able to use the sports field for a period of about two hours. On Sundays, prisoners were expected to return to their cells after breakfast to write letters, to make and mend, and to prepare for voluntary church services should they wish to attend. Church services normally began at 10.00, by which time prisoners were again on association for the rest of the day. Again it was possible to use the field, and in the evening film shows and other entertainments might be held. Lock-up was at the same time at weekends as it was during the week.

Laid out in this way, there was nothing in the routine that could be described as oppressive and hardly anything that was even very uncongenial. But the paper outline is rarely the same as the substance of daily life, and there certainly were problems. Staff were particularly concerned about the situation at night when prisoners collected supper. Unlike other mealtimes, when each hall went separately and under supervision to its own dining hall, prisoners from all halls went to supper at the same time and were able to mix freely in a situation that could not easily be supervised. If trouble were to occur it was at this time that staff expected it; and when we observed activities in the halls there was little doubt that this was the most tense period of the day. Staff and prisoners alike were concerned about the uneven pace of the routine. Early in the morning and last thing at night there was scarcely enough time to accommodate all the activities, but in between when prisoners were not at work there were not enough activities to fill the time.

Although welfare interviews and psychology interviews and the like were organized, according to the blue print, to fit into the non-work hours, they by no means fully occupied the time of prisoners.

And it is not difficult to imagine the problems of the tutor-organizer who was expected to find part-time staff to take morning classes which would have to be duplicated in the afternoons. Although persons were eventually found, mostly retired school teachers, who were able and prepared to conduct such courses, this was only half the battle. At nights the tutor-organizer had to arrange classes to accommodate not only industrial shift-workers who could only attend in alternate weeks, but also domestic shift-workers who could not attend day-time classes but who were available for evening classes every week. The chaplain found it similarly difficult to maintain group work on this basis. Case officers were supposed to be doing case work during these periods. They could often be seen chatting with prisoners, but case work activity was much less clearly specified than supervision, and we rarely saw staff writing up case notes. Indeed, many Albany files were completely blank, and in those that had been written up training plans were often difficult to discern.

There were also difficulties in providing adequate recreational activities. On 3 September 1967 the governor had remarked in his journal that off-work periods were extremely dull and that he hoped some way out of the impasse would be found as they went along. Football was at times rather dangerous on the uneven and heavily crevassed field left behind by the contractors, although the prisoners beat the staff 4 – 0 in one game which was organized in the early days. Darts matches were also arranged between the halls from time to time. Discussion groups with members of Brighton College of Education, a performance of *The Crucible* by players from the same college, and even recitals from a string quartet provided moments of interest, but they were the highlights in an otherwise monotonous round. It was difficult to obtain enough films for regular showing on Sundays, and no immediate ways could be found to finance a record club which had been proposed. Even a decision to allow prisoners to have budgerigars in their cells was blocked by a standing order which apparently prohibited anyone from actually buying one. Though the film supply was improved, the record club started, and ways found to introduce not only budgerigars but also tropical fish, there were still insufficient activities to fill the hours of association with pursuits that might be construed as contributing to social training. If it was fine prisoners preferred to be outside, and if it was wet they preferred to play cards. Though prisoners told us that they enjoyed the freedom and the frequent opportunities to be in the open air, they also complained that changing from shift to shift was unsettling and did nothing for the prisoners' perpetual problem: constipation. On one occasion in August 1967 the men from B hall had refused to go to work, and were only persuaded to leave the hall after the intervention of the chief. But they continued to complain, especially when they worked the late shift: in the mornings they had too much free time when it was not even possible to watch television, and in the evenings there was no time to do anything, especially to watch television. The reduction in working hours for the late shift in June 1968 did something to ease this problem.

The two-shift system also created some problems in the workshops. With so many short-run orders it was difficult to arrange the work efficiently, and in practice each shift worked on a separate contract and so had to clear its work and materials away each day before the next shift started. When we observed the workshops, this activity usually began half an hour or more before the end of the shift. As one contract finished it was often not practicable to switch the shift to work on an existing contract, even though work was available, and some unevenness of work-flow resulted. This could become especially marked on occasion because the shifts became lop-sided as a result of receptions, discharges and changes of labour, with sometimes twice as many workers on one shift as the other. And in spite of the fact that welfare interviews and so on were scheduled for periods of off-duty, workshop interruptions were by no means eliminated. The governor had made it clear as early as July 1967 that while interruptions for things like dental treatment might be inevitable, prisoners were only to be allowed to leave the shops for valid reasons that could not be embraced elsewhere in the routine. But some interruptions persisted. It is probable that many of the interruptions were engineered by prisoners. Whereas at first the prisoners were content enough to have any occupation, even in the needle trades, their interest waned as products such as overalls and pyjamas gave way to coinbags and bandoliers; they were certainly not anxious to spend their time on the machine sewing of mailbags. Instructors were soon complaining that men tried every means possible to get out of the shops. The numbers reporting 'special sick' went up, and at one time there were 14 men in the textile shop who had been forbidden to sew on the grounds that their eyesight did not permit close work. Applications for changes of labour similarly increased.

Several measures were considered to help to improve matters in
the shops. Greater control was exercised over the initial process of
labour allocation, and limits were imposed on changes of labour
applications. To counteract what was seen as the declining quality
of the work by new receptions, proposals were made for a training
shop. And to counteract the limited positive inducements to hard
work, some negative sanctions were proposed in the form of a
'fall-out' shop where the work would be even less congenial.
Incentive earnings were under discussion but were not introduced
until Albany was work-studied some time later. However, an
employment exchange was introduced in May 1968 in which
vacancies in the forthcoming carpentry shop were advertised, and
this lightened some of the gloom that often descended upon the
industrial scene.

There was no doubt that operating the halls and workshops
around the two-shift system brought with it many problems.
Opinion appeared to be quite sharply divided among the staff,
however, between those who thought the effort should be made to
solve the new problems and those who did not. As best we could
judge on our early acquaintance most, though not all, of those
concerned with staff training were committed to making the
system work. This group perhaps comprised about half or more of
the central management meeting. Among the staff on the industrial side there were some who still thought the system made
economic sense, though rather more who found it either complicated to administer or inconvenient. Most of the discipline staff
appeared to be either indifferent to, or against, the prisoner shift
system. Interestingly, when we spoke to opponents of the two-shift
system among the staff, they often cited the disapproval of the
scheme among prisoners to support their case. But when we spoke
to prisoners they were much more dissatisfied at the nature of the
work they were required to do and at the poor level of remunera-
tion. The most frequent complaints that we heard were that
prisoners had been 'conned' at Wandsworth into believing that in
Albany they would be able to do carpentry and would earn up to a
pound a week. In fact most were earning a good deal less than half
that amount at the ubiquitous needle trades. As far as the shift
system itself was concerned, as many prisoners told us of its
advantages as its disadvantages, both of which were very real from
their point of view.

The state of social order

One thing that almost everyone was agreed upon when we arrived in the prison was that Albany was a relaxed and flexible place which had built up a substantial reservoir of goodwill between staff and prisoners. But it had taken time to establish good relations between the two sides, and not everyone approved of it.

The very first prisoners from Parkhurst had presented a real test of the Albany style of management, as well as a glimpse of what was to happen in the future when the prison became a category-A establishment. They arrived on 26 April and quickly decided that they did not like what they saw, nor what was expected of them. The following morning they demanded to see the governor to make their complaints, and the meeting which followed went on into the afternoon. They objected to having to live with young prisoners from Wandsworth; and they objected to what they saw as a young and inexperienced staff who had an obsessive concern with smartness and who tried to impose unnecessarily petty or restrictive rules. They pointed out that the screws did not have to live there twenty-four hours a day, and that all these regulations might be suitable for the young cons from Wandsworth but not for seasoned prisoners like themselves who had been used to some comforts and privileges which were accorded to long-termers at Parkhurst. When it was pointed out that hall management was in the hands of the hall staff they made it clear that they dealt with the governor and not with the screws, and that if they could not do that here then they wanted to go back to a proper prison.

The complaints of the men from Parkhurst, though often expressed apparently in hysterical terms, could not lightly be dismissed. They *had* enjoyed privileges at Parkhurst; they *were* expected to abide by the same rules as short-term prisoners; and the staff *were* predominantly young and inexperienced. Moreover the new staff were undoubtedly nervous when faced with prisoners who had spent much more time in prisons than themselves. This showed up in their determination to enforce the letter as well as the spirit of the regulations. Thus the chief, mindful of an earlier incident at Parkhurst where a prisoner had been stabbed while watching television, introduced a rule that a light should be kept on during the time that the television was on. Basic-grade staff in the hall interpreted this so literally that even on a sunny May afternoon they insisted on keeping a light on, much to the contempt of the prisoners. In this situation the governor had little choice but to give the staff his support – they were, as they said, carrying out the chief's orders – but the need for exercising discretion and responsibility was also pointed out.

The need to exercise discretion and responsibility was more easily pointed out than carried out. As far as the staff were concerned the Parkhurst prisoners had declared their position, and any approach to the governor on the part of the inmates was to be seen as 'wedge-driving', an attempt to undermine the exercise of any authority by discipline staff no matter how responsibly it had been discharged. And often enough that is just what it was, or at least that was its effect. As far as the prisoners were concerned they were in prison anyway and it might as well be a real one as a fancy one; screws were for banging people up, and the real decisions should be taken elsewhere. Even the most reasonable request to the governor, if granted, could serve to put the screws in their place. In the circumstances the staff were hardly going to rush out on to a limb from which they might be toppled, when sticking to the rules guaranteed them a position they could defend. The Parkhurst men treated the Albany facilities with studied indifference and ignored the discipline staff. They made their applications direct to the governor, as they had every right to do under Rule 8 of the Prison Rules. While they were satisfied with the food they were sore about everything else, from the initial lack of tea-making facilities to the alleged fear of victimization by the screws. With great patience and considerable skill the governor discussed each application in general terms but then referred the matter back to hall principal officers for specific decision. At first this only reinforced the belief of the prisoners that the prison was run by the screws. Dissatisfied with the governor's response they began to petition the Board of Visitors and the Secretary of State, and one prisoner periodically went on hunger strike 'until the management of this prison is investigated'. The governor too had his doubts. In his journal he wrote 'The Albany rules are badly drawn. I let them go so that we can see they are bad in action . . . At present I feel sure I must refer the decision-taking to the effective levels, and in the halls this must be the POs. But if they take unwise decisions can we wait?' But in time the policy paid off. Judicious concessions were made; the staff at middle-management level both in the halls and the workshops began to co-operate more effectively; consultation in the halls began to erode the natural wariness of prisoners and officers in their day-to-day contacts; and the prisoners from Parkhurst settled down.

The price of this devolution of authority and flexibility of approach, however, was a continuing degree of uncertainty and inconsistency. By May 1968 the halls were administered with as few rules as possible in a conscious attempt to reduce the 'aggro' between staff and prisoners, and the regulations were interpreted as generously as the facilities allowed. To quote a relatively trivial example, prisoners were formally required to bath once a week; but there was no set time for this in the routine and no procedure for checking that it had been carried out. In practice, with the prisoners unlocked from early in the morning until comparatively late in the evening and with access to the bathing facilities at any reasonable time, they could bath as much or as little as they liked. On the whole both staff and prisoners approved of this relaxed and more dignified method of administration.

At the same time real difficulties could be encountered over the interpretation and implementation of rules. Because of the design of the prison, close and detailed supervision of the prisoners while they were unlocked in the halls was not practicable and it was not attempted. While it was the usual practice to turn a blind eye on most activities so long as they constituted no direct threat to good order and discipline, the rules could be invoked at any time by any member of staff. Behaviours that were tolerated by some officers could attract a disciplinary report if they were noticed by a new member of staff unfamiliar with the practice in that hall. Sometimes the regulations were permissive rather than mandatory and it was perfectly possible for them to be interpreted differently in different halls, or by different shifts in the same hall. The regulations on dress provide a case in point. Prison garb is not the most self-enhancing apparel and the rules were designed to give prisoners some limited choice, from what they had available, about what they wore and when they wore it. From time to time, however, disagreements arose as to what was the proper dress to be worn for meals. One prisoner, who found these disagreements particularly irksome, thought the staff were being deliberately provocative: he told us 'there is one good shift and one bad shift in this hall – they must have organized it special'. Others agreed with this view and, like the Parkhurst prisoners before them, wanted to return to a proper prison. Many of our first contacts among the prisoners told us that they would rather be back in Wandsworth:

'it's stricter there, but at least you know where you stand and what you can do'. Even some prisoners who were otherwise enthusiastic about the virtues of the Albany regime could not resist coming down in favour of a return to Wandsworth on these grounds.

Knowing 'where you stand' in relation to the likely behaviour of staff is an important element in any prisoner's approach to 'doing time'. If the lines beyond which he may not step are clearly drawn, then he can tread safely inside those boundaries without fear of disturbance. Any unnecessary anxiety only intrudes on the peaceful oblivion that can come from simply following the routine, and this makes time harder to do. Some prisoners rightly perceived that the regime at Albany was intended to disturb them out of that peaceful oblivion, and resented it. But some expressed their resentment automatically and without conviction: they were perfectly capable of maintaining themselves inside whatever the staff might do. And probably most prisoners had effectively adapted themselves to their situation and had come to learn where they stood with the Albany staff. The long periods of unlock and the closer contact in the halls, after all, enabled them to sound out staff as well, or better, than it permitted case officers to review their cases. As a result they were able to base their behaviour on their own assessment of what would be tolerated and what not. On the whole most prisoners seemed to regard Albany as imperfectly administered but genuinely humane.

It was not only prisoners who wanted to know where they stood. Anyone who pushes responsibility and decision-making on to the shoulders of subordinates himself assumes a responsibility for the way they discharge it, especially if they were unwilling to take it in the first place. As we went round the halls it was our impression that many staff were happy enough with the responsibilities placed upon them. But it was also clear that some had tried unsuccessfully to push the decision-making back up the line. Thus, when it was noticed that prisoners were making substantial alterations to the styling of prison clothes, and therefore defacing prison property, the whole issue of clothing and what could be worn on which occasions was brought before the governor. Eventually, after much discussion, a governor's order was issued – but the order was limited to the alteration of garments, and the question of proper dress was left to be resolved in the halls. One or two officers hinted that they would not try to take matters before the governor any more because they would 'get no satisfaction there'.

Albany had its fair share of reports for disciplinary offences, and friction did exist, as it always does exist in prisons, not just between staff and prisoners but also among the prisoners themselves. One prisoner told us: 'You can't trust anyone here – blokes pinch more stuff in here than they do outside.' An officer warned us that there was more gambling – and so more baroning – at Albany than at previous prisons where he had worked: 'This is a gambling community; even though it's against the rules, men do gamble. There is a sort of understanding that it's not too serious to be caught with betting slips and there's a lot of betting going on. This leads to men in debt, and appeals for protection from the barons. We've got the two richest barons on punishment in Y block at present, and we've also got two men on Rule 43 there who can't pay their debts.' Violence is the great enforcer of gambling debts in any prison, just as it is outside; it also enforces moral standards and adjudicates in struggles for power. It is rare for the reasons for violence to reach the surface, though the results are usually obvious enough: one prisoner 'slipped and fell because of the bad placing of equipment in the kitchen'; another was found with a serious eye injury; and when a child-rapist was received he was assaulted within minutes of his arrival, it was thought by another prisoner on the same escort.

When discipline offences were brought to official notice and found, within the limits of prison justice, to have been proved they were usually punished by loss of earnings or by confinement to cells. The punishment block, Y hall, was directly under the supervision of the chief officer, and staffed by two experienced officers from each division who worked there on a more or less permanent basis. The staff there were encouraged, somewhat against their own judgment, to rule lightly and sympathetically, using boredom rather than briskness as the deterrent. The governor thought the policy in Y hall was successful and none of the staff or prisoners we spoke to contradicted that.

Great vigilance was exercised in relation to all security matters, and anyone who could be identified as constituting a threat to security was dealt with firmly. Some months before the research began information was received that there would be an attempt to 'spring' one of the members of the Richardson gang, and he was discreetly but swiftly moved to Parkhurst. Two prisoners who scampered towards the fence were quickly apprehended and received loss of remission and a long spell in cells. Even so, with contractors constantly on the site carrying out work of one kind or another, security was a constant headache, and some movement of contraband and information, if not prisoners, was inevitable. Once a file was lost and was assumed to have got into the possession of a party of visiting labourers from Camp Hill prison, though it was never traced. But most prisoners, perhaps contrary to popular belief, neither thought much about attempting to escape nor had any serious intention of doing so. They mostly regarded the increasingly elaborate arrangements to keep them inside either with indifference or contempt, though a few were prepared to quote the new wisdom that a secure perimeter permitted greater freedom inside.

We had no way of telling how representative the views expressed to us were, nor at that time did we particularly try to find out. Instead we were content to let members of the prison present the situation to us as they wished. If we had to summarize our impressions of the atmosphere in Albany in the middle of 1968 we would have to say that our first impression was of widespread, if not universal, enthusiasm, but that this was tempered by our second impression of an underlying ambivalence and doubt. Probably two-thirds of the staff we spoke to after our early meetings in the prison, including many discipline staff, conveyed their commitment by speaking of Albany as 'our' prison, and of what 'we' do here. The many changes in the prison, which in our formal meetings had been put forward as problems the research would have to solve, were now discussed with us as problems which they themselves had, or would, overcome. Perhaps a third of those we spoke to were less happy about Albany, and at first they kept their own counsel. Not all were from the discipline grades. When they did speak they emphasized their distance from the prison by speaking of what 'the governor' wants, or what 'they' do here. They often implied and occasionally said, that some of the plans and changes from tradition in Albany were pointless and even childish.

When the governor's promotion was announced in the Press on 8 June 1968 it seemed that the underlying uncertainties quickly rose to the surface. Much had been achieved in less than eighteen months of office, but there was a feeling that it was mainly the energy and determination of the governor that held the achievements together. Many expectations had been raised, though few as yet had been realized. Those that had been realized did not seem sufficiently established to survive a concerted attempt to change them. There was also a feeling that talk at all levels had been a substitute for action. The principal officers, for example, had received much propaganda about their role, but no machinery to support them as effective middle managers had been devised, other than *ad hoc* meetings to deal with particular issues as they arose. Those members of staff who by inclination, or by conversion, were convinced of the wisdom of the Albany philosophy were uncertain as to whether they would be allowed to continue to exercise their new-found responsibilities, and what support would be forthcoming if they did, under a new regime. And those who were not so convinced could not help hoping that a period of discomfort was coming to an end and that the burden would soon be lifted from them. What effect the change of governor would have on the concept of social training was also of concern to senior managers. Here again much discussion had generated awareness and understanding; but few nuts and bolts had been provided to help convert the design into a functioning structure. The assistant governor's review board was operational but hardly established. Whether it would or could become an effective instrument of training and evaluation was still very much in the balance.

In short Albany was poised on the brink. But of what? No one quite knew. It had come a long way and it was still broadly on the path which the governor had charted for it. But everything so far was by way of preparation, and successful operation was still in the future. There were those among the staff who wanted a continuing effort to push forward with what had been started, and there were those who felt they had been pushed far enough and would settle either for things as they now were, or a return to what they thought of as normal prison conditions.

Interestingly enough this ambivalence was shared by the prisoners. Some liked the prison simply because it was new and free from unpleasant associations; as one prisoner told us: 'The walls don't ooze generations of other people's feelings.' Some professed indifference. Some were certainly anxious, though how therapeutic their anxiety was there seemed no way of knowing. But the overriding impression to emerge from the various shades of feeling expressed to us was that the prisoners were puzzled. It was not a proper prison, and the screws did not behave in the ways that all screws were supposed to behave. This did not mean that underneath they weren't really screws, of course, who were not to be trusted. But they found that they did trust some of them, or at least they talked to them. And they found themselves enjoying Albany and its facilities, in so far as one can enjoy any prison, almost against their will. And when they realized that, it seemed that it would be better if they were back in a proper prison. Though they weren't quite sure why, they knew that they were vulnerable. Since one prisoner took the trouble to put his thoughts on paper, we will leave the last word with him: it captures the spirit of what many prisoners conveyed in discussion. We have, without permission, corrected spellings and added punctuation but made no other amendments.

An honest inventory of Albany Prison

I came here from Wandsworth nearly a year ago. My first impression was surprise. I mean by that the way things are allowed to be run. Let me say first of all that the difference between the two prisons is like day and night. At first I did not like the place. That was because I had never known the like of it before. Here we are allowed to run about half dressed whereas in Wandsworth you can be up in front of the governor if one of your buttons is undone. Albany Prison is more like a borstal than a borstal. Most of the men here object to being treated like naughty little boys. They would, I think, much rather be treated as men. If they do wrong let them be punished for their wrongdoing.

When I came here first, as I said, I was surprised. Coming through reception was funny. When I first entered into this place my name was taken, my personal kit was taken note of. I was then issued a complete new prison uniform, was told to dress in one of the empty reception cells and wait until I was called in to see the chief officer. Meantime I got acquainted with some of the lads who had come with me. They then called us in number to see the chief officer. This was my first surprise. When I entered the little room I told my name. He was actually smiling. He said in a friendly voice, 'Sit down, lad.' He then told who he was and that he was just having a chat and bidding me welcome to Albany; telling me for the first couple of weeks I would be working as a cleaner until I was through with interviews, and where I was to work for the biggest part of my sentence. Well, I started off working in the administrative offices and was there for about a month. I was then taken up for an interview with all the workshop bosses and it was said that I would work in the tailor's shop for several months and then I could get another job outside – working on the gardens or something. I started working there and Mr ——— who is the boss of the tailors got me a job as he said he would outside. I worked in the said shop for about seven months. Well, at first I was told to work one of the machines but I could never get used to the sewing and asked to do some other type of work. I was taken to the cutting shop to cut lengths of nylon material into new mail bags. I was a bit more interested in this sort of work but unfortunately I was just there to fill a vacancy. The chap who had been sick came back and I had to go back to my original shop, but I had a taste for using the scissors and was put to pattern cutting. I was very happy while this lasted. But like all things there was no more to be cut so I was told to give the storeman a hand. And that is what I was doing when the chief officer told me I had gotten a job out in the fresh air. It worked rather well. The good weather had just started and now I am out from eight till twelve, have lunch and go out again at two o'clock.

I will now fill you in on the kind of things that I have been doing since leaving the shop. The very first day me and few more lads in the party were sweeping the main drag when into the prison came my chief officer around nine o'clock. He stopped and said to the officer in charge of our party that on the football field there is an old brick toilet that needs pulling down. So the lads and I picked up our shovels and brushes and made haste to the garden shed where we picked up a couple of heavy hammers, a spike, and odds and ends. Went to the place where the old cassey was and started to knock hell out of it. The poor building hadn't an earthly. We had it flat in about one hour flat. All the rubble was left lying and all the wood was burned. We had a lovely fire going. For a good bit of the time we mucked about there until we were again asked to do another job. We were told to dig a trench for the GPO and we done this so fast that we left ourselves nothing to do, except carry on sweeping the driveway. We are allowed to walk around the nick stripped to the waist and with good weather it is giving us a nice tan. When we leave here, if people ask where have you been, we can just say we have been overseas and we won't be telling lies. Just lately we have had a little trouble not knowing what we are supposed to do. There are far too many people with different opinions but I don't think I can go into that. I do not want to leave myself open to some trumped-up charge.

Part III

The rise and rise of Albany fences

6   Consolidation, consistency and new priorities

Perhaps in no organization is the position of general manager, and the person who fills it, of such concern to all the organizational participants as it is in the prison. Even the ablest delegator, or for that matter the governor who merely seeks seclusion and the quiet life, has to be seen in his prison from time to time and has to be accessible in some degree, both to front-line staff and to prisoners, as well as to his heads of departments. Through tours of inspection, through hearing applications and through making adjudications, his administrative style reaches out at first to those directly involved, but quickly thereafter by reputation to the rest of the prison: for everyone is interested to know how he handles each situation.

The governor opening a new prison faces quite different problems from the governor who takes over an established institution. But Albany was not yet an established institution, and the task of following in the footsteps of David Gould in the summer of 1968 could not have been easy.

A new style of government

When Brian Howden took over the prison on 8 July, Albany had been open a mere fifteen months. There was no serious evidence of overt tension. Nor was there any history of disturbances to live down. There had certainly been no time for stagnation. The new governor must have known before his arrival that the physical structure of the prison was still unfinished and that its future place in the system was still uncertain. If he did not know in advance he must soon have realized that the social structure of the prison had not yet fully been formed in the image created for it. Given the exigencies of the opening up of the prison from scratch, and according to principles which departed from the traditional model, it would have been impossible for David Gould to have maintained a low profile even if he had wanted to: both his philosophy and his general strategy for implementing it were well known. It would have been surprising had they received universal acceptance and, of course, they did not. But so long as the prison was moving forward on so many fronts, there was a degree of indulgence extended towards the innovator, perhaps born of the joint struggle to overcome the many teething troubles, which could hardly be expected to apply to his successor. Brian Howden must have quickly become aware that there was a keen desire to learn not just what the Home Office plans were for Albany but also how he defined his task and how he would set about it. Anxieties had been raised since the announcement of David Gould's promotion and there was pressure to relieve those anxieties. As observers we were as anxious as anybody. Our own research had scarcely begun, and an unsympathetic or hostile governor could, if he wished, have effectively terminated the project. As soon as decently possible we invited the governor to the University, where we discussed the research once again in some detail. Our fears were quickly laid to rest. The governor expressed both an interest in the research and a willingness to tolerate any threat that it might constitute. He noted that sufficiently wide-ranging contacts had already been made with both prisoners and staff to have revealed any likely problems that might have given him concern. He assured us of his full support which was, in fact, always forthcoming.

The pressures from the staff, however, were obviously more demanding of the governor's time and attention. Although Brian Howden had experience of taking over relatively new establishments – he had previously been governor at Kirkham open prison and at Bela River – the usual expectations regarding divisions between discipline staff and the other staff did not provide good guidelines for the situation at Albany. While such divisions undoubtedly continued to exist, the involvement of basic-grade discipline staff in the social training structure and the use of senior discipline staff and the governor grades in functionally separate managerial roles, produced a somewhat modified pattern of alliances, anxieties and conflicts. Moreover, many of the staff at Albany paid more than just lip service to the idea of rehabilitation and training: there was liable to be more dispute about how it might best be achieved than whether it should be attempted at all. In the circumstances any radical changes in policy would have run the risk of sacrificing the reservoir of goodwill and enthusiasm which had been built up under David Gould. At the same time there was sufficient disagreement in matters of administration to give almost any decision a much wider significance than its nominal scope would suggest. Seemingly small details of routine brought to the governor for resolution could be regarded as a test of his intentions and thus be given far-reaching implications. The granting of an apparently innocuous request from one quarter might heighten old tensions elsewhere or raise new problems that could not have been foreseen.

Not surprisingly Brian Howden trod carefully at first. When he arrived the prison had for three weeks been under the effective command of the deputy governor during the terminal leave of David Gould. The new governor began with a few days of information-gathering, in the course of which he was able to take initial soundings of attitude and opinion within the prison and to give general assurances about his intentions in return. He made it clear, for example, that he would give full and firm support to the staff, and that he would also endeavour to preserve the achievements of the Albany pattern of working, for which he expressed his admiration. He was then confident enough to leave the prison once again in the hands of the deputy governor and the senior management for a further period of three weeks while he took his own annual leave.

It is not clear whether the absence from the prison of successive governors for a total period of some six weeks was brought about by a carefully thought-out policy, or a routine take-over procedure without particular thought for the consequences, or whether it merely resulted from coincidentally prearranged holiday plans which had to be honoured. It is clear that the period was an unsettling one for the prison. What caused particular concern was a memorandum from headquarters saying that 40 cells were to be strengthened against the contingency that Albany might become a dispersal prison. Ever since the Radzinowicz sub-committee had reported unfavourably on the Alvington concept there had been sporadic speculation that Albany, with its island setting and electronic systems, would eventually be required to cater for category-A prisoners. So when it fell to the deputy governor to pass on the contents of the memorandum to the central management meeting on 24 July the speculation became endemic. Thus far there had been no official confirmation that the dispersal policy would even be implemented (it came the next day in answer to a parliamentary question), let alone that Albany was earmarked for this purpose. Inevitably the change of governor was interpreted by some as part of a process to firm up the prison for a new role. One or two members of the management team told us that it was unfortunate that the governor was not there in person to deal authoritatively with the matter.

It was indeed unfortunate that such an important memorandum should have arrived in the absence of the governor, although had he been there he would probably have been unable or unwilling to provide more information about the future of Albany because, officially at least, its status remained obscure for several weeks. In other respects the period between the departure of the first governor and the effective arrival of the second seemed to serve useful functions. There was in fact no real reason why Albany should not have been able to function effectively for six weeks without a governor. The senior staff were able and by now experienced; and leaving them to get on with the job demonstrated confidence in their capacity to govern and de-emphasized the importance of the change of governor in the life of the institution. The gap between the last decisions of David Gould and the first decisions of Brian Howden also served to reduce the visibility of the differences between the two men, both in terms of management style and policy. The transitional period under the deputy governor formed, as it were, a kind of temporal no-man's-land. But perhaps most importantly of all, the brief initial encounters between the new governor and his staff, followed by a substantial period of leave, served to reduce the scope for inter-personal conflict during the crucial and consequential change-over period. The governor was able to sound out his staff and then to reflect on strategy before having to confront them with, or be confronted by, major decisions. He was also spared the embarrassment of having to acknowledge any staff reactions to his arrival. The staff were able to seek basic reassurances and then to work out their anxieties either separately or through mutual discussion and speculation. In this way, on the basis of expectations engendered by their first impressions, they were able to anticipate and to prepare themselves for possible developments before they had actually to meet them in reality, and without the need for possibly uncomfortable face-to-face interaction with their new master.

As it happened, after Brian Howden returned from leave there followed a period when major changes were accomplished with remarkable speed and little opposition. Perhaps we should begin by describing the changes in central management. At the CMM on 7 August – a critical meeting to which we shall have to return later – the governor began by asking that in future heads of department should meet with him each Monday morning for a short briefing about the events of the week. The governor thought that such a meeting would help him in the early stages of his administration, and he said it was not intended to replace the central management meeting itself. He asked if there were deep-rooted objections to the proposal. There were none. But privately some members of the meeting thought the new governor had created ripples in the smooth surface of the Albany pool and others thought he was making waves. Briefing meetings were part of the common stock of experience in the traditional pattern of management by governorial fiat; central management meetings of the kind established at Albany were not. In spite of the governor's assurances they feared that his proposal signalled the end of the central management meeting as a serious body for the exchange of views and the formulation of policy. Their fears were buttressed by the recognition that other members were apparently willing to forego the opportunity for debate that the CMM offered. The administration officer, for example, had welcomed the governor's suggestion of a briefing meeting, and in turn suggested that the CMM be moved to Mondays to be combined with it. This idea was strongly resisted by both the assistant governors, and the topic was dropped; the governor reiterated his assurances and the meeting moved on to other business, with an agreement to commence the briefing meetings in the following week. In the event the fears, as expressed, were unfounded. The briefing meeting was to last much longer than 'the early stages' of the Brian Howden administration and it became an established part of the management process. But it did not lead, and was probably never intended to lead to the demise of the CMM. When Brian Howden did change both the form and function of the central management meeting, it emerged as a stronger body, with a much more clearly defined place in the management structure. And those who had earlier expressed reservations to us were prepared to accept those changes when they came.

It seems likely that Brian Howden may initially have entertained a number of possible alternatives to the central management meeting as the main instrument of government. But if so he did not reveal them. Instead he watched the operation of the meeting carefully for several weeks before becoming convinced of its utility. Not surprisingly, however, he began to refashion it to deal more explicitly with the administrative problems as he saw them. Once the briefing meeting was established it hived off much of the information-giving function of the old-style CMM and systematized the process of communication. Routine departmental matters, which in the past had sometimes been squeezed out of central management discussions to be dealt with in private consultation with the governor, were now reviewed in a regular and business-like way at the briefing meeting with all heads of department present. The central management meeting was thus freed to concentrate on longer-term inter-departmental planning. Before introducing any changes, however, Brian Howden consulted his senior managers and found that they were very ready to consider proposals to reform the meeting, especially if these would result in its becoming more of an executive body.

On 18 September the most far-reaching changes for the meeting were proposed and accepted. Symbolically the meeting was held in the more formal board room in Y hall instead of the staff rest room where the meetings had customarily been held. The governor proposed that all future meetings be held in the board room to promote a more business-like atmosphere, which would be in keeping with the more explicit emphasis on making decisions which he wanted to bring about. The main tasks of the meeting in future would be to make joint decisions after due discussion, and to see that they were carried out. If meaningful decisions were to be reached, discussion would have to be more limited than in the past and a closer correspondence between those responsible for the ideas and those responsible for carrying them out would need to be brought about. This might best be achieved by reconstituting the meeting as a somewhat smaller group, perhaps limiting it to members with 'genuine' departmental responsibilities, and by adopting a more 'severe' approach to accountability than had so far been apparent. Decisions reached by the meeting would have to be subject to a veto power vested in the governor because of his legal responsibilities, but they would otherwise be regarded as binding and they would not be changed without reference back to the meeting. Where action was required, individuals would be nominated by the meeting for seeing that the action was carried out, and would be held to account at later meetings. To go with the greater formality of Y hall board room, the meetings would henceforth have a properly constituted agenda; and a shorthand writer would attend to take minutes, which would be circulated. Matters arising from the minutes would be raised formally at the beginning of each meeting. Finally, it was proposed and agreed that, under the new arrangements which were expected to expedite business, the frequency of meetings could again be reduced to once a fortnight.

On 30 September the revised arrangements for the meeting were announced in an internal circular, and the first new-style meeting took place on the following Wednesday. The membership was reduced from thirteen to eleven, comprising the governor, the deputy governor, the two assistant governors, the chief officer and the senior chief officer II, the administration officer (who was made responsible for preparing the agenda), the principal psychologist, the senior welfare officer, the foreman of works and the industrial manager. The tutor-organizer, the chaplain and the medical officer were thus dropped, while the industrial manager was introduced to the management group for the first time.

It is worth analysing why these changes came about. In retrospect, most sequences of events can seem to be explained either as the development of a consciously formulated policy or policies by one or more of the participants, or as the unfolding of a more or less inevitable process which transcends the individuals who participate in it. No doubt there is some truth to be found in both views, but even in the controlled organizational world of prisons contingent short-term factors probably play a major, if not the most important part. Certainly at the time the events occur – and this is so for the observer no less than the participants – the motivations of others seem much more ambiguous, the outcomes of action much less certain than the broad sweep of history suggests.

The changes in structure and personnel of the CMM did signal some marked changes in the Albany regime, which amounted to a more or less explicit change of policy away from the dual mandate of social and industrial training towards a new mandate of security and industrial production which was to play an ever-growing part in the development of Albany. Some such change in policy had presumably already been developing in Prison Department before Brian Howden was appointed; and the changes in management structure which he effected undoubtedly facilitated the introduction of the new policy. But it is unlikely either that headquarters had then sufficiently thought through the consequences of the emerging policy to have requested those changes in the administrative structure, or that Brian Howden was merely fashioning a structure which would best fit the anticipated consequences. Certainly the full import of the change of policy did not become clear until October, although the general direction towards which events were moving was evident enough. It seems somewhat more likely that the process of organizational development would eventually have required changes in the central management meeting even if there had been no change in governor. After all, the longer the prison had been in operation the more it would be expected to account for its progress and the more necessary it would become to define and apportion responsibilities. Whatever weight one gives to these factors, however, it was also the case that the administrative changes also provided a means for dealing with the problem of succession.

The lack of accountability in the old-style central management structure was the price that David Gould was prepared to pay for keeping long-term goals and the concept of therapeutic anxiety before his fellow participants. The loosely structured and informal meeting provided the ideal setting for turning questions back on the questioner, which was the essence of David Gould's style in relations with staff. He was able to use the meeting as something of a group therapeutic session, now as a safety valve for discontents, then as a sounding board for new ideas, but always ultimately working towards developing a sense of personal responsibility in the mutual pursuit of common goals. However much he spoke of the need to clarify roles and to specify tasks, in the event he was always more concerned to get staff to look beyond short-range difficulties and conflicts of interests to the larger issues. A sense of Delphic ambiguity constituted his defence against the possibility that staff would merely operate within the safety of routine procedures. It was as though he saw the staff as an unintegrated social force and his energies were devoted to mobilizing them behind an integrative ideal. He was fond of quoting Emerson's dictum that 'Nothing great was achieved without enthusiasm': and there is no doubt that he did generate the enthusiasm he sought.

Brian Howden did not share the same vision. And it would have been manifestly impossible for him to have maintained the central management meeting on its existing pattern even had he wanted to. He had to find an alternative basis for establishing respect for his leadership in his own right, if the prison was not to lose confidence and momentum at a critical period of its development. As it happened, he was able to capitalize on the feeling among both staff and prisoners that they needed 'to know where they stood'. As we have indicated, those feelings were expressed in several ways. The prisoners felt that somehow Albany had gone beyond the bounds of what they understood as a proper prison. Hall principal officers, faced with prisoners who objected to the different ways in which staff exercised their initiative, looked both for support in what they had done and for guidance in choosing between alternatives. Central management personnel felt frustrated that they could not always be sure whether or not a decision had been reached by the meeting, and if it had that so little action seemed to flow from it. It is certainly fair to say that Brian Howden would have ignored such feelings at his peril. And it may even be the case that he had no real alternative but to move in the direction that he chose. In any case his administrative style was ideally suited to allaying these staff fears and he was quick to sense that correspondence.

Throughout his term of office, but especially in the early stages, he was careful not to enter the arena of penal philosophy which had been so much the domain of David Gould. In so far as he was concerned with such matters it is probable that Brian Howden believed that behaviour changing was as likely to be brought about through the carrot and the stick as by talk and introspection. If confidence in such a system was to be upheld it would be necessary for everyone to know what the carrots and sticks were, and who wielded them under what circumstances. Clarity in organizational relations was therefore the prerequisite for goal attainment. Howden praised the achievements of his predecessor and insisted that he would do his utmost to keep the prison on the course that Gould had charted. Those achievements would best be consolidated, he argued, by bringing them within a more consistent framework of routine administration. And in the name of consolidation and consistency Albany moved into a very different phase of development.

The demise of social training

Perhaps the clearest need for consolidation and consistency was at middle-management level, especially in the halls. Indeed attention was being focussed on this area even before the reform of the central management meeting. At the CMM on 28 August the assistant governor was invited to discuss the current state of thinking on the role of hall principal officers. He outlined a proposal for a series of fortnightly meetings which would be concerned with two aspects of their work: the routine administration of their halls and the process of helping prisoners to help themselves. He thought that the emphasis should be on the second aspect because, whereas principal officers had now developed some experience in their custodial or hotel functions, they needed considerable guidance in the area of social training. He argued that it was essential that the meeting should be held and attended regularly, regardless of the difficulties. He proposed that the meeting should be under the chairmanship of the governor with the principal psychologist and the two assistant governors in attendance. The principal psychologist indicated his agreement. He pointed out that the prison had always been too preoccupied with other things in the past to get the meeting off the ground, and that the opportunity should be taken of instituting it before the prison became completely absorbed in the change-over from a category-C to a category-B prison. Broad agreement was reached on the need for action; and a new middle-management meeting for principal officers was duly announced, with the constitution and functions which had been suggested by the assistant governor. It too was to be held in Y hall board room, with a written agenda and circulated minutes. The new central management group was to meet on the first and third Wednesdays in each month, and the principal officers' meeting was scheduled for the first and third Thursdays, so that decisions and information could be speedily and fully communicated from one level to another.

The first principal officers' meeting (POM) was held on 3 October 1968, and it quickly became a feature of the management structure. Although it was still functioning when we returned to the prison some three years later, under Mr Gifford Footer the meetings gradually became less and less frequent, eventually being called together only as required. The AG for staff training had expected that the first few meetings would take the form of 'gripe sessions', but that the meeting would soon settle down into a more general discussion group. He hoped that it would provide an opportunity for staff training, and especially that it would at last be possible to make some real progress in the specification of staff roles. The first few meetings were undoubtedly gripe sessions. But the POM never really assumed the nature of a training forum, and role specification was not attempted in that context. The principal officers were simply much more interested in ironing out the problems in the domestic routine of their halls than they were in grappling with wider issues. The minutes reveal the constant pressure towards greater consistency in the control and management of prisoners.

Two long-standing issues provide good examples of the kind of concern which led to the growth of middle management and then sustained it; the serving of supper, and the dress of prisoners.

As we have noted earlier, prisoners left their halls to collect supper at the end of evening association, and returned to their halls to eat it before being locked in for the night. Prisoners from different halls could and did mix freely at this time, and there was no real attempt to exercise supervision over their activities. Although no serious incidents had occurred staff were noticeably more tense at this time, and they told us they felt particularly vulnerable. Representations to change the procedure had been made to central management by the hall POs through the chief and the POA, but without effect. Not surprisingly these representations were renewed with the arrival of the new governor, who made proposals that would be in keeping with the liberal policy of his predecessor but which would also go some way towards diminishing the threat to good order perceived by the hall staff. He suggested that at supper prisoners should be given the choice of taking the meal or not. This might reduce the numbers to be supervised and provide the staff with a barometer for assessing the level of feelings and tension in the halls. Those who did not want supper could stay behind and watch television; those who did would eat it in the dining room before returning to the halls. A suggestion by the chief that all movements to supper should be staggered by sending each hall separately was resisted on grounds that such regimentation would be inappropriate at Albany and was not justified by the situation. In discussion, however, it emerged that not all halls adopted the same practices at other meals. Thus the PO in A hall said the new procedure at supper would present no problems for him because he already gave prisoners the choice for all meals. The governor was quick to point out that it might be desirable to give prisoners such a choice, but if so all prisoners should have it. Inconsistency between one hall and another was not desirable, he said, and the hall POs should get together to agree what procedure should apply. Otherwise it would appear that staff were 'buggering the prisoners about for the sake of buggering them about', and prisoners could reasonably ask the hall staff to 'make up their bloody minds'.

The new arrangements for supper were put into immediate effect, and prisoners thus had to choose between taking supper and watching television.   We were in the halls on the evening that the new scheme was implemented, and large numbers of prisoners chose not to take the meal. The remainder were checked out and back by an officer on the gate of each hall. A few prisoners complained to us, and the next day to the governor, about the new checking out and checking in procedures, though most prisoners seemed happy enough about the new element of choice. Complainants were dismissed by staff as 'troublemakers who complain about anything' and the situation was expected to settle down quickly enough. Indeed it did, and the numbers attending supper gradually rose.

Shortly after his arrival the governor raised the question of the manner in which prisoners were dressed. He wanted to hear how others felt, but he declared his own position to be that the present policy of allowing considerable latitude created a situation which offended his military eye. The discussion which followed generated a good deal of heat. The chief officer agreed that the way a prisoner dressed was very important and that high standards should be expected and enforced. But others felt the matter was irrelevant to an understanding of why people became criminals and how to train them to be law-abiding. The governor hoped that staff at central management level would give the matter further thought. He asked the POs to try to come up with an agreed policy about dress in the halls, and pointed out that he would expect prisoners to be clean and neatly dressed whenever they appeared before him.

When the principal officers met they decided that 'in the interests of hygiene' overalls should not be worn at meals. For B, C and D halls, where prisoners were on shift work, however, those prisoners working the early shift would be permitted to wear overalls at breakfast because they would not have time to change before going to work. In A hall, where prisoners worked both in the mornings and the afternoons, overalls could be worn at breakfast and lunch, but not at tea or supper. In no hall would prisoners be permitted to wear overalls during association periods, on grounds that the wearing of overalls had 'caused the easy chairs to get in a filthy condition'. The hall POs put up notices to this effect in their halls, and their decision was duly communicated to the governor. But the need for formalizing the communication process at different management levels was illustrated a day or so later when the chief officer accompanied the governor on a tour of inspection. On seeing A-hall prisoners going to lunch in their overalls, the chief reprimanded the senior officer on duty and instructed him that in future prisoners should be made to change into their prison 'greys' before going to meals. That afternoon the hall POs met with the chief to attempt to clarify the position. They pointed out that they had been given authority to reach a decision by the CMM, and that now they found that their decision was countermanded. They were told that they had 'jumped the gun': that they should have made a recommendation to the governor and then waited for his circular before taking action. Although the POs had themselves asked for authoritative guidance they were none the less disconcerted by this apparent return to the use of governor's orders. When the circular appeared, a few days later, it made no mention of the exception for A-hall prisoners at lunchtime, so that the regulations on dress at mealtimes were the same for all halls.

When the new rules on dress were put into effect most prisoners agreed that 'a new broom' had entered the prison. Several prisoners said that the new governor was trying to turn Albany back 'into an ordinary nick'. When we pointed out that a few weeks earlier some had complained that David Gould did not run 'an ordinary nick', and that they had wanted to return to Wandsworth which was 'a proper prison', they agreed that this seemed inconsistent. But one prisoner pointed out that 'when it comes right down to it, it doesn't matter what *they* do – you're still doing bird'. And another observed that while it was true that prisoners wanted to know what the rules were, this did not mean that the rules had to be drawn in an undignified, inconvenient or restrictive way. The flexibility about dress in Albany had at times puzzled some prisoners but it was also one of the freedoms which many enjoyed. What they were really concerned about now, he said, was that there would be a general tightening up which would mean the end of the liberal regime at Albany.

Prisoners' fears that Albany would become an ordinary nick were not entirely unjustified. The governor had let it be known at central management level that there was a general feeling in the prison service that while Albany could deal with low-security-risk prisoners using its present methods, it might not be able to cope with the more sophisticated population that it could expect in the future. There can be little doubt that Brian Howden had this consideration in mind throughout his drive to achieve consistency, and this was reflected in POM discussions. Proposals were made for more inspection of the halls, and arrangements for tightening up visiting procedures were made long before any high-security-risk prisoners were received. At the same time, whenever it was possible within the framework of the emerging policy for Albany, the governor seemed genuinely anxious to preserve as much as possible of the freedom of choice that had typified Albany in its early days. In any case it was well recognized that the design of the Albany halls was such that any increase in supervision had to be focussed on easily identifiable externals such as dress.

It is probable that Brian Howden always envisaged a practical management focus for the principal officers' meeting, rather than any longer-term training function in which the role of the hall staff would be further explored. Although the framework within which the POs were required to operate was made much more explicit, this is not to say that their power was diminished or that the governor sought to diminish it. Indeed, they remained fully responsible for the management of the halls and, in so far as their joint meetings provided them with a source of support and leverage, their power *vis-à-vis* other members of the prison staff probably increased. Thus the POs voiced a number of complaints against the welfare department, about what was seen as an indiscreet use of the telephone on behalf of prisoners and an over-generous policy with regard to welfare visits. As a result it was agreed that the governor would discuss the use of the telephone with the department, and that recommendations for welfare visits should be referred to one of the governor grades for approval. The net effect of the introduction of the middle-management meeting, then, was to shift the prison staff into a rather more traditional posture. The attention of principal officers was re-focussed, away from a consideration of what the ends of their own activity should be and on to the means whereby certain external policies might be implemented. The burden of self-justification which had been left firmly with them by David Gould had now been removed.

Along with the removal of anxiety among principal officers the whole notion of 'therapeutic anxiety' as a lever for changing prisoners gradually disappeared. And though the case-officer system remained very much part of the vocabulary it became increasingly a matter of form rather than substance. The case-officer system had never been very effective at monitoring and guiding change among inmates, not just for lack of training (which was the official explanation for its deficiencies) but because no one had a clear understanding of how that task could or should be conducted. It was soon to become a pale shadow of what had been intended, partly because of lack of inclination to pursue the matter further and partly because other more understandable tasks appeared to take up the time and attention of almost everyone in the prison. Moreover, since progress in the new tasks of securing the prison and rearranging its industries could readily be assessed, staff received regular and reinforcing feedback as to their effectiveness which had not been available in their case work efforts.

At the important central management meeting on 7 August 1968 it became clear that there was a crisis of confidence as to the nature and purpose of social training. Though doubts had, of course, been discussed before, it was not until the governor began probing what he thought of as the weak spots of the regime that the true extent of those doubts emerged. The governor complained that in spite of the best efforts of staff in the past, there seemed to be very little for the prisoners to do during the long hours when not at work, especially in the mornings. In the first statement of a theme to which he was to return on many subsequent occasions, the governor pointed out that 'boredom in prison is a killer: it disturbs prisoners and produces unnecessary trouble for the staff'. He had talked to the tutor-organizer about the inadequacies of the classrooms for their purpose or to accommodate prisoners' hobbies, and of the depressing difficulties in arranging classes. Was there anything, he asked the meeting, that could be done? The only real suggestion came from the principal officer in charge of physical education, who pressed for making games and physical training compulsory. The assistant governors argued that this would undermine the Albany principle whereby prisoners should make their own decisions, and the governor rejected the proposal as a backward step when what was required was to consolidate and then to move forward by finding new activities and opportunities. Several members of the meeting felt that Prison Department had lost interest in social training at Albany in favour of concentration on security and industry, and the governor confirmed that such feelings were not without justification. To murmurs of approval, the chief expressed the general indignation by suggesting that headquarters be told 'give us the tools and we will get on with the job'. But when the senior assistant governor challenged the meeting to specify just what tools – apart from classrooms – they needed to get on with the job, there was no answer. The long silence was indicative of the paucity of ideas for mechanisms that would bridge the gap between staff and prisoners in such a way as to bring about behavioural change. The meeting ended with an agreement that the governor would try to stimulate interest at headquarters, while the CMM would set up a sub-committee to see how far they could help themselves.

As the weeks went by the sub-committee decided to use one of the dining halls as a games room until more adequate and permanent accommodation could be provided. Its use would present problems of hygiene, and inevitably of supervision, but there was no real alternative. Games such as Monopoly and Scrabble were purchased, though it was recognized that even if they were used they would probably only encourage further gambling. A record-player was acquired and so were communal birdcages and fish tanks. All of these may have done something to relieve the boredom, but they scarcely filled the vacuum in social training.

In October the full attention of central management was diverted to making new arrangements for the organization of industry and preparing for the eventual reception of category-A prisoners. By Christmas this change of emphasis in Albany had become obvious to the prisoners. In the first, and very much delayed, edition of the prison magazine *Albany Argus* an article appeared under the title 'Where is my case officer?' The author, with a heavy sense of parody, echoed the sentiments which prisoners had expressed with increasing frequency since our arrival at the prison. He wrote:

It's rather sad that he seems to have gone as I was just getting to know him. Of course I am going back a bit now, over a year in fact. Why, some of these new drafts haven't even heard of a case officer. It makes you feel sorry for them in a way, missing out on the 'deep meaningful human relationships' and 'officer involvement'. Perhaps it was a bit of a romp: a Home Office 'frolic', never intended to be taken too seriously, but it was fun while it lasted.... Take interviews... no stone was left unturned to lay a sound basis for your rehabilitation! Once it required three quarters of an hour of 'in-depth' probing and much deliberation but the man stuck with it – the soft-toy class would help in my rehabilitation! I still sometimes have a twinge of remorse at a missed opportunity!

In the next edition the assistant governor in charge of social training replied. Mistaking a deep-rooted cynicism about the yawning gap between rhetoric and reality for defensiveness, the AG offered a rebuke to the author and an affirmation that the case officer was alive and well. The question that puzzled him, he wrote, was:

Why did you think he had disappeared, when he's been on the landing all the time? Perhaps you don't know him. Perhaps you don't want to know him. Anyway, what does he do that is useful to you? If you knew him that's a question you could ask him.... Your case officer is here to *help you help yourself.*

By trivializing a philosophical issue into personal terms the AG did little to ease the problem, and in the correspondence that followed the original author pointed out that it was incumbent upon would-be helpers to show what goods they have to offer. Other prisoners joined in claiming that the scheme was 'abortive', of 'nil achievement', and that 75 per cent of the population had no idea who their officer was.

In spite of his reply to the *Argus* article, the assistant governor evidently had his own misgivings; and in January 1969 he sent a memorandum to the governor in an attempt to codify the aims and methods of social training and to improve the working of the case-officer system. Ironically it was the first document of its kind to be produced in Albany since David Gould had made his declaration of intent in May 1967. A modified version of the document was issued as an internal circular to all staff the following month. The circular was re-issued, with amendments, in May 1970.

The codified social training structure was divided into three parts: induction, casework and pre-release. The induction period, progressively reduced in the three versions of the document from three weeks to ten days, was concerned with diagnosis, assessment and allocation. The casework was to be carried out by case officers whose case loads would be reorganized. Instead of each officer being allocated four to eight prisoners, as had been the system in the past, four officers, two on each division, would be jointly responsible for all the 24 prisoners on their landing. It was hoped – vainly as it turned out – that this would ensure greater continuity and encourage consultation between officers which would revitalize the system. In fact it became more difficult for prisoners to know who their case officer was under the new pattern of divided responsibility. And, here as elsewhere, the process of codification led to an emphasis on form rather than substance. When it came right down to it the only definitive duties that could be laid at the door of case officers was 'that the case file of each prisoner is annotated with a minimum of three entries per month'. Hall POs were required to inspect the files on a regular quarterly basis and to ensure that the files were properly used, though what constituted 'proper use' was nowhere spelled out. After discussion about the difficulties experienced with the assistant governor's review board, the 1969 circular required hall POs to hold two review boards per month, each to be attended by one division of their staff and an appropriate representative from central management. That the POs' boards went the same way as the AGs' boards before them is indicated by the fact that this requirement was dropped entirely from the 1970 circular. The pre-release phase included discussions on parole, employers, unions, government agencies, marriage guidance and other matters, as well as the use of home leave facilities.

While the social training structure as described in these documents was almost certainly as good as or better than anything that was offered in other prisons, it was already too late to be anything more than a formal framework. The priorities in Albany had simply shifted elsewhere: to security and industrial production.

The changes which had been wrought from within by a new governor with a different administrative style were undoubtedly far-reaching, although they did represent an attempt to maintain the existing Albany programme within a more consistent organizational framework. The upgrading of the security so that the prison could receive category-A prisoners, and the shift to a policy which, within the limits set by security considerations, gave an unambiguous priority to industrial production were, of course, imposed by headquarters. More than anything else it was these developments which reflected the revolution in Prison Department thinking since the days of Paterson and Fox. But they were scarcely compatible with a management structure devised with quite different ends in view, or with buildings designed for a different purpose, and it should not be surprising that difficulties arose.

Upgrading the security

Three weeks after the deputy governor had passed on the contents of the Home Office memorandum about the strengthening of 40 cells at Albany, the central management meeting was told that Brian Howden had been asked to join a working party to consider arrangements for the dispersal of category-A prisoners. Though no public announcement about the future of Albany was made until October, there could be no lingering doubts in the prison that it would receive top-security prisoners. The only questions were: how many would there be, when would they arrive, and what security measures would be required to prepare for them.

It is clear that thinking at headquarters about the consequences of dispersal had not gone far before the working party was set up. When the deputy governor first spoke to the CMM on the eve of the government's disclosure that the Radzinowicz proposals had been accepted, his remarks on the likely effects in Albany almost certainly reflected the official view. But nobody at the meeting really believed his argument that the regime would continue unaffected apart from some extra supervision for the occupants of the special cells, which were to be distributed evenly among the halls It seemed much more likely that special prisoners in special cells would demand special attention that would, in turn, have extensive repercussions. The mood was similarly sceptical three weeks later when the deputy governor again insisted that category-A prisoners would be 'absorbed' into the population 'perhaps with one or two, but only one or two, special precautions'.

The proposals for upgrading the physical security at Albany were eventually to prove far more extensive than even the most pessimistic participant in those early meetings could have feared. The first indication of the nature and extent of precautions thought necessary emerged at a central management meeting early in October 1968. By then Brian Howden had talked with the governors of other potential dispersal prisons at the working party. He indicated that the function of the working party was to consider the practical implications arising from the policy recommendations of a steering committee on dispersal – which itself had only been established after the Radzinowicz proposals were accepted. He gave the meeting what, in the event, turned out to be just a preliminary list of the work that would be necessary to lift Albany from its present lowly standard of category-C security to a state fit for receiving up to 35 category-A prisoners by December 1969. A group of officers would be dispatched immediately to attend a dog-handling course and on their return Alsatian dogs would be housed in the prison for the first time. Top priority would be given to the building of a control room, and the erection of a second fence seventeen feet high around the perimeter. The installation of the electronic locking system in B hall, which by now was seen as a security device as well as a means for providing night sanitation, would be completed to a higher specification and would definitely be extended to all halls. It would, perhaps, eventually be controlled by a computer, thus making Albany one of the most sophisticated prisons in the world. Work was also to begin on a segregation unit of the kind discussed in the Radzinowicz report. Much confusion about the dispersal policy, however, arose at that meeting. The minutes suggested that the segregation unit would be used 'so that category-A prisoners could be kept strictly apart from other prisoners' and had to be corrected subsequently to make it clear that 'category-A prisoners would be dispersed in the same way as other incoming prisoners', and that the segregation unit would be used for the removal of 'any inmate who misbehaved antisocially'.

On 30 November 1968 six dogs and their handlers began duties in Albany. Instructions were issued to all staff that nobody other than the handler should attempt to touch a dog or come into close contact with him; that in no circumstances should anyone approach a handler; and that in case of emergency the pursuit and detention of a prisoner should be left entirely to the dog and his handler since 'cases have been reported where dogs attack staff who are trying to assist'. No such incident occurred in the course of any emergency while we were at Albany, but shortly after the dogs arrived one of them bit a civilian cleaner attending to her duties in the administration building.

Only gradually did it become clear that the overworked and

understaffed works department, as well as outside contractors, would be virtually continuously employed on security projects for more than two years. This in a new prison, which in the eighteen months since it opened had never been without the presence of workmen repairing or adding to the fabric. As the governor said in his annual report for 1968, echoing the sentiments of his predecessor, 'Albany is completely overshadowed by works projects and future building and development. . . and maintenance'.

The year 1969 began with the completion of the first security fence and ended with the completion of the second. In between came months of construction in which many other projects were begun and a few were finished. The central management staff, and especially the foreman of works, were fully occupied by the nightmare task of integrating all the various jobs that had to be carried out, a task that was made much more difficult by staff shortages, the apparent lack of any critical path analysis, and constant delays in delivery dates and in getting decisions from headquarters. It seemed as if the completion of one project at Albany was always dependent upon the completion of another, and delay in meeting any one deadline soon produced chaotic disruptions elsewhere. And as if the new works were not enough there was the constant problem of carrying out repairs and modifications to the original buildings and facilities, because of poor site preparation and inadequate quality control. It would be tedious in the extreme to attempt to recount all the projects that were undertaken and what went wrong with them. The trials and tribulations that were caused for both staff and prisoners by this 'massive strengthening operation', as the governor referred to it, were fully recorded in his annual report for 1969. And again in his report for 1970, because the work continued through the greater part of that year also. Suffice it to say that the December 1969 target for the reception of category-A prisoners came and went. So did the next deadline of March 1970. It was not until October 1970 that the prison was finally ready. During all that time the main functions of the dog patrols were to guard the contractors' equipment and to prevent people from falling into the holes and trenches that punctuated and criss-crossed the prison grounds.

Even though our information is now some years old it would probably be undesirable to make a detailed report on security here, and in any case unnecessary. For obvious reasons we did not seek permission to attend security meetings, and many of the detailed arrangements were known to only a selected group of staff. But we did continue to attend central management meetings where security matters were discussed in general terms, and we did have access to circulars outlining security precautions. For present purposes it will be enough to review the main outlines of the security provisions which had been achieved, and some that were still planned, in October 1970 when the first category-A prisoners were received. They can be considered under three headings: the perimeter; internal security; and routine and emergency procedures.

The perimeter consisted of two security fences, each seventeen feet high, each with an overhang at the top and surmounted by barbed wire. A zig-zag wall to the south of the main gate had been replaced by a straight wall. The twelve-foot fence with the wooden screening along part of its length which, in 1966, had been thought sufficient for Albany's needs, had been pulled down. The two security fences were separated by a cleared hard surface some twenty feet wide, and geophonic alarm devices were installed which could be triggered when the fences were approached from inside. A new wooden screen was erected at the front. Along the length of the fence, and at various points in the yards, including the sports field, floodlights were fixed eighty feet high at the top of masts the bases of which were concreted into the ground. The lights flooded the yards and perimeter so that television cameras, also mounted on masts, could survey both the inner and outer fences by night as well as during the day. Several changes were made to the original gate house and others were planned. Strengthened accommodation was provided for the gate staff, who were now protected by bandit-proof glass. A modern PABX telephonic communications system was installed. New vehicle gates were introduced to the vehicle compound and the main gates were to be motorized. Various breaches to the fences which had been necessitated by construction work were repaired.

Inside the prison manganese steel bars, which had first been introduced at strategic points following Mountbatten's visitation, were eventually used to replace the original mild steel bars almost throughout: in the halls, the gymnasium, the chapel, the workshops and wherever prisoners had direct access. The strengthening of the halls had greatly interrupted the electronic installation, but work on the more advanced central automatic control system

(CACS), which would permit the locking and unlocking of the entire prison using a computer in the control room, was nearing completion. Unfortunately A hall, which was still operating on the ELSA system, would have to be re-wired to higher standards. The most important development inside the prison was the reconstruction of the punishment block into a new segregation unit. In the process part of the first floor of E hall was separated from the rest of the hall and joined to the punishment cells to form an extended unit which provided space for 43 prisoners, an association room and a workshop.

The control room, later to be called the emergency control room, was to become the focal point of routine as well as emergency planning, especially after the arrival of category-A prisoners. It housed a generator, two-way radio equipment, the television monitors, a master location panel for the prison, and would in time contain a computer and the control panels for the central automatic control system. It was surrounded by a chain link security fence, and staffed by teams of four officers, drawn from a group of specially trained control-room staff under the leadership of a senior officer. The expanded perimeter defence force, including five fixed observation posts and a prison dog section now numbering twelve dogs and their handlers, provided routine coverage of the prison. They maintained regular UHF radio contact with control, using special call signs to indicate the nature of any incidents. Alarm devices were fitted to the staff quarters so that off-duty officers could be called back to the prison in cases of emergency. And plans were drawn up whereby the staff from the three island prisons, Camp Hill, Parkhurst and Albany, as well as the local police, could be speedily mobilized in the event of an escape or serious disturbance.

Throughout 1969, and much of 1970, of course, most of the population at Albany were classified in category C, and some prisoners who had watched the first fence being built around them now had to watch a second. To them, as well as to ourselves, the element of overkill in the mounting security arrangements seemed, at times, little short of paranoia. Not only had there been a massive increase in the security of the perimeter, which had been at the heart of the Radzinowicz proposals, but also a major strengthening of the internal buildings. These buildings, following the Blundeston design, had already been the main security barrier, so that, if anything, freedom within the Albany perimeter was reduced rather than increased. Together these changes began to produce something which seemed to differ only in appearance from Mountbatten's plan for the rejected Vectis. Except, of course, that Albany was much larger, and but one of several similarly secure establishments across the country. And that even when it assumed its dispersal role it would continue to house more than 100 category-C prisoners for whom, in the words of Mountbatten, 'simple basic security procedures...will be sufficient' since 'they do not have the ability or resources to make a determined escape attempt'.

To the staff, of course, category-C prisoners were not a significant problem. Contrary to the early assurances which had been communicated by the deputy governor, attention was focussed quite single-mindedly first on category-B prisoners, and then on category-A prisoners. The apprehensions of the discipline staff were dealt with by inculcating 'good security procedures'. As the governor noted in his annual report for 1968, the staff were 'encouraged to operate with a higher degree of security in mind than perhaps is really necessary' and he regarded the next few months as 'a useful time for training the dogs and their handlers to a high standard of readiness'. By February 1969 the governor was prepared to receive category-B prisoners who were not thought to be a security risk, and after discussion at central management the staff were informed of this development by a circular notice. Wandsworth had been asked to help to maintain the balance of Albany's population by sending prisoners from a variety of age-groups. No special difficulties were encountered with the category-B men; and what finally changed Albany from a 'caravan in a meadow' to a category-A dispersal prison was the completion of the segregation unit in September 1970. As part of his plans to heighten the security awareness of the staff the governor had issued a circular renaming the punishment cells in Y hall as the segregation unit as long ago as June 1969, when the plans for the unit were first approved. And even before that the regime in Y hall had been tightened up to demonstrate the way in which Albany would have to develop in the future. David Gould had described the regime in Y hall as using 'boredom rather than briskness, coupled with willingness to talk and listen', and he found it to be successful. Brian Howden introduced what he called 'some slight alterations' whereby 'every effort was made to differentiate between the normal everyday life in the prison and the stricter regime of the punishment cells'. The 'firm and consistent, yet reasonable and humane treatment provided' was sufficient, he found, to 'deter men from making a habit of visiting this part of the prison'.

The first category-A prisoners were received on 26 October 1970, and, up to the time of writing at least, there have been no escapes from Albany Prison.

Industrial production
By far the most important changes in the Albany regime, however, came as a result of the shift in emphasis from industrial 'training' to industrial 'production', and the official establishment of a clear priority for economic goals over social training. Its importance extended far beyond the boundaries of Albany. For the decision marked the implicit, though none the less fundamental, re-interpretation of Prison Rule 1; and perhaps the only possible way of coming to terms with the new philosophy of security as this came to be applied in dispersal prisons.

The considerations involved in this change at Albany were complex, and deserve careful analysis. Albany had always been involved in industrial production. Though half of its original dual mandate involved the pursuit of industrial 'training', that aim was always narrowly conceived. There was never, for example, any vocational training of the kind intended to fit a person for a trade outside prison. Instead, training was geared to teaching the simple skills required for the production workshops in textiles and tailoring, and later in carpentry. The only sense in which what went on in the Albany workshops could be construed as 'training' involved the puritanical conception that economic achievement itself was a training of the character, as Lord Stonham had indicated in his speech at the opening ceremony.

While Albany had a commitment to some kind of industrial production, it was not and could not be a wholehearted commitment. The other half of Albany's mandate was to provide 'social training'; and the foundation on which both industrial and social training structures were built was the two-shift system. On the one hand the two-shift system provided plenty of time for staff to try to meet the social, medical, welfare, educational, physical and spiritual needs of prisoners, in so far as those needs could be met at all within a custodial institution. On the other hand it represented a reasonable approximation to outside work activities, with alternating work shifts, assembly-line production techniques, and so on. As a bonus it offered advantages in terms of capital costs: by dividing the population approximately in half fewer work spaces were needed and there was less pressure on recreational facilities. There was little doubt that the compromise worked somewhat unevenly in favour of 'social training' depending on what shift one was on, and always somewhat against industrial production. But so long as the dual mandate was maintained the compromise probably worked well enough. Certainly when we first entered the prison the nature of the compromise itself did not seem greatly in question: the problem was to make it work. Opinion was divided as to whether it would ever work, but in spite of all the difficulties there were some people at central- and middle-management levels who thought that the scheme was just on the brink of success.

Looking back, however, it is hard to resist the conclusion that any interest that Prison Department may once have had in two-shift working had simply been overtaken by events. By the time Albany opened it was in receipt of the 'Folkestone-Worksop' report about the incompatibility of pursuing both social training and industrial production in the same prison – although in fact Albany's industrial difficulties were to come not from its organizational structure but from the failure of headquarters to win contracts and to provide instructors. Soon, the Department was looking forward to the establishment of Coldingley as the prototype industrial prison where a 40-hour five-day week would be worked by all prisoners. The feedback from Gartree, where the two-shift scheme had first been tried out, was unfavourable. None of these developments came in time for any alterations to be made in the initial mandate for Albany, but it is clear that no enthusiasm was shown for it by headquarters once the prison opened. No priority was given to getting instructors or work so that the two-shift system could be developed, and no genuine attempt was made to evaluate its success or failure.

When Brian Howden raised some of the difficulties of two-shift working with the regional office shortly after his appointment, he was able to report back that the Department was 'committed to the two-shift system in Albany'. But neither he nor anyone else had much confidence in that. He also noted that Gartree had abandoned their attempt to operate the scheme in June and that the Department was concerned to 'stabilize' the situation. No one quite understood the meaning of that remark, for at that time only the governor knew the context in which it made sense: that both Albany and Gartree had been nominated as dispersal prisons for those prisoners the Radzinowicz sub-committee had thought two-shift working 'unsuitable'. In any case the governor continued to be concerned about the problem of boredom during non-work time, and in September 1968 he asked headquarters whether a change to single-shift working might not provide the solution. At the beginning of October the steering committee on dispersal had reached much the same conclusion, and by the end of the month the decision had been taken to abandon two-shift working. Brian Howden was asked to calculate the detailed changes that would be involved, and make a time-table, and to report back so that headquarters could undertake discussions with the POA and other staff associations on matters that affected them. A working party was set up for this purpose and to consider the implications of the change. Ironically it was only during the next few weeks that sufficient instructors were finally recruited to start a second shift in the tailoring and carpentry shops.

When it became clear that Albany was to change over to single-shift working, the research team set down what effects they thought would be likely to flow from it. All of us felt that the decision would have far-reaching consequences: indeed that it would possibly produce a prison unrecognizable from the one we had entered only five months earlier. Of course, there would be major as well as minor alterations in the routine that would affect the lives of staff and prisoners. Apart from the new working hours, it would be necessary to consider introducing simplified unlocking procedures and fewer mealtime sittings, for example, and perhaps changing the arrangements for the taking of applications and so on. The change would certainly require different arrangements for the work of the psychology, education, welfare and PE departments so that their activities could be conducted outside normal working time. If an incentive earnings scheme was also introduced, which linked pay more closely to productivity, this would probably lead to tighter control over workshop interruptions and perhaps to a quickening in the pace of work. But most importantly it seemed to us that the change-over to single-shift working would affect the nature of relationships between different groups of staff, and ultimately the quality of mutual co-operation that could be expected. The very process of working out the new time-tables was bound to be divisive. Discipline staff would probably have to work new duty hours and would presumably look inwards to trades union considerations. As specialist and ancillary staff sought to find a place in the time-table whereby their services could reasonably be accommodated, conflict with the industrial personnel would be difficult to avoid. And any compromise that could be worked out would have to be compatible with the control and security considerations raised by the discipline grades. In short the appearance of the traditional divisions between industrial, specialist and discipline staffs, which had thus far been successfully held in check at Albany by structural and ideological constraints, now seemed inevitable. Moreover, the development of a clear priority for industrial production over social training would mean that the original management structure devised to cope with the dual mandate would scarcely be appropriate any longer. The changing balance of power had already been reflected in the appointment of the industrial manager to the CMM, and the exclusion of the tutor-organizer, the chaplain and the medical officer. And we now wondered how long it would be before the division of responsibility at the central management level would have to be examined anew. The division between the two assistant governors and their respective chief officers, with one pair dealing with staff resources and training and the other with social training of the prisoners, now seemed only tenuously related to the new priorities and thus particularly vulnerable.

As expected, the discipline staff were quick to see that any rearrangement of the working day for prisoners would affect their own duty hours, and a number of tentative schemes were worked out and sent to headquarters for approval. It soon emerged that the duty hours in Albany were the subject of direct negotiations between the Home Office and the national executive of the POA, and thus no longer a local matter. The negotiations of the POA for a five-day week for discipline staff, and the determination of the Home Office to cut down on the enormous amount of overtime worked throughout the service, came to form part of the backdrop against which the new working arrangements for prisoners were introduced.

The Albany working party met for the first time on 14 November 1968 with the governor in the chair. From the beginning it was clear that what the working party would be discussing was the meaning of Prison Rule 1: 'The purpose of the training and treatment of convicted prisoners shall be to encourage and assist them to lead a good and useful life.' Most members of the working party were aware that the deputy chairman of the prisons board had recently suggested to a conference of prison governors that Rule 1, which had done valuable service in the past, had 'now served its term'. None the less the governor reminded the working party that Rule 1 still existed and that they had to pay attention to it. While industrial work was not the beginning and end of treatment and training, he pointed out, neither was social case-work. He hoped the members of the working party would be generous in devising arrangements that would give the best blend of their various interests, bearing in mind that the Department required them to provide prisoners with 'as near as possible an 8-hour day for five days a week'. He told the meeting that the workshops were to be work-studied and prisoners paid on an incentive earnings scheme which would be based on a minimum working week of 37 hours. The meeting then set to work.

For a time it looked as though the transformation to an industrial prison with an otherwise traditional routine was purely a formality. Under the guidance of the chief officer a time-table was produced which ensured that prisoners had their allotted span in the workshops, but required that all other activities be carried on in competition with the television during the evening association period. Then the senior welfare officer suggested that an effort be made to create time for other activities, for example by shortening the lunch hour and letting prisoners take sandwiches to work, or by starting the day earlier. From that point on a remarkable rearguard action emerged in an attempt to salvage what had been the main benefit of the two-shift system: a clear division between the periods to be devoted to industrial activity on the one hand and social training on the other. The co-operation that went into devising two ingenious schemes that met this objective promised to overcome the divisions which threatened. For several weeks the staff were united in a struggle that must have resembled the resolve of the advance party under David Gould 'to lick this muddy bloody mess into passable working order'. But their efforts were in vain because the prisons board vetoed both schemes. When the struggle was lost the staff accepted the defeat with an air of resignation, and the tide of mutual support that had sustained Albany so far began slowly to ebb away.

The first scheme was proposed initially by the senior assistant governor, but all departments agreed that it offered a viable compromise. It involved each prisoner working sufficient hours to participate in the incentive earnings scheme but within a 4½-day week, leaving one free half-day in which to avail himself of whatever the ancillary services had to offer. It was agreed that the activities of the chaplaincy, the welfare, psychology and physical education departments would be carried on with the minimum interruption of the working week. The greatest difficulty would be experienced by the welfare department, but it was thought that once problems had been identified during the induction process, routine matters and ongoing case-work would be dealt with by making appointments for prisoners on their next half-day off. Where interruptions to the working day were necessary it was proposed to give the workshops advance notice so that work could be planned accordingly. This would be done through a new information service that would take over much of the old discipline office function and which was then in the planning stage. Though narrowly mistitled the labour control unit (LCU) the new service would be responsible for collating information about each prisoner and making it available to those who needed it. Dates of reception, discharge, home leave and parole eligibility as well as other sentence data, together with information on medical status, location in halls and assignments to work parties and so on would be kept up to date, stored on punch cards and displayed on peg-boards. One of the main difficulties in the 4½-day week scheme was how to arrange the rota by which prisoners had their half-day off. Discipline staff wanted each hall to be off work on a different afternoon to facilitate arrangements for staffing and supervision, even though such a plan would disrupt all shops to some extent every day. Not surprisingly, the industrial staff argued for the opposite arrangement. The suggestion that this problem could be resolved by putting all prisoners from the same shop in the same hall was rejected on the ground that it was bad enough for prisoners to have to live together, let alone to make them work together as well. In the end the choice between hall-based rotas and shop-based rotas was resolved in favour of the latter.

On 22 November the proposal was submitted to Prison Department, together with the suggested duty hours for instructors and discipline staff. The governor sent a covering minute making it clear that the scheme devised by the working party had the full support of himself and the central management group. He pointed out that they had studied the implications of the change to single-shift working 'in considerable detail, at length and with great care'; and that if the prison were properly to implement Rule 1 then it was 'not practical to require a prisoner to work a 40-hour week in five days and then devote only the evenings to the many other aspects of his prison life that should go to provide a full, complete and, we would hope, constructive prison environment'. As a result, he said, 'we have come to the firm and final conclusion that this can be done only by providing prisoners with a 37½ hour working week incorporated in 4½ days, thus leaving half a day . . . for all the other necessary activities. . . which are provided for his rehabilitation'.

Brian Howden was not optimistic that the proposal would be accepted and he said as much to his management group. A week or two later he had heard, unofficially, that the scheme had not been well received. The Albany duty hours for instructors were out of step with a new national agreement that was soon to be introduced, and the 4½-day week was embarrassing in view of Lord Stonham's public commitment to a five-day 40-hour week for prisoners. However, the prisons board had not yet met to decide the matter and there was still time to submit a modified proposal. The working party was re-convened and a new scheme quickly emerged. Staff duty hours were kept within the national agreement for workshop instructors, and the 4½-day week was abandoned. Instead, using the same rota system as before, each shop was to close 1¾ hours early on one afternoon a week to allow at least some earmarked time for the work of the ancillary departments. This modified proposal was also submitted for the attention of the prisons board at their forthcoming meeting.

The prisons board met on 16 December 1968 and rejected both proposals. A week later official confirmation of the decision was sent by letter to the prison. After praising the initiative and ingenuity of the Albany staff it said:

> They [the prisons board] would like the staff to know that the advantages and disadvantages of the proposed scheme were fully gone into and that they recognised the difficulties of devising a regime that makes fair provision for all the facilities needed for training 'the whole man'. After this searching examination, the board came to the conclusion that it would not

be right in present circumstances to base the new regime at
Albany on a 4½-day working week. In their view the aim should
be to experiment within the framework of a 5-day working
week.

The letter ended by inviting the governor to meet officials at the
Home Office early in January, where a member of the POA
national executive would join in the discussions. The occasion of
introducing a five-day forty-hour week for prisoners had become
the opportunity for both the Home Office and the POA to
negotiate just that for prison officers as well.

Experimenting within the framework of a five-day week apparently meant that the Department was prepared to tolerate
workshop interruptions, for prisoners could be made available for
interviews with ancillary staff on a rota basis if required so long as
the workshops were not closed for this purpose. When the working
party met to consider the time-table yet again they found that
there was little alternative to the one originally proposed by the
chief, who was chided by the senior assistant governor for looking
'so jubilant'. The industrial manager was successful in his insistence that interruptions be limited to the last part of the afternoon,
as agreed in the latest proposal of the working party, and not
during the whole afternoon as was implied in the letter from the
prisons board. The specialist departments agreed to try to keep
within this constraint while reserving their right to call prisoners
from work at other times if necessary. But, as the governor said,
the implication of the board's decision was that 'industry takes
precedence over everything else'.

The new timetable was agreed and submitted to headquarters
with the suggestion that it be implemented in the week beginning
17 February 1969, by which time the LCU and the new induction
scheme would have been brought into operation. But it was noted
that one of the most immediate consequences of the change would
be that prisoners would find themselves working an extra ten
hours a week for the same pay! It was not until January 1969 that
the work-study team entered its first workshop to begin the long
slow process of evaluating the procedures in tailoring. The first
incentive earnings for prisoners were introduced in that shop in
June 1969, and at the end of that month eight prisoners had earned
the maximum of one pound per week. Most workers in the shop,
however, earned about half that amount, and in the carpentry

shop skilled workers could still earn a maximum of only 7s. 6d. It took many months for the scheme to reach other shops, and more than a year before it was applied to non-industrial workers.

Single-shift working did begin on 17 February, but not without still more modifications to the programme. The final version was not decided by the working party at all. It was, in effect, imposed by headquarters following their negotiations with the POA about the introduction of a five-day week for discipline officers. In return for conceding the five-day week for officers, Prison Department wanted to introduce a scheme of functional group working through which they hoped 'to obtain maximum effective utilization of staff' and to reduce the amount of overtime worked. The functional group working scheme rested on the principle of dividing the staff into specialist groups: a control and security group, a treatment group, a small quasi-management group, and a support group which could provide relief in each of the other categories. Officers would serve limited tours of duty in their chosen group, with the possibility of continuing for a longer period, before being transferred to other duties. Although functional group working was quite practicable within the twelve-day fortnight which Albany staff had so far worked, the complexities of combining it with a five-day week, as the POA wanted, were considerable. It was not fully implemented on a five-day week basis in Albany until October 1970, just before the first category-A prisoners arrived. But in the meantime several compromise schemes were tried, and it was on the basis of one of these that Albany changed over to single-shift working for prisoners. As a result of the new duty hours for discipline officers the working day for prisoners was trimmed by ten minutes each day, producing a maximum working time of 39 hours and 10 minutes a week.

Our expectation that the division of responsibilities at central management level could not be maintained once the emphasis had changed towards industrial production was substantially borne out by events. The AG for staff resources and his chief officer were able to continue their concern with staff training; but the AG for social training, in spite of his debates in the *Albany Argus,* spent more and more of his time developing the labour control unit. In this he collaborated with the industrial manager and the administration officer, but it also took much of the time of his chief officer as well. The labour control unit did, through its appointment system, help to keep the work of the welfare department going, but the social training programme continued to look much better on paper than it did in reality. The deputy governor effectively relinquished his trouble-shooting role and gradually took on many other duties instead, namely, the chairmanship of the hostel, home leave, and labour allocation boards, the chairmanship of the local security committee and responsibility for dog-handling, as well as supervision of the prisoners' canteening and earnings. With these shifts in role emphasis the central management structure continued satisfactorily enough until further pressures built up to resolve the residual ambiguities after the arrival of category-A prisoners.

What was quite unforeseen was the emergence of a new problem at middle-management level. The new duty hours for discipline staff, among other things, required principal officers to work on a shift basis along with their subordinates. This meant that it was no longer possible for one principal officer to take effective charge of each hall. Four principal officers were nominally assigned to hall duties – one for each of the halls in use – but with two of them off duty at any one time each PO in fact had to supervise two halls while he was in the prison. This dispersion of authority was in theory offset, but in practice occasionally exacerbated, by the deployment of two senior officers, one on each shift, to each hall. These senior officers inevitably took some of the daily management decisions which hitherto had fallen to principal officers. After so much effort had been put into bolstering hall management this weakening of the system, coming in the crucial run-up period before the reception of category-A prisoners, was to cause many difficulties later on.

As we have said, it seemed to us that the decision to abandon two-shift working had important consequences, not just for Albany but for the implementation of Rule 1 throughout the prison system. Moreover the rejection of Albany's 4½-day week proposal represented an untimely blow to the morale of staff who had striven to give meaning to the concept of social training. In 1972, long after the dust had settled and when Albany was an established dispersal prison, we wrote to Prison Department asking why the two-shift system had been abandoned and why the prisons board had rejected Albany's compromise schemes.

We were told that the reasons for abandoning two-shift working were simply economic: 'It was originally thought that there would be strong economic advantages in this, but detailed examination had shown the contrary.' It had been calculated that 'in a prison where 240 prisoners were employed in reasonably efficient work-shops the net annual profit under double-shift working would be under £20,000 and under single-shift working nearly £30,000'. Since such a calculation was available to anyone who cared to make it long before the two-shift system was introduced, this scarcely seems a sufficient reason for ending it after less than two years. In fact the real reason for trying it in the first place had been to facilitate social training while still maintaining a real measure of industrial activity. The decision to abandon it has to be seen, therefore, as a change of policy whereby industrial activity assumed precedence over the implementation of Rule 1 through social training.

Although we asked to see the minutes of the relevant meetings of the prisons board we were told that these were not available. But the reason given for the rejection of the Albany counter-proposals again bears out the changed attitude to Rule 1. It was said that although the 4½-day week 'had its attractions as a single-shift method of working it was far from an answer to the problem of making time for non-industrial activities. These activities could not be packed into a half-day each week for every prisoner; and some things, for example, a welfare interview, could not always await the prisoner's off-duty afternoon.' What is quite remarkable about such reasoning is that no credit at all is given to the fact that under the Albany schemes at least *some* time was made available for these activities, whereas the solution imposed by headquarters eliminated the possibility of carrying out *any* of these tasks except during the evenings and weekends or by interrupting the work-shops. The special irony is that the Albany schemes could have operated, imperfectly no doubt, but at negligible cost to the length of the working week. The 4½-day week guaranteed a minimum of 37 hours and 10 minutes in the shops; the revised proposal reduced the minimum to 37 hours; the Home Office solution gave a theoretical maximum of 39 hours and 10 minutes but in practice, because of interruptions, the expected average working time was 37½ hours. It is tempting to conclude that the advantages of the 4½-day week were sacrificed in order to secure the politically expedient appearance of a five-day week favoured by Lord Stonham, regardless of its other consequences.

However, it is clear that there was another reason for rejecting the Albany proposals, namely, the implementation of the dispersal policy. We asked the Home Office specifically to comment on this aspect of the changes, but they made no mention of it in their reply. The Radzinowicz sub-committee had been lukewarm in its praise for the two-shift experiments at Gartree and Albany, and was not convinced that such a system would be suitable for a long-term prison, though the implication that it might be suitable for a short-term prison was left unexplained. In spite of the Radzinowicz sub-committee's reservations, two-shift working at Albany would probably have been successful if only the Prison Department had supplied enough instructors and enough work, for the staff had worked long and hard to bring it to the brink. And there is little doubt that the 4½-day week could have worked well enough once the two-shift system had been abandoned; even the prisons board had applauded the ingenuity and resource that had produced the scheme. But once the dispersal policy was accepted, a new principle that the dispersal prisons should be substantially similar in their regimes, ruled the scheme out of court. Actually the Radzinowicz sub-committee was undecided about the degree of variation that should exist between the regimes in the selected prisons. On the one hand they did not want regime differences to be so great that allocation procedures might contravene the principle that even (sic) long-term prisoners should go to prisons in their own regions (para. 171). On the other hand they expected some natural variation to occur in the regimes and so far as was reasonable they wanted to encourage that (para. 172). It was probably inevitable that the Home Office should have leaned heavily towards the idea of maintaining similar conditions in all its dispersal prisons, with its implicit notion of fairness and, of course, its apparent ease of administration. Certainly the negotiations with the POA seemed to have been dependent on achieving common duty hours in all the dispersal prisons. And, most significantly, the circular instruction issued on 7 February, to announce the detailed arrangements for single-shift working on 17 February, bore the title *Standard Category-A Regime*.

It is interesting, though fruitless, to speculate about what might have happened had the two-shift system not already been abandoned in Gartree after precisely the same difficulties that bedevilled Albany: lack of instructors and lack of work. There would then have been one Midland and one south-eastern region dispersal prison with a two-shift scheme of work. This would have provided a compromise between regionality and variety that might have commended itself to the Radzinowicz sub-committee, apart from the objection to the use of a two-shift scheme as such. The sub-committee may well have been right in its assumption that such a scheme was not suitable for a long-term prison. All that we can say for certain is that we shall never know. The scheme was abandoned in both Gartree and Albany long before they became long-term prisons. And nobody replicates an 'experiment' which can be shown to have 'failed'.

7   The standard category-A regime

By the summer of 1969, when we embarked on a formal programme of interviewing with staff and prisoners, a kind of stability had settled on Albany. It is true that the prison was still in a state of physical disruption, at times bordering on chaos, as the security and other modifications were carried on, but many of the psychological uncertainties had been removed. The new governor had stamped his style on central and middle management, the transition to single-shift working had been accomplished, work-study was bearing fruit in the first incentive earnings for prisoners, and the future role as a dispersal prison had become clear. Albany was still a long way from being a traditional prison, and underlying all the changes there had been a measure of real consolidation for the innovative patterns of working relationships evolved by David Gould. The air of excitement and raw enthusiasm tinged with anxiety, that we had found a year earlier had given way to a sense of purpose and confident preparation for the arrival of high-security-risk prisoners. Although the confidence arose, at least in part, from the process of practising to be a dispersal prison with a population that was still predominantly drawn from category-C prisoners, it was none the less widespread. Only a small group of staff were really worried about whether Albany could stand up to the task ahead.

In the present chapter we seek to convey something of the character of the Albany regime at this time, and in the next we try to show how both staff and prisoners adapted themselves to it. But first we should say something about the research programme on which our account is based, and of the methodological problems involved in characterizing prison regimes.

The research programme
When the research team arrived in the prison in May 1968, as we noted in chapter 2, both staff and prisoners raised doubts about the validity of the research exercise. The prisoners, ironic as it now

seems, told us that they feared we had been sent by the Home Office to see the showplace of the prison service. The staff similarly advised us that Albany was not a typical prison and that therefore our work would be of little relevance to the rest of the system. While the typicality of Albany was not crucial for the research programme, because we planned to carry out a comparative study of other prisons at a later stage, there did in fact seem to be some advantage for a long-term study of prison regimes to start in a showplace institution. For in a prison where a new regime was in the process of being created, the persons involved were likely to have a heightened consciousness about what they were doing, and of the ways in which it differed from tradition. But the staff also went on to point out that Albany was changing so fast that we would not be able to keep up with events; that whatever we studied and reported on would quickly become out of date. It was no less ironic that what the staff had in mind then was the introduction of experimental locking and unlocking procedures, the development of the case-officer system, the operation of the two-shift scheme of working and the involvement of principal officers in hall decision-making rather than the introduction of dogs, the erection of fences, the virtual abandonment of social training and the arrival of category-A prisoners. However, irony apart, this was a real issue from the point of view of the research. The task of actually characterizing a regime that was changing before our very eyes proved to be a daunting one. As things turned out we did indeed spend a great deal of time catching up on past history and keeping abreast of current events. Much of our data collection took the form of recording what happened at central- and middle-management meetings; reading through the governor's journal, planning files, workshop records and the minutes of past meetings; talking to key members of staff and prisoners about the history of the establishment and new developments as they occurred; and simply being in the halls and workshops to observe what happened and to discuss why it happened. The field notes from these ongoing procedures have formed the basis for the material presented in the preceding chapters.

We were also concerned to devise and test instruments for collecting systematic information about regimes for use in our future studies. Our examination of the regime at Albany began from first principles because we could find little in the existing prison literature to guide us. There had been a number of excellent case studies of prisons and of aspects of inmate response to imprisonment (for example, Clemmer, 1940; Schrag, 1944; Sykes, 1958; Wheeler, 1958, 1961; Garabedian, 1963; Morris *et al.*, 1963; Atchley and McCabe, 1968; Cline, 1968, among several others) which were, in their various ways, of great value in sensitizing us to the kinds of issues we should look out for in Albany. But our longer-term aim was to develop a framework for the analysis of prison regimes that would enable us to make reasonably precise and meaningful comparisons between one prison and another. Although there had been several attempts to measure the extent to which inmates became 'prisonized' we could find no systematic measures of the regimes they experienced. Occasionally differences in the degree of prisonization found in different studies were speculatively attributed to differences in the respective prison regimes (see Atchley and McCabe, 1968) but the exact nature of the regime differences were not specified.

There was, of course, much discussion in the literature, both administrative and academic, about 'treatment-orientated' institutions and 'custodially-orientated' institutions (for example, Cressey, 1965). This often mirrored the distinctions between therapeutic communities and custodial mental hospitals; but we could find no empirical studies of prisons that provided any substantial accounts of these differences, let alone tried to measure their extent. In any case, the 'orientation' of all English training prisons had for many years been governed – officially at least – by the notion of treatment as enshrined in Prison Rule 1, so that it seemed unlikely that we would be able to distinguish major differences between prisons by using this dichotomy. Moreover it quickly became apparent to us that *all* prisons are first and foremost custodial, whatever else those concerned in their management might also say. Even where specific treatment or training programmes were in operation it seemed likely that these would account for only a small proportion of the prisoner's day, and that as in mental hospitals 'the other twenty-three hours' might be just as important (Stanton and Schwartz, 1954). Indeed it was not long before studies appeared which demonstrated that prison 'treatment' could also be a subtle but powerful form of control (Kassebaum *et al.*, 1971). Any methods devised to compare regimes, therefore, would have to attempt to discriminate among different 'treatment' orientations and among different 'custodial' orientations, as well as between these two broad types.

Even if such an approach were possible, there were important problems to be resolved with regard to just what was being compared. Thus one of the most interesting studies, albeit of juvenile institutions, by Street *et al.* (1966) distinguished several different types of institution range along a custody-treatment continuum. The typology was based partly on the expressed goals of the chief executive of the institutions concerned and his strategies for achieving them, and partly on the perceptions of staff and inmates about the emphasis of the institution. After we had begun our work at Albany another study of juvenile institutions appeared (Moos, 1968). In this study staff and inmates were asked to rate the 'social climate' of their institutions in group-administered pencil-and-paper tests. Respondents had to indicate the extent to which the environment appeared to them to foster certain kinds of activities or processes, such as 'insight', 'submissiveness', 'aggression', and a total of twelve dimensions of the social climate of institutions were assessed in this way. Both these approaches seemed to offer fruitful avenues for further investigation; but neither got to grips with the actual regime that was operated for different groups of inmates. Although we could hardly fail to be impressed by the importance of the aims of the respective governors at Albany and their administrative styles, we were all too aware that major differences could occur between the intentions of the governor and what actually happened in the halls: witness the constant demand for the strengthening of middle management and the strain for consistency in dealing with prisoners that we have already reported. Indeed it seemed likely to us that, in some institutions at least, there might co-exist several different regimes even if these were not intended as matters of policy. Thus the intentions of the governor might be differentially interpreted and acted upon by subordinate members of staff, or some individual prisoners or groups of prisoners might successfully resist the application of certain policies and so construct an alternative regime for themselves. Moreover, while we were interested to know *how* staff and prisoners rated their institution, it also seemed important to try to discover *what* procedures or features of the establishment gave rise to perceptions that it was one kind of institution rather than another. There seemed no alternative, therefore, but to embark on a programme of observation and questioning about the mundane daily routine of the prison.

It was only after several months that we began to conceptualize the prison regime not as a simple entity, nor even as a well-defined orientation, but as the more or less varied application and use of the rules, routines and resources that were designed to govern the lives of prisoners. But to recognize that the regime was to some extent the outcome of negotiation between different groups of staff and between staff and prisoners, and that possibly several regimes may exist within the same institution, was also to raise rather complex methodological considerations: about the units for comparison, about the sources for data collection, and about the interpretation of results. While we ultimately wished to characterize whole institutions and to compare one prison with another, it clearly would not be meaningful just to ask general questions of either staff or prisoners about 'the prison' as a whole, for this would scarcely do justice to any internal differences that might occur. The judicious selection of sub-units such as halls or wings, or of identifiable groups of prisoners such as long-termers or short-termers, might overcome this problem; but there could be no guarantee that internal regime differences would be ordered along these lines. An alternative strategy of asking a sample of prisoners and staff about their own individual experiences of the regime would certainly capture any differences that might exist, but would possibly present problems of how to interpret those differences. For example, where prisoners reported common experiences these might have resulted from the rigid application of rules by staff, or from the exercise of similar choices by prisoners in a situation which allowed them some discretion. It would also be necessary to aggregate the data in some way if comparisons were to be made between prisons, and difficulties of interpreting individual responses might lead to inappropriate procedures of aggregation.

With our longer-term objectives in mind we regarded Albany as a pilot study in which to explore alternative methods for collecting data which might meet these methodological problems with the minimum cost in terms of research time and resources. Accordingly we decided to select halls as the basic unit for analysis in the expectation that, since prisoners spent the greater part of their time in them, the main differences in regime would occur as between one hall and another. We conducted interviews with the senior officer in charge of each shift in each hall about the routine practices that applied while he was on duty. We framed questions as specifically as possible, focussing on the detailed application of the rules within the general framework laid down for him. For each set of questions we probed to see whether there were exceptions in relation to any particular prisoners, and if so what applied to them. The advantage of this approach was that it yielded a great deal of information from very few respondents. But one of the difficulties was that in order to deal comprehensively with the matters we were interested in, the interview took a long time to administer and respondents found it hard to cope repeatedly with all the exceptions we wanted them to cover. (The schedules used in the study are too bulky to reproduce here, but copies may be obtained from the authors on request.) The procedure provided a good enough outline of the routine in each hall, but in an attempt to get more detailed information from the point of view of prisoners we decided to ask a limited range of questions of the sample of prisoners which we describe below. In these interviews we asked about the personal belongings they had in their possession, the contacts which they had had with various members of staff, and about how various routine matters had been applied to them. These interviews took less time with each respondent and, since the matters discussed were of immediate concern to the interviewees, there was a greater readiness to provide detailed information. But a disadvantage here was that there was a considerable degree of duplication involved for those practices over which little variation occurred.

In an attempt at providing an independent verification of some of the information supplied in interviews we conducted a small programme of systematic observations in each hall. We observed two time periods: from the time that prisoners were unlocked in the morning until the time they went to work, and from the time they returned from work in the evenings until they were locked in cells for the night. Observations for these periods were conducted on four separate occasions in each hall. Since it was not possible to observe everything that happened in the halls we decided to focus on the activities of staff and the way they interacted with prisoners. Accordingly the observer followed the activities of the officer in charge and randomly selected basic-grade staff by turns in a prearranged fixed sequence. Each officer was observed for two minutes at a time before the observer passed on to the next. We also explored the possibility of observing various other situations that occurred more or less frequently in the prison routine, but

these were carried out less systematically, and since they sometimes caused embarrassment for the persons being observed we
decided to curtail them.

Finally, in assessing the regime at Albany, we conducted
interviews with the specialist staff about their contacts with
prisoners and we also 'sat in' on a number of occasions when they
were interviewing prisoners.

On the basis of our experience in Albany we decided that wings
and halls should form the unit of comparison in our subsequent
studies and, in spite of the costs in research time and the
duplication that might be involved, that our data should be
collected mainly from prisoners. In these later studies a longer and
more comprehensive interview schedule was devised for use with a
sample of prisoners drawn from each living unit in order to provide
data for characterizing the regimes. A shorter, and more general,
schedule was used for interviewing officers in charge of halls to
provide a check on the probable scope for variation in prisoner
responses. Reluctantly it was decided that observational studies,
though desirable, were not practicable in prisons unless, as in
Albany, the research workers could first spend a very long time
establishing their role.

In our comparative studies, and using the information collected
from the prisoner samples, it was possible to scale the differences
found in the routine handling of prisoners in their respective living
units along a number of dimensions. It was also possible, in some
respects, to aggregate scores according to categories of prison
employment and categories of security rating and length of
sentence, regardless of the living unit, or the prison, in which the
respondents resided. Some of the findings using these quantitative
measures have been reported elsewhere (King, 1972; King and
Morgan, 1976), and other findings will be published when further
analysis is completed. But it is perhaps worth making a few general
comments here about the extent to which differentiated regimes
occur. First, prisons are governed by rules and regulations that are
probably more comprehensive and more explicit than could be
found in any other institutions. While there is no guarantee that
the rules are always applied, there is likely to be a central core of
more or less common practice in most institutions within the same
prison system. Second, within that framework of rules there is
scope for variation in which a distinctive style of approach can be
displayed. But the impact of that style and the meaning of those

variations is likely to depend on the past experiences of both staff and prisoners who are subject to them. Thus, although we frequently found differences in regimes both between prisons, and among the living units within prisons, that were highly statistically significant, it seemed that some variations were valued highly and others not at all by the persons experiencing them. Third, it is likely that, whatever the general rules provide and whatever may be the particular style of the prisons concerned, certain categories of prisoner and prisoners in certain types of employment experience much the same kind of regime no matter where they serve their sentence – though it should be remembered that our data were not collected in the most suitable way to test this, and that in any case our analysis is still incomplete.

In our studies at Albany, of course, our measures of regimes had not yet become available and we here provide a more qualitative account, calling on the results from several of the techniques which were then in the pilot stage.

Having established some of the details about the Albany regime we also wished to discover how staff and prisoners responded and adapted to it. For this purpose we selected a sample of staff and a sample of prisoners for further structured interviews. Everybody in Albany had previously been in at least one other prison and we asked all respondents to rate Albany in comparison with other prisons of which they had experience. We then explored why they rated Albany in the way they had chosen and asked how they felt about various aspects of the regime in Albany and about the changes that had occurred in the prison since their arrival. We will give more details about these interviews in the next chapter when we report on the patterns of staff and prisoner adaptation. For the present we will describe the characteristics of the Albany staff establishment and prisoner population and the samples we drew from them.

The prisoner population and sample

The numbers of prisoners in Albany had grown slowly over the past year, from 315 on 1 May 1968 to 348 on 1 May 1969. No less than 128 prisoners who were in Albany on the former date were still there on the latter, and the general characteristics of the population had changed only in a few respects. The great majority of the prisoners were still classified in category C. One prisoner who had formerly been rated as category A was still in the prison and was still so classified, at least according to his F 1150. There were eight prisoners in category B, whereas there had been none a year earlier; while the numbers deemed suitable for detention in open conditions in category D had fallen from six to one. For some prisoners we could find no information as to security rating in the records. Albany still contained a mainly young recidivist population with a significant minority group of older prisoners. As before, about half the prisoners were under 30 years of age while one-sixth were 40 years old or more; two-thirds had six or more previous convictions, and half had been in prison on four or more occasions. Again two-thirds had left school before their sixteenth birthday, a quarter had finished their education in approved schools, and about half of those on whom we had information had graduated to prison through approved schools, detention centres or borstals. Albany had become even more of a London satellite in the interval, with four-fifths of its intake being transferred from Wandsworth compared with three-quarters in 1968. The numbers coming from other local prisons declined proportionately, but there was a slight increase in the numbers of long-term prisoners transferred from Wormwood Scrubs, Parkhurst and Dartmoor. As in 1968, two-fifths of the prisoners had never married or cohabited; and the remainder were more or less equally divided between those who were still married or cohabiting and those who no longer had such liaisons for whatever reason.

Although the intake of high-security risk prisoners had scarcely begun, there was none the less a noticeable change in the seriousness of the offences which had brought prisoners to Albany. Most were still imprisoned for offences in Class II, property offences with violence; or Class III, property offences without violence. But whereas in 1968 there were 14 Class II offenders for every 15 Class III offenders, by 1969 there were nearly four offenders in the former category for every three in the latter. The numbers imprisoned for Class I offences against the person had also gone up by rather more than half. These differences in offences committed were reflected in the sentences received, so that the proportion serving comparatively short sentences of two years or less had fallen from two-thirds to two-fifths, while the proportion serving comparatively long sentences of four years or more had risen from an eighth to a quarter. There were also three persons serving life sentences compared with one a year earlier. Thus by 1969 there had been an important change in the 'mix' of prisoners in Albany: in May 1968 there had been five short-term prisoners for every one long-term prisoner, now there were only three for every two.

From this population we selected a stratified random sample of 18 prisoners from each of the four residential halls in use: 72 prisoners in all. Six prisoners had to be replaced because they were discharged or transferred during the interval between sample selection in May and the interviewing some weeks later. In the event, three prisoners declined to be interviewed.

Our sample of prisoners included the one prisoner in Albany rated as suitable for open conditions, and four of the eight classified as category-B prisoners. On four prisoners we could find no information recorded as to security rating. The great majority, 63 or 87.5 per cent, of course, were rated as category-C prisoners.

Rather more than half the sample were 30 years or younger, with about one-fifth aged over 40 years. Both these groups were slightly over-represented in the sample at the expense of the 31-40 year olds, as is shown in Table 7.1.

Table 7.1 Percentage age distribution of the sample and Albany population: May 1969

Age in years	Sample N=72	Population N=328*
21–25	27.8	27.1
26–30	27.8	26.2
31–35	15.3	18.0
36–40	8.3	10.4
41–45	11.1	10.1
46–50	6.9	4.9
51–55	2.8	3.4
All ages	100.0	100.1

*No information cases excluded.

The proportions of persons never previously married, and no longer married were similarly greater in the sample than in the population as a whole, and this possibly reflects the differences in age. The data are given in Table 7.2.

*Table 7.2   Percentage distribution by marital status:
sample and population*

Marital status	Sample N=72	Population N=343*
Never married	48.6	42.0
Now married	12.5	22.2
Widowed	2.8	2.0
Divorced	13.9	11.7
Separated	13.9	14.9
Cohabiting	8.3	7.3
All groups	100.0	100.1

*No information cases excluded.

Less than two per cent of the sample had their last-known address in Hampshire or other counties close to the Isle of Wight. Forty-four per cent came from the London postal district, 43 per cent from the home counties, and the remainder from much further afield. Less than a third were known to be employed at the time of arrest, and for half the sample there was either no information in the records about normal employment or else it was clear that employment was on a purely casual basis. The most frequently cited occupation was in the building trade, which accounted for one sixth of the total, while the remainder were fairly evenly divided among manufacturing industry, retail shops, catering, and services such as hairdressing and laundry work.

Just over half our sample had been convicted for Class II property offences with violence, mostly for burglary or aggravated burglary, compared with just under a half in the population as a whole. Correspondingly a lower proportion in our sample had been convicted for Class III offences against property without violence, mostly for simple larcenies of one kind or another, than could be found in the population. The details are given in Table 7.3.

Not surprisingly, in view of the slight exaggeration of serious offences amongst our sample, the prisoners we interviewed were somewhat more likely to be serving sentences of four years or more than were the prisoners generally to be found in Albany, as is shown in Table 7.4.

Table 7.3   Percentage distribution by current offence:
sample and population

Offence class	Sample N=72	Population N=348
I Offences against person	8.3	8.0
II Offences against property with violence	52.8	48.3
III Offences against property without violence	31.9	36.2
IV Malicious injury to property	2.8	0.9
V Forgery	1.4	3.4
VI Others	2.8	3.2
All offences	100.0	100.0

Broadly speaking, it was the younger prisoners who were more likely to be serving shorter sentences, while the older prisoners were more likely to be serving longer sentences. But although

Table 7.4   Length of sentence: sample and population

Sentence	Sample N=72	Population N=348
24 months or less	37.5	40.8
25–48 months	38.9	41.6
49 months or more	23.6	17.6
All groups	100.0	100.0

there were readily identifiable groups of young short-sentence prisoners and older long-sentence prisoners at each end of the spectrum in our sample, there were also many cases which did not fit this pattern. The details are given in Table 7.5.

Youth, however, was no guarantee of institutional inexperience,

Table 7.5   Age in relation to length of current sentence

	24 months or less %	25–48 months %	49 months or more %	Total %
30 years or under	26.4	22.2	6.9	55.5
31–40 years	6.9	11.1	5.6	23.6
41 years or over	4.2	5.6	11.1	20.9
Total N=72	37.5	38.9	23.6	100.0

and by any standards the prisoners in our sample must be regarded as substantial recidivists. Only 11 per cent had never been to prison before, 22 per cent had been imprisoned once or twice, 36 per cent on three to five occasions, 22 per cent had been in prison six to ten times previously, and eight per cent had served between eleven and fifteen separate sentences of imprisonment before their current term in Albany. Of those who had previously experienced prison, a little more than a fifth had been given sentences in the past whose nominal terms totalled two years; at the other extreme almost a quarter of the sample had accumulated prior sentences which in total exceeded ten years in nominal length.

Most of the prisoners in our sample had already had a good opportunity to get to know Albany Prison. Only one prisoner had been in the establishment for less than four months, and more than three out of every five had served more than six months in Albany. Because all prisoners in Albany, like those in other training prisons, had spent some time in local prisons before they were transferred, only about one-fifth of them were still serving the first third of their sentences. The remainder were equally divided, with two-fifths in the middle period and two-fifths in the last third of their sentence. While over half our sample could look forward to discharge in the normal course of events within six months, more than one in ten had no prospect of release, barring the unlikely favourable intervention of the Parole Board, for at least another two years. The information about length of time served and time left to the earliest date of release is summarized in Table 7.6.

It is possible that some selective factors involved in the distribution of prisoners between the halls account for the differences between the sample and the population, but the

Table 7.6   Time served and time left to earliest date of release

	Time served in Albany %	Time left to EDR %
6 months or less	38.9	54.2
7–12 months	33.3	22.2
13–24 months	27.8	12.5
Over 25 months	0.0	11.1
Total N=72	100.0	100.0

differences were quite small and the sample we interviewed was broadly representative of the population in Albany in the summer of 1969.

The staffing establishment and sample

To deal with its growing population of more difficult prisoners Albany had enjoyed some increments in staffing, most notably resulting from the appointment of 13 senior officers who were introduced into the prison from October 1968 onwards. Some of them were promoted from the more senior basic-grade officers within Albany (who had sometimes been referred to as landing officers), and some had been drafted in from other institutions. The numbers of staff in post in the various discipline grades for May 1968 and May 1969 are given in Table 7.7.

Table 7.7   Discipline staff May 1968 and May 1969

	May 1968	May 1969
Governor	1	1
Deputy governor	1	1
Assistant governors	2	2
Chief officer I	1	1
Chief officers II	2	2
Principal officers	12	12
Senior officers	0	13
Basic-grade officers	109	105
All ranks	128	137

Although the numbers of senior discipline posts had not changed, several of the incumbents had. Not long after Brian Howden succeeded David Gould as governor, one of the chief officers II died and was replaced; and in February 1969 a new deputy governor was appointed, following the promotion of his predecessor who had helped to open up the prison.

The 'treatment' staff at Albany remained much the same in 1969 as it was in 1968, with the exception that the post of senior welfare officer was now a full-time Albany appointment instead of one which was shared between the three island prisons. He was assisted by two welfare officers. The psychology department consisted of a principal psychologist, assisted by one psychologist; during the year a psychological tester had joined and left. The medical officer still had the support of a psychotherapist, a dentist, an optician and an ENT specialist, and was assisted by two hospital officers. The education department utilized a changing number of civilian teachers under the supervision of the tutor-organizer and his assistant. Spiritual matters were in the hands of a full-time Church of England chaplain with ministers from other denominations and other religions attending on a part-time basis.

Elsewhere the most important developments in staffing had taken place in the works department, reflecting the growth in the number of projects started in the intervening period. In 1969 the foreman of works and his three engineers employed a staff of 29 civilian workmen and officer trade assistants compared with 20 a year earlier. The administration officer had gained one executive officer in addition to the three already in post, and there were still 12 clerical officers who worked in various parts of the prison under his authority. The industrial side had added one more instructor to the 19 civilian and officer instructors who worked under the industrial manager. Finally the prison employed one farm foreman as before, but the complement of temporary officers, civilian storemen and cleaners had been reduced from 11 in 1968 to 8 in 1969.

We selected 95 members of staff for interview, and all of them agreed to co-operate. Staff were first divided into four broad functional groupings according to whether they were primarily concerned with 'discipline', 'treatment', 'administration' or 'industry and maintenance', and then further subdivided according to grades of seniority. Because the resulting categories varied considerably in size, different sampling fractions were employed. For groups which were particularly small or specially important a census was taken, although in some cases we decided to exclude staff who were engaged on purely specialized tasks that did not bring them into contact with prisoners. Otherwise a random sampling technique was used. Among the uniformed staff our sample of 48 was selected as follows: all three chief officers, 7 of the 12 principal officers, 10 of the 13 senior officers and 28 of the 105 basic-grade officers. In addition we interviewed all the governor grades, all the specialist 'treatment' staff, all the senior administrative and industrial staff, and a sample of civilian and officer instructors, trade assistants and civilian workmen. For most of the description and analysis, however, we will be concerned with the uniformed staff on the discipline side and will refer to other staff categories only from time to time as required. Somewhat to our surprise, we found that the 6 officers who were working as shop instructors did not seem to differ in any significant way from other uniformed staff, and so for all practical purposes we have included them with basic-grade officers, bringing their numbers up to 34 and the total for the whole uniformed group to 54.

Promotion for uniformed staff in the prison service is notoriously slow, and is based at least in part on qualifying periods of service. It was hardly surprising, therefore, that we found that the mean age of staff rose with each step in the promotional ladder: 32.5 years for basic-grade officers, 42.6 years for senior officers, 45.8 years for principal officers, and 52.7 years for chief officers. The details of the age distribution are shown in Table 7.8.

Table 7.8 Percentage age distribution of Albany uniformed staff sample

Staff grade		Age in years				
		21–30	31–40	41–50	51–60	All ages
Basic-grade	N=34	35.3	50.0	14.7	0.0	100.0
Senior officers	N=10	0.0	50.0	30.0	20.0	100.0
Principal officers	N=7	0.0	0.0	71.4	28.6	100.0
Chief officers	N=3	0.0	0.0	33.3	66.7	100.0

As we shall be reporting later, many prisoners, but especially the older prisoners, thought that there were too many staff in

Albany who were too young: they resented being supervised by persons younger than themselves with whom they found it difficult to relate. But even more important than mere youth was inexperience. Principal and senior officers, as well as prisoners, complained that many basic-grade officers did not have the requisite experience to deal with recidivists, some of whom had been in prisons many times and for many years in the course of their lives. There was certainly some substance to the view that basic-grade staff were inexperienced, for half of our sample had spent less than four years in the prison service, and three in every ten were either still in their first probationary year of service or had only just completed it. Although direct comparisons are not possible with the material reported by Morris *et al.* (1963), it seems that Albany had proportionately fewer probationary officers than was the case in Pentonville ten years earlier. On the other hand Albany compared unfavourably in this respect with the four prisons we studied subsequently, where the proportion of probationary staff averaged less than one in five. Just under a third of the basic-grade officers had been in the prison service between four and eight years, and a fifth had served for more than nine years.

Experience may be measured not just by length of service but also by such matters as the number and type of institutions in which staff have previously worked, the background from which staff are recruited, and the amount of training received.

The Morrises reported that 34.6 per cent of their respondents had served in no other prison establishment besides Pentonville, and of those two-thirds had been in Pentonville for more than two years. Moreover, the Morrises believed that a high proportion of the staff who refused to be interviewed (36 per cent of all those whom they approached for interview declined) were also from the 'Pentonville only' group but with longer periods of service (Morris *et al.*, 1963, pp. 75–6). In Albany, which had only been opened in 1967, anybody with a total period of service of more than two years had to have had experience in other prisons. Even so this experience did not extend very widely across the range of Prison Department establishments. None of the basic-grade staff in our sample had served in remand centres, for example, and none in open prisons. Twenty-six had served in only one other type of establishment: 13 in local prisons, 12 in closed training prisons, and one in a borstal. Five had worked both in local prisons and in closed training prisons, and two had worked in closed training establishments as well as borstals. For those who had been less than two years in the prison service, the experience of other establishments was extremely brief, most having been transferred to Albany immediately after completing the basic training course at the Officer Training School. All but one of the higher ranks among the discipline staff had seen service in at least two other kinds of establishment within the system.

Prison staff, like other occupational groups, come from a variety of backgrounds, but there has always been a strong tradition of recruitment to the prison service from persons with military experience. The Morrises discussed the preference expressed by the Pentonville selection board for ex-servicemen (Morris *et al.*, 1963, p. 80), and the preference expressed by at least some prisoners for screws who had come from 'ordinary' life (pp. 265–6). All the staff interviewed at Pentonville had spent periods in the armed services, but it is likely that many of them – perhaps a third of the total – had either been national servicemen or wartime conscripts. Even so two-thirds had served for more than seven years, a period which must have included some professional peacetime soldiering. Perhaps a different recruitment policy had been adopted at Albany because of its experimental status, for the proportion of regular peacetime soldiers there was very much lower. Indeed, as far as basic-grade officers were concerned there were fewer men from this background in Albany than we found in any of the prisons we studied later. National service having been abolished, more than a third of the basic-grade staff had no military experience whatever. The details are given in Table 7.9.

Table 7.9   Military service of uniformed staff in Albany

	Basic-grade N=34	Higher ranks N=20
None	35.3	5.0
National service	20.6	15.0
War service	0.0	40.0
Peacetime regular	44.1	40.0
All types	100.0	100.0

In spite of a growing emphasis on training in the prison service in recent years there seemed to be little difference in the training experience of Albany officers from that of Pentonville officers ten years earlier. All basic-grade staff had attended the initial training course at the Officer Training School: one had had a three-week course some years ago, the remainder had attended for at least one month of training, and most of the more recent recruits had attended for eight weeks. The training periods for higher ranks had often been extremely brief and, of course, had taken place in the somewhat distant past. Thus two of the chief officers had had little more than a week of formal training for the job when they joined the service more than twenty years previously. One in three of the basic-grade staff and one in two of the senior, principal and chief officers, had since attended refresher or other specialist courses of various kinds, which lasted from five days up to three months. It is inevitable that such short periods of formal training should pale into relative insignificance when placed alongside the learning process from colleagues and bitter experience in the course of a career. But although we made no special study of the staff response to training it was our impression that this was a good deal less negative than was reported for Pentonville officers.

The regime
The standard category-A regime was introduced at Albany, simultaneously with the change of prison work to single-shift, on 17 February 1969. It soon underwent a number of changes as various troubles were ironed out, and by July 1969 when our interviews were conducted the basic outline of the routine was as follows:

Standard category-A regime: Albany, July 1969

Staff	*Prisoners*
MORNINGS	
06.35 Early shift on duty	06.35 Roll check and unlocking
	06.40 Slopping out
06.50 Night staff off duty	
07.10 Staff to supervise dining halls	07.10 Prisoners to breakfast in dining halls

07.15 Internal search: one
officer from each hall
Party officers to
breakfast

07.50 Shop instructors on
duty

07.55 Staff line route to   07.55 Prisoners to labour, A
supervise movement to   hall followed by C, D
labour   and E halls

08.10 Various staff groups to   08.00 Labour commences:
09.45 breakfast   shop and parties

AFTERNOONS

12.10 Staff line routes from   12.10 Cease labour: shop and
labour and thence to   all parties
dining halls

12.15 Governor's   12.15 Prisoners to dinner in
applications   dining halls

12.20 Shop search: one   12.30 **Roll check in**
officer from each hall   **dining halls**
Shop instructors to
dinner   12.50 Prisoners return to halls

                                   12.55 Voluntary exercise

13.00 Late shift on duty

13.10 All parties to labour   13.10 All parties to labour

13.20 Shop instructors from
dinner
Early-shift officers off
duty

13.25 Staff line routes to   13.25 Exercise ceases: to
labour   shops

	13.30 Resume labour
16.15- 17.00 Staff to early tea	
17.10 Staff line routes from labour	17.10 Cease labour: shops and parties
17.15 Staff to late tea	17.15 Roll check in halls
17.20 Staff to dining halls	17.20 Tea served in dining halls
	17.45 Return to halls: association commences

EVENINGS

18.00 Staff from late tea	18.00 Classes
	18.15- Outside recreation 19.30 in summer
	20.00 Classes cease
20.05 Staff to dining halls	20.05- 20.20 Supper in dining halls
20.55 Locking up	20.55 Locked up
21.00 Night staff on duty	21.00 Roll check
21.15 Late shift off duty Key check	

All halls were governed by this broad schedule of events, but there was still scope for quite important differences to occur.

Perhaps the most notable differences arose out of the work situation of the prisoners. Thus a party of five prisoners in A hall who worked in the officers' mess were regularly wakened half an hour before the rest of the prisoners; and the kitchen party consisting of 15 prisoners in C hall were wakened almost an hour

earlier, at 05.45. In all halls two dining room orderlies were
similarly wakened somewhat earlier so that they could be on duty
before the other prisoners started breakfast. The early rising
involved for these jobs was often the subject of complaint, but the
perquisites attaching to them could sometimes be considerable.
Preparing, serving and clearing away food for other prisoners was
not popular work, but kitchen workers and dining orderlies could
supplement their own rations. Their access to supplies of food,
however, could sometimes mean that they were subject to
pressures from tougher men. Only particularly 'trustworthy'
prisoners nearing the end of their sentences were selected for the
officers' mess party, because Albany House was outside the
perimeter fence. This occupation thus offered the enormous
advantage of a complete change of environment outside the
prison, and these prisoners took all their meals except supper in
the officers' mess. While some prisoners in the main complex
perceived the task of cooking and waiting table for the screws as
beneath their dignity, this did not seem to weigh heavily with those
who actually worked in the mess. Indeed, while the formal niceties
of a master and servant relationship were observed there was a
real sense in which, for once, the power balance was tipped in
favour of the prisoners. On the many occasions when we ate in the
mess the possibility of the adulteration of food was often raised in
banter between officers and prisoners, and sometimes in the
uneasy jokes that were told to the research workers. Officers could
not afford grievances to be held in such circumstances, though
prisoners, aware that they could be quickly removed back to the
main prison, were equally careful not to give offence. The job
provided many opportunities for acquiring scarce goods and
contraband items, but possibly above all it offered information.
Staff were off duty and talked over the matters of the day with
colleagues. Gossip about the domestic affairs of staff was also
common. Occasionally visitors such as ourselves opened up the
horizon to the world beyond the prison. It was not necessary for
the prisoners to solicit news, they merely had to keep their eyes
and ears open.

While these jobs necessitated the most significant departures
from the daily time-table in the halls, there were marked
differences in work situation between the various labour alloca-
tions which constituted important regime differences in their own
right. Only 213 men, or 61.2 per cent of the population of 348

prisoners, were employed on industrial work of any kind on 1 May 1969. This compared with 179 men or 56.8 per cent of the population a year earlier, but it was fewer than might have been achieved had the two-shift system, with its more intensive use of workspace, come into full operation. The numbers employed in the tailor's shop, which had only ever operated alternate shifts, remained much the same. On average about 55 prisoners worked there, producing pyjamas, overalls and similar items. The tailoring shop was the only workshop geared up for production-line working, although it never lived up to this aspiration either before or after the shift change because of the continuing problems in getting contracts, and because of the blockages that occurred in the production line when key men were absent or inadequately trained for the job. Nor was the pace of work comparable to what might be found in outside industry. At first prisoners resented the extra hours of work for no extra pay which followed on the shift change, and few of them liked the work or the working conditions. Smoking was prohibited, except at tea breaks and unofficially in the recess. The work was more regimented than in other shops, and the serried ranks of prisoners sat in a somewhat sullen semi-silence, tending their machines. The main noise in the workshop, apart from the hum and chatter of the machines, was the incessant background music broadcast over the Tannoy. The pace of work speeded up after the introduction of incentive earnings, but higher pay did not solve the problem of motivation, and instructors continued to press for the return of some prisoners to the training and fall-out shop. Though it was sometimes possible to make illicit alterations to prison clothing, out of sight of the officer instructors, there were few other perks available. On one occasion some magnets were removed from the sewing machines and used to interfere with the ELSA system, but for the most part the only contraband to be had was a ready supply of needles and thread.

The tailor's shop contrasted most markedly in its working conditions with the growing woodwork industry, which in May 1969 employed on average 62 prisoners. Of these 13 were in the old woodmill, 33 in carpenters I, where washstands and other articles of cell furniture were assembled, and 16 in the new spray finishing shop known as carpenters II. The woodmill had previously operated with two shifts, but an expansion of work places meant that it was able to continue with much the same numbers as before. The assembly shop had never operated on a two-shift basis, and the spray shop was only opened after the change-over to single-shift working. While the operations performed in these shops obviously differed they had much in common in terms of atmosphere. The work was not regimented, and prisoners had considerable control over their task and their pace of work. Prisoners appeared to smoke at will and to move freely about the workshops, and it was common to see several horse-playing around. It was in any case difficult to supervise their activities; and the possibility always existed of making 'useful' items, or of secreting tools and attempting to smuggle them back to the halls. Not surprisingly, the carpentry trades, which were also seen as involving more dignified work, were popular among prisoners, even though the incentive earnings scheme had not yet been introduced for those workshops. To the uninitiated outsider, brought up on public stereotypes of the violent criminal, the apparent disorganization of the carpentry shops and the variety of potentially dangerous weapons that were available must have seemed quite threatening. Such stereotypes are seldom far beneath the surface even for initiated insiders, but there was no move as yet to place supervisory discipline officers in the shops.

The cutting shop and the light textiles (now renamed tailors II) fell somewhere between the regimentation of tailors I and the disorganization of the woodworking shops. Both had previously worked fully on a two-shift basis and so had only half the work places available for single-shift operation. The cutting shop employed 12 prisoners on average in May 1969. They were engaged in cutting out materials for use in both the tailoring and light textiles shops. The light textiles shop was working on part of the pyjamas contract in addition to a further order for nylon mail bags. It employed, nominally, much the same numbers as previously: 81 on average in May 1969. But in fact nearly half of these men were separately housed in what had become the training and fall-out shop, and so were not really engaged in industrial production as such. None of these shops had yet been work-studied, and the prisoners were still working for longer hours at the old rates of pay. The training and fall-out shop attracted the lowest pay of any job in the prison, and the work, by common consent, was the least interesting to be had.

The remaining 135 prisoners, or 38.8 per cent of the population on 1 May 1969, were employed on the numerous domestic and maintenance parties throughout the prison or else on a few specialized tasks. We have already mentioned the officers' mess party, the kitchen party and the dining room orderlies. Apart from these the main parties were the inside and outside gardens, the inside and outside works, the trenching party, the workshop carrying party, the disposal party, the quarters, roads and yards party, and, of course, the ubiquitous cleaners. Most offered some variation in routine or advantages of one kind or another. Thus party workers, in spite of what was stated in the formal blueprint, typically began work a quarter of an hour later and finished ten minutes earlier than prisoners in the workshops, and while they were at work there was often little pressure to exert themselves. The size of each party was usually quite small, and the tendency was to exercise only the lightest of supervision. The officer in charge of a party sometimes knew his prisoners in the residential context of the hall as well as the work situation, and it was common for relaxed joking relationships to develop.

Not all the jobs involved in party work were equally congenial, nor did they all offer the same opportunities to acquire items that might be used either indirectly as currency within the prison, or directly to make life a little more comfortable. At one extreme, employment on the outside gardens party, which tended the grounds outside the gatehouse, and on the quarters party, offered some of the advantages that obtained in the officers' mess. Prisoners for these jobs also tended to be trusted men, though not necessarily at the end of their sentences. At the other extreme, the disposal party involved little more than removing the waste from the workshops and the kitchens; and while there were sometimes pickings to be had it was less than pleasant work, about on a par with the various cleaning parties. During the summer the gardens parties, outside works and so on were especially popular, but they lost some of their appeal in the winter months.

Finally, there were a few prisoners engaged in occupations which enabled them to construct rather special regimes for themselves. Two men, for example, were employed on indexing the 1871 census on what was known as the deputy governor's record party. These prisoners, like the assistant librarian, were able to derive some intrinsic satisfaction from their work as well as to enjoy generally pleasant working conditions. They felt they had earned the respect and confidence of the staff, with whom they were able to maintain relationships that resembled those that might be found between colleagues in the outside world. To some extent this also applied to several prisoners who worked for various members of staff in a clerical capacity. Occupations such as the canteen clerk, or storemen, also provided their incumbents with a sense of responsibility and sometimes power over other prisoners, as well as the opportunity for securing rather better provisions for themselves.

All told, the employment offered in Albany in the summer of 1969 was rather more varied than might be found in most prisons, and the prisoners had a fairly clear idea of what was available to them. When we asked our sample of prisoners to rank the various occupations according to those that they would most prefer to do, or least like having to do, there was less than universal agreement among them. It was clear that in choosing jobs, prisoners performed much the same kind of calculus as anyone else when weighing pay, perks and working conditions in the scales. There was a generally expressed resentment, among our prisoner sample, that the incentive earnings scheme had been introduced on such a piecemeal basis, and staff confirmed that they were embarrassed by the anomalies that had been produced. But pay was rarely the most important consideration for prisoners, except when confronted with otherwise equally unattractive choices. Some occupations were rated very highly by some prisoners but given very low priority by others, a case in point being the officers' mess party which we have already discussed. To take account of this, and in order to reach some kind of consensus, we counted one plus point for each time a job was ranked first and one minus point for each time it was ranked last. On this basis, and beginning with the most popular, the top ten jobs were: outside works (+13), inside works (+9), library clerk (+8), education clerk (+6), gymnasium orderly (+5), inside gardens (+5), canteen clerk (+4), hospital orderly (+3), carpentry shop (+3) and storemen (+3). Almost without exception the jobs most frequently cited as the best were the ones which had the most obvious perks and regime advantages of the kind we have discussed. Only three jobs were rated worse than the workshops, and these bestowed unfavourable regime elements such as early rising, or else were contaminated in the eyes of the prisoners by too close an association with the more odious aspects of imprisonment. Beginning with the least favoured, the bottom ten jobs were: kitchen party (−12), segregation unit orderly (−8), hall cleaner (−7), training and fall-out shop (−6), light textiles (−6), tailors shop (−5), woodmill (−4), disposal party (−4), spray shop (−3) and the cutting shop (−3). When we asked prisoners to choose only between the workshops, the tailor's and the carpentry shop were placed equal at the head of the list with a score of +17. It seemed that if one had to be in a workshop, one might as well work for the money in tailoring or the more satisfying and constructive task of woodworking. The spray shop (+7) came a poor third, followed by light textiles (−1), the cutting shop (−4) and the woodmill (−5). The training and fall-out shop had evidently achieved the reputation that was intended for it, with a score of −31.

We had expected that differences in pay and in access to perks of one kind or another afforded by different occupations might be reflected in the number and quality of personal possessions that prisoners acquired. Accordingly we compiled a detailed inventory of all the items to be found in the cells of our sample prisoners; this was carried out with their permission and in their presence. The items were classified under four headings: clothing, food, utilities and luxuries. In the course of this procedure we sought to establish the sources from which the items originated, and many unauthorized articles came to light. Most prisoners seemed very ready to explain to us how they had obtained them. There was a slight association between prison income and the number of items possessed, at least for some foods and utilities that could be bought from the canteen. But purchasing goods from prison earnings was only one method of acquiring possessions and was not necessarily the most important. Many 'possessions', including all clothing, items such as razors and toothbrushes which we classified as utilities, and carpets and bedspreads, for example, which we classed as luxuries, were supplied by the institution. And it was also possible to buy some goods from private cash or to have them supplied by relatives and friends. Having goods sent in was obviously the most effective way of getting the more expensive luxury items, such as personal radios, and the longer prisoners had served the more likely were they to have developed a range of luxury goods in the course of their sentence.

There were also a number of illicit and unofficial methods of acquiring personal possessions. Even clothing and other articles supplied by the prison were not equally distributed. Some prisoners reported that items had been lost or stolen and not replaced, or simply that they had not wanted to take their allocation. Others had obtained more than the official provision, sometimes simply by asking for more and getting it, sometimes through operating fiddles at the times when goods were handed out or exchanged, and sometimes by theft. There was certainly evidence to support the view that different jobs afforded different opportunities for supplementing what was officially supplied and what could be bought. In some cases goods were acquired by pilfering, as with needles, thread, pieces of cloth, wood and tools taken from the workshops, or supplies of tea, sugar and food from the kitchens. In others the goods were regarded as unofficial but 'legitimate' perks, as with the tips of tobacco in the officers' mess, or the taking away of left-over prepared foods from the kitchens. In still others extra possessions were generated out of the close working relationships between certain prisoners and members of staff: for example, when books, magazines, pencils and paper were passed on to help prisoners who had expressed particular interests. But there was no clear-cut relationship between prison occupation and the number of items acquired in these unofficial ways for two reasons. First, not all prisoners in a given occupation responded to the opportunities presented in the same way. The decision to take advantage of any opportunities offered seemed to be part of the wider process of adaptation to the prison regime, and we return to this matter in the next chapter. Second, goods did not always remain in the possession of the person who first acquired them, but were distributed more generally through the process of theft, the settlement of debts and the bestowal of gifts. While prisoners were subject to searches on returning from work, and all cells were routinely searched by hall staff, the main concern was with items that might constitute a threat to security or good order and discipline. Staff were well aware that many prisoners had unauthorized articles in their possession and that these were often exchanged within the prison community. But there were tacit understandings that this was acceptable in the interests of harmonious working relationships and there was no systematic attempt to impose the letter of the law. Occasionally, when what was found in cell searches could not be ignored, or when a new member of staff applied the rules in ignorance or disregard of the common understandings, the disciplinary action which followed caused temporary ill feeling.

As Albany became more security conscious, and industry assumed a higher priority, so the notion of providing social training had progressively declined. Nevertheless prisoners had access to a number of specialist staff who had more or less definite roles to play on the social training side. The new induction scheme was also in operation and the case-officer system continued, at least in name, throughout the summer of 1969.

Most prisoners at least saw the heads of the various specialist departments when they first arrived at Albany, if only on the other side of the desk at a reception board. But we were interested to find out the extent of any ongoing contacts. We therefore asked the 69 respondents in our prisoner sample whether they had been in touch with any members of the specialist staff since reception, and more particularly whether any contacts had been made during the two months preceding the interview date. The results are presented in Table 7.10.

Table 7.10   Contacts with specialist staff since reception and during two months preceding interview. Prisoner sample N=69

Staff member	No of prisoners with nil contact since reception	No of prisoners making contact in preceding two months	Mean number of contacts in two months
Welfare officers	4	30	2.0
Medical officer	1	29	3.3
Assistant governor	30	25	2.9
Chaplain	7	18	6.8
Ed. tut. organizer	16	6	3.7
Psychologists	53	4	2.3

In calculating the average frequency of contact we have excluded three prisoners who came into daily contact with either the chaplain or the education and tutor organizer in the course of their occupations. The higher frequency of contact with these two members of staff is otherwise accounted for by a small number of prisoners in our sample who attended remedial education classes or the regular weekly sessions of Alcoholics Anonymous and the padre's hour. Most of the contacts with the assistant governor were not directly concerned with his social training role, but arose out of prisoner applications which could not be dealt with at principal officer level. The higher proportion of prisoners who had recently seen the welfare officers and the doctor – more than two-fifths of our sample in both cases – was confirmed in interviews with the members of staff concerned. The medical officer had more than 100 consultations each week, mostly, we were told, either for the treatment of petty ailments or for the purposes of routine reporting to various boards. Many of his consultations involved the same patients on repeated occasions, and it was common for prisoners to report sick in the hope that this would lead to a recommendation for a change of labour. The welfare officers similarly reported more than 100 consultations between them weekly. About two-thirds of the appointments with the senior welfare officer occurred during the induction process, whereas two-thirds of those with the other two officers usually resulted from the requests of prisoners to deal with welfare problems that had arisen during the sentence. The remaining consultations were either for routine reporting purposes, or else had been made at the request of the welfare officer, usually to impart information to the prisoners. The most surprising finding was the very low level of contact with the psychologists, but this too was confirmed when we spoke to the staff concerned. In the week preceding our interviews the principal psychologist had seen no prisoners, except as part of the induction procedure, and his assistant had seen only two. Indeed, 53 prisoners in our sample claimed never to have had contact with the psychologists since their reception at Albany, which suggests that little attempt was made to monitor progress once any initial diagnosis had been made during the induction period.

The majority of the prisoners in our sample were either indifferent to the induction programme or else thought it a 'meaningless waste of time', in which 'impertinent questions' were asked and 'useless tests' administered. Staff were generally in favour of a closely supervised induction period. Several argued that it showed how well the prisoners were looked after and how much thought went into planning their stay. Others were extremely cynical about the use to which any of the information collected would – or could – be put. As to the case-officer system, about one-third of our prisoners thought it a good idea in principle and that it worked well enough in practice as far as they were concerned. Another third approved in principle but claimed that it did not work well, if at all. They commonly complained that they did not know their case officer, or that they rarely saw him. The remainder were either indifferent or else felt strongly that 'screws should not poke about in matters that don't concern them'. Interestingly enough, these views were mirrored closely by the staff and in approximately the same proportions. Nearly three-quarters of the discipline officers from all ranks voiced approval in principle, but of these about half thought it worked well and half thought that it did not. Among the latter group, staff complained that they did not have enough time to carry out their 'case work', and that the task had become much too fragmented once the hall staffing had been reorganized. About a quarter of the discipline staff felt no sympathy for the system at all and wished that they could opt out. We suspect that in practice they did.

If the formal development of training plans and the case-officer system did not amount to much, there were still several positive aspects of staff-prisoner relationships that had been fostered under David Gould and which continued to characterize the Albany regime. Indeed what staff, prisoners and the research workers came to think of as the core of the regime, and the essence of the Albany approach, consisted of three elements which were closely interlocked: the provision of a long period of association in which prisoners were able to take responsible decisions about personal and collective activities; the development of close relationships between staff and prisoners in which officers exercised a discreet and unobtrusive supervision; and the responsible use of delegated authority by hall principal officers in the drawing up and interpretation of the rules to govern routine procedures. The extent to which these core elements were applied, however, varied somewhat from hall to hall.

Prisoners were required to take decisions for themselves as far as this was possible within the limited circumstances of their confinement. Since prisoners were out of cells from early in the morning until quite late in the evening there were many opportunities for them to do so, even though they spent less time in the halls once the two-shift system had been abandoned. There were no set routines for bathing or hair-cutting, for example, and it was left to prisoners to decide when and how frequently these activities should take place. Similarly facilities were provided for ironing and pressing clothes, so that prisoners could take advantage of these if they chose. Hardly any restrictions were placed on movement within the halls. Cell doors were left unlocked and prisoners could choose to remain in their own cells, to visit the cells of other prisoners, or to use the communal landings, association room or quiet room for their activities. The communal facilities were less than adequate for the needs of recreation, bearing in mind that Albany was a new prison, but they were better than could be found in most older establishments. There was no suitable place for playing table-tennis, hence the pressure to use one of the dining halls as a games room, and makeshift arrangements were made on the landings. An effort was made to maintain the tranquillity of the quiet room; and the large association room was used for television viewing. Since there was no accommodation for a second television set the choice of programme was made by television committees in each hall – though this did not eliminate occasional disputes.

Few other matters required communal resolution at hall level, though staff-prisoner liaison committees were occasionally convened to deal with matters as they arose. Each hall could send elected representatives to a number of prison-wide committees, but E hall did not send delegates to all the committees available. Apart from the messing committee and the general purposes committee there were three others which met on a more or less regular basis: one decided on the disbursement of monies from the common fund to which all prisoners contributed a nominal weekly sum; another arranged occasional tournaments of various kinds between the halls; and the third organized entertainments and films for periodic viewing in the gymnasium. Movement outside the halls during association was more restricted, in spite of the growing perimeter security. Prisoners could not go outside their halls at will, and visits to the games room, the gymnasium and the sportsfield were time-tabled and subject to supervision. Even so, most prisoners felt that the provision in these matters was quite generous; and prisoners could be seen in the outside recreation areas on most weekday evenings and for substantial periods at weekends, whenever it was fine. Prisoners were encouraged to attend as many educational or hobbies classes as they could fit in, and in the summer of 1969 there were 32 separate classes with a total enrolment of 321 members. The eight daytime remedial classes had an attendance record of 68 per cent of the nominal roll, while the 24 evening classes enjoyed only 47 per cent attendance. Many prisoners were enrolled in several classes.

Staff exercised only a light, and generally distant supervision. There were no parades for counting heads, and roll checks were taken discreetly as prisoners left and returned to their halls. When prisoners went to and from work discipline officers lined the route at intervals, but there was no attempt to regiment the prisoners from place to place. Inside the halls, of course, close supervision was ruled out by the design of the building; but in any case the policy was to intervene as little as possible. During association periods card schools could be found on the landing in all halls and tables were provided for this purpose. Gambling was part of the everyday scene and, in addition to cards, some prisoners would bet on the outcome of games of darts, dominoes, draughts, table-tennis and any number of other activities. It was common to see clusters of prisoners sitting around the racing pages of newspapers perusing the results. Just as staff exercised their discretion over unauthorized possessions in cells, much the same attitude was taken in regard to gambling in the halls. So long as staff felt that they knew what was going on and where, and that the activities were conducted in a reasonably orderly fashion, then no action was taken. The idea was to watch and contain rather than to control and possibly provoke.

The pattern of relationships between staff and prisoners throughout the routine activities of the day was, for the most part, characterized by a quite remarkable degree of tact and delicacy from both sides. Of course, incidents did occur from time to time, and no one could forget that they were in a prison, but Albany was blissfully free from the kind of interpersonal aggravation described by the Morrises at Pentonville. Thus one way in which some staff at Pentonville needled prisoners was by ignoring the cell bells which provided prisoners with their only means of communicating with staff once they had been locked up. Usually the ringing of the bells at Pentonville signalled that a prisoner, often sharing a cell with two other prisoners, wanted to be let out to go to the recess rather than to use one of the chamber pots provided (Morris *et al.*, 1963, p. 262). This particular situation scarcely arose in Albany. Prisoners were unlocked for the greater part of the day and when they were in cells at least they had privacy. But in all prisons the locking and unlocking of prisoners serves to emphasize the relative power of the staff, and potentially conflict is always possible at these times.

Unlocking, followed by the daily ritual of prisoners filing to the recess to 'slop out' the contents of chamber pots, is an unpleasant element of prison life that is degrading for staff and prisoners alike. When it is handled insensitively, tensions arise which are sometimes resolved by prisoners throwing pots on the floor or at officers before being removed to the punishment cells. From the evidence of our observations, as well as the reporting of staff and prisoners, the unlocking and slopping out procedure in Albany was conducted in a non-provocative way. In A hall, of course, where one member of staff could unlock the prisoners a group at a time from his position at the ELSA control panel, this difficult face-to-face contact was avoided, a fact for which both prisoners and staff were duly grateful. We were somewhat surprised to discover that, although the ELSA system had been devised to effect night sanitation, several prisoners preferred to use pots and to slop out in the time-honoured way. Slight variations occurred in the procedures adopted in other halls, but the usual practice was as follows. Two officers on each landing first checked that all prisoners were in cells, and as they did so slid back the bolts from the cell doors. They then reported back the numbers to the senior officer, who checked the roll and gave the order to unlock. Meanwhile the prisoners, having heard the bolts being drawn, knew that they were expected to get up and accordingly prepared themselves. The officers, returning to their stations, then went round the cells unlocking them with the key and pushing the doors open. At no time in C and D halls did staff talk to prisoners, though when we carried out observations in E hall we sometimes heard officers from one division giving instructions to prisoners to get up. Only after all the cell doors were opened did one officer move round the landing to check that prisoners actually were getting up. Prisoners moved to the recess as soon as they were ready, to slop out, wash and shave before going down for breakfast. While there was little enough time for these activities, it was left to prisoners to organize themselves and there was no regimental procession to and from the recess.

'Banging up' at night was organized in much the same way. In A hall prisoners were effectively responsible for shutting their own cell doors, and whether they had done so or not was shown on the control room panel. All that officers had to do was to make a visual check that each prisoner was in his own cell before reporting the roll to the senior officer in charge. In the other halls also prisoners made their own way to cells. Two officers were allocated to each landing (if there were enough officers to go round) to supervise the process. If there were insufficient staff on duty then two officers were assigned to the landings furthest away from the hall office, and one officer to the closer landings. Locking-up officers first ensured that men were in their cells, then locked and bolted the doors, and finally checked through the cell observation windows before reporting the roll. Once again, whenever we observed the process, hardly anything was said between staff and prisoners, and face-to-face contact was largely avoided. Neither staff nor prisoners raised adverse comments about locking or unlocking during the course of our interviews.

We attempted to assess the level and character of contact between staff and prisoners in the halls in two ways. First, we asked the prisoners in our sample whether they had spoken to hall officers on any of ten defined occasions on the day preceding the interview, and if so for how long the conversation lasted and what it was about. The situations included mealtimes and the various periods of the day when prisoners were freely associating in the halls. Very short contacts that were concerned solely with the giving or receiving of instructions or information (such as might occur during the issuance of razor blades, for example) were excluded in the hope of getting at more social contacts. A score of 1 was assigned for each contact established, and a score of 0 when no talking took place in the situation as defined, so that each prisoner could score between 0 and 10. Individual scores were then summed to produce hall scores. These 'social distance' scores clearly differentiated between the halls, and an analysis of variance showed the differences to be statistically significant ($F = 4.71$, $p < 0.01$). Table 7.11 gives the results.

Table 7.11   Staff-prisoner contact scores by halls

	A hall	C hall	D hall	E hall
Total hall scores	66	36	27	44
Mean prisoner scores	3.7	2.1	1.6	2.6

Since the interviews in each hall were spread out over several weeks, and in any case one prison day is much like any other, there is no reason to suppose that the results present an atypical picture. By eliminating what we took to be the shorter, more formal contacts, however, we have probably underestimated the overall level of contact between staff and prisoners on these occasions. It seems unlikely that the systematic variation, which differentiates A hall quite sharply from C and D halls with E hall occupying an intermediary position, could be explained by the personal characteristics of the staff and prisoners concerned, for this would require that such variables had been taken into account before staff and prisoners were allocated to halls. More probably it indicates the different ways in which officers interpreted their roles within the general framework laid down for them (cf. King *et al.,*

1971).

Some confirmation for these results was found when we used our second measure. For this we utilized our observations of hall staff during the evening association period which we described earlier. We observed A hall officers for 174 observation intervals, C hall officers for 172 intervals, D hall for 154 intervals and E hall for 177 intervals. We then calculated the proportion of these intervals in which staff were in the presence of prisoners so that interaction could theoretically take place, and found very little difference between the halls; no hall had fewer than 50 per cent of the intervals as potential interaction situations, and none had more than 55 per cent. Differences were found, however, in the proportion of potential interaction intervals in which interaction – specifically talking between staff and prisoners – actually took place. A hall was again sharply differentiated from the other three halls, and although the differences between C, D and E halls were really quite small the rank order was the same as that which resulted from the questions we asked prisoners. We also attempted to rate the quality of the interaction by categorizing the situation as either formal or informal. In order to maintain reliability it was necessary to take rather obvious indicators of 'informality' – such as laughter, participants smoking cigarettes together, officers not wearing caps or jackets, and so on – as criteria for the rating, with the result that we almost certainly underestimated the degree of informality. Nevertheless, this measure showed very little difference between A, C and D halls, all with around 30 per cent of contacts being rated as informal while E hall lagged very much behind with only 10 per cent of the contacts being rated in this way. The results are given in Table 7.12.

Table 7.12 Frequency and quality of observed staff-prisoner contacts during association

	Total observations	Proportion of potential interaction situations %	Proportion resulting in actual contacts %	Proportion rated as informal %
A hall	174	53.5	64.5	30.0
C hall	172	50.0	55.8	31.3
D hall	154	51.3	54.4	27.9
E hall	177	55.4	57.1	10.7

We conducted too few observations to warrant further statistical analysis, and we would not wish to draw conclusions based on this alone. When we returned to the halls a week or two later with a revised observation schedule it was clear that our respondents had had enough, and for the first and only time in the research, staff and prisoners jokingly behaved in ways which were obviously not part of the normal pattern. But if the results from interviews with hall staff, prisoners and our observations are combined, the picture emerges that although the formal rules governing interaction between staff and prisoners did not vary much, real differences could be discerned at the behavioural level: specifically, that A hall, and to some degree E hall, exhibited a rather higher frequency of contact between staff and prisoners than C and D halls; but that whereas in A, C and D halls such interaction as did take place was quite often of an informal kind, this was much less likely to be the case in E hall.

Perhaps the greatest problems in the Albany regime arose from the exercise of delegated authority by hall principal officers in devising and operating routine procedures. There had been a continuing attempt to achieve greater consistency in the pattern of routine functioning in preparation for the arrival of category-A prisoners. To some degree this had been successful. For example, hall senior officers now reported to us complete agreement on the regulations concerning what prisoners should wear at meals – a topic which, as we indicated in chapter 6, had been the subject of much discussion at the principal officers' meeting. With the end of two-shift working it had become possible for all prisoners to change into and out of overalls before and after all meals, and overalls had thus been banned at mealtimes. In all halls prisoners were required to wear prison 'greys' – uniform trousers and shirts – to meals, though they had the option of wearing jackets and ties, and shoes or slippers. In so far as we could tell the rule was always applied, and anyone improperly dressed was sent back by the officer on duty. But the drive for consistency had been set back by the new working arrangements for principal officers, which left each hall under the effective command of a different senior officer on each shift. Inevitably there were differences of interpretation over various matters as between one hall and another, and most noticeably in E hall between one shift and another. Many of the differences were quite trivial, though they were sometimes enough to cause comment from prisoners and basic-grade officers. Possi-

bly the most glaring example was over the compulsory or
voluntary attendance at meals, a matter over which Brian Howden
had remarked many months earlier that it might appear as if the
staff were 'buggering the prisoners about'. Far from achieving
uniformity of practice, the situation had become even less
consistent than before. D hall had now adopted the formula which
had always been used in A hall, whereby all meals were regarded
as optional, in the sense that any prisoner who did not wish to eat
could report to the senior officer and remain in the hall. In C and
E halls, however, breakfast, the midday meal and tea were
regarded as compulsory, so that all prisoners had to go to the
dining room and queue for their food. Then any prisoners who did
not want to eat could either refuse to take it from the counter, or
else take it to a table and subsequently return it, depending on
which member of staff was on duty.

While the fact that prisoners now ate supper in the dining rooms
did make that occasion rather more orderly, prisoners could and
did leave the dining room as soon as they had finished eating,
returning to their halls with steaming mugs of tea and cocoa. On
occasions the process of returning to halls could become extremely
disorganized, and staff continued to feel vulnerable. Moreover,
staff in A, C and D halls treated supper as an optional meal along
the lines which had earlier been agreed, but in E hall it was still the
practice to make all prisoners go whether they wanted to eat or
not. In fact, most prisoners went to supper anyway unless there
was something very gripping on television, but it was inconsistencies of this kind that led some staff and prisoners to complain that
'you never know where you stand in this prison'. Sometimes,
especially if a prisoner had been transferred from one hall to
another, such inconsistencies led to incidents and altercations.

There was little doubt that of the four residential halls A hall
enjoyed the best reputation among prisoners, and the question of
how to resist the growing volume of applications for transfer into
A hall was regularly discussed at the principal officers' meeting.
As the only hall yet fitted out with electronics, and the hall which
housed the induction scheme, it was the most shown part of a
show-piece prison. And in addition to these advantages a much
higher proportion of A hall prisoners worked on the more
favoured parties around the prison than in the industrial workshops. A-hall staff tended to regard themselves as something of an
élite, who perhaps more consciously tried to live up to the

expectations placed upon them. Some officers elsewhere, however, viewed A hall somewhat cynically, as presenting a propaganda or public relations exercise. There was little to choose between C and D halls, but again both staff and prisoners looked on E hall with reservations. We found it to be the least consistent hall in its routine procedures and in the interpretation of rules, and the hall with the most formal pattern of relationships. Interestingly, prisoners thought that E hall was different because of the attitudes of the officers, while staff attributed the differences to the immaturity and over-sensitivity of the prisoners.

The punishment block in Y hall, of course, was something else again. The governor issued his circular renaming it the segregation unit just as our interviews began. Several distinct categories of prisoner could be held there. Some prisoners were contained in the segregation unit under the provisions of Rule 43 of the Prison Rules, which permits the governor to remove prisoners from association with other prisoners for up to 24 hours on his own authority, and for periods up to one month, renewable from month to month, on the authority of the Board of Visitors or the Secretary of State. Rule 43 prisoners were in one of two categories: those removed for their 'own protection', either at their own request or on the decision of the governor; and those removed as 'subversive' because they were seen as a threat to the maintenance of good order or discipline. In addition to Rule 43 prisoners, the segregation unit housed prisoners under Rule 48, who were awaiting adjudication in respect of charges for alleged offences against prison discipline, and prisoners who were undergoing cellular confinement as punishment, usually awarded by the governor under Rule 50 of the Prison Rules, but exceptionally by the board of visitors under Rules 51 and 52 dealing with 'grave offences' and 'especially grave offences' respectively.

Prison Department had not yet developed the uniform procedures for the operation of segregation units in dispersal prisons, but Brian Howden had already introduced some 'minor changes' that tightened up the regime. Broadly speaking, the staff distinguished between prisoners undergoing punishment and those awaiting the hearing of charges on the one hand, and the two types of Rule 43 prisoners on the other, for most practical purposes. Thus the unlocking procedure was as follows. Two discipline officers would unlock punishment prisoners and those awaiting adjudications one at a time, escort them to the recess for slopping out, and then return them to their cells. Only after the last punishment prisoner had been returned to his cell did one of the officers then begin to unlock the Rule 43s, who were allowed to proceed to slopping out as a group. The presence of two officers during the unlocking of each prisoner undergoing punishment or awaiting a hearing was justified to us on two grounds: first, that if a prisoner made trouble he could more easily be restrained; and second, that should a prisoner attempt to fabricate a case against an officer there would be two witnesses against him. On the occasions when we were observing in the segregation unit there was no doubt that there was a rather heavy atmosphere even if it could not be described as particularly tense, but perhaps not surprisingly we saw no incidents.

For all prisoners in the segregation unit locking and unlocking was a regular and frequent part of the daily round, and each time it followed much the same pattern that we have described for the mornings. Prisoners undergoing punishment were allowed out of their cells only for slopping out, for the collection of some meals which were then eaten in cells, and for periods of exercise. Rule 43s did have a substantial period of association, though not as much as prisoners in other halls, and they too ate all meals in cells. Both punishment and Rule 43 prisoners worked in cells, and were visited daily by the governor and the medical officer. At weekends the regime in the other halls was varied to take account of the facts that only a few prisoners engaged on essential jobs were required to work, and that the staff worked shorter duty hours. This meant essentially that the day started later and that more time was spent in association and recreational activities. But in the segregation unit it hardly mattered that the day started later. The rest of the routine was the same except that there was no work to do. As the governor said, the regime was firm enough to 'deter men from making a habit of visiting this part of the prison', at least during the summer of 1969.

8   Doing time in Albany Prison

In the present chapter we seek to convey how the staff and prisoners evaluated Albany Prison, how they 'made out' or 'got by' in the course of their stay there, and how they felt about the various changes that had taken place while they were there.

On doing time

Nobody likes doing time. Of course, almost every total institution holds to the belief that it provides something of a constructive nature for its inmates, and the modern prison is no exception. Virtually every prison or borstal governor we have spoken to has been able to point to some former inmate who has expressed his gratitude for a new life which he discovered in the institution. Indeed to the extent that anyone is able to change the direction of his life it would be surprising if some did not achieve such a change within prisons. And it is important to note that many of the prisoners we have spoken to *expect* their captors to provide them with an opportunity to reform or be rehabilitated. Regardless of whether they view the aims of the prison system, and the means which it offers to achieve those aims, with sympathy, cynicism or indifference, prisoners are apt to feel that the opportunity to reform, to be treated or to be rehabilitated is theirs by right. If the prison system stakes those claims, they suggest, it should be judged accordingly. But even those few prisoners who do 'reform' or who are 'rehabilitated' do not, in our experience, actually enjoy the process as it occurs in prison. However much they might look back on it as useful or even necessary, in general they would have preferred to be elsewhere and doing something else.

Every prison or borstal governor can also point to those who, far from being reformed or rehabilitated, seem to be completely dependent on the structured environment of the prison to maintain some semblance of balance and security in an uncertain, even hostile, world. It is said that when they are released they soon return, either by default because they are so inadequate on the outside that they can no longer function there, or by design because they so miss the security of the inside that they deliberately engineer a further conviction. Often, though by no means always, such persons are said to have a long history of institutionalization. But even though some prisoners seem to 'need' prison in this way, they are also, in our experience, acutely aware that they 'ought not' to need it. It seems likely that they feel at least the same kind of guilt about the use they make of prison, that was so eloquently expressed in the letters of James Blake (1970) about his repeated sojourns in *The Joint*. And if this is so, whatever benefits they receive must be somewhat mitigated.

But perhaps we should simply admit exceptions and say that hardly anybody likes doing time. For it is not vital to the argument. The central point is that *time*, for good or ill, is the very essence of imprisonment. Every person who receives that sentence from the courts has to come to terms with the fact that he or she has time to serve. And from the point of view of the prisoner it is not 'his' time that he is serving, for it is not of his choosing. His time was spent in his own way before he came into prison, and will be again when he gets out. The time he is serving now is but an interregnum, someone else's time imposed upon him, to be got through as best he can. Cohen and Taylor (1972, p. 93), in their excellent analysis of time and deterioration in long-term imprisonment, have expressed the view of the lifer: 'One may be serving life, but one is not serving my life.' For the prisoner the most important questions are: How much time? and how do I serve it? Most prisoners feel that they are serving too much and look for ways to cope; these may conceivably include such things as reform and rehabilitation. Even those prisoners who are dependent on the prison do not escape the bind of time. For not only may they find difficulty in admitting the fact that in some sense they benefit from prison in a way with which their peers are unlikely to feel sympathy, but sooner or later they may find that they are serving too little, that their time has come. Prison argot, on both sides of the Atlantic, is replete with time-laden concepts: 'hard time', 'good time', 'short time'; and no one is immune from the invasion of present consciousness by future dates: home leave boards, parole eligibility date, earliest date of release, and so on.

It is a commonplace of the prison literature that the prison staff are confined in and by the prison almost as much as their captives.

This is true in at least two senses: not only is the prison officer physically locked into the particular institution where he works, he is also metaphorically locked into the ways of thinking which direct the system as a whole. But it would be foolish to lose sight of the crucial difference between staff and prisoners, which is, of course, that the staff have the keys. They can and do leave the institution at night or when their duties are finished, and they can and do leave the system if, and when, they come to disagree with it. While the irony is not lost on prisoners that the staff spend their working hours in substantially the same physical conditions as themselves, they cannot overlook the fact that the staff are there of their own choosing. To the extent that anyone's job is 'their life', this is the life that prison staff sought out, or at least for which they were prepared to settle. Whether all or any custodial staff enjoy their time in prison is a moot point. Certainly at times of tension many staff have reported to us that they do not look forward to going into the prison, as we will be discussing later. But what is clear is that time has a different meaning for them than it has for prisoners. The time that prison staff spend in prison is their own, in a way that the prisoners' time is not. It is their job, and the time they spend on it is both useful and used. To be sure there are some staff, in prisons no less than in other career occupations, who, though they may be far from retirement, will report that they are now only marking time. For them 'time' may begin to resemble 'time' as it is perceived by prisoners. But they still have options open to them which are not available to prisoners, and they do not lose a conventional concern with hours of work and overtime. In the final analysis the opportunity to do something else at one's own discretion distinguishes spending time or marking time on the one hand, from doing time on the other. Both staff and prisoners are well aware of the distinctions.

Some writers have drawn other parallels between staff and prisoners. In the United States, for example, Sykes (1958) found cultural affinities between captor and captive at Trenton, New Jersey, although in upstate New York the Commission on Attica (1972) noted that such affinities, if they ever existed, had largely been obscured by racial differences. Similarly in England the kinds of commonalities between staff and prisoners at Pentonville described by the Morrises were either not found in the security wing at Durham by Cohen and Taylor or else were overshadowed by considerations of the status and notoriety of such prisoners as the train robbers. It is not altogether clear what the implications of social differences and similarities among staff and prisoners might be: the similarities at Trenton may have facilitated the corruption of authority of the guards, whereas the inability of rural white guards and urban black prisoners to communicate with each other may have been one of the main causes of the disaster at Attica. No doubt there will often be some similarities between staff and prisoners because of temporal, geographical and social factors affecting recruitment to both groups. But it is doubtful whether such similarities would lead, on their own, to the kind of 'problems of identity' which are suggested by the Morrises at Pentonville (Morris *et al.*, 1963, p. 100). For there are major differences in the conceptions of each other by custodial staff and prisoners which help them to maintain the social distance which is structured into their situation. Thus, in an ingeniously designed study of a state reformatory, Wheeler (1961) was able to show that in spite of close similarities in privately expressed attitudes to common problems, staff and inmates were none the less able to maintain widely divergent expectations of each other's responses. Moreover, inmates did not expect 'treatment' staff to respond differently from 'custody' staff; both were viewed as equally custodial.

Institutional staff, for the most part, are able to view their charges as morally inferior merely by virtue of the fact that the cons have been deemed by the courts as suitable cases for imprisonment. Whether imprisonment involves punishment or treatment makes no difference to the inferior status of the prisoner: he is still a suitable case for attention. The staff, on the other hand, have been deemed, at least inferentially, to be morally superior. They are, presumably, the exemplars of the 'good and useful life' enshrined in Prison Rule 1. It is on behalf of the Home Office and society, no less than themselves, that staff become locked into their environment, and it is in terms of these wider identifications that their time is to be viewed as usefully used. The prisoners, characteristically, are able to entertain a similar negative stereotype of the screws. In a system devoted to changing the moral outlook of one group by another, the moral stance of both is bound to be called into question. Given that the task of the staff involves locking, keeping and watching over, people in cages – no matter whether designed to punish or treat – the prisoners may feel justified in making a presumption that their custodians are at worst sadistic, or at best insensitive. Now that their own crimes are no longer visible, the prisoners may be able to ascribe the label of moral inferiority to staff as effectively as that label is applied to themselves. It would be surprising if such ideal-typical conceptions were universally held, and of course they are not. No doubt they are more widely held in some institutions than in others, but no one acquainted with prisons at all can have failed to have come across them. The point is that unless such stereotypes have been broken down to some degree and replaced by something else during the growth and development of any particular institution, it is unlikely that common background, or even common values, on the part of some prisoners and staff would be sufficient to cause major problems of identity for either side. Almost certainly the relationships between staff and prisoners in any institution will have to be interpreted in the light of the specific history and traditions of the particular prison as well as the social backgrounds from which the two groups are drawn. Cohen and Taylor have made much the same point in their analysis of the brief, but spectacular and traumatic, history of the security wing at Durham.

Throughout our discussions with staff and prisoners at Albany, and our subsequent more formal interviews, we were very conscious of the unique character of the institution in which we were working, and of the rapid changes it had already undergone and could expect in the future. We were anxious to discover in some detail how they felt about the regime which they had helped to create, and about the many events which were changing, perhaps even destroying, that regime. Our focus was thus a narrow one, and our approach grew out of the natural history of Albany Prison rather than from the existing literature about prisons and prison culture. We make no claim that our findings have any significance beyond the fences of Albany, for it was not our purpose to seek generalizations about imprisonment in any wider or more abstract sense. This has not stopped us from relating our findings to those of other researchers where we have felt justified in doing so. Nor would we wish to claim that there is any special virtue in our approach. Given the usual limitations on time and resources, however, it would quite simply have been a waste not to have explored the unique and changing situation of Albany as far as we could. The approach did enable us to gain some insight into the ways in which prisoners and staff adapted themselves to

Albany, and it did also help us to make sense of the events which occurred in Albany after we left. Perhaps we should say, however, that we do feel the study of the responses of prisoners, and especially of staff, to prisons is still in its youth if not its infancy, and that studies in the past have sometimes generalized findings prematurely with insufficient regard to the context in which they occurred. Just as the study by Cohen and Taylor is bounded by the context of very long sentences served in very secure conditions, so our study is bounded by the very newness of Albany and the experimental nature of its regime. What is clear, we believe, from both these studies is that a detailed knowledge of the context is vital to an understanding of the way in which persons adapt to imprisonment. They have to adapt not merely to imprisonment as such but also to the particular prison in which they work or are incarcerated.

An evaluation of Albany
We began our interviewing of staff and prisoners only after we had been in Albany for many months. We were then well known throughout the prison and perhaps the majority of our respondents were known personally to one or other of the research workers. There was little doubt that the part of the programme which our respondents enjoyed most was the opportunity to evaluate Albany. In the course of structured interviews with each member of our samples we talked about Albany in relation to other prisons they had spent or done time in, and we asked them to rate Albany as best, better than most, about the same as others, worse than most, or worst of all, in their experience. We then asked them what made Albany better or worse than other places in their view. Since we had by now a fair idea of what many liked and disliked about the prison we included a number of specific probes in order to get systematic data about the extent and strength of feeling on these issues. Everyone was also encouraged to raise any other matters of liking or disliking that we had not included. Finally, we asked every respondent whether they approved or disapproved of the various changes that had taken place in Albany since they had been there, or whether they were merely indifferent to them; and again we asked for reasons for their responses.

If most prisoners do not enjoy doing time, they are still aware that they can scarcely avoid doing it. None of the prisoners we spoke to entertained serious hopes of going 'over the wall'. Since that is the case, *where* they do time becomes an important consideration, and prisoners know only too well that some places are better than others. Almost all our sample were able to base their evaluation on the bedrock of extensive prison experience: even the 11 per cent who were undergoing their first sentence of imprisonment had been in at least one local prison before being transferred to Albany. The remainder had sampled many of Her Majesty's institutions: none had been in fewer than two local prisons before, and some had done time in four or five locals as well as three or more training prisons. Certainly their experience was at least as varied as that of the staff, and probably a good deal more so; if anything the self-reported details of prisoners' previous experience underestimated rather than overestimated the number of other prisons they had passed through.

All told, there was a quite remarkable consensus among both staff and prisoners in the summer of 1969 that Albany was a good place in which to do or spend one's time compared with other prisons. Not surprisingly, eight members of the central management meeting thought it the best prison they had been in and three, including the governor, thought it better than most. The three ex-members of the CMM also evaluated Albany as the best prison, while all the administrative and specialist staff we interviewed rated Albany favourably, with one exception who regarded it as an average prison. Approval of Albany was even more marked among prisoners than it was among uniformed staff. More than four out of every five prisoners in our sample, and nearly two out of every three discipline officers, thought that Albany was either better than most prisons or the best prison they had known. Indeed for both prisoners and uniformed staff the biggest single response category was that Albany was the best prison they had ever been in. The details are given in Table 8.1.

When we looked at these results in terms of the characteristics of our respondents we found that, among the prisoners, those who disliked Albany were, on average, younger, serving shorter sentences, more likely to have passed through approved schools and borstals before getting their main experience of imprisonment in local prisons, and less likely to have regular contact with the outside world through letters and visits than those who liked

Albany. Among the uniformed staff we found that liking of Albany was closely associated with seniority, higher ranking officers being much more likely to approve of Albany than basic-grade staff. Seniority, of course, was in turn related to age, length of service, and the number and type of previous institutions experienced. But when we examined the basic-grade staff separately those with service in several other prisons, and especially in in other training prisons or borstals, tended to like Albany whatever their age. Those with service in only one or two other establishments, almost always local prisons, tended to dislike Albany.

Table 8.1   Evaluation of Albany: prisoners and uniformed staff

Evaluation	Prisoners N=69* %	Uniformed staff N=54 %
1. Best prison	46.4	35.2
2. Better than most	36.2	29.6
3. About average	4.3	20.4
4. Worse than most	4.3	3.7
5. Worst of all	8.7	11.1
All responses	99.9	100.0

*Three prisoners declined to be interviewed from our sample of 72.

However, the liking or disliking of Albany was only a summary evaluation, apparently arrived at after weighing carefully the pros and cons of spending or doing time in the establishment. It was clear that there were many reasons for liking or disliking Albany, and many ways of coming to terms with it, which seemed to be associated with characteristic patterns of previous experience for both prisoners and staff. We discuss these in more detail below. But before doing so it is worth noting briefly how those who liked or disliked Albany in our samples were distributed among the halls and employment categories, which, as we indicated in chapter 7, offered different living and working conditions for the persons involved.

Prisoners and discipline officers were most likely to evaluate Albany highly if they lived or worked in A hall, and least likely to do so if they lived or worked in E hall. Among the prisoners in our sample from A hall, 89 per cent rated Albany as the best prison, compared with 72 per cent of prisoners from E hall, and 78 per cent from each of C and D halls. Thirty-five officers in our sample were regularly assigned to hall duties, excluding the principal officers who were formally responsible for the halls. A-hall officers were 7 to 1 in favour of Albany, C-hall were 6 to 2 in favour, D hall were 5 to 3 in favour, while E hall had only 3 in favour and 6 against. The two officers who worked in the segregation unit both viewed Albany negatively. It seems possible that both officers and prisoners here may have been responding to much the same things. The use of the ELSA system in A hall and the inconsistencies in the E hall routine were experienced by prisoners as real differences in regimes; for staff they represented real differences in their work situation.

Perhaps more important than hall differences were job differences. Among the prisoners, those who rated Albany highly were five times more likely to have changed jobs since they had been in the prison than those who rated Albany as an average, or worse than average prison. The difference was partly a function of length of time served in the prison, but when the number of jobs held was expressed as a ratio of time served, the former group had still changed jobs twice as frequently as the latter. This suggests that those who liked Albany may have been influenced in their evaluation by their greater success, through whatever means, in getting a job that suited them. Certainly well over half of this group were employed on jobs that had been rated as the more preferred, whereas three-quarters of the second group were employed in the tailoring industry which was generally viewed with disfavour. Even though the earnings among the latter were, on average, 25 per cent higher than those for the rest of the sample it seemed that income was only a comparatively minor element in the overall evaluation of Albany. As far as the staff were concerned, we have already noted that favourable evaluations of the prison were more likely to come from staff in the more senior ranks. In some cases the enthusiasm of higher-ranking officers may have been a diplomatic expression of loyalty because of their position in the management structure. But it may also reflect the fact that their rank ensured a greater social distance between themselves and the prisoners. Basic-grade staff, on the other hand, had no escape from daily contact with the inmates, in which they bore the brunt of implementing the Albany regime. Clearly this played some part in their evaluation of the prison, and negative views were much more frequently expressed by these officers.

Making out and getting by: strategies of prisoner response

Before we carried out our interviews many prisoners had already told us about why they liked or disliked Albany, and we tried to find out how widespread those views were. We encouraged our respondents to tell us in their own words what made Albany better or worse than other establishments. Where necessary we probed to ensure that we covered the following: the work situation, pay, amount of association, the administration of rules, type of supervision employed, ease of welfare contacts, relationships with officers, relationships with prisoners, ease of making applications, and ease of access for visitors. Not all of these were of equal importance, of course, and when respondents thought that they had no influence on them we took careful note of their indifference. Several matters were raised by respondents, and of these the one most frequently cited was the physical plant and amenities of the prison, which were welcomed by many prisoners.

Analysis of prisoner responses soon revealed that the same elements that we earlier referred to as the core of the Albany regime – the amount of association, the way the rules were interpreted and implemented, the type and amount of supervision employed, and the quality of relationships with officers – provided a focus around which the attitudes of prisoners crystallized. For the most part, those who disliked Albany regarded these features as operating seriously to the prison's detriment, whereas those who liked Albany felt that they worked in its favour. Further analysis, however, showed that the reasons for approval or disapproval differed quite widely among different groups of prisoners, and we were able to use their responses to the core elements of the regime as a basis for classifying modes of adaptation to the prison. We should mention that one other factor seemed to have an important bearing on the way prisoners reacted to the Albany regime: namely, their attitude towards other prisoners. As the New Jersey State prisoner explained to Gresham Sykes, 'the worst thing about prison is you have to live with other prisoners' (Sykes, 1958, p. 77). Few prisoners in Albany had anything favourable to say about their fellows. But whereas most of those who liked Albany managed to maintain a steady indifference towards other prisoners, half of those who disliked Albany expressed very negative views about their peers. The remaining areas about which we probed in the interviews did not differentiate our sample in any significant ways. Even though they were important to some individuals they seemed to matter much less to our respondents than the physical facilities and recreational opportunities which so many of them mentioned spontaneously.

Just as we knew in advance of our interviewing something of what prisoners liked and disliked about Albany, we could not help learning how some of our respondents had developed strategies for coping with what Sykes called the 'pains of imprisonment', and which enabled them to 'make out' or at least to 'get by' during their time in Albany. We were anxious to discover how far we could classify such strategies, and what, if any, relationship they bore to liking or disliking Albany, and to the experiences of prisoners before embarking on their present sentences. Neat conceptual classifications have a habit of falling apart when confronted with stubborn 'facts', and usually the more facts one has at one's disposal the less satisfactory does one find any conceptual categories. We had known some prisoners over a substantial period and in many situations, so that we 'knew' them in a way that is not often the case in sociological research. This knowledge, together with the statements offered by our sample in the course of our structured interviews, constituted a body of 'soft', but we think quite powerful, data. We had also collected a good deal of harder, factual data from prisoner records, class registers, letters and visits sheets, records of applications, and interviews designed to elicit frequency of contact with specialist staff, which could be used to validate and complement material gathered or acquired in other ways. Our preference was to move from these data to organizing concepts, rather than the other way around, especially since we suspected that Albany posed problems for prisoners that have not been dealt with in the literature before.

Nevertheless, one classification emerging from the work of Irwin and Cressey (1962) and developed later by Irwin (1970) seems to capture such fundamental aspects of criminal identity and prisoner response that it assumes almost an ideal-typical status. In spite of what seem to us quite wide divergencies between the cultural patterns to be found in English and American prisons, there is much in their classification of relevance to Albany.

Irwin notes that all prisoners are basically doing time, except those who are so unable to cope with imprisonment that they commit suicide or sink into psychosis. Those who do cope may be divided into prisoners who identify with, and orient themselves primarily towards, the world outside prisons and those whose horizons are bounded by the prison walls, within which they orient themselves to the inmate culture. Prisoners whose basic orientation is to the outside world may be further subdivided into those who wish to maintain their life patterns and identities untouched by the experience of imprisonment, and those who use the prison as an opportunity to make significant changes of identity and pattern of life. In effect, then, Irwin distinguishes three broad classes of prisoner who are likely to respond to prison in rather different ways. The professional thief, it is argued, regards prison as an unfortunate, but temporary, break in his outside career. He is oriented to the thief culture in the outside world and has no wish to change. His concern is to *do his own time* as quickly and as comfortably as he can. He will avoid trouble, secure a few luxuries if he can, find things to occupy himself, and do whatever he thinks is required of him by the authorities to secure his release at the earliest possible moment. By and large he knows how to do this, either from experience or from the hints he has picked up in the thief culture outside. Some prisoners, however, especially since the expansion of educational, training and treatment opportunities, do decide to attempt to change their life-styles, and follow an adaptation which Irwin describes as *gleaning*. In what is often a cumulative process such prisoners seek out every chance they can get to take courses, join self-help groups or attend therapy programmes in an effort to 'find themselves' and start anew. Sometimes professional thieves, aware that 'having a programme' may carry some weight with the parole board, or simply because they wish to 'retire', may turn to such avenues; but the adaptation is said to be most likely taken up by hustlers, drug users and the like. Finally, those prisoners who do not retain or never developed any real commitment to social worlds on the outside tend to make a world for themselves out of the prison and its culture. In the prison they become involved in the inmate social system of barter and exchange, in struggles for power and prestige, in the concern to acquire goods and services, and in the organization of gambling and rackets. This response is termed *jailing* by Irwin, and is said to be characteristic of 'state-raised youths' whose career through institutions from childhood has amply fitted them to grow into the role of 'convict'.

Of course, a number of prisoners fit none of these patterns, most notably perhaps the 'square john': a term for which we have found no general English equivalent which appears to command consensus in English prisons, nicely describing the conventionally upright man, not well acquainted with criminal behaviour systems, who finds himself in prison for a comparatively isolated offence such as embezzlement, incest, buggery, rape, or domestic murder. He typically finds prison life repugnant and experiences difficulty in operating by any of its standards, official or unofficial.

Irwin makes the point, and we must strongly reinforce it, that adaptations to prison are fluid. Though there is an element of strategic choice about these adaptations, the choices are not mutually exclusive. Most prisoners probably adapt in different ways at different times, and many follow elements of several adaptations at one and the same time. Irwin described the largest group in his sample as 'disorganized criminals' who, with no distinctive criminal life-style on the outside, were like 'human putty' on the inside, responding to forces outside their control. We suspect that every prisoner probably makes some effort at *doing his own bird* in English prisons, for at least part of his sentence, provided he is sure that he will be coming out within the reasonably foreseeable future (cf. Cohen and Taylor, 1972). It may well be that *doing time,* or something approximating it, is more common in England where the prisons are still largely populated by thieves, than it is in the United States, where the proportion of professional thieves in the prison population appears to be dwindling as the number of other, more militant, groups grows.

We have said that we preferred to move from our data to concepts rather than the other way round, and we should now say something about the way in which our classification was developed. The starting point for classification was provided by the comments offered by prisoners in their response to Albany evaluation questions. As we sorted these responses into groups, characteristic patterns of adaptation began to emerge. We then looked at other series of data, both 'hard' and 'soft', which could either offer some validation for the classification we were making or else could provide contextual information against which the responses could be interpreted. Some of the categories we derived seemed specific to Albany – at least we have not been able to discover them reported elsewhere in the literature – and we will discuss them more fully below. Others corresponded closely to the categories put forward by Irwin, and it will be helpful if we indicate at this point the operational definitions we employed for them. Prisoners were only counted as exhibiting the *gleaning* adaptation if what they told us was consistent with the picture we have described above *and* if they met certain criteria by way of attendance at classes and involvement with 'therapeutic' staff. We had data for class attendance for all the prisoners in our sample, as well as information about their contacts with the welfare officer, the chaplain, the psychologist and the tutor-organizer during the last two months before interview. We ignored contracts with the medical officer since we knew from what he told us that most of these were routine consultations. We did not count any contacts that were initiated by staff since these too were mostly for routine purposes. Nor did we count visits to the welfare officer at the prisoner's request when we knew that these were designed to cope with sudden domestic difficulties. Only prisoners who had themselves initiated the highest rates of contact with specialists, including those who were regular attenders at Alcoholics Anonymous, were deemed eligible to be included as adopting the *gleaning* response.

Again prisoners were only classed as having adapted by *jailing* if what they told us was compatible with an involvement in the inmate culture *and* if we could find additional evidence which independently corroborated such an involvement. It seemed to us that a most valuable indicator, though clearly not the only one, was the possession of contraband items. We have described earlier how we undertook a detailed inventory of every item contained in the cells of our sample prisoners, which was carried out with their permission and in their presence. In the course of this many unauthorized articles came to light: items of clothing, workshop equipment, food, stocks of tobacco, and so on. Most prisoners in possession of such items were very ready to tell us how they obtained them from the workshops, from stores, by smuggling them in on visits, or through 'deals' with other prisoners. Others showed us how they had refashioned uniforms so that they demonstrated their status within the prison community.

Some prisoners appeared to exhibit *jailing* and *gleaning* in approximately equal measures. For reasons we discuss more fully later we christened this category *opportunism*. Others exhibited *jailing* or *gleaning* to a minor degree, or only intermittently; and where other forms of adaptation were clearly more dominant we assigned them to the more dominant category.

We must be the first to admit that there is nothing hard and fast about the groupings we offer below. One or two prisoners possibly warranted marginal consideration for classification in one of the other categories as well as the one in which we finally located them, and there is inevitably some small measure of overlap. The differences are primarily differences of emphasis, and may be open to other interpretations besides those we have considered here. For this reason we have not attempted to subject our material to any statistical analysis. None the less we are confident that the classification does justice to the very full amount of data we had at our disposal. When we confronted our emerging classification with all the different kinds of data in the way we have described, some initial responses seemed more ambiguous than they had at first sight, and in these cases we preferred to make no classification. Since we erred on the side of caution, eight prisoners, or 11.6 per cent of our sample, remained unclassified at the end of the analysis.

Before describing the adaptations we should mention the operational definitions we employed for two concepts that we had taken over from Irwin. 'State-raised youths' were defined for our purposes as prisoners who had passed through either Home Office approved schools or borstals or both before coming into prison. In a few cases clear evidence of an institutional background in the care of local authorities or at reform schools in Scotland was also taken as a criterion. Nearly 54 per cent of the sample were state-raised youths on this definition, though it should be noted that many had long since lost the bloom of youth. 'Orientation to the outside world' was defined by the frequency of contacts through letters and visits. Prisoners who had close to the maximum permitted number of letters and visits were given a score of 2;

those with irregular letters or visits, or who received regular letters but no visits, were assigned a score of 1; and those who had hardly any such contacts or none at all were given a score of 0.

Adaptation 1: Uncertain negative retreat
Not all prisoners who cannot cope with prison sink into psychosis or commit suicide. They may instead attempt to cope, fail, and then proceed to what we have termed an *uncertain negative retreat*.

This adaptation was characteristic, in varying degrees, of all those prisoners who disliked Albany and who accounted for 17.4 per cent of our sample. Though these 12 prisoners can scarcely be regarded as a group, because their response to Albany was a somewhat solitary one, they shared certain characteristics in common. They were younger than the rest of the sample, on average, by five years, and indeed were younger than any other adaptive group in the prison, with a mean age of 26.9 years and a range from 23 to 34 years. Eleven of them were state-raised youths and, with a mean score of 0.42, they had fewer contacts with the outside world than any other group except one. But they had not made a world for themselves inside the prison, as Irwin's work would suggest. It may be that their lack of contact with the outside world was strategically decided, in an attempt to make doing their time easier; for some of these prisoners found waiting for letters and visits much too anxiety-provoking. Certainly with these prisoners, as throughout the sample, rates of outside contact bore little relationship to marital status or area of residence. It is true that seven of these men were currently in the middle stage of their sentences, a time when the 'pains of imprisonment' are said to be at their height and reliance on inmate culture at its strongest; but we could find no evidence, from what they said or independently, that any of them were currently involved in the inmate social system. In any case for these men the pains of imprisonment would not last much longer, for they were among the shortest-serving prisoners in Albany. None was serving longer than 36 months and the mean sentence was 29.3 months. Nor were they experiencing the shock of imprisonment for the first time: all had been in prison before and some had been 'inside' many times. However, their experience of imprisonment was almost entirely confined to short sentences served in local prisons, usually in Wandsworth. When we looked at their criminal offences we found that all but one were serving time for various forms of breaking and entering or relatively straightforward larcenies, and as far as we could tell from lists of previous convictions they had been consistently oriented to these kinds of theft for some time. The single exception was a prisoner sentenced for obtaining goods by a false pretence. These were not disorganized criminals, in Irwin's sense of that term, for they had well-defined patterns of crime and firmly established criminal identifications. Nor did they present the devil-may-care attitude towards 'fucking-up' the authorities that Irwin associates with disorganized criminals. Some of them did seem to show, however, the defeatist attitude described by Irwin that they were 'born to lose', even though their basic identification was with more successful thieves than themselves.

None of these prisoners liked Albany. Almost half of them disapproved of the amount of association because there was too much of it. It was argued, sometimes with vehemence, that so much association made the 'bloody time drag' or the 'day too long', because 'time passes quicker when you're banged up'. Patrick was serving three years for burglary. (We have provided false names, and sometimes changed minor details to protect the identity of respondents.) He told us that 'if you are unlocked all day you are open to discipline, aren't you: if you are banged up you're away from all that'. David was also serving three years for burglary and made much the same point: 'there is too much aggro here whenever you come out of your cell'. Although as many approved of the amount of association as disapproved, it was usually welcomed on purely instrumental grounds. The comment of one prisoner was typical: 'I don't want to know about association but I like to have the door unlocked so I can go to the john without asking.'

Ten disapproved of the officers in Albany and the way in which they administered the rules; and while fewer disapproved of the type of supervision most of the remainder were indifferent rather than approving. Some of their views on these matters had already been anticipated in earlier responses. Officers were seen by some as young, inexperienced and interfering. As Patrick said, 'the screws here are children playing with something that they don't know how to use' – a view which appears to contain a reference to the case-officer system. By others they were seen as two-faced: 'they preach one thing and do another'. In large part the trouble with the officers had to do with the way in which they interpreted the Albany rules and the way they exercised supervision. The comments came thick and fast, and a few brief quotations give some idea of the depth of feelings involved: 'you can't win here, there just aren't any basic rules and you feel that someone is going to pounce on you any time'; 'you don't know where you stand here – I think they make up the rules as they go along'; 'they are always changing their minds about what you can do – I'm sure they only do it to stir you up'; 'there is too much niggling and pettiness here'. Perhaps David summed it up best when he said, 'I wish they'd make their bloody minds up; I'd go back to Wandsworth tomorrow if I could, at least I know where I stand there.'

What added to the difficulties of these prisoners was that they found their fellow-inmates a problem and a threat. They thought of them as 'nutters', 'grasses' or 'fairies', or simply as 'untrustworthy'. One said that 'with so little supervision you just are not safe with these queers about', while another, who echoed the sentiments of several of his peers, told us that 'everything gets nicked in here, you can't trust anybody and nobody does anything about it'.

It is hard to resist the conclusion that these prisoners were not having difficulty in coping with imprisonment – they had after all experienced that before – but they simply could not come to terms with the particular regime in Albany. Had they been in Wandsworth, they argued, they would have had no difficulty in 'doing a bit of quiet bird', sticking to the rules and making few contacts with either staff or prisoners. They tried to do that in Albany, but felt that it just was not a proper prison in which they could carry it through. A few had tried jailing; and Patrick had even attempted to glean for a time, but then dropped out of classes and resorted to writing an occasional complaining letter to the prison magazine, the *Albany Argus*. When they ventured out of their cells they felt subject to interference from staff and to provocation from other prisoners. If they could not rely on their fellow-prisoners, the problem of living through long periods of association which, as they saw it, were poorly supervised by inexperienced or two-faced staff who made up the rules as they went along, made them yearn for a return to Wandsworth. But they could not return to Wandsworth, and they reacted with differing degrees of negativism, sometimes involving truculent outbursts with staff or prisoners, only to beat an uncertain retreat again into the safety of their cells. We suspect, from the accounts we have come across, that much the same kind of response was made by the so-called passive inadequate preventive detainees when they were exposed to the new regime in Blundeston some years ago.

Adaptation 2: Secondary comfort indulgence
What the uncertain negative retreatists lacked was any visible strategy which could enable them to make out in Albany. Some prisoners, who otherwise resembled the retreatists in their negative evaluation of the core elements of the regime, were able to get by during their stay by indulging themselves in the *secondary comforts* that the prison provided.

Eleven prisoners, accounting for 15.9 per cent of our sample, took this form of adaptation. They made much the same kinds of comment about the association in Albany, about the officers and the way in which they interpreted the rules and supervised the halls, as did the retreatists. But they were much less inclined to hanker for a return to Wandsworth. Charlie, an older prisoner doing three years for attempted buggery, particularly resented the disjunction between the promises of the case-officer system and the reality. He described his experiences with staff as 'painful'. He, and several others, saw the staff as 'interfering' and the general philosophy of the management as 'too ambitious'. The members of this group were less likely to see their fellow-prisoners as a personal problem. When they did refer to other prisoners it was often in terms of some conception of the welfare of the community. A fairly typical remark here was voiced by Nick, a false pretender who had got three years for his latest offence: 'Some of the others don't appreciate what they have got here: everything gets kicked and broken – it would be better if they had to earn some of their privileges.'

If others did not appreciate the facilities that were available in Albany, these prisoners certainly did, and it was in their spontaneous expression of enthusiastic approval for the amenities that they principally differed from the retreatists. Whereas Patrick among the retreatists grudgingly admitted that the facilities in Albany were quite good, this did not influence his overall evaluation of the prison. For Charlie, on the other hand, the physical environment of Albany was enough to make his life bearable and to enable him to evaluate Albany favourably in spite of his rejection of its basic philosophy. Charlie was particularly pleased about the new design and the general cleanliness of the buildings, which, he said, did not make one feel 'that generations of poor wretches had been through here before'. Other comments were that the living accommodation was 'superior', the prison was 'more spacious', the sports and recreation opportunities were 'better and much more widely available', and that the bathing, washing and toilet facilities were 'much more hygienic and you can use them when you like'. Some of these prisoners especially appreciated the access to night sanitation in A hall, even when they did not benefit directly themselves. One or two prisoners seemed to be helped through their otherwise negative feelings towards Albany by having a good job in the prison – Charlie, for example, worked on the records party for the deputy governor – or by their earnings, though these factors seemed to weigh less in the balance than the sheer physical amenities of the prison.

The prisoners who adapted in this way had little in common apart from their response to Albany, and they did not in any sense form a cohesive group. They ranged in age from 22 to 44 years with a mean age of 31.9 years. They came from a variety of social backgrounds: although four had been 'state-raised' only one of these could still be regarded as youthful. Between them they had committed offences which covered almost the whole range from sexual offences, woundings and arson, through embezzlement and receiving to burglary and theft. Moreover, except in one or two cases, there was no consistent pattern in their criminal histories.

All but one were serving short sentences of between 18 and 36 months – the exception being a prisoner serving five years for receiving – and the mean sentence was 30.3 months. Two had not been to prison before. But the remainder had served a few moderate sentences in the past, and all but two of these had spent some time in other training prisons with which they could compare Albany. There were almost as many prisoners who maintained regular contact with the outside world through letters and visits as there were who did not, so that the mean contact score for the group was 0.91.

We were left with the feeling that many of the prisoners who took this adaptation were in fact 'square johns' who would have had difficulty doing time almost anywhere else. In a more traditional prison, with their often fussy conventional attitudes, they would have been oppressed by the staff, by their fellow-prisoners and by the general drudgery of the routine and the meanness of the conditions. Few of them had anything pleasant to remember about Wandsworth. When they came to Albany, however, they found that its new facilities were in striking contrast to what they had come to expect of prison. They saw in Albany hotel-like qualities which provided a link with more civilized living on the outside, and this enabled them to get by. There were also some persistent thieves, however, like James, the E hall cleaner who was serving yet another sentence for burglary, who adapted in this way. They were insufficiently cool not to show their extreme resentment at the intrusions into their privacy, but unlike the retreatists they were well able to recognize the comforts available and to take advantage of them.

We should make it clear that other prisoners in Albany also liked the physical environment, but for them the facilities were not the one redeeming feature in an otherwise bleak landscape. We should also point out that for all their emphasis on secondary comforts, the prisoners we have described here did not see the use of the facilities as an opportunity to reconstruct their lives. None of them was involved in gleaning. Many did not regard themselves as criminal and therefore saw no need for change. Those who did have established criminal identities would have been happiest if they had been left alone, and did not wish to change. If anything, then, this adaptation was a variant of doing time, though the prisoners who took this course lacked the careful detachment which was exhibited by some prisoners who were more skilled at doing their bird.

Adaptation 3: Jailing
Both the preceding types of adaptation seemed to be somewhat Albany-specific in character. *Jailing,* however, is a more universal phenomenon in the prison world, and Albany provided excellent opportunities for anyone who wished to adapt in this way. Eleven prisoners, or 15.9 per cent of our sample, were so categorized.

They would probably have responded by jailing in whatever prison they were in, though all of them expressed their satisfaction at being in Albany rather than elsewhere. They did find them-selves in something of a dilemma, however, when they came to assess Albany in more detail. As self-conscious carriers of the inmate culture they could scarcely subscribe to the formal aims of the Albany regime. Albany was 'not a proper prison' in the eyes of any self-respecting con and they felt bound to say so. They ridiculed the induction scheme and the case-officer system, complained about the staff who were 'always changing their minds', and said that they would rather be back in Wandsworth. But they did not really mean that, and their flippancy mocked the earnestness with which the retreatists had used the same words. It was clear that they were aware that confusion over the rules and as to where people stood could work to their own advantage. Almost without exception they applauded the freedom afforded in Albany and the virtual impossibility of supervising the halls. In interview they made dark hints about their activities and sought to imply their involvement in the inmate social system through a studied and knowing understatement. John, a burglar serving two years, was employed as a centre cleaner, a job that gave him access to staff and the chance of acquiring information which he felt could be used to manipulate others. He told us 'there is virtually no supervision here' and, winking broadly, that this gave him 'plenty of scope'. Gerry had spent his childhood in care and his youth in approved schools and borstal. He was now serving 21 months for housebreaking. He had got himself a job in the clothing stores, which gave him a ready-made sphere of influence among those prisoners concerned with smartness and style. He was surprised that he had 'so much freedom to move around and make contacts' and that there was so little 'comeback' for any of his activities. John and Gerry, like others in this group, thought the physical facilities in Albany were excellent. They regarded them as a bonus which they were happy to use, but which they could have as easily done without.

While those engaged in jailing did not constitute a self-contained group, they were at least known to each other. Together with other prisoners outside our sample they formed a number of interlocking cliques, sometimes in competition with one another in the illicit market for goods and services within the prison. A large number of prisoners in our sample had at least one contraband item in their cells, if only sewing thread that originated in the tailoring shops. And it was common for prisoners to inherit such things as books, pin-ups and so on from prisoners being discharged, or else to exchange goods among themselves. As we have noted, hall staff did not try to keep a check on these matters. But the prisoners we have characterized as jailing had an extensive range of contraband in their cells, and apparently well-established sources for obtaining further supplies. Several prisoners admitted to stealing from other cons as a way of acquiring wealth. Some also claimed that they had collected goods with the permission or the connivance of staff. One prisoner stated that he acquired things from other prisoners returning from home leave, another that he had material brought in from outside by various means. Most of these prisoners were involved in gambling, either in the card schools to be seen in the halls each evening, or in racing, or both. Many items thus changed hands in settlement of debts. Tom, a prisoner serving five years for larceny as servant, continued his criminal life-style in Albany by stealing from the hospital where he worked. Gerry had spare overalls and clothing above the standard issue, as well as articles he had made from materials taken from the stores. He had exchanged clothes for soap and razor blades and had 'sold' clothing for tobacco, which he had in turn used to buy himself further material comforts. John told us, while we were taking his cell inventory, that he had built up substantial 'invest-ments' for his release through his activities as a tobacco baron. He claimed that he first bought and saved tobacco out of his earnings. He then sold it in small quantities to other cons on condition that they first arranged to send money (£1 for half an ounce) to his private cash account from their resources outside the prison.

We did not entirely believe in John's exploits, though they clearly played an important part in the image he created for himself in Albany. For all the talk and swagger there seemed to us to be no real 'tough guys' among this group, and we sometimes doubted whether performance matched up to aspirations. We certainly found a good deal of immature posturing – Gerry, for example, laid claim to the affections of a female member of staff – but we could find little evidence of leadership or organization either among our sample prisoners or among other members of their cliques. From time to time isolated incidents of violence occurred among these prisoners, but there was no persistent or systematic use of intimidation to secure the payment of debts or to enforce inmate rules during our stay in Albany.

The immaturity of this group is not surprising, for only the uncertain negative retreatists were younger and had more prison-ers from institutional backgrounds. Those who adapted by jailing ranged in age from 21 to 34 years with a mean age of 28 years. Seven of the 11 were state-raised youths who had graduated from borstal. These were not recent graduates, however. All but one had been to prison before, and most had been in adult prisons on more than four occasions. Unlike the retreatists, their previous encounters with prison had usually included training prisons, and thus they could make comparative judgments about Albany. They were neither shocked nor greatly impressed by the Albany philosophy, though some were mildly surprised that it should have gone so far. They did not expect it to be successful, since their own previous exposure to treatment and training had had little effect. As far as they were concerned Albany simply provided even more of a good thing, and if they were now back on the inside again they might as well take advantage of it.

Two prisoners had been convicted for robbery and one for malicious damage, while eight were doing time for various forms of breaking and entering offences and larceny. Although many of them seemed well established in their thieving they were hardly successful thieves. Some were undoubtedly disorganized criminals of the kind who make up a pool of criminal labour waiting to be recruited for jobs by more sophisticated thieves. John, for example, had a record stretching back for 12 years, in which occasional breaking offences were interspersed with offences of indecent exposure and drunkenness. Several had been hell raisers with a pattern of taking and driving away, and hooliganism, before settling down to breaking and entering. Some of the swagger adopted by these men in prison seemed to provide a cover for the expectation of failure on the outside: the attempt to maintain an image of running the prison themselves offered them a more viable method of appearing successful than their criminality. At least it gave them an opportunity to 'mess up the authorities' or to 'screw the screws' from time to time. Be that as it may, these prisoners had begun to attract the displeasure of the courts, and were serving sentences ranging from 18 to 78 months with a mean of 39.6 months.

In Albany jailing was not restricted to those who had failed to develop or retain their commitments to the outside world, as Irwin suggests. Six prisoners maintained very frequent contact through both letters and visits, and one wrote and received letters regularly but saw no visitors. Only four prisoners in this group had little or no contact with the outside world. Indeed the contact score for this group was 1.18, one of the highest for any adaptive category in the prison. It was the professional time-doer who, whatever his commitment to the outside world, cut himself off from the community while he was in prison, as we shall be reporting later. As for other categories of prisoner, contacts with the outside were not related to marital status, area of residence, nor stage of sentence. Only a few of the prisoners we have categorized as jailing were in the middle portion of their sentences, the majority being quite close to release. This, of course, does not constitute evidence one way or another in relation to the so-called U-curve hypothesis (Wheeler, 1961; Garabedian, 1963), for we have no way of knowing how many other prisoners may have moved towards the jailing response and then away again in the course of their sentences.

Adaptation 4: Gleaning

As the facilities in prisons improve and the numbers of specialist staff employed in them increase so the possibility of adapting to imprisonment by *gleaning* becomes more attractive. The philosophy of Albany was, in effect, designed to promote the gleaning response. As initiated by David Gould, the concept of therapeutic anxiety was intended to motivate prisoners to contemplate their situation and to think about the possibilities of changing it. Any prisoners who could thus be provoked into desiring a change in their life-style should be provided with the facilities with which to bring it about. Under Brian Howden, and especially after the abandonment of the two-shift system of working and the upgrading of Albany security, the official emphasis changed. Instead of provoking prisoners into action the task was redefined as the provision of tacit support for prisoners who sought help, in so far as this was compatible with the new emphasis on security and industrial production. Had Albany continued along the path first mapped out for it, the gleaning response would probably have been more frequent. In fact, it was much less common than jailing. Only six prisoners, or 8.7 per cent of our sample, could be classified as gleaners.

In general gleaners found Albany greatly to their liking. The core elements of the regime were seen as an attempt to treat prisoners as responsible and intelligent human beings. In so far as complaints were raised, these were voiced not against the philosophy but the efficiency with which it was implemented. Stanley had a long record of petty offences and was now serving two years for larceny as servant. Though he had been to prison before this was his first time in a training prison, and he saw

Albany as offering him his first real chance for reform. He was critical of the case-officer system, not because of its intrusiveness but because he could not see enough of his case officer: 'If you're going to have a case-officer system it's got to be organized so that it works better.' Alex was a gambler. He had a short, but persistent, record for larceny as servant and was determined to kick his habit and qualify for a different job. His only complaint was that some of the younger officers did not match up to his experience with some of the older and, in his view, more sympathetic officers. Most of these prisoners liked the facilities and amenities in Albany, though they were mainly concerned with making satisfactory contacts with staff. All the prisoners we classified as gleaners had made regular and frequent contact at their own request with one or more of the specialists: psychologist, welfare officer, chaplain, psychotherapist and education and tutor-organizer, in an attempt to 'find themselves'. All had also attended at least two educational classes a week during their stay at Albany, usually with a view to getting a qualification at the end of the course or when they were released.

The prisoners who adapted to Albany by gleaning ranged in age from 24 to 48 years with a mean age of 34 years. They were serving sentences of between 24 and 84 months, with an average of 45.5 months. They came from a variety of backgrounds and were currently sentenced for a mixed bag of offences, from buggery through larceny as servant to shopbreaking. Only one was a state-raised youth, and he was now aged 35 years. All except one had been to prison before, though none had previously experienced a training prison. What they seemed to share in common was the recognition, or perhaps it was only the hope, that Albany offered them a real chance to re-establish themselves after release. How realistic their hopes were is another matter, but what is important here is that their expectations were sufficient to sustain them during their sentence. As might be expected from such an optimistic group, oriented to their future on the outside, these prisoners also had the highest rates of contact through letters and visits of any groups in the prison, with a score of 1.33.

Before leaving this discussion of gleaning we should mention that the concept is not without its problems, and that these are of no less importance for the prison authorities than they are for research workers. As we have noted, the formal rhetoric of the prison system suggests that gleaning is a preferred adaptation as far as the authorities are concerned. But since it is the only adaptation which requires a major identity change on the part of the prisoner, those who seek to use it are likely to have their motives called into question. In deciding whether or not to include a prisoner in this category we were aware of framing the question 'is this *real* gleaning or merely the representation of such for some ulterior motive?' By using the rather stringent criteria of interview responses combined with records of attendance at classes and visits to specialist staff we probably excluded one or two 'genuine' if less diligent gleaners from our category. It seems likely from our data, in any case, that many other prisoners had made attempts to glean from time to time but, for whatever reason, were not able to sustain the response, and after a time resorted to alternative modes of adaptation. There were certainly a number of prisoners who gave every indication of both the jailing *and* the gleaning response. After careful consideration we finally decided that this was essentially a variant of jailing and that the gleaning was not oriented to a change of identity but to an opportunistic use of the facilities available. We discuss this response more fully below. But, if the research was faced with such questions, much the same problem must be regularly presented to all those concerned in the treatment of offenders as they evaluate their charges. Many 'genuine' gleaners may thus be put off if their motives are put in doubt at the first hesitant step.

The problems are not limited to an evaluation of motives. As far as the authorities are concerned at least two practical problems can arise. The first is the problem of rationing. If everybody gleaned the resources could not meet the demand. Already the prison medical service is no longer so willing as once it was to remove tattoos, even though prisoners may claim that these interfere with their rehabilitation. The second, albeit a less immediate problem, is that if prisoners persistently gleaned the general level of educational achievement among prisoners could begin to exceed that of the officers who guard them. In the circumstances it would not be surprising if the authorities gave blessing in principle but backpedalled in practice as far as gleaning is concerned.

Adaptation 5: Opportunism
Six prisoners met the objective criteria which we set up for both the jailing *and* the gleaning adaptations. That is to say they had substantial quantities of contraband in cells, participated in

gambling, altered their uniform so as to appear more modishly dressed and so on, yet they also attended classes regularly and made frequent contact with specialist staff. All of them were thieves, mostly of long standing, and five of them were state-raised youths. In these respects, as well as in the degree of contact with the outside world, they closely resembled those who took the jailing response. But they were somewhat older, with an average age of 30.2 years, and were serving substantially shorter sentences, on average 27.5 months, than their jailing counterparts. Two had only been to local prisons in the past, but the remainder had all had previous experience of training prisons. These prisoners did not brag about their exploits. Indeed their involvement in the inmate social system was often not at all apparent during interview and did not emerge until we discussed cell inventories. But their approach to the facilities and staff in Albany was much more cynical than that put forward by those who maintained themselves by gleaning. As Robbie, who had been in and out of institutions for 25 years since he first went to a reform school for stealing a bicycle, remarked: 'I don't like discussing my private affairs with anyone, but if they want to run a case-officer system I'll find something to tell them.' And Don, who was already doing his second stretch in Albany, told us that 'you get good hospital treatment here, you know, better than other prisons and better than outside'. Many prisoners go to classes to fill in time, or to see what it is like, though often they attend one or two sessions before dropping out and trying something else. Don, however, attended classes voraciously: 'Some of these blokes are very interesting you know. I try to get to as many classes as I can.' But he was not seeking qualifications, not did he hope to effect any change in his way of life. Classes, of course, did fill the time, and Don got very bored at weekends when there was nothing much to do except gamble. But he was aware that classes were an approved activity: 'It can't do you any harm if they think you're getting a bit of an education, can it?' During the week he could usually make contact with the staff for one reason or another. Again it filled the time, and nothing was lost by chatting up the welfare staff.

Although these were far from successful criminals, they seemed a more sophisticated group than those who adapted by jailing alone. They were well versed in prison culture and knew how to obtain what they needed in the inmate social system. Indeed jailing was their own basic response, but they were more subtle in their approach, and they could see more fruitful ways of presenting themselves in public. They took full advantage of whatever opportunities presented themselves.

Adaptation 6: Doing your own bird
At the opposite end of the spectrum from the retreatists there were nine men, accounting for 13 per cent of our sample, who had no difficulties whatever in coping with Albany. As far as we could judge they responded no differently to Albany than they would have to any other prison. They did not have problems about knowing where they stood, because they drew their own lines which were well within anything demanded of them by the authorities and behind which they could stand with relative safety from the intrusion of others.

It is not particularly illuminating to quote from the interviews with these men because they sometimes used words as much to conceal as to reveal their views. Doug, for example, responded with such apparent enthusiasm that Albany sounded far too good to be true. Alf, on the other hand, was cool and objective and gave us a very detailed analysis of what was happening in the prison, though he was not in the least concerned that any of this really affected him. Alf was, in fact, one of our key contacts in the prison, a man to whom we often turned for diagnostic comment and opinion. Most of them, like Edward, simply regarded Albany as an easy nick whose regime was really a matter of indifference to them.

By and large, we established that they would have preferred less interference in their lives from both staff and prisoners, but they did not let it trouble them and they accepted it as the price they had to pay for a more relaxed environment. They enjoyed such comforts as were provided and were happy to operate within the official system to better their lot if they could. But they did not expose themselves to risks through direct participation in the inmate social system. And if life became less comfortable, well, they could cope with that too. Thus George had made several unsuccessful applications for a change of labour until, so he said, he had finally made contact with one of the instructors who was able to recommend him for the job he wanted in the carpentry shop. Alf had secured for himself one of the most comfortable jobs available in Albany, which brought him into daily contact with prisoners from other halls as well as with important members of staff. He saw himself, and was seen by others, as a political bridge between staff and prisoners, being one of the few men who could talk to, and command the respect of, both sides. Alf still hoped to pull off the big job one day when he got out, and if he succeeded he would retire. If not he had no illusions that he would be back, though that held no terrors for him. We had no doubt that Alf was a shrewd manipulator of men within Albany. But he was careful never to be involved in anything that was likely to attract attention to himself – and he had never been on a discipline charge. Alf, like several of these men, could sense the aggro coming from whatever quarter, and he always managed to avoid it.

We came to think of these prisoners as the 'top men' in Albany – at least in 1969. Had they wished to do so they could have utilized the younger opportunists and the jailers quite effectively for their own ends, but they were more interested than most in keeping the place a quiet and easy nick. Though they were resilient enough to hold their own in any company, and would not have been pushed around, it is doubtful that we would have considered them 'top men' in a number of other prisons, or indeed in Albany at a later date. They were established professional thieves, though one had lately turned to blackmail, and they were neither particularly notorious nor especially successful in their criminal careers. But they had made a living out of crime, they did have a lot of experience in the criminal world outside, and they knew how to handle themselves in prison. Unlike the opportunists and those engaged in jailing, who are regarded as 'hotheads', 'tearaways' and 'borstal boys', the top men were respected for their coolness in any situation, their capacity to survive and their ability to do their bird quietly.

With the exception of Tim, a scrap merchant who had made a living by seeking his own supplies of lead, brass and copper and who had, to his delight and surprise, been sent down for only 18 months, all these men were serving between 48 and 84 months. The mean sentence for the group was 66.7 months. They were older men, aged between 28 and 53 with a mean age of 41.9 years. Between them they had vast experience of the prison system, mostly accumulated in a few, well-spaced, heavy sentences rather than the more familiar pattern of many short periods of confinement. They had the lowest contact rates of any group in the prison, with a mean score of 0.33. Again this was not related to marital status, area of residence, or stage of sentence; and the breaking of contact with the outside world seemed to be a deliberate act of policy on their part. They were better able to do their time if they maintained the sharpest possible distinction between life inside and life outside.

Other adaptations

As we pointed out earlier, there is nothing very hard and fast about the way in which prisoners adapt to their situation. Most tried to get on with the business of doing time, but they probably tried out a number of strategies before settling into a mode of adaptation that seemed viable or at least open to them. Three prisoners in our sample could best be described as in the process of *finding their feet.* None had been in Albany for very long and they presented themselves rather diffidently expressing cautious approval of the prison. Two were among the youngest prisoners in Albany and both had been convicted of theft. On the basis of their responses in interviews it was clear that they identified with prisoners who adopted the jailing response, but neither had yet become significantly involved in the inmate culture, presumably for lack of opportunity. The third was the oldest prisoner in our sample and had been convicted for embezzling. He had been assigned to work as the chapel cleaner, possibly because he expressed strong religious beliefs. From what he told us in interview he seemed very likely to adapt by gleaning, but thus far the only positive step he had taken in this direction was his attendance at church services.

There were two prisoners who passed at least some of their time by *campaigning,* but since both of them achieved a successful outcome, this did not become a way of life. One, sentenced for buggery and working in the library when we knew him, had in fact conducted his campaign to achieve a change of labour from the workshops. He had made frequent applications to see the hall PO, the deputy governor and the governor, and had even petitioned the Home Office. Once the campaign succeeded he seemed to maintain himself, at least partly, by writing stories, articles and letters for the prison magazine. The other was a young man in prison for simple larceny. He had developed something of a missionary zeal and began a campaign lasting several months to get permission to make tape recordings for broadcasting to geriatric patients in St. Mary's Hospital opposite the prison. The campaign was successful, and regular recording sessions were in fact held. The very success of this campaign provided the prisoner concerned with a viable method of adaptation throughout the rest of his stay.

Finally, one prisoner seemed to be in a class by himself. He claimed to be involved in the inmate culture, though he was certainly not attached to any of the cliques we identified. He attended classes regularly and came to some of our research meetings, though as often as not he interrupted the proceedings or walked out. He had opinions on everything and these were noisily expressed in public outbursts. He responded instantly to all provocations, and he had often been to 'the block' for infringing disciplinary rules. On one occasion it was alleged to us that he had been beaten up by a group of staff known as 'the heavy mob' while in the segregation unit. He was universally held in low esteem by staff and inmates because he just could not keep his cool. We could not help but think that his response of *blowing his top* was a very hard way of doing time.

There remained eight prisoners, 11.6 per cent of our sample, whom we were unable to classify. There was nothing distinctive about the responses of these prisoners when considered as a group. Often their remarks in interviews seemed mildly inconsistent if not contradictory, which suggested to us that they had no strong identifications of their own but were repeating a hodgepodge of views that they had picked up from staff and fellow prisoners. With one or two exceptions we did not get to know these prisoners well. We suspect that some of them may have contributed to the stereotype held by several officers that Albany prisoners were whining children, unable to look out for themselves. And some were probably viewed by other prisoners as 'nutters' or 'fairies'. Judging from the information we had on criminal careers and social backgrounds, at least half of them could be regarded as rather inadequate and disorganized criminals, and two were classic examples of 'square johns'.

Adaptations in context
In Table 8.2 we have tried to set out in summary fashion the interconnections between biographical background variables and modes of adaptation for our sample of prisoners when faced with the specific features of the Albany regime.

Table 8.2   Modes of adaptation by prisoner sample: N=69

Adaptation	Response to Albany	Biographic characteristics
1. Uncertain negative retreat N=12 (17.4%) Low community contact (Mean score 0.42)	Dislike the prison Reject core regime Indifferent to facilities	State-raised youths Mainly thieves Previous local prisons Mean age 26.9 years Mean sentence 29.3 months
2. Secondary comfort indulgence N=11 (15.9%) Mixed community contact (Mean score 0.91)	Like the prison Reject core regime Enthusiasm for facilities	Mixed backgrounds All offence classes Previous training prisons Mean age 31.9 years Mean sentence 30.3 months
3. Jailing N=11 (15.9%) Mixed community contact (Mean score 1.18)	Like the prison Cynical approval of core regime Accept facilities	State-raised youths Disorganized thieves Previous training prisons Mean age 28.0 years Mean sentence 39.6 months
4. Gleaning N=6 (8.7%) High community contact (Mean score 1.33)	Like the prison Enthusiasm for core regime Enthusiasm for facilities	Mixed backgrounds All offence classes Previous local prisons Mean age 34.0 years Mean sentence 45.5 months
5. Opportunism N=6 (8.7%) Moderate community contact (Mean score 1.17)	Like the prison Cynical approval of core regime Cynical approval of facilities	State-raised youths Mainly thieves Previous training prisons Mean age 30.2 years Mean sentence 27.5 months
6. Doing your own bird N=9 (13.0%) Low community contact (Mean score 0.33)	Like the prison Indifferent to core regime Accept facilities	Mixed backgrounds Thieves Previous training prisons Mean age 41.9 years Mean sentence 66.7 months
7. Other adaptations N=6 (8.7%)		
8. Unclassified N=8 (11.6%)		

We have repeatedly emphasized the importance of viewing prisoner adaptations in the context within which they are found, and it may be helpful to look at the classifications developed by Irwin in California and by Cohen and Taylor in Durham in the light of our findings at Albany. It seems to us that the population described by Irwin in California was a good deal more varied than the population in Albany, the great majority of whom were thieves albeit sometimes of a rather disorganized kind. Perhaps it is not surprising, therefore, that almost half our sample were adapting in one or another way by attempting to do their own time. Whether or not they were successful seemed to depend partly on experience and partly on the regime to which they had to respond. The nine top men were undoubtedly the most successful, but twelve much younger thieves – most of whom were state-raised youths and who had not previously been in a training prison – could not cope with the regime and simply retreated into their cells. Another group, who were mostly not thieves at all and who would have had a hard time in most prisons, were none the less able to do time in Albany because they were able to focus on the secondary comforts available. Although Irwin lays stress on the identification of the professional thief with the outside world, this identification was not carried over into actual contacts by such persons in Albany. The top men and the retreatists had the lowest rates of community contact of anyone in the prison. It seemed that maintaining a strict separation between the outside and inside worlds was a considerable aid to the task of doing one's own time.

On the other hand, whereas Irwin argues that those who take the jailing response have either not maintained or never developed community identifications, the prisoners who jailed in Albany were more likely than most to keep up their contacts by letters and visits. Though they did make a world for themselves inside Albany, this did not require that they cut themselves off from the world outside. It was certainly the case that jailing was an adaptation most frequently taken up by state-raised youths. But in a prison which presented many alternative possibilities, jailing was not the only adaptation used by such youths. Most of the retreatists were graduates from borstal institutions, as were the opportunists, and there were one or more state-raised youths who took each of the other adaptations. Given the frequency with which state-raised youths may be found in the English prison system it would be surprising if some did not respond in other ways. More than a quarter of our sample were state-raised youths under the age of 25 years at arrest, compared with less than a sixth of Irwin's sample. If those over 25 years are included, more than half our sample had been state-raised. For what it is worth, the youngest of our state-raised youths retreated, the oldest adapted opportunistically, while those in between jailed. It may be the case that such persons change their style of adaptation as they get older and gain more experience of adult institutions.

We had too few cases in our gleaning category to suggest any

typical background that was particularly conducive to this response. Certainly none of them were 'heads' or 'hustlers' in Irwin's
sense of those terms. As one might have expected, however, our
gleaners had the highest rates of contact in the prison; and what
they mostly had in common was a first confrontation with an
institution whose philosophy and facilities made a change of
direction possible. We suspect that gleaning is an adaptation that is
open to anybody, given the opportunities and the strength of will
to carry it through. We noted earlier some of the dilemmas
associated with gleaning from the point of view of determining
motivation and providing enough facilities. It is worth pointing out
that most research projects in prison offer some gleaning possibilities to the inmates, and none more so than the work of Cohen
and Taylor at Durham prison which grew out of the sociology
classes they were teaching.

The research of Cohen and Taylor was published some years
after we had collected our data. Nevertheless we have reviewed
our material with a view to discovering whether the classification
they developed could be applied in Albany. It seems to us that
their classification is heavily determined by the special conditions
obtaining in the maximum-security wing, which Cohen and Taylor
so rightly emphasized. The prisoners in the top-security wing at
Durham had on the one hand to live up to, or live with, the images
of themselves created by the notoriety of their crimes, and on the
other to come to terms with very long sentences indeed. Such
conditions hardly applied in Albany, and none of the categories
used by Cohen and Taylor proved helpful in understanding our
data. Thus we had three robbers in our sample, though their
crimes had received little publicity and they were not well known
in the prison. Two of them adapted by jailing, but they were not
specially rebellious nor did they harbour serious hopes of escape,
as was apparently the case in Durham. There were no real
campaigners in Albany, other than those we have described, and
certainly none on the scale of Robert in the Durham special wing.
Those in our sample who approached this style of adaptation were
not also subverting in their response, as had been found at
Durham, but were really rather conventional in their attitudes.
They were not involved in organized crime or protection rackets
on the outside. Although some of our thieves retreated in Albany,
and others jailed, the real professionals were quite capable of

doing their own time. The tendency to give in at Durham almost surely resulted from the much longer time scale to which they had to adjust. Finally, we could find no evidence that sex offenders in Albany were given to mystical retreat so that they could meditate on their private sins in the way this was reported at Durham. One or two of our sex offenders remained unclassified, but we had no difficulty in assigning several other cases along with non-sex offenders to the categories we described earlier.

Making out and getting by: strategies of staff response

Making out in Albany was not such a problem for staff. Although many persons had been drafted into senior positions with varying degrees of enthusiasm, most of the discipline staff had chosen to apply for a transfer to Albany. It is true that for some the decision to apply was not entirely free from career pressures as far as promotion was concerned, and others almost certainly applied more for the benefits of living on the Isle of Wight than for the prospects of working in Albany. But even if the job was not to their liking they had the luxury afforded to all working citizens of time off.

We asked all staff the same questions that we put to prisoners in their evaluation of Albany, and once again we encouraged them to raise any matters which were important but which we had failed to include. Not surprisingly, the matters raised spontaneously by staff were concerned with their working conditions, which included the physical facilities of the prison mentioned by so many prisoners, and with the virtues or otherwise of establishing a non-work life on the Isle of Wight.

The members of the central management meeting, and the other specialist and administrative staff whom we interviewed, varied only in the degree of approval with which they regarded Albany. They had, after all, been involved to a greater or lesser degree in creating what was now being evaluated. In our interviews with them they frequently mentioned the strength of the organizational achievements at Albany as a key factor in their evaluation. That they still did so in spite of a change of governor bears testimony to the human skills with which that operation was, in the end, accomplished. This did not mean that they were completely uncritical of the regime or the organization structure. The governor, for example, told us of his misgivings about the time spent in association because prisoners were often bored and this led to tensions – a view freely expressed at central management meetings, as we reported earlier. The deputy, and some others, were concerned at the difficulties involved in supervising the halls. The foreman of works also felt that there was insufficient supervision in the workshops, and hoped that discipline officers would one day be employed in the shops as well as instructors. One or two members of the management team thought that the rules in Albany now lacked the flexibility that had obtained under David Gould and which had been thought to promote a more responsible attitude among discipline staff and prisoners. Such a view was offset by others who welcomed what they saw as a stricter process of enforcement. Welfare staff, who felt that they had lost out during the change-over to single-shift working, thought that the industrial emphasis made for difficulties in arranging inter-views with and visits to prisoners. Fairly or unfairly, some Albany managers expressed their disappointment at the quality of the discipline officers who, in their view, had not responded to the challenges as well as had been hoped. Perhaps most importantly, particular doubts were raised about the effectiveness of the organization structure at middle-management level where, it was argued, policy sometimes broke down. None of these matters, however, seriously detracted from the sense of achievement and modest success that underpinned their positive evaluation of Albany.

In fact, the majority of the uniformed staff, as we have already reported, also thought that Albany was the best prison they had been in or better than most. But there was a substantial minority, amounting to nearly half of the basic-grade officers we inter-viewed, who rated Albany as only an average prison or else saw it as the worst, or worse than most in their experience. As with our prisoner sample it was the core elements of the Albany regime around which the attitudes of uniformed staff crystallized, and we were able to use their responses to these matters as the starting point for developing a classification of modes of staff adaptation.

For staff, of course, especially those who were in the front line of duty in the halls, what we have called the core elements of the regime represented the essence of their job specification: the use of light supervision in the course of close working relationships with freely associating prisoners. While staff were often divided as to whether free association made for a more contented population or merely created problems of supervision, it was clear that the Albany rules provided the most contentious issue. Several members of the staff raised other aspects of their life and work in Albany as important. But whereas prisoners had been very ready to comment on the characteristics of their fellows and their guards, discipline officers often maintained an impressive professional indifference both to their colleagues and their charges. A few older officers referred to the youth and inexperience of other officers, while some younger staff complained of the 'bloody-mindedness' and 'bigotry' of their elders. But for the most part they took the view that officers were 'moulded by the demands of the regime', that they 'did what they were told anyway', and thus that it did not greatly matter who was wearing the uniform. Several commented on the 'childishness' and 'demanding nature' of Albany prisoners, but they also thought that 'the type of prisoner you get is not very important – you just do your job whoever they are'.

In the analysis which follows our attention is confined to the uniformed staff sample. The total sample is reduced to 51 because we excluded the three chief officers on the grounds that it would have been impossible to preserve their anonymity. We followed the same procedure that we have described for the prisoner classification, except that we had no independent or objective measures of behaviour that could be used in any systematic way to corroborate what we were told in interviews. However, we knew many of the staff well and had seen them at work over months of informal observation in the prison. We were often able to draw on this impressionistic evidence before finally assigning an officer to one category of adaptation rather than another. Once again we should state that there was some possibility of overlap between different modes of adaptation, and that staff could move from one mode to another in the course of their careers. We did feel, however, that staff responses seemed somewhat less likely to change than those of prisoners. With these provisos in mind there were some quite remarkable similarities between the ways in which discipline officers responded to the Albany regime and the modes of adaptation we reported for prisoners.

Adaptation 1: Uncertain withdrawal

Some of the younger basic-grade officers, especially those in their probationary period of service, had as much difficulty in coming to terms with the core elements of the regime as did the uncertain negative retreatists among the prisoners, and they made much the same kind of adaptation to their situation.

There were five such officers in our sample. Perhaps it should not be surprising that they experienced difficulties, given the problems we described earlier about providing an adequate staff training programme. Their biggest complaint was over the interpretation of rules, and they felt that they did not know when they should turn a blind eye and when they should not. And they were inclined to think that whatever they did was likely to be wrong. As Harry put it to us: 'The laxity in the rules always rebounds on us in the end. We are never backed up and we don't get enough support from the senior staff.' Thrust into case-officer relationships with prisoners who sometimes knew much more about the system than themselves, they felt uneasy and vulnerable. After faltering attempts at exercising their own initiative, often with the uncomfortable feeling that they were being manipulated by prisoners, they sometimes tried to take a firm line only to find themselves losing face for being petty-minded. Without clear guidance they tended to withdraw into themselves, having nowhere else to retreat to.

These young officers were not so much rejecting of the Albany regime as puzzled by the way it was supposed to operate. They came to Albany with no experience of military service, and none of the prison system save the prison at which they joined up and the Officer Training School. More often than not they wished to be involved in the process of treatment and training, and they tended to approve, at least in principle, of the case-officer scheme. But they felt that it needed to be applied in a more structured situation, which they were powerless to provide. These officers seemed to find no compensatory advantages in the prison, nor in their social position on the Isle of Wight. They did not like Albany, and would have preferred to be elsewhere, though they had to rely on second-hand accounts from other officers as to what alternatives were available. We suspect that some of these officers soon resolved their dilemma by taking jobs outside the prison service.

Adaptation 2: Secondary comfort indulgence
Another group of basic-grade officers found that, although they

rejected the core elements of the Albany regime, they none the less liked working in the prison because of various secondary gains that attached to the job. In this they so resembled those prisoners who responded through the indulgence of secondary comforts that we have used the same term to describe the staff adaptation.

There were seven officers in our sample whom we categorized in this way. They were somewhat older than the first group, with a mean age of 32.3 years, and they had all passed through their probationary period of service. There was no common background for these men before joining the prison service, though most had served in both training and local prisons before coming to Albany. They were thus in a position to make meaningful comparisons and they knew when they were well off. Albany came out badly, in their view, as far as such matters as the rules, the kind of supervision and so on were concerned. Some, like Reg, one of the younger and shorter-serving members of the group, had much the same kind of puzzlement about the regime that was expressed by the probationers. Others, like Tony, a 37-year-old ex-soldier, were frankly rejecting of the whole Albany philosophy. But they also found a number of other factors on which their present situation compared very favourably with what they had experienced elsewhere. Several mentioned the same hotel-like qualities which had appealed to their counterparts among the prisoners. Others mentioned the possibility of amassing earnings through overtime working. As Tony said: 'It's a good shift system, you get plenty of overtime and the working conditions are fine. Why should I move?' But what seemed to weigh most heavily for nearly all of them was living on the Isle of Wight. Brian, a 38-year-old family man who had applied for Albany because he wanted to live on the island, spoke for many: 'It's a good location here, near the seaside and in the country, a pleasant place to live if you've got kids. And we're lucky – we've got nice new quarters.' Such factors were enough to outweigh their discontents with what happened inside the prison.

Of course many other officers appreciated the working conditions and living on the Isle of Wight, but usually these were regarded as additional bonuses rather than the main or sole benefits to be had.

Adaptation 3: Negative detachment

Two men who actively disliked living on the Isle of Wight were included among a group of five basic-grade officers in our sample whose response to Albany may be described as negative detachment. These men rejected the core elements of the regime, and finding little else in their job or their location from which to draw comfort, they detached themselves from the official policies of the establishment and sought to operate within a more traditional framework. There was no direct correspondence with any single mode of adaptation among the prisoners. But there were some noticeable parallels between the methods used by these officers for coping with what they found uncongenial about Albany and the strategies adopted by various groups of prisoners. Thus they shared with the uncertain negative retreatists, and many other prisoners, their desire to return to a proper prison such as Wandsworth, though in the absence of that possibility they did not beat an uncertain retreat. Instead what they tried to do was to bring a little bit of Wandsworth into Albany. In their capacity to disregard what was specific to Albany and to behave as though it were actually more like Wandsworth, they somewhat resembled the top men who drew their own lines behind which they could do their own time.

All five of the officers in this category had been regular peacetime soldiers before joining the prison service, and four had served for substantial periods in local prisons before coming to Albany. The mean length of prison service was 7.6 years. They ranged in age from 33 to 37 years and the mean age was 34.8 years. Mike was the youngest of the group, and he had spent four years as an officer in Wandsworth when he answered the trawl notice for recruitment to Albany. He pointed out that the rules were 'much too ambiguous' and in any case 'too leniently applied'. He had no time for the concept of therapeutic anxiety, and little for the notions of incentive earnings and industrial production. 'A prison should be a prison' was his motto: 'If the inmate is uncertain about what he can do, then this upsets him and that upsets us. The only way to keep everyone happy is to run a tight nick. This isn't a tight nick. You don't get whining in Wandsworth.' Mr Phelps (a false surname because we never did get on Christian-name terms) was a former army sergeant. He pointed out that the rules didn't make sense to staff, let alone the prisoners, and went on to say: 'Officers compare their situation to the con's situation.... In Albany the scales are tipped in favour of the prisoner and against the staff, and that can't be right.' Though we had no independent measures of the behaviour of these officers it was our impression that they stuck to the letter of the law when there were clear rules, and kept prisoners at a distance in all situations where ambiguity arose. Certainly some of them had this reputation among the prisoners. Little attempt was made by these officers to work the case-officer system, and indeed they expressed indifference or contempt for such methods during interviews.

The researchers at Pentonville ten years earlier had suggested that the popular image of the prison officer was of a 'harsh disciplinarian who joins the Prison Service in order to continue the pleasure of ordering other men around which he has hitherto enjoyed as a non-commissioned officer in the armed forces'; and that at Penonville there were 'a few martinets who have merely exchanged a khaki uniform for a blue one' (Morris *et al.*, 1963, p. 77). Of all the officers from regular peacetime military service backgrounds in Albany, we suppose some of the officers in this group must have approached that stereotype. In this we were surprised, for we had expected that such an outlook might have characterized older rather than younger officers from military backgrounds. Older ex-army men in fact seemed to respond rather differently, as we report below. Even with this group, however, it is worth noting that it was not just the inability to give orders that troubled these men, but the fact that they rarely received clear orders from above. Like so many prisoners they felt that they did not know where they stood without them.

As we have said, the response of negative detachment pursued by these officers had no direct counterpart among the prisoners. But before leaving this discussion we should mention that there were a few officers known to us in Albany, though none as it happened came into our sample, who followed this pattern of adaptation in an extreme form and with certain additional elements in a way which rather resembled jailing among the prisoners. These men were known by both staff and prisoners in Albany as 'the heavy mob'. They were big, burly men who had a reputation for being provocative but who regarded themselves as key men should trouble arise. What they shared with prisoners who adopted the jailing response was the capacity to make of the prison a world of their own. And within that world they saw themselves as the bearers of the staff side of prison culture. Such men viewed Albany with negative detachment, and thought that the only way to run a prison was by running a tight nick. But they also seemed to regard prisons as places in which prisoners occasionally needed to be 'taught a lesson' to ensure that they did not get out of line. When we ate in Albany House, or went for a drink in the staff club, we sometimes heard them swapping stories which became more outrageous in the course of elaboration. No doubt most of the stories were little more than barrack-room folk tales, and clearly some were told directly for our benefit. In fact, most of it was probably just talk, because the prisoners reported very little in the way of 'needling' or 'aggro', as we have said, and there were very few incidents. But the talk also served as part of the initiation for new recruits fresh from the training school, and as a powerful antidote to the official philosophy of the prison. In different circumstances, of course, talk could turn into action.

Adaptation 4: Implementing Rule 1

Eleven officers, the largest single group in our uniformed staff sample, liked Albany, expressed enthusiasm for the core elements of the regime, and in their spontaneous comments during interviews laid stress on the humanitarian qualities of the prison. Their adaptation to Albany thus involved the acceptance of its philosophy, and of their part in carrying it into effect. In short, they saw themselves as implementing Rule 1. Thus Charles, a 42-year-old principal officer with 18 years of prison service behind him, told us: 'It's Utopia really. It's clean, it's modern and it's fair. There is free association, relaxed relationships, unobtrusive supervision, and if some of it is a bit tongue-in-cheek no one comes to any harm. It is a sight more pleasant to be here than anywhere else, whichever side of the bars you are on.' Thomas was a 44-year-old senior officer, with 16 years' experience in several different types of prison. He said: 'There is more consideration here both for staff and prisoners. We all have to work to bring that about, you know, but it does work.'

Only one of the 11 men was a basic-grade officer. The remainder were drawn equally from the ranks of senior officers and principal officers. All had military service experience, though only two had been regular peacetime soldiers; the others were wartime or national service recruits. These were the oldest, longest-serving men in our sample, and between them they had more experience of Prison Department establishments than any other group. They ranged in age from 35 to 56 years with a mean of 45 years. The average period spent in the prison service was 16.2 years. Virtually all had previously served in other closed or open training prisons or borstals, in addition to local prisons.

Since implementing Rule 1 was obviously the preferred response among staff exposed to the formal rhetoric not just of Albany but of the prison service as a whole, this adaptation was analogous to gleaning among the prisoners. As with gleaning, however, the very pursuit of such an officially approved path perhaps calls into question the authenticity of the adaptation and the sincerity of those adopting it. Though the question was raised in our minds, as it must be in the minds of anyone concerned with staff training, of whether some officers may have been paying mere lip service to the official ideology while concealing other feelings, we made no attempt to answer it. For what it is worth, from the evidence at our disposal, we saw no more reason to doubt this adaptation than any of the others we identified.

Adaptation 5: Making a career

A small group of officers expressed much the same degree of liking for Albany, and of approval for the core regime, as those we have described as implementing Rule 1. But their approval of the regime was expressed in somewhat less euphoric terms, and when we invited them to offer their own comments they stressed the encouragement given to younger officers to exercise responsibility and take decisions. Mac, a basic-grade officer who expected promotion in the near future, said: 'As a member of staff you can use your initiative here: it takes some of the weight off the governor, and when staff have responsibility and take an interest in their work you get more amicable relationships all round.' Taffy, a young officer, particularly welcomed the 'chance to learn about prisons, prisoners and techniques of interviewing' that would stand him in good stead in the future. Mr Williamson, after praising the system of communication and distribution of responsibilities generally, went on to say that he would be very willing 'to take on much of the work done by the specialist staff, given the facilities'.

These officers certainly embraced the official thinking about the implementation of Rule 1, but they seemed even more concerned with the prospect of making a career within the prison system; and we have characterized their adaptation in those terms. While they did avail themselves of the opportunities offered in Albany it would be fanciful to compare their adaptation with those prisoners whom we described as taking the opportunist response. Making a career, of course, is just as officially approved as implementing Rule 1 and quite compatible with it. If anything, then, the gleaning adaptation once again provides the most direct comparison among prisoners. It is probable, however, that making a career is even more understandable as a response, and thus less likely to be called into question, than implementing Rule 1; and it is possible that officers may move on to the Rule 1 adaptation once their careers are made. In any event the officers whom we included in this category were younger and still climbing the promotional ladder.

Of the six officers taking this mode of adaptation, four were from the basic grade and two were senior officers. Two had been regular peacetime soldiers, two had done national service and two had no military experience. The mean age was 36.5 years with a range from 25 to 49 years. All but one had served in training prisons or borstals as well as local prisons before joining Albany, and the mean period of prison service was 9.5 years.

Adaptation 6: Marking time

If those men we described as implementing Rule 1 and making a career could pride themselves on doing a good job, the officers we characterized as marking time quite definitely saw themselves as 'just doing a job'.

Ten officers in our sample came into this category. They were basically indifferent to' Albany, saw its regime as 'nothing special', and indicated to us in interviews that it didn't really matter much what establishment they were in because they just got on with the job in hand. Mr Edwards really spoke for them all: 'Like anything else it's what you make of it. I don't take too much notice of all the fancy talk. I just do what I'm told: all the staff fall into the routine sooner or later.'

All but one of these men had been regular peacetime soldiers, and the exception had seen military service during the war. They were found in all ranks from the basic grade up to principal officer level. The mean age was 40.6 years with a range from 32 to 54 years. All had been in other types of establishment as well as local prisons before coming to Albany, and the mean period of prison service was 11.3 years.

We suspect that the strategy adopted by these ex-professional soldiers and now long-serving prison officers, was the more typical response of the military man who moves over to the prison service. While they preferred tidiness and order and discipline, they did not seem to make a relentless pursuit of these aims. Nor did they seem particularly to seek the pleasure of giving orders, as is implied in the Morrises' conception of the 'military martinet'. Rather they seemed able to bend whichever way the wind blew without this affecting their fundamental outlook. Thus while they remained indifferent to the Albany philosophy they were none the less able to conform to its outward requirements, to 'fall into the routine'. In some ways their mode of adaptation resembled that of the top men among the prisoners who simply got on with doing their bird. Like them they had seen everything before in a wide variety of settings, they knew how to handle themselves in difficult situations, and, crucially, how to head trouble off before it happened. Though they were marking time, prison for these men was more than just an interlude in their lives as it was for prisoners, something to be got through as best they could. Being in prison was their life, or a large part of it. In pacing themselves through it they had learned to absorb the changing fashions for one or another method of treatment or training, without ever losing sight of the underlying realities of what prison was about: the daily ritual of locking, unlocking and watching.

Other adaptations

Three young basic-grade officers in our sample, two in their probationary period of service and one who had just completed it, seemed, like some of the prisoners, to be still in the process of finding their feet. We tentatively characterized their response as uncertain acceptance, but it was by no means clear that their uncertainty would finally be resolved in favour of Albany. They resembled the other probationary officers who responded by uncertain withdrawal in virtually all respects, except that they were younger and at the time of our interviews still found Albany to their liking. But Simon felt anxious when he spoke to prisoners lest he be 'accused of skiving' by older officers, and Philip said that he found it 'very difficult to live up to the ideals of David Gould', even though he had only served under the first governor for a few weeks. The third of these men, Ken, was attracted towards the network of officers who made up the heavy mob. He was perplexed at the disjunction between what he heard in the course of training and what he heard in the officers' mess. Though he liked Albany and the idea of the case-officer system, he also told us that 'the rules are too flexible here; one simply doesn't know how far you can go with the prisoners'.

At the end of our analysis there remained four officers whom we felt unable to classify for one reason or another. In Table 8.3 we have tried to summarize the relationships between modes of staff adaptation in Albany and some of the biographic characteristics of the officers concerned. Once again we should stress that there is nothing hard and fast about this classification. We had no objective or independent measures of staff behaviour that we could use to validate interview responses in the way that we did for prisoners. While there is some degree of overlap between the various modes of adaptation, the categories we have identified do reflect the differences of emphasis expressed in interviews and are consistent with the impressions we gained during the course of our long period of fieldwork.

Reactions to change

We had been warned that Albany was changing so fast that we would have difficulty in conducting our research. It is fitting therefore that we should report how our respondents felt about those very changes which had occurred between the spring of 1967 and the summer of 1969.

Many prisoners, and not a few staff, were unaware that certain changes had taken place, or else were unable to say how they had been affected by them, if indeed they had. And some matters, changing or not, were simply of no interest either to staff or prisoners. In the discussion which follows we concentrate on those matters which seem of greatest importance to us, in the light of the frequency and strength of views expressed, rather than attempt to provide a complete and detailed account.

Nearly everyone who had been in the prison in July 1968 – and many of the prisoners in our sample had not – had strong views about the effect of the change in governors. Only four prisoners who had served under both governors thought that the succession had made no difference. Among the remainder there were three prisoners who thought the change was for the worse for every one

*Table 8.3   Modes of adaptation by uniformed
staff sample: N= 51*

Adaptation	Response to Albany	Biographic characteristics
1. Uncertain withdrawal N=5 (9.8%)	Dislike the prison Puzzled by core regime Indifferent to other matters	Probationary basic grade No military experience Local prisons Mean service 1.6 years Mean age 26.0 years
2. Secondary comfort indulgence N=7 (13.7%)	Like the prison Reject core regime Like IOW, conditions, overtime	Basic grade officers Mixed background Training prisons Mean service 3.1 years Mean age 32.3 years
3. Negative detachment N=5 (9.8%)	Dislike the prison Reject core regime Indifferent to other matters	Basic-grade officers Regular peacetime military Local prisons Mean service 7.6 years Mean age 34.8 years
4. Implementing Rule 1 N=11 (21.6%)	Like the prison Enthusiasm for core regime Stress humanitarian aims	Principal and senior officers War or national service Training prisons, borstals Mean service 16.2 years Mean age 45.0 years
5. Making a career N=6 (11.8%)	Like the prison Approve of core regime Stress staff responsibility, etc.	Basic grade and senior officers Mixed backgrounds Training prisons, borstals Mean service 9.5 years Mean age 36.5 years
6. Marking time N=10 (19.6%)	Indifferent to prison Indifferent to core regime Stress just doing a job	All grades Regular peacetime military Training prisons, borstals Mean service 11.3 years Mean age 40.6 years
7. Other adaptations N=3 (5.7%)		
8. Unclassified N=4 (7.8%)		

who thought otherwise. The minority who preferred life under
Brian Howden did so because they felt that they knew better
where they stood when the prison was run on a tighter rein. But
the majority were firmly agreed that David Gould had been closer
to the men in the cells and was prepared to listen to them. As Alf
told us: 'Gould worried the screws much more than he did the
cons.' Judging from the response of the staff, Alf may well have
been right. Half of all the uniformed officers we interviewed

welcomed the new leadership. They felt that 'morale had improved' and were apt to say that 'the cons used to run this prison . . . they don't quite so much now'. Most officers expressed respect for both men as well as a degree of personal warmth, but rightly or wrongly Gould was seen as 'leaning too far towards the needs of the prisoners', whereas Howden was regarded as a 'staff man'. As a result, like some of the prisoners, they began to feel that they knew where they stood. When difficulties arose and they went to see the governor they felt that they would receive an answer rather than be faced with another question. Less than a tenth of the discipline staff maintained a personal allegiance to the first governor, though some, including a few who now expressed indifference to the whole affair, had clearly experienced his departure as tantamount to an act of betrayal. These officers thought that Gould had been 'a man of inspiration and ideas', 'a progressive governor who was full of interest and understanding' for both staff and prisoners. A fifth of the officers claimed that the change was of no consequence to them, while the remainder felt unable for diplomatic or other reasons to express an opinion.

About a third of the uniformed officers accounted for this first momentous change in the life of the prison in terms which were similar to the judgment expressed by most of the central management team. This held that the two governors had been given different tasks to fulfil and that different men with different qualities were required to carry them out. Gould, a charismatic figure capable of keeping certain ideas and goals before his audience and motivating staff to achieve them, was thought ideally suited to open up a new prison. Howden, an administrator with an eye for detail was needed, however, to put the nuts and bolts on the organization structure, to consolidate policy and to carry it through. Some officers also linked the change to the upgrading of the prison from its category-C status: 'You can't run a security prison the same way you run a borstal.'

By contrast, hardly anybody noticed the change of deputy governors in February 1969, and those who did evaluated it purely in terms of personal relationships. Similarly no one was very impressed at the introduction of the new grade of 'senior officers' in October 1968. Prisoners scarcely distinguished between uniforms at this level; and while most staff were prepared to voice mild approval even those who had just been promoted were still more or less sceptical about the career structure. Both staff and prisoners acknowledged that the opening of the woodmill in June 1968 had widened the work opportunities in the prison, but no one thought that the upgrading of the light textiles shop to tailoring some six months later involved anything more than a change of name.

Opinions were sharply divided again over that most important of changes: the abandonment of the two-shift system of working in February 1969. Interestingly enough, although we had been told repeatedly by staff that prisoners did not like the two-shift system because there was nothing for them to do in their mornings off, and too little time to watch TV in the evenings, we found the opposite to be the case. Forty-eight prisoners in our sample had experienced both systems in Albany. Two out of every three among them preferred the two-shift method of working because it gave them 'better access to the welfare', 'better opportunities for recreation', and because it was 'much better for visits'. It is true that many *had* complained about the two-shift system at the time, but now they felt the routine was 'very rushed', that there was 'no time to sort anything out any more', and that now 'no one wants to listen anyway'. In spite of the rush they felt that time dragged by even more slowly under the new system than it had under the old one: 'Each day goes by all right, but you can't tell one week from the next.' Most of those who did not actually disapprove of the change professed indifference to it rather than approval. Only seven prisoners in our sample gave responses that even approached those attributed to them by the staff.

The overwhelming majority of the uniformed staff – almost 85 per cent – viewed the introduction of single-shift working with approval. There was a very high degree of consensus among officers of all ranks that the change had brought many benefits. The prisoners now had 'a full working day' and, with 'less time on their hands', they posed 'less of a threat to security'. Moreover the change had meant that the organization of the halls could be rationalized, so that things were now 'easier for staff working' and there was 'greater continuity of relationships in the halls'. Most officers argued that the change had had little effect on welfare activities. Only a few discipline staff thought that the time-table was now too overloaded to do justice to visits, welfare appointments, applications and so on. One officer told us that he was disappointed that Albany had not been able to rise to the challenge of providing training and industry by persevering with the two-shift system. In this, of course, he had the sympathy of some members of central management who had tried to meet that challenge. The central management team, for the most part, still held to the views that they had expressed nearly a year earlier, for they had accurately predicted the effects on their own interests.

From an analysis that we were able to carry out in some workshops before and after the change, it was clear that workshop interruptions that could be attributed to social training purposes did increase considerably as a result of the introduction of single-shift working. In the period immediately preceding the shift change, workshop interruptions for these purposes accounted for an average of 4.5 hours a week or 0.2 per cent of total work time. After the shift change they accounted for an average of 152 hours a week or 3.4 per cent of total work time. Two-thirds of the time lost resulted from the time-tabling of remedial physical education during working hours, and the remainder was attributable in approximately equal proportions to welfare and governor's call-ups, appointments with medical and other specialists, remedial education classes, and visits. However, the introduction of the labour control unit did cut down on other interruptions to working time, through discharges and labour changes, for example, which nearly offset the increases due to social training needs.

Work study, which accompanied the change to single-shift working and preceded the gradual introduction of the incentive earnings scheme, was viewed with mild approval by staff and prisoners, largely on instrumental grounds. There were, however, a number of grumbles that the piecemeal development of the scheme led to injustices. The labour control unit was also developed at the time of the change in shift working. Prisoners, if they had heard of it, were largely indifferent to its effects. Staff, at all levels, were generally approving on grounds that an aid to efficiency was also an aid to security. A few complained that it made extra work for officers, and several admitted to finding the whole apparatus of labour control rather confusing.

Staff and prisoners were almost unanimous in their approval of the ELSA method for locking and unlocking. Although there had been setbacks in the plans for extending the use of electronic locking, much experience had been gained in A hall since the prison had opened. Both staff and prisoners were grateful for the improved sanitary arrangements, even though some prisoners still used their plastic pots. And both felt the benefit of reduced contact and tension during the most sensitive periods of the day. Prisoners felt less dependent on staff, and staff felt glad to be rid of keys. The ELSA scheme was not introduced on security grounds, but although there was always the risk of electronic failures and sabotage, the security considerations were not lost on either staff or prisoners. All the halls were eventually to be fitted with a more sophisticated system of electronic locking, with security very much in mind. Several prisoners and at least two officers viewed the use of electronic aids in prison with a deep sense of foreboding. It was known, or guessed, that television cameras would soon follow; and the era of remote control, they thought, would only serve to 'dehumanize' the situation still further – the 'zoo-like' character of the prison was gradually being enhanced. The central management group approved of ELSA, but several members had reservations: about the loss of association space brought about by the enclosure of stair wells, and the possible creation of social distance between staff and prisoners. One of them was beginning to get the first intimations that Albany might become what he was later to describe as an 'electronic coffin'.

If the ELSA system had not initially been concerned with security, there was no mistaking the purpose behind the commencement of the second fence and the introduction of dog patrols. Prisoners who had watched the high-security fence being built around them were either unconcerned or disapproving of it. They mostly argued that it was a ludicrous waste of money. Not only had they no intention of escaping, they none of them had the resources to get off the island even if they got out of the prison. One or two realized that it would be essential when category-A prisoners arrived in Albany, and a few took comfort from the fact that Prison Department had not chosen, or could not afford, to build a wall. They did not know, of course, that walls were to come later! More often than not, among prisoners, the fence was the subject of derision. Dogs were another matter. Even though the atmosphere in Albany was still relaxed and easy in the summer of 1969, the introduction of dogs more than anything else had sown the seeds for a deterioration in moral climate. Dogs were seen as unnecessary by prisoners; but they were also deemed to be 'degrading', 'dehumanizing', 'provocative' and 'dangerous' as well as just plain 'noisy'. Less than a third of the prisoners even attempted to maintain an air of indifference on this issue.

More than three-quarters of the uniformed officers welcomed

both these changes on grounds of improving security: dogs provided 'a powerful deterrent' to potential escapers, whereas the strong perimeter fence would enable them to 'relax the regime within the prison' – a bitter miscalculation of what was to follow later. Several staff had no strong opinions on these matters but were inclined to think that they included an element of 'overkill', while one officer was mainly conscious that the fence was an 'eyesore' and that the dogs would give the prison service in general, and Albany in particular, a 'bad name'. The governor thought that both the dogs and the fence had helped to improve staff confidence and morale. The rest of the central management group tended to accept, with varying degrees of reluctance, that the fence was a necessary step in the build-up of a category-A establishment. But seven of them, including representatives from the uniformed staff, expressed their qualms about the use of dogs. One suggested that introducing dogs showed how far the prison had 'lost its sense of direction'; another merely commented that it was a 'barbarous development'. It was argued that 'dogs should only be used at night', thereby keeping a low profile and 'minimizing tension'; but it was equally argued that dogs were simply 'incompatible with the idea of training'. Several members of the management group were concerned that dog handlers had become progressively isolated from other staff and prisoners. They were alarmed at how ready some men were to opt out of face-to-face contact and to 'hide behind' dogs. Others were concerned that the dogs provided a general hazard to everyone in the prison.

The building of fences and the use of dog patrols only made sense against the impending arrival of category-A prisoners and the establishment of Albany as a dispersal prison. For nearly a year Albany had been moving steadily towards that objective, an objective very different from that held out for it on its foundation. It had been many months since the arrival of the first category-B prisoners, and the structure of the population of Albany had already begun to change. We asked staff and prisoners how they viewed the proposed influx of long-sentence, high-security-risk prisoners. We were fascinated by the responses we received.

One member of the central management group felt that it was a good thing to mix prisoners of different degrees of sophistication and serving different lengths of sentence. Others were frankly opposed to the policy of dispersing high-security-risk prisoners and would have preferred them to be 'concentrated', either in Albany or elsewhere. Most agreed that it was right to use Albany's facilities for long-term rather than short-term prisoners, and having accepted that the decision had been taken anyway, felt they had done all that reasonably could be done by way of preparation. One or two members expressed their doubts, however, as to whether the discipline officers would have received enough training or experience to be able to cope. Time assuredly would tell.

The great majority of the uniformed staff, to our surprise in view of the official POA view on the dispersal policy, welcomed the prospect of getting more long-termers, apparently on the grounds that 'they settle down to their sentence better' and were 'easier to cope with'. Several officers responded with quiet confidence because they felt that they would be able to do 'more constructive work' than had been possible with the typical Albany prisoner. Many officers took the view that long-termers deserved the better facilities in Albany rather than the cramped conditions of the special wings, and many more said that it made no difference who the prisoners were because 'you simply get on with the job'. Only eight expressed serious anxieties. All felt that the prison needed to be 'tightened up' if it was not to be 'taken over' by subversives. Two were firmly of the opinion that it was a grave mistake to mix long- and short-sentence prisoners.

Many of the prisoners in Albany who were already serving long sentences said they would be glad to have more long-termers in the prison to keep them company. They thought it would help to 'cut out some of this borstal childishness' on the part of both prisoners and staff because 'these cons just won't stand for it'. Some prisoners, especially those who indulged in the secondary comforts of the prison, also thought that Albany was a good prison to put long-termers. The largest single group of prisoners, a third of the sample, thought that it would not make much difference to them, especially as many of those prisoners now in Albany would be released before the category-A prisoners arrived. But nearly a fifth of the sample predicted trouble ahead, either for the prisoners or the staff, as more sophisticated criminals arrived in Albany. They saw one, or both, of two difficulties arising. First, men serving long sentences would become very unsettled living alongside a changing population of short-sentence men. Second, no really tough or experienced prisoner would stand for the kind of ambiguities and inconsistencies perpetuated by the staff in

Albany. Unless something was done to keep short- and long-sentence prisoners apart, and unless the staff were able to get themselves together about running the halls, then it was argued that some disturbance was bound to follow. It was recognized that this might be as uncomfortable for prisoners as it would be for staff. Perhaps we should leave the last words with Malcolm, if only because they came so close to the truth.

> This is not a good place to send high-security men. For one thing long-termers and short-termers don't mix: it will just get under their skin seeing these short-termers going out. I'm doing long-time myself, so take it from me. Another thing they will not stand for is this borstal-type way with screws. I just hope I will be out by the time they come. This place has been tightening up for a year now; fences, dogs, all that stuff. Soon it will be nothing but a penal colony. Things are OK now, but the whole atmosphere will change. And when it does there's going to be trouble. I tell you there'll be a riot.

9   The electronic coffin

In September 1969, our fieldwork completed, we left Albany to embark on our comparative studies in other prisons. We left a full year before Albany received its first category-A men, and much of the work to upgrade the security which we described in chapter 6 still remained to be done. Indeed, when we departed, the prison resembled nothing so much as a rather secure labour camp in which the main activity appeared to be digging trenches. Apart from a small number of prisoners and a substantial minority of basic-grade officers, the overwhelming verdict of the participants was that if you had to do or spend your time in prison, Albany was the best, or better than most places to do it in. As observers, with experience between us of observing prisons as extensive as that of many of our respondents, we would have to endorse that verdict. We were not alone either for, not long after we left, Albany was accorded the highest rating – four arrows – in the *Good Jail Guide* (Oversby and Hill, 1970). It was said to be 'under progressive management' and the envy of other HMP establishments.

By the summer of 1971, when we first tried to write up this part of the project, Albany had been housing category-A prisoners for over six months. It had also undergone yet another change of governor and it was beginning to become the subject of adverse publicity. Before starting to write we discussed our work with both David Gould and Brian Howden, the first two governors. It was clear from these discussions, and from our informal contacts which we maintained with the prison, that Albany had become a different establishment from the one we had entered three years earlier. Whilst our data seemed to go a long way towards accounting for the latest developments, we felt that there were still a number of gaps in our knowledge of the prison that we would like to fill. Accordingly, we approached Mr Gifford Footer, the new governor, to see if we could re-establish access to the prison to fill those gaps. Shortly afterwards we also sought permission from Prison Department to examine files at headquarters on the planning and setting up of Albany. Both requests were readily granted.

In fact, when we returned periodically to Albany we were welcomed back. The same co-operation and facilities were extended by Mr Footer as by his predecessors. Old relationships were quickly re-established and we were soon brought up to date with events. Our presence was intermittent, and on a much reduced scale than formerly, but we were able to keep ourselves abreast of a progressively deteriorating situation even after our last official visit in 1972. By 1973 it seemed that a new pattern of social order had been established in Albany, and it seemed safe to begin writing once more. In the present chapter we seek to describe and account for some of the developments up to the end of that year.

The events

It will be helpful if we give a narrative, chronological account of the major events as we understand them to have happened, before we attempt too much by way of analysis. Only some of the incidents received wide publicity at the time, and then not always accurately.

Between August and October 1969 there were protests at a number of other prisons, especially those containing the so-called 'special wings', by the families of category-A prisoners. The protests were sparked off by a new Home Office requirement that only approved persons, who had to submit photographs and obtain identity cards, could visit these men. Albany would not have been involved except that the protests led, at least in part, to one of the most serious prison riots in modern times, at nearby Parkhurst Prison on 24 October 1969. The noise of the rioting could be clearly heard in Albany cells, where there were ripples of sympathy among the prisoners. Stories were freely circulated that many old scores had been settled, by both staff and inmates, during the course of the riot and its aftermath. Some Albany officers were drafted into Parkhurst to help to restore order, and when witnesses and defendants at the 'Parkhurst trial' were subsequently lodged in Albany during 1970 there was some uneasiness. Their presence provided a symbolic representation of the sharp divide that can be exposed between prisoners and staff in any institution: perhaps it could even happen in Albany.

On 26 October 1970 the first category-A prisoners arrived. A few days later the local Press published an article on the role of the prison officer in Albany under the 'Prison officers are far removed from the turnkeys of yesteryear', and it was clear that the Albany image remained untarnished:

> No longer is the simple aim just to isolate the wrongdoer from the community whose laws he has broken. It is also to prepare and fit him to take his place within the community again – only this time as a good and useful citizen.... All these aspects of the prison life call for a more professional type of prison officer than the old-style warder whose image they hope will...fade for ever from the public's mind (*The News*, 30 October 1970).

But the article also drew attention, melodramatically, to the dangers of working in the country's newest maximum security establishment:

> ... working among some of the toughest and most hardened convicted criminals of our modern society...in Britain's newest Class A high-security establishment.... Outnumbered by the villains they guard, unarmed (unlike their counterparts in other countries) and without even the deterrent of capital punishment for a prisoner who might fatally wound them, today's prison officers have to be a special breed of men.

Even so the report was chiefly notable for the remarks attributed to one of the POA representatives at the prison. While he indicated that there had been some 'tightening up' to take account of the new security role, he still felt able to conclude that: 'There is a friendlier relationship between staff and prisoners here at Albany than at any other prison where I have served.'

It was not long, however, before the first signs of tension began to show. The police were called to investigate incidents of fire-raising. An escape attempt was quickly foiled. And the numbers of prisoners applying to be removed from association under Rule 43 so that they might be protected from intimidation by others began to rise, from about six or seven daily in October 1970 to twice that number in March 1971 and three times that number in June. There was no great publicity until May 1971, when the POA held its annual conference. The same representative who had spoken of the friendly relationships just six months earlier, now stated that cells had to be searched day and night for fire bombs, and that the staff had to answer an enormous number of alarm calls. He concluded this time that 'someone soon will be severely hurt or even killed if this goes on'. He blamed the unrest in Albany on the implementation of the dispersal policy; and the conference, not for the first time, reaffirmed its support for the Mountbatten proposals for concentrating high-security-risk prisoners. The conference then went on to lament the dwindling recruitment to the service, the low basic rate of pay, and the need to work overtime in excess of the 14 hours a week agreed with the Home Office in order to man the prisons and to earn a satisfactory wage. Such matters were to become ever more important in the next few years. In fact both sets of dissatisfactions had been brought together in Albany some months earlier, when the first proposals for a work-to-rule were put forward by the local branch of the POA. Such a device would not only bring industrial power to bear on a trades union dispute, but would also, or so it was thought, have the effect of limiting the amount of time that prisoners could spend in association and thus cut down the scope for aggro in the prison.

The aggro had indeed reached a new peak shortly before the conference when the prison underwent its second change of governor. Brian Howden was posted to headquarters on 19 April. Gifford Footer took over the prison on 4 May. Whereas the six-week interval between the departure of David Gould and the arrival of Brian Howden in 1968 had been characterized by rumour, the two-week gap before Brian Howden was replaced was filled with action. Several incidents were dealt with by the first extensive use of Rule 43 to deal with so-called 'subversive' prisoners.

Under Rule 43 the governor was able to remove any prisoner from association and into the segregation unit when this seemed desirable for the maintenance of good order and discipline, as well as for the protection of a prisoner in his own interests. The use of Rule 43 requires the authority of either a member of the Board of Visitors or the Secretary of State if the prisoner is removed for more than 24 hours. In practice it is rare for the governor's decision to be challenged by either of these authorities. The segregation of subversive prisoners does not require that they be charged with any offence. The absence of even those slender elements of 'due process' which are involved in the adjudication of offences against prison discipline is greatly resented by prisoners. On the other hand, prison officers often feel that they know, even if they cannot prove, that certain prisoners 'make the bullets for others to fire'. When faced with this situation they frequently press for action to be taken under Rule 43. The use of Rule 43 is almost certainly double-edged in its effects. If it is used sparingly and early, some situations can be effectively nipped in the bud. If it is used frequently or on a large scale it is likely to be counter-productive. Most governors probably regard the resort to Rule 43 as signifying the failure of more dignified methods of control. Be that as it may, the numbers held at any one time as subversive under Rule 43, since the arrival of category-A prisoners, had been kept to an average of two by Brian Howden and never exceeded five. Shortly after Brian Howden left, the deputy governor was asked to segregate a notorious category-A prisoner – whom we shall call Mr X – on grounds that he was suspected of being involved in intimidatory practices. The prisoner was duly removed; whereupon several other prisoners protested at his 'martyrdom', and one of them climbed on the roof to do so. These prisoners in turn were also segregated, and when Gifford Footer took over the reins there were already nine such prisoners in the block.

By 9 June all 'subversive' Rule 43s had been returned to their halls; but on the following day a letter smuggled out to the National Council for Civil Liberties (NCCL), one which had been circulated by Radical Alternatives to Prison, was published in the *Guardian*. It alleged, among other things, that: 'Out of the total amount of long-termers here at Albany about one fifth is now in solitary confinement' (*Guardian*, 10 June 1971). A Home Office spokesman, in reply to this charge, told the Press that there were only 21 prisoners in the segregation unit: two in punitive solitary confinement, two who were being held subject to police enquiries, and 17 under Rule 43 at their own request and for their own protection. We assume these figures related to the date of the statement, – i.e., 9 June – and our examination of the segregation unit records for that date indeed confirms those figures. The Home Office spokesman also estimated that the numbers in *punitive* solitary confinement in Albany usually varied between two and a dozen. That too we were able to verify from the records. But the spokesman failed to provide figures for other categories of prisoner held in the segregation unit, most notably those held under Rule 43 for suspected subversive activities. Nor did he discuss the situation in the segregation unit as a whole for the recent past, the period to which the smuggled letter presumably referred. Thus, in the two months prior to the Home Office statement the numbers held for *subversive* activities varied between 0 and 12, while the average population of the segregation unit was 27 prisoners. On one occasion, just before the new governor came into post, there were 35 prisoners, or 11 per cent of the population, in the segregation unit. We do not know what length of sentences these men were serving. But since 12 of them were category-A men, of whom there were fewer than 30 in the prison as a whole, the allegation that a fifth of the long-termers had been in solitary confinement was probably not far from the truth.

The author of the letter claimed that the use of solitary confinement was part of a continuing 'backlash from the Parkhurst trial'. He alleged that quite 'a lot of the staff here were involved in beating and clubbing those Parkhurst prisoners into submission', and that since the Parkhurst riot long-term prisoners had become 'the targets for discrimination and victimization'. One specific case, which was cited in the letter, involved a long-termer who 'spent the whole Christmas during a 21-day seclusion in confine-ment for having two slices of bread in his hand when leaving the dining hall. He lost all his privileges for that period and was fined five shillings out of his very small weekly wage for that very trivial offence.' The Home Office spokesman, in trying to set this matter straight, only succeeded in highlighting the problems associated with the use of Rule 43: the prisoner in question was put in solitary confinement over Christmas for his subversive activities and was 'merely' fined for the dining hall offence.

The prisoner complained that there was no longer any effective rehabilitation or treatment in Albany: 'It would be a lot cheaper to bury us in an allotment somewhere because the results are about the same – we are slowly but surely becoming vegetables.' At least one member of the central management team also had doubts as to whether Albany was really concerned with the systematic planning of a long-term prisoner's sentence, though his choice of metaphor was perhaps more apt for the Albany setting. He argued that there was no point in the psychology department making detailed plans if no one read them or had any intention of acting upon them. Yet if the prison did not concern itself with long-term plans, then it would be hard to repudiate the criticism that Albany was nothing but an electronic coffin. Actually such a criticism would have been premature, for the electronics were still not complete and the computer was not yet installed.

The BBC tried to maintain interest in the smuggled letter by interviewing an ex-Albany prisoner, who predicted a riot there if conditions did not improve. But the transcript of the interview which was supplied to us was less than coherent; and Albany got little further attention from the media for the next three months, until 7 September 1971. On a number of occasions just before that date prisoners had refused to eat their food once they had asked for it. It was said that the prisoners involved had been intimidated into making such protests. Certainly at that time two prisoners found that their pet budgerigars had been set on fire in their cages. It was believed that these incidents amounted to a more or less systematic campaign against the catering staff, and the principal officer in charge of catering was indeed twice absent from duties for substantial periods through sickness. The incidents led to the first real explosion of violence, and the renewed use of Rule 43 to confine subversive prisoners to the segregation unit. On 7 September, when suspected subversive prisoners were removed to the segregation unit, fighting took place; and the next day disturbances in the segregation unit resulted in more serious injuries to several staff and at least one prisoner. One officer had his head cut, another had his wrist caught in a slammed cell door. All told, over the two days of violence nine officers were hurt, though in many cases the injuries were of a minor nature. The prisoner, whom we shall call Mr Y, was serving a life sentence for what had been described in the Press as underworld executions. He sustained a broken bone in the face, a cut lip, two black eyes and numerous bruises. The whole prison was locked up for two days as a result of the disturbance, with all prisoners confined to cells. Five prisoners were charged with offences which were heard by the Board of Visitors, and two lost part of the remission due on their 12-year sentences and were confined to the segregation unit for 56 days. Six prisoners, including Mr Y, were transferred to other prisons, and a rather uneasy peace was restored. However, in October 1971 Mr Y, who had claimed that he was assaulted by several officers, was brought back to Albany to face charges that he had made 'false and malicious allegations' against the staff. Mr Y alleged that 'staff were out to get prisoners in the segregation unit', and that twice as many officers as usual were on duty. Staff did not deny that more officers were on duty, but pointed out that they had every reason to expect trouble. They claimed that the incidents began when the prisoner threw the contents of his chamber pot at officers supervising slopping out. No unnecessary force, they said, was used in returning the prisoner to his cell, even though he struggled against them. Prisoner Y said that he threw his pot on the floor when he saw the officers coming towards him, and that he was then beaten and carried back to his cell, where he was flung bodily into it, causing his head to strike the water pipe. None of his allegations against the staff were upheld. But the Board of Visitors expressed some disquiet about the insistence of Prison Department that Mr Y should be charged with making 'false and malicious allegations' instead of with 'assault'. Three charges of assault had in fact been dropped, even though the board felt satisfied that there was ample proof that the prisoner had assaulted officers. As it was, the medical evidence in respect of the injuries to Mr Y was not incompatible with his allegations that he had been thrown into his cell. In the event the prisoner was found guilty of the offence but, bearing in mind the circumstances, he received a relatively mild sentence and lost no remission.

It is not our purpose to comment on the truth or falsity of any of these allegations, for we were in no position to do so. The point is that allegations such as these, which were almost unheard of during the main research programme, were now beginning to become almost commonplace. There is also a sense in which, considerations of justice on one side, it hardly matters who is right or wrong. For once the charges are made they serve to perpetuate the situation of tension. Both sides sooner or later come to believe in the validity of their versions, and see in them sufficient legitimation to justify any further provocation or retaliation. The publicity did not help matters. The national Press took full advantage of the notoriety of the prisoners involved, and the *Daily Telegraph* broke the story under the headline:'Kray gang men in prison battle' (8 September 1971). It was claimed that notorious criminals had 'gained control of prison consultative committees' and that a number of prisoners had been injured after 'falling down stairs'. 'It is understood,' the report continued, 'that some of the more powerful prisoners have radios, radiograms and records sent in from outside, and several take up to £2.50 worth of newspapers each week.' The next day a report in the *Daily Mail* was headlined 'Mafia gang blamed for jail violence', and the *Telegraph* repeated that theme: '"Mafia regime" imposed by high risk prisoners'. In both stories the general secretary of the POA was quoted as blaming the dispersal policy for the Albany troubles. One of the local newspapers noted the difficulty of maintaining discipline among hardened prisoners 'when cases of rank insubordination are "punished" by a fine of 25 pence', and then went on to predict worse troubles ahead (*Southern Evening Echo*, 8 September 1971). Another stressed the need for reform: *The Portsmouth News* ran a front-page headline – 'MP urges get tough policy over jails' – and in an editorial called for better pay and conditions for prison officers as the costly but necessary answer to the 'Albany Prison Outrages' (9 September 1971). None of these reports was particularly well informed.

Nearly a year elapsed before Albany was the subject of extensive news coverage again, but this did not mean that the prison had returned to a state of social order. Two stories did leak out. In January 1972 it was reported that the police had been called to investigate an alleged assault by four prisoners on a 'top-security prisoner' who was found bleeding from a gash in his left cheek. Later that month firemen attended a fire near the segregation unit, to the accompaniment of cheers and whistles from the inmates; it was the twelfth fire in as many months. These were by no means the only events in a progressively deteriorating situation.

In October 1971 the thermostatic controls in the segregation unit heating system had broken down and the temperature rose to 84°F. Prisoners broke windows to improve the ventilation, and then refused to leave the unit to attend their own adjudications. The governor tried to reduce the numbers held in the unit as subversives from the new peak of 13 which had been reached in September. But it was a slow process. Not until February 1972 had the numbers been cut back to an average of two or three prisoners, and by then the situation in the segregation unit was precarious. Prisoners were given to making noisy demonstrations, and from time to time we heard complaints that prisoners had been beaten up. It was said that the staff could not be identified because the attacks were carried out by officers brought in from another part of the prison. One prisoner did get as far as making his complaint to the Board of Visitors, but he was unable or unwilling to name names. We have no direct evidence one way or another about these matters, although some members of staff to whom we spoke were unofficially prepared to admit that such things could happen. They pointed out that it is very hard to control all potentially violent situations, especially where there had been sustained provocation or a residue of past bad feeling.

When prisoners did demonstrate by shouting and banging this was dealt with by attempting to remove the ringleaders to a special cell (variously known as 'the strong cell', 'the box', 'chokey' or 'the hole') under Rule 45 of the Prison Rules. Early in March 1972, a prisoner whom we shall call Mr A had broken off the leg of his chair and used it to lead a demonstration in the segregation unit, during the course of which food trays were thrown out of the cell windows. Prisoner A continued his demonstration even after the others had quietened down; and the governor authorized his removal to a special cell. He was duly removed. However, discipline officers later decided, without prior approval, to remove another prisoner, Mr S, who had also been involved in the demonstration. When Mr S refused to leave his cell the officers decided to remove him forcibly. In fact no injuries were sustained in what probably amounted to a fairly minor piece of manhandling. Nevertheless the governor found it necessary to state that the decision to remove Mr S by force was open to criticism. He reminded his staff that standing orders required that removal to a special cell should be authorized by the most senior officer present in the establishment and that it should be supervised by a principal officer throughout.

On Friday, 17 March 1972, St Patrick's Day, during one of our periodic visits to the prison, two separate but probably related disturbances occurred. One of the chief officers who had recently joined Albany was called urgently to the carpentry shop, where seven long-term prisoners, four of them from D hall, were refusing to work. They claimed that as Roman Catholics they could not be obliged to work on a religious holiday, and they had tried and failed to organize a sit-down by the whole shop. The chief explained that St Patrick's Day was not a feast of obligation in England and was not therefore observed in English prisons. The prisoners thus had no grounds for protest and should return to work. After a lengthy dialogue, the chief told us later, the men did return to their benches, even if they could not be described as working. Later that morning we spoke to the catering principal officer. He had already explained the difficulties experienced in the last year, arising from the constant and concerted complaints of prisoners about the monotony of the vegetarian diet and, it seemed, about all meals which included fish. That day being

Friday, fish was again on the menu. As we were talking the deputy governor visited the kitchen, sampled the food and expressed himself satisfied. For what it is worth, though we did not try the fish on that occasion, whenever we had eaten in the prison in the past the fish was among the more palatable of the dishes provided. We left the kitchen and were discussing the refusal to work incident with the chief officer when he was called away to the D hall dining hall, where prisoners were refusing to eat the fish. We learned later that the prisoners had successfully held out until the governor instructed that an alternative meal be provided. That evening there were further complaints about the tea in D hall. Again an alternative menu was provided.

We did not return to the prison for several days, but it was clear that the prison had been very tense in our absence. Throughout the weekend the prison was described as 'restless' and 'uneasy', albeit without overt trouble. Then on Monday there was an orchestrated complaint about the vegetarian diet. When the matter was reported to the governor he again gave instructions for an alternative meal to be provided, which caused some dislocation in the work of the kitchen. By the time we returned to the prison the catering officer, under renewed pressure, had taken a period of leave, and he was subsequently transferred out of the front line to another prison.

Later that week the extent of intimidation among prisoners was vividly brought home to us. Prisoner X, whom we discussed earlier, had been transferred to another prison, where he subsequently died. A collection was organized on behalf of his wife. A lifer, who wanted nothing more than to do his time quietly, was asked to donate to the fund. He refused on the grounds that he had regarded the activities of Mr X as contributing to the mounting aggro in the prison. He told us that he was then visited in his cell by three prisoners who threatened: 'You contribute five bob or be down the block tonight.' So he paid out 25p, about a third of his weekly income. On the same day one of us was in the B hall office. A prisoner knocked and entered to talk to the principal officer. He explained that his budgie was missing from its cage, even though it was unable to fly. Sensing further trouble, the prisoner asked if it would be possible to change halls. The principal officer said he would take the matter up, but he also pointed out '*you* know the situation, there's not much we can do to stop it'. The prisoner departed with the words: 'Well it looks like the block for me then.' The next day he was in the segregation unit on Rule 43 at his own request.

Albany was not the only prison facing problems. In May, after months of rumblings and rumours, Preservation of the Rights of Prisoners (PROP) was unveiled, as an organization of ex-prisoners, radical reformers and academics dedicated to becoming 'the most effective pressure group for penal reform this century' (*Telegraph*, 12 May 1972). Already the organization had claimed to have handed in petitions protesting about the conditions in Brixton and Pentonville, and to have planned a three-day hunger-strike at Hull. For the next few months hardly a week went by without one or more of the prisons in the system experiencing a demonstration of one kind or another. In June, 102 prisoners in Albany staged a 24-hour demonstration by staying in their cells. It passed off peacefully. It is not clear whether the demonstration was organized with outside help from PROP or not, although it was certainly aimed at bringing about recognition for that group. But the disturbances which continued in the dining halls almost certainly had no connection with the activities of the new 'prisoners' union'.

The arrival of a new catering officer effected only a temporary respite in the complaints over meals. Within four months he too was transferred. The most serious incidents occurred on four consecutive days at the end of July 1972. On each day the protests took much the same form. Prisoners carried their meal trays from the dining halls and threw them on the floor. Relatively few prisoners were actually involved, mostly from B hall, while the majority ate their meals quietly. But large numbers of prisoners refused to go to work that week in sympathy with those protesting about the diet. One prisoner, Mr Z from E hall, apparently discovered a bag, which was subsequently learned to have come from Camp Hill farm, on which was stencilled the words NOT FIT FOR HUMAN CONSUMPTION. He waved it overhead, shouting, and produced an immediate reaction from the other prisoners. Mr Z was seen by the governor and warned that such subversive behaviour would not be tolerated in future. On each of these occasions order was restored quite quickly, prisoners returned to their halls, and the normal routine was resumed by the evening. Then, on the last day of July, a group of 12 prisoners broke away from the main body on outside recreation and sat down in the exercise yards. Nine of them stayed out all night, returning to their cells the following day.

Throughout these disturbances it was alleged that the prisoners involved were acting under the instructions of prisoner W in B hall, though he himself did not participate. Not surprisingly, the demands were made once again to use Rule 43 to isolate the subversive prisoners. The governor resisted some demands and acceded to others. The incidents were undoubtedly unpleasant and frightening, even though no violence was offered to staff. And some prisoners who had gone to work as usual found that their beds had been soiled with excrement or soaked with urine when they returned to their cells. One prisoner, whom we had known slightly in 1968 and who was now back in Albany for a second time, felt that Albany was now effectively managed by a small group of prisoners. He warned that it was only a matter of time before people got badly hurt.

Meanwhile the PROP campaign was approaching its climax: a national prisoner strike. On 4 August 1972, according to official figures, some 5,500 prisoners in 28 establishments participated in demonstrations which took various forms: refusing work, sitting in cells, dining halls and exercise yards. The like of it had never been seen in British penal history. The strike at Albany was 100 per cent effective. It had been advertised well in advance and was apparently peaceful. The governor and chief officer chatted to prisoners and reported that the demonstration was being conducted in a good-natured way. It was made clear that the protest was aimed at improving the situation of people in prison generally, rather than specifically at conditions in Albany. Moreover, Prison Department had issued instructions that peaceful demonstrations were to be handled with velvet gloves: 'the Department's policy was to seek to contain . . . without needless confrontation or provocation' (Cmnd 5375, 1973, para. 149). But goodwill had been steadily evaporating in Albany, and it is not surprising that staff found it difficult to make fine distinctions between the different kinds of protest. Indeed at its annual conference in May 1972 the POA had already voiced its concern at the thin dividing line between passive demonstrations such as those envisaged by PROP and the violence of the Parkhurst riots (*Guardian,* 27 May 1972). As far as they were concerned, one thing led to another. When it was announced that the Home Office had agreed to meet representatives from PROP to discuss, without prejudice, specific complaints (*Guardian,* 5 August 1972) prison officers were apt to feel their own complaints about pay and conditions were being neglected. A new feeling of militancy among members of the POA was led by officers from Albany.

On 5 August, the day following the PROP strike, the governor left Albany for his annual summer leave. On Wednesday, 16 August, three prisoners were discovered in an escape attempt, and a fourth was found in possession of escape equipment. An improvised ladder and grappling iron, items of civilian clothing and about £30 in cash had been concealed in various places, including a record-player and the base of a large birdcage. When the governor returned from leave on Monday, 21 August he faced an angry staff, who demanded much firmer action against subversive and security-risk prisoners. The following day reports leaked out of a struggle for power in Albany, and these were picked up by the national Press. On 23 August *The Times* reported that Albany officers had told their national executive that discipline 'had been assumed by some of the country's most violent criminals' who were said to be terrorizing 'the staff and weaker prisoners'. Unless the Home Office took immediate steps to restore the situation the officers said they would work to rule, ban overtime and even go on strike, leaving the prison 'at the mercy of a score of hardened criminals'. Two senior officials from the national executive announced that they would visit the prison for talks in the hope of averting such action. But it was also announced that representatives from 50 other institutions had pledged support for Albany officers. After a three-hour meeting in London the executive committee of the POA drew up a policy statement designed to guide members in coping with emergencies caused by inmate demonstrations. Among other things it suggested that officers should report all infringements of prison discipline, no matter how trivial, for adjudication. It was later reported that the Home Office was willing to discuss the matter with the Prison Officers' Association. In the *Guardian* that day it was noted that an offer by PROP to discuss the situation had been rejected by the POA, which did not recognize its existence. PROP, no doubt with tongue in cheek, subsequently offered to call a prisoner strike in sympathy with the officers' action for better conditions! The *Daily Express* carried a long interview with an unidentified Albany officer under the headline 'Locked in with the Prison Mafia'. He spoke of a 'victory by fear campaign' waged against the staff, of 'tough young men who openly scoff in your face', and of mealtimes when 'you feel as if at any moment all hell might break loose'. Six months earlier a number of officers had spoken to us in much the same vein. They told us that they 'felt sick at the prospect of going to work' and that they were now 'frightened to go into the halls' on their own.

Meanwhile, back in the prison, a stormy staff meeting was held on Wednesday, 23 August, and this was followed next day by the meeting between national and local representatives of the POA and the governor. At that meeting the governor was pressed to give an assurance that if staff decided a prisoner was subversive then the governor would use his powers to segregate him under Rule 43, or else arrange for his transfer elsewhere. The governor said he would give careful consideration to their views but declined to give any assurance which would abrogate his responsibility to use his discretion in such matters. In the course of the meeting the governor was presented with a list of 24 grievances, in which it was claimed that he had failed to give the staff the support they required to maintain order: for example, by failing to insist that 'escape list' prisoners should change cells when this was thought necessary on security grounds, and for taking no action over some of the recent incidents in the dining halls. The threat of a work-to-rule was not averted, even though the chairman of the POA had 'left the governor in no doubt' about the feelings of his members (*The Times*, 25 August 1972).

The scene was now being set for the most cataclysmic event yet in Albany's short history. Hardly had the national representative of the POA departed, when the governor was advised by members of his staff that in view of the recent find of escape materials, and as a result of information received about the possibility of further escape attempts, it would be prudent to carry out a complete security search of the establishment. The governor agreed in principle, but thought it better to wait until after the August Bank Holiday weekend. The staff stressed the urgency of the situation, and advised that in any case a complete search of the prison could be carried out in one day and would thus be over before the weekend started. Early on Friday morning the staff were briefed and prisoners were returned to cells after slopping out, so that the whole prison was locked up, and the search began. Prisoners did not know that a security check was being carried out and many assumed that the POA had begun their work-to-rule. Some prisoners thought they would be compensated for time lost at work, and so did not mind being banged up – at first.

It soon became obvious that the search could not be completed in one day. As prison officers began their search the rules regarding unauthorized articles in cells were, for the first time, interpreted according to the letter, and the long-standing flexibility that had characterized hall management in the past was finally reversed. By Friday. night less than one-third of the occupied cells had been scrutinized, and it was clear that, once begun, the operation would now have to continue throughout the weekend. The governor decided that it would be necessary to provide some compensation for the loss of expected activities among the prisoners.

On Saturday prisoners were let out of cells only once to go to the recess. As the day wore on, and it became clear to prisoners what was happening and how long it would take, the tension mounted. By that evening less than half the cells had been searched. The tension snapped and the prison erupted. One prisoner, released on home leave, later told the Press that the trouble was precipitated by the provocative remarks of the staff and the insensitivity with which they handled prisoners' possessions. 'They made it clear that they would keep the search going as long as possible, so that they could keep us locked up,' he said. 'On Saturday night the tea was hours late and the screws were going round the block ripping picture boards and fitted furniture off the cell walls with a crowbar and a hammer. About 7.30 a man shouted, "The bastards have ripped the board off the wall, two photos are missing and the one of my wife is torn up." He picked up his chair and started smashing the glass. Then about six fellows began to follow suit, and one man, who had been in the prison only about four days, set fire to his mattress and threw it out of the window' (*The Times*, 31 August 1972). Whether this account of the beginning of the riot is accurate or not we do not know. Certainly the discipline staff were in no mood to stand any nonsense, and it seems to have been the case, judging from the many conflicting accounts that we have heard and read, that some members of the 'heavy mob' went about their task with excessive zeal. Indeed, it would be surprising in the circumstances had they not done so. Even if all the staff had acted with the greatest circumspection throughout, and probably most of the moderates among the officers conducted themselves with considerable restraint, a remark such as that quoted by the prisoner on home leave would have been enough to induce the mass hysteria that followed among inmates who had all been locked up for 48 hours.

The rioting continued on and off for two further days and nights until Tuesday morning: windows were smashed, cell furniture was broken and burned, mattresses and clothing were set on fire and flung from the windows. Indeed a great variety of objects were thrown into the yards below, some of them, no doubt, to avoid detection in the search which was still going on. Since all prisoners were locked in cells the staff were in no great physical danger. But the prison was reduced to a squalid state. One prison officer was reported as saying: 'The din was frightening and today the prison is in a shambles. One can only describe the last 48 hours as an orgy of defiance and destruction. In the present mood of unrest we dare not let the prisoners out' (*The Times*, 28 August 1972). The sanitary recesses, for those permitted to use them, got 'filthier and filthier' (*The Times*, 31 August 1972). Conditions for those who had smashed their own furniture were even worse, for they were not let out to empty their pots. Prison officers pointed out that nothing would be done to improve the conditions until the prisoners began to behave. One visitor said: 'They are being locked up day and night like animals. My husband has not even got a mattress to sleep on.' When asked why, she replied: 'Because he burnt it during the riot, didn't he?' (*The Times*, 29 August 1972). Over the Bank Holiday the wives of Albany officers, concerned at what might happen when the 'lock-in' ended, picketed the wives of Albany prisoners as they visited, in an attempt to 'stop the rot'. There were renewed demonstrations on the Monday night, but by Tuesday morning the search was completed and the prison was quiet.

The riots in Albany were widely reported. 'Cells damaged and fires started at jail after mass escape plot foiled' was the complex headline in *The Times* (28 August). The *Daily Mirror* was shorter and even more dramatic. 'Siege at the Jail of Fear' (28 August). In the next few days the headlines changed as prisoners in Parkhurst, Camp Hill, Chelmsford, Gartree, Dartmoor, Maidstone, Liverpool, Cardiff and even Peterhead climbed on to roofs and stayed there, partly in sympathy for their fellows in Albany, partly in renewed pressure for the recognition of PROP.'Parkhurst prisoners scale 60 ft to signal to Albany jail, said *The Times* (29 August). 'NOW IT'S PRISONER POWER' roared the *Express* (30 August). But, contrary to the impression given in most reports, very little evidence was discovered for the existence of a 'mass escape plot', and nothing of major significance was revealed in the great search apart from a small supply of money. It is true that items of escape equipment had been found before the search began, and that a large number of technically unauthorized, but previously tolerated, articles were removed from cells. Some of these could have been used as weapons; but, as any policeman knows, there is scarcely any object which in some circumstance could not be construed as an offensive weapon. Press accounts also differed as to the amount of damage done in the riots, the numbers of prisoners involved and what proceedings were taken against them. There is no doubt that the damage was extensive, with furniture and bedding destroyed in between 50 and 100 cells. Many more had broken windows and minor damage. According to the prison records, about two-fifths of the prisoners were actually charged with offences, and many of them had multiple charges against them. All told, 158 prisoners were dealt with on 654 counts, mostly by the governor, although a few cases were heard by the Board of Visitors. Several prisoners were immediately transferred to Wandsworth; and most of the remainder received punishments reported as ranging from a caution to a fourteen-day loss of remission (*The Times*, 1 September 1972).

If the search had not produced much material evidence for substantiating the existence of an escape plot, it had provided a clear show of strength on the part of the staff. They had, through confrontation, forced on the governor, the Home Office and the public the need for firm action to regain control of the prison. In the aftermath of the riot the governor had little choice but to accede to requests to 'weed out' the troublemakers. Some were transferred to other establishments. But on 13 September, two weeks after the uproar, the numbers of 'subversive' prisoners held on Rule 43 had reached the staggering total of 67, a fifth of the Albany population. The segregation unit had only 43 cells, and these had to cope with prisoners undergoing punishment, awaiting hearings or segregated for their own protection, as well as subversives. Virtually the whole of E hall had therefore to be taken over as an extension to the segregation unit. By that time the Home Secretary had announced a review of the dispersal policy and a review of the system of rewards and punishments available to maintain control in prison (*The Times*, 6 September 1972).

At the end of the riot the staff were firmly in control – so long as the prison remained locked up. Two weeks after the riot there were fewer than 60 prisoners working, and these were employed only on essential jobs. The workshops and the dining halls had been closed before the Bank Holiday and remained so. Meals were served in cells. Prisoners were unlocked at 07.40 for slopping out and were then returned to cells. The minimum statutory exercise period of one hour was provided, for prisoners not under segregation, during the course of the morning. For those in the segregation unit and E hall special permission had been obtained to reduce the exercise period to half an hour a day. Prisoners not under segregation were allowed a limited period of association in the evenings until 20.00 hours, but education classes had stopped and access to the library was curtailed. For most of the time everyone was locked in cells. It is fair to say that many prisoners by now preferred to be banged up than to be let out. But equally the staff were reluctant to open the prison up lest their position be undermined.

The governor was anxious to restore the prison to a state of normal functioning, and representatives of the Board of Visitors offered to meet representatives of the local branch of the POA to see if they could help. The meeting took place on 15 September. The POA representatives said that they too were concerned to get the prison back to normal and that they would co-operate with the governor to this end. Indeed, they had already agreed to ease prisoners out of cells over the coming weekend and to recommence the industries in the following week. But the officers stressed that in their view the hard-core discipline problems remained. If order was to be maintained they would have to move forward step by step. In any case the new 'normality' could not be a return to the situation prevailing three months earlier. There could be no going back, for example, to associated meals in the dining halls. Pending the outcome of the Home Office reviews recently announced, however, the officers said they would call off their threatened work-to-rule.

Albany never did return to what had been normal prior to August 1972. The workshops were re-opened, but ironically they never achieved a working week that was significantly longer than under the original two-shift system. Because of restrictions in the daily routine the workshops were opened on a 30-hours-a-week basis instead of the 39 hours which had been the *raison d'être* of the single-shift system. Prisoners were compensated for the 9 hours of work lost at the basic rate under the incentive earnings scheme and, interestingly enough, were said to achieve the same output as formerly. The dining halls were never used again – at least not for eating in. Meals have been served in cells ever since. Complaints about the fish and the vegetarian diet, though not eliminated, were soon overshadowed by complaints that the food was cold, and in October 1972 hotplates were installed in all halls. The amount of time spent in associated activity was greatly curtailed. Instead of the all-day unlock which had operated in the past, prisoners now had to be let out for particular activities and were returned to cells immediately afterwards. Access to washing and toilet facilities was thereby also reduced, and this became an irritating source of complaint. Education classes were resumed in October, and the evening association period began to operate more or less as before, if for shorter periods and under closer supervision. Staff training, which had been run down since the earlier troubles of 1971, stopped altogether in August 1972 and did not begin again until March 1973.

During October 1972 the segregation unit still overflowed into E hall and the number of subversives held there remained high. The prisoners made frequent complaints about their conditions. They were permitted a weekly bath, and could slop out morning and night, and were provided with a bed and a chair. But they were not permitted to keep cage birds, and the exercise period remained half an hour a day. It was not until the end of 1972 that the exercise period for these prisoners was restored to the statutory minimum. At the beginning of November, however, fifteen prisoners who had been continuously in the segregation unit since the August disturbances barricaded themselves in their cells. Two of them even managed to break down the partition walls which separated them. Considerable damage was done and once again the segregation unit was the centre of noisy demonstrations. The situation was contained and the protesters disciplined, but further action was required if tension was to be reduced. For the first time some systematic variation in the use of the residential halls was introduced. D hall was to be operated with a tightly controlled regime, less strict than the segregation unit but more closely supervised than the rest of the establishment. Some of the so-called subversive prisoners were moved into D hall pending a return to the general population. By the end of November the remaining 27 subversive prisoners could be contained in the segregation unit, thus allowing E hall to be handed over to the workmen who were now in the final stages of fitting up the electronic locking system.

There were only 12 prisoners on Rule 43 as subversives at the end of December, though some of these were still so detained in March 1973 some seven months after the riots. In spite of the measures taken to reduce tension the staff remained jumpy. Perhaps under the influence of the recommendations of the national executive, officers reported every infringement of the regulations, no matter how trivial, as a disciplinary offence. In the course of the year Albany had clocked up 2,148 offences, 800 more than any other prison, and three-quarters of them had been reported in the last four months. With 6.2 offences per head, Albany reported exactly twice as many offences as Aylesbury, its nearest rival, and well over five times the national average for closed prisons for men. Even if the 654 offences resulting directly from the riot were excluded Albany would still have been top of the league by a clear margin. Yet in the preceding five years Albany had been in no way exceptional in this respect. Even in 1971 when the first serious troubles arose only 1.9 offences per head had been reported.

The opening months of 1973 saw some progress towards a more peaceful atmosphere in Albany. Serious incidents were fewer and the intervals between them longer. Even some escape equipment which was found on the recreation ground was thought to have been discarded because it was 'too hot to handle' rather than hidden for subsequent use *(Guardian,* 24 April 1973). Many staff and prisoners wanted to let bygones be bygones and to maintain a state of truce. But there was a significant number of 'subversives' on both sides of the bars, and the situation remained edgy. Some prisoners were as likely to empty their chamber pots out of the cell windows as in the recesses so that the yards were in a semi-permanent state of squalor. Some officers were anxious to promote industrial action in Albany whenever trouble emerged in other establishments. The prisoners continued to make complaints about the conditions. The staff continued to report every infringement. Albany was once again the prison with the most reported offences per head in 1973, with 3.97 offences compared with 3.22 at Swinfen Hall which came second, and 1.15 which was the national average.

On 11 May, in a written Parliamentary answer, the Home

Secretary, Robert Carr, announced the results of his review of the dispersal system. He concluded that it would be 'undesirable and unsafe to concentrate in a single prison those prisoners who are most likely to cause trouble or who are in the highest security category' (Hansard, vol. 856, cols. *215-6*). Instead he proposed to increase the number of dispersal prisons from six to nine. Where they were lacking at present segregation units would be built, and the existing buildings and perimeters would be further strengthened. Tighter limits would be imposed on the number of prisoners allowed to congregate at work, meals, or during association periods. Essentially this would mean the organization of institutions on a unit or wing basis. Management would be strengthened, staffing levels and staff training in the dispersal prisons would be kept under review. For prisoners who could not adequately be contained within the existing facilities two further measures were announced: the provision of secure cells in local prisons for the temporary transfer of troublemakers, and the setting up of two 'control units' for confinement for longer periods until a return to normal prison life was justified. The control units, it was later learned, were to be built at Wakefield and Wormwood Scrubs; and although no details of the regime were then published, it was said that it would be 'strict'. Not surprisingly, these plans were widely, and often somewhat wildly, reported in the Press. Rather less publicity was given to the results of the review on rewards and punishments revealed at the annual conference of Boards of Visitors the following month.

Shortly after the Home Secretary's announcement it was revealed that the coefficient of security at Albany was to be raised yet again. The dividing walls between cells in the segregation unit were to be reinforced to prevent any repetition of the destruction of November 1972. And, incredibly, work was to begin on a process of guniting which would turn the outer fence into a solid wall! In other ways the outcome of the Home Secretary's review had already been anticipated. The basis for allocating prisoners to halls in Albany had been undergoing reconsideration since the turn of the year. In April the completion of the re-wiring in E hall meant that, at last, all five halls could be available, thus increasing the scope for any reorganization. By the summer the new functional arrangements became clear. A hall was to become a discharge hall, housing prisoners in the last eight months of their sentences; it was hoped to develop pre-release programmes there.

Elsewhere the aim was to separate short-term from long-term prisoners as far as possible. B hall was to take the short-termers, while C and D halls were to accommodate the long-termers. Most, though not necessarily all, of the category-A prisoners, and those serving the longest sentences, would be in D hall. E hall was to become the new induction unit. The only thing that prevented the new arrangements from being brought fully into effect was a shortage of staff.

The whole question of staffing levels in Albany, as throughout the service, was a complex one. The manpower control team which visited Albany in July and August 1971 had recommended an establishment of 190 officers for the operation of all five halls. Two years later there were still only 150 officers in post. On the other hand, in June 1973, when Albany was the subject of a full-scale Prison Department inspection, the inspectors suggested that the prison was being run with unnecessarily high manning levels, especially in view of the rather restricted regime which now obtained in the prison. Prison officers in Albany, however, were not prepared to accept lower manning levels; and they claimed that even to keep the prison operating on the existing pattern required much more than the 14 hours of weekly overtime which was the agreed maximum that prison officers could be required to work. Many officers complained publicly and privately about the disruption to family life, and the reduced vigilance at work, which could result from excessive overtime. Very long periods of overtime working also produced anomalous disparities between the pay of newly-recruited basic-grade staff and their chief officers, who were not paid on hourly rates. The situation in Albany was, in this respect, not so very different from that at other establishments. And with low recruitment and high wastage no improvements in the staffing situation could be expected. In July 1973, on the day that the Prison Department published its annual report, the POA finally called for an official ban on overtime beyond the agreed limit, to be imposed for a period of one month beginning in August. The implementation of the overtime ban in Albany could only result in a further curtailment of associated prisoner activities, even though the inspectors had called for the restoration of a full working week and a return to communal dining for at least some prisoners as soon as possible. In fact the working day for prisoners was trimmed by a further quarter of an hour, and evening association by half an hour, for the duration of the work-to-rule.

In the middle of the staff work-to-rule it was announced that Albany was to have yet another governor. Mr Footer was to be transferred to Risley remand centre as from January 1974, and his place in Albany would be taken by Mr Carnegie. But by that time two further incidents of a serious nature had led to a deteriorating atmosphere in the prison.

At the beginning of July the electronic coffin metaphor took on a macabre reality when a prisoner burned to death in his cell. One evening, after being told of arrangements for transfer to another prison, the prisoner began to smash up his cell. This was observed by the night patrol and reported to the orderly officer. The usual procedure in such circumstances was followed, which was to give the prisoner some twenty minutes or so to let off steam before taking any action. A short while later, however, the control room received an alarm call to say that there was a fire in the hall. Five minutes elapsed between the receipt of the call and the opening of the cell by the night patrol, by which time the fire was firmly established. The prisoner died next day. At the inquest a verdict of accidental death was returned and no criticism was made of the staff, although the coroner felt that one officer per hall was insufficient for night patrol purposes. It was not the first death to have occurred in Albany (there had been at least two successful suicides since the prison had opened), but it left its mark, especially on those in adjoining cells who had listened, helpless, to the screams.

The second incident occurred towards the end of August. For the first time a member of staff was taken hostage and held at knife point for several hours. The officer was eventually released unhurt when the prisoner was allowed to see his wife, who was then held in custody in London. Once again the tension began to mount, although for a time the moderate elements on both sides seemed to prevail. The prisoner concerned received little sympathy from his fellow-prisoners in D hall, who were prepared to support the staff so long as there were no reprisals. The staff acted with restraint and the prisoner was later brought before the Board of Visitors; they ordered that he forfeit 360 days' remission.

But the situation threatened to get out of hand as the work-to-rule went on, and both prisoners and staff seemed ready to respond to what they saw as provocation. On one occasion only the long-term prisoners in D hall were allowed to stay up to watch the whole of an international football match on television. Prisoners in other halls had to switch off at the usual time, half way through the match. The following day those prisoners who had been deprived staged a sit-down demonstration. In the now familiar pattern the staff asked the governor to weed out the troublemakers and place them on Rule 43. The governor resisted, pointing out that the protest had been passive and orderly. But further incidents followed, and it was soon clear that a new confrontation was brewing between prisoners and staff and between the staff and the governor. Towards the end of October the wives of prison officers, apparently accompanied by some of their husbands, again picketed the prison calling on the governor to take firmer action against disruptive prisoners (*Guardian*, 26 October 1973). The officers prevailed. Numbers in the segregation unit began to rise again, and the prisoners contained there renewed their complaints. One of them set fire to his cell, and early in November it was reported that a number of fire bombs had been discovered in the course of a routine search (*Guardian*, 3 November 1973).

Before the end of the year a second member of staff, a civilian instructor, was taken hostage, this time in an escape attempt. The escape was quickly foiled and the prisoner was subsequently charged, brought before the courts and sentenced to a further two years' imprisonment. By then, one of the leading actors in the dramatic events that had been played out at Albany had left the stage. On 9 November 1973, at the height of the latest confrontation and just seven weeks before he was due to end his tour of duty in what had become the most difficult prison in the country, Gifford Footer collapsed and died.

Interpretation

If one is to understand the events which occurred at Albany it is essential to make clear distinctions between certain matters which remained confused in the public reporting of them.

The first of these concerns the nature of the events involved. In our view the often violent disturbances which occurred in Albany in 1971, and which recurred and spread to other dispersal prisons in 1972 and 1973, were events of a quite different order from the usually peaceful demonstrations organized by, or in sympathy with, PROP. The former had to do with the specific conditions of custody for long-term prisoners and had antecedents in the Parkhurst riot of 1969 and the problems generated by the special wings. The latter were always more broadly based, being concerned with the conditions for all prisoners, and their rights both inside and outside prison. From time to time these movements overlapped as one seemed to feed off the other in a kind of symbiotic process. But this in no way invalidates the essential independence of the two developments. Many of the disturbances in Albany hardly rose above the level of underworld in-fighting, though they increasingly took the form of direct power struggles between the uniformed staff and the inmates. The disturbances were essentially local in scope and, in spite of what was sometimes said, events elsewhere in the system were of little real significance to the participants. In any case the disturbances began long before PROP got off the ground and would have continued whether or not that organization had ever existed. The prisoners' rights movement, however, always aspired to the arena of radical politics, even if sometimes those aspirations were subverted. The strategy was to use civil disobedience techniques in an attempt to bring pressure on the Home Office first for recognition and then for reform. Demonstrations were often locally based, and sometimes geared to specific complaints, but the intention was always to use particular cases to point up wider issues. The publicity given to the conditions for long-term prisoners in the special wings was an undoubted stimulus to the emergence of PROP. But that organization would probably have followed much the same natural history with or without the riots in Parkhurst, Albany and Gartree. Unfortunately the participants – prisoners, prison officers and the Home Office – were, for various reasons, either unable to make these distinctions at the time or else found it to their advantage to obscure them. So it is hardly surprising that newspaper coverage was often confused. To the outsider, and in retrospect, it is easy to identify the sit-down demonstrations in Albany of 2 June and 4 August 1972 as having to do with the aims of PROP, whereas the incidents on St Patrick's Day and the concerted disturbances in the dining halls in July of that year, for example, clearly had other motives behind them. But it is fair to point out that these events followed one another quite closely, and some prisoners possibly played a leading part in events of both types. In the circumstances it must sometimes have been genuinely difficult for many prisoners to distinguish between them. And if the staff did see a distinction, it is perhaps understandable that they were afraid it would turn out to be a distinction without much of a difference.

In fact the uniformed staff were much more worried about the problems of control in relation to long-term prisoners, and it was undoubtedly they who released stories to the Press which referred to an attempted take-over by the prison 'mafia' (*Telegraph,* 9 September 1971). When subsequently PROP-inspired demonstrations took place in Albany and elsewhere, it was in the interests of discipline officers to use these larger-scale protests as ammunition, at the local level in their struggle with the governor for tighter control in the prison, and at the national level in their campaign to have the dispersal policy reviewed and reversed. Certainly the general secretary of the POA exaggerated the connection between the two kinds of event when he was interviewed by the *Guardian* on 23 August 1972. In an article which first made it clear that the POA did not recognize PROP, the unrest in prisons was then attributed to failure to carry out the recommendations of the Mountbatten report. The general secretary was quoted as saying: 'The really violent men are responsible for organizing these disturbances, *after getting word from outside*' (emphasis added).

It was not just the prison officers who blurred the distinction, for they were aided and abetted by spokesmen from the Home Office. The Prison Department was no more enamoured of publicity which suggested the emergence of a mafia-style take-over than it was of reports about the existence of a widespread prisoners' rights movement. It sought to play down both issues by denying them. In a letter to the general secretary of the POA published, in part, in *The Times* on 25 August 1972, the Department stated: 'Contrary to what has been said in the Press, we have no reason to believe that the demonstrations in prison this summer have owed their origins to what have been described as mafia-type groups trying to take control within the prison community.' But, confusingly, the letter also said : 'Most demonstrations have been more or less spontaneous and related primarily to matters of local concern within the prison.' Quite how such a statement could have been sustained in the light of the national strike on 4 August, and the Department's own preparations for that event, is not clear, except that requests for the implementation of a national prisoners' charter may be more easily handled if they can be construed as 'matters of local concern'. In any case, the POA were quick to see the inconsistency, and the general secretary retorted that spontaneous local actions were 'exactly what we mean by mafia-style attempts to gain control of discipline in some prisons'.

Nothing is to be gained by denying the existence of these two separate movements, nor by confusing one with the other. In the pages which follow we hope to throw some light on those disturbances which arose specifically in Albany out of the circumstances in which long-term prisoners were held. We are not concerned here with those events that were inspired or organized by PROP.

The second source of confusion concerns just who was involved in the disturbances. The impression to be derived from the Press reports was that the trouble in the dispersal prisons was caused by the very category-A prisoners who had been dispersed there from the special wings. When the Albany disturbances were reported, the usual practice was to rehearse the names of the more notorious criminals housed there and the crimes for which they had been sentenced, regardless of whether these prisoners had anything to do with the events actually under review. Of course some category-A high-security-risk prisoners were involved in intimidation, in struggles for power, and in subverting the authority of staff. But just as many took no part whatsoever in these events. And still others were much more likely to find themselves in the segregation unit on Rule 43 at their own request and for their own protection, than they were to be placed there for subversive activities or as a result of disciplinary offences under Rule 47 of the Prison Rules. Many of those who were involved in the disturbances were not category-A prisoners nor ever likely to be classified as such. Prison officers, of course, were aware of this. But perhaps in their anxiety to link the troubles in prisons to the implementation of the dispersal policy they did little to clarify who the participants were. Or perhaps their explanations fell on deaf ears. Thus the prison officer who was 'Locked in with the prison Mafia', as the *Express* put it spoke of 'young toughs' and 'Big Men' without, of course, specifying who they were. We do not know precisely whom he had in mind, but the probability is that the 'young toughs' at least were category-B or even category-C prisoners, who were serving sentences for unspectacular crimes that had received little publicity at the time. Nevertheless, the published article listed five 'big criminal names' all of whom were classified in category A, and left the impression that if these were not the actual men concerned then it was men like them who were responsible. While one of the men named was indeed suspected of being a moving force behind some of the incidents, another was virtually permanently segregated for his own protection, and a third was well known and respected by insiders as being among the most moderating influences in the prison community. The Prison Department were also aware that security-risk prisoners were not always troublemakers in prison. They were, in any case, to be reminded of it periodically. But, as we have seen, at the time of the troubles officials seemed more concerned to deny the existence of any 'mafia groups' than to give an inkling of who was behind the 'spontaneous' disturbances.

All this is not to say that the troubles in Albany were not directly attributable to the implementation of the dispersal policy, because we believe that they were. But it is to say that there is a vitally important distinction to be made between prisoners who constitute a risk to security and prisoners who constitute a threat to the good order and discipline in the prison. Of course some prisoners do fall into both categories, but there are probably more who come into only one or the other, and for the great majority of prisoners these categories are almost irrelevant. In so far as this distinction has important implications for policy we return to it in our final chapter.

It is impossible to avoid the conclusion that the dispersal policy was responsible for the massive deterioration in the quality of life in Albany between 1969 and 1972. The real question is, what aspects of that policy and its implementation in Albany brought such a transformation about. We can divide our analysis conveniently into two parts. First we will try to show how the policy was implemented and its immediate effects in the Albany setting. Secondly we will attempt to examine what might have been done to prevent the adverse effects, or at least to contain them.

When we left Albany in 1969 the prison community was wide open. As we have shown in the preceding chapters the regime had been tightened up somewhat in anticipation of receiving more difficult prisoners, but it remained by prison standards a flexible and humane establishment. The prisoners were unlocked from first thing in the morning until last thing at night, and had free association within their halls for most of the day when they were not at work. There were further opportunities to associate with prisoners from other halls at work, on the way to and from meals, and during outside recreation periods. The halls were loosely supervised and a blind eye was turned on many activities, if only because of the impossibility of doing otherwise given the physical layout of the halls. Prisoners responded to all this in a rich variety of ways: from what we earlier described as *uncertain negative retreat*, through the *indulgence of secondary comforts,* to *gleaning* and *doing one's own bird.* Some prisoners were involved in *jailing* and still others adapted by what we called *opportunism,* a calculated mixture of jailing and gleaning. Although these prisoners could reasonably be described as 'difficult' recidivists, as far as management was concerned they were nuisances rather than real villains. The most notorious prisoners had been convicted of fraud or domestic murder, rather than anything that would have caused an outcry had they escaped. And much of the jailing and opportunism involved attitudinizing and posturing: it enabled prisoners to make out but it posed no great threat either to institutional control or the safety of other prisoners. There were some long-sentence prisoners in Albany who were well versed in crime and prison culture. These were capable of organizing and manipulating others; but they preferred to do their own time and were strong enough to resist temptations or pressures to do otherwise.

As the coefficient of security was raised, and especially after October 1970, so the character of the population in Albany changed dramatically. In May 1969, at the time we took our sample, there were 348 prisoners in Albany, of whom one was classified (presumably anachronistically) as category A, and 24 had no security rating in their records. Eight prisoners, little more than two per cent, were classed in category B; the overwhelming majority, 314 prisoners, were classified in category C, with one prisoner in category D. By the time we returned to the prison in September 1971, according to the figures then supplied to us, there had not only been the dispersal of 28 category-A prisoners but also a vast influx of category-B prisoners, who now numbered 204. Between them these categories accounted for two-thirds of the Albany population. The numbers in categories C and D had been reduced to 119, and these accounted for only one-third of the population.

There were rather more prisoners in the youngest (under 21 years) and oldest (over 51 years) age categories, and fewer in the intermediate ranges in 1971 than there had been in 1969, but the differences did not reach statistical significance. There were also fewer prisoners with no previous convictions and more with over 10 previous convictions in 1971; but again the differences were not statistically significant. On the other hand, more prisoners in 1971 had passed through approved schools, borstals or detention centres before coming to prison than was formerly the case, and these differences were significant at the five per cent level. These prisoners would come within our definition of state-raised youths which we used in chapter 8. The most striking changes, however, were in the nature of the offences for which prisoners had been currently sentenced and the length of sentences they were serving. It is these factors, of course, that are reflected in the higher security rating of the prisoners. The figures supplied to us for offence and length of sentence were not in the same form as when we had collected our information two years earlier. On current offence we were given separate figures for Class I offences against the person, and Class II offences against property with violence, but the offences in Classes III to VI had been grouped together. Nevertheless when we grouped our data for 1969 in this way for comparative purposes, a sharp increase in Class I and Class II offences at the expense of other categories was shown, and the difference was statistically significant at the one per cent level. The trend we had observed between May 1968 and May 1969, whereby Class II offences had displaced Class III offences against property without violence as the main offence class, had been further exaggerated. The details are given in Table 9.1.

Table 9.1   Percentage distribution by current offence: 1969 and 1971

Offence class		May 1969 N=348	Sept. 1971 N=351
I	Offences against the person	8.0	23.7
II	Offences against property with violence	48.3	51.6
III-VI	Other offences	43.7	24.8
All offences		100.0	100.1

$x^2 = 45.44$ df = 4, p < 0.001

No direct material on length of sentence was available for the population in 1971. For internal administrative purposes, however, the population had been classified according to the length of time left to serve until earliest date of release (EDR); that is, until release with normal remission deducted from the sentence. It was only possible for us to calculate comparable statistics for our sample prisoners and not for the whole population in 1969. When this was done it was clear that only a substantial increase in the length of sentences could explain the differences found, which again were significant at the one per cent level. The comparison is shown in Table 9.2.

Table 9.2   Percentage distribution by time left to serve until EDR: 1969 and 1971

Time to EDR	May 1969 (sample) N=72	Sept. 1971 N=351
9 months or less	69.4	34.2
10-15 months	9.7	17.4
16-21 months	8.3	12.3
22 months or more	12.5	36.2
Total	99.9	100.1

$x^3 = 31.82$, df = 3, p < 0.001

There is no doubt that the spirit of the dispersal policy was followed through faithfully in Albany. In the document *(Some Notes on Albany Prison)* which Brian Howden left for his successor, Mr Footer, he wrote: 'We do not locate all the long-term prisoners together: we tend to distribute them in the four halls available as equally as possible . . . we have tried hard not to differentiate between a category-C prisoner serving 18 months and a category-A prisoner serving life, except that the privileges that are accorded by the rules to long-term prisoners are allowed.' And as far as possible an attempt was made to run much the same kind of liberal regime that had always been applied in Albany. 'Prisoners are in constant association from 6.30 am to nearly 9.00 pm. We do not restrict them from going into each other's cells, it would be futile to try and do this. They do gamble, they do play cards, in fact they do a lot of things in the halls which perhaps are, technically speaking, against the rules, but which we know about and we try and keep a reasonable measure of control on.' But there is also no doubt in our minds that the implementation of such a policy in the conditions prevailing at Albany was a recipe for disaster.

It would be surprising if amongst the new arrivals there were not some prisoners who were able and willing to exert their influence in a situation which was neither dominated by existing inmates nor yet firmly controlled by the discipline staff. We did not have an opportunity to study the adaptations of prisoners when we returned to the prison in 1971 and 1972. But in the light of our earlier analysis of prisoner responses to Albany, our subsequent discussions with key staff and prisoners, and our persual of various records that were made available to us, it is not difficult to make a hypothetical, and occasionally speculative, reconstruction of how things developed.

The new prisoners included an even higher proportion of persons who had previous experience of approved schools, borstals or detention centres, so that the proportion of state-raised youths in the population as a whole was increased. It is reasonable to assume that, other things being equal, these men would react to Albany in much the same way as other state-raised youths before them; that is, either by uncertain negative retreat, or by jailing, or by opportunism. In the past negative retreatism had been adopted by younger state-raised youths, whose adult experience of institutions had been limited to local prisons. When faced with the freedom, and the potential aggro of Albany, they wanted to go back to Wandsworth. Older state-raised youths, who had learned what training prisons were all about, responded differently. In general, the longer their sentence the more likely they were to jail; and the shorter their sentence the more likely were they to think it worth their while also to go through the motions of gleaning, for the benefit of staff, in an opportunistic response. Given the increase in length of sentences in the Albany population generally, the new state-raised youths were probably also serving longer sentences. And it is not unreasonable to assume that the longer their current sentence the more likely they were to have been to training prisons before, because this relationship held generally for the population in 1969. If these assumptions are sound, then probably the largest single group among the new state-raised youths sent to Albany were those most likely to respond by jailing. It is not hard to imagine that they joined, or more likely competed with, those prisoners who were already actively, if somewhat aimlessly, jailing in Albany. The newcomers whose offences and length of sentence had justified a category-B security rating were almost certainly more sophisticated operators than the existing incumbents, and so perhaps were more likely to survive in the ensuing struggles. In any case those on the losing end, and those reluctant to compete, would certainly be forced to seek alternative modes of adaptation. Our expectation would be that, as the aggro mounted, more and more prisoners would be pushed into negative retreat, leaving the victors in control of small cliques with fairly well-defined spheres of influence.

Manoeuvring of the kind we have suggested evidently began quite soon after we left the prison in 1969. The first category-B prisoners had been admitted earlier that year, and throughout 1970 their numbers steadily increased. In his annual report for 1970 Brian Howden remarked that 'Many men find the pressures of hall life very trying and difficult. The weak become the prey of the strong. Groups form, rackets develop, gangs emerge and violence is always present. It is the life of the jungle. . . . The staff are very sensitive to the difficulties and give sympathetic support but they are powerless to keep more than a superficial control over the situation.' It was undoubtedly cliques and gangs like these that the prison officer had in mind when he spoke to the *Daily Express* about the 'young toughs' in Albany.

Not all the newcomers to Albany were state-raised youths. There was obviously also an increase in the numbers of older, experienced, professional thieves and robbers serving very long sentences. These prisoners were more likely to have violent offences against the person in their criminal records than was the case for the 'top men' we described in chapter 8. Some, by virtue of the spectacular nature of their crimes and the possible conse- quences of escape, were classified in category A. Some, lacking this notoriety but otherwise sharing much the same characteristics, were classified in category B. The expected response for these prisoners, judging from their counterparts in 1969, would be for them to do their own time. But the longer a prisoner's sentence and the further away his release date, then the less point he may see in settling down to do his bird. Indeed, as Cohen and Taylor (1972) have shown, he is likely to entertain serious doubts as to whether he *can* do his bird. Most of the new prisoners in this group were serving very long fixed sentences. A few were serving life sentences with or without minimum terms recommended by the courts. In these circumstances it would not be surprising if alternative adaptations seemed more attractive. A prisoner might, for example, take to gleaning in the hope of off-setting the deterioration which he feared might overtake him. Or he might feel that he had so little to lose of his prospects for a future existence in the outside world, that he might as well manipulate the world inside prison to his present advantage.

We knew of prisoners in both category A and category B who, from the accounts given us by staff and prisoners, were doing their own time. Others were gleaning, and still others had begun to operate for themselves by manipulating and using the ready pool of young, tough, state-raised youths who dominated the halls. But the implementation of the dispersal policy in Albany actually contrived to make a subversive, manipulative response more likely than it otherwise might have been. Thus, the allocation of both long- and short-term prisoners to the same halls only served to remind the long-sentence men just how long they still had to do. It was unsettling and a constant irritation, an irritation predicted by many of the prisoners we had spoken to in 1969. The resentment of short-term prisoners felt by long-term prisoners was one of the main problems mentioned by Brian Howden in the notes that he left for Mr Footer. If the mixing of long- and short-termers meant that it was harder to settle to do one's own time, the insistence that long- and short-termers be treated alike as far as possible created other pressures towards nonconformity. When the dispersal prisoners arrived in Albany, far from approving of the facilities they found – as many staff and prisoners had predicted they would – they frequently complained to the staff, the governor and the Board of Visitors that they did not get the same privileges they had enjoyed in the special wings. When it was explained to them that they were not 'special' prisoners in the eyes of the administration it is not surprising that they should have been angry. They knew only too well, whatever they might now be told, that they *were* special: it was for people like them that the whole elaborate machinery of security had been set up. Since the authorities forced them to mix with short-term prisoners, what more appropriate tool could there be for striking back at the authorities? Even if a prisoner was reluctant to follow this logic he still had to mix with other prisoners who, because of his reputation outside or the way he handled himself inside, sought to cast him in an anti-authoritarian role.

The number who did come to operate for themselves in this way was never clear to us. There is no question that there were 'Big Men' of the kind that prison officers spoke about to the Press. But they worked behind the scenes, and did not show their hand unnecessarily to other prisoners, let alone the staff. In his annual report for 1970 Brian Howden commented that 'some prisoners must spend long periods of their sentence in the segregation unit', but such men, he said, were 'thankfully few in number'. The following year, in his *Notes on Albany Prison,* he pointed out that 'we are getting some very difficult and unco-operative men'. He predicted that there were troubles ahead and warned that 'the situation could arise from time to time when there is a definite bid for power'. He was, of course, right in his predictions. But we have little doubt that the staff assessments of the number of subversive prisoners were subsequently greatly exaggerated. It is testimony to the manipulative skills of prisoners that staff became so fearful of their activities that a massive and often indiscriminate campaign was mounted to deal with them. As we reported earlier, at times in 1972 as many as 67 prisoners were labelled subversive and held under Rule 43. They overflowed the segregation unit, and E hall had to take the surplus. Most of them must have been lieutenants rather than generals and many of them, in the opinion of Mr Footer at least, constituted no real threat to the community when left to themselves.

As the situation in Albany deteriorated, certain modes of adaptation became less tenable for prisoners and eventually nearly impossible. Thus when the time allowed for association was cut down, communal dining abandoned, and access to baths and toilets restricted after the riot in 1972, there was clearly very little opportunity for the indulgence of secondary comforts. And since education classes were put under pressure at a time when staff training and the case-officer system had been completely run down, gleaning must have become a very difficult adaptation to follow. In any case with more aggro than ever when one was out of cells, the pressures for prisoners to retreat into their cells must have have been greatly increased. Finally, as control began to pass from staff to prisoners, the advantages of doing one's own time must have seemed less real, and some top men who had formerly got on with their bird may well have been tempted to join the struggle for power.

It is important to note, in view of our earlier findings, that after

Albany became a dispersal prison the adaptations of long-term prisoners began to correspond more closely with those described by Cohen and Taylor (1972) in Durham. Our evidence for this period in Albany is necessarily somewhat impressionistic. Nevertheless some changes were obvious. In 1969 we had no difficulty in assigning sex offenders to the same modes of adaptation used by other criminals. None was so preoccupied with private sins to the extent that he underwent a mystical retreat. In 1971, however, at least one sex offender, whose crimes had been given the widest possible publicity, appeared quite unable to live with any other people and opted for nearly total seclusion. We have already noted that whereas in 1969 the top men had all been concerned to do their own time, in 1971 some were certainly engaged in subversive activity as a strategic response, while others sought to forestall deterioration by gleaning. There were also some prisoners who spent a large part of their time campaigning, an activity that had been very nearly absent in 1969. The subjects of campaigns varied, but usually involved matters such as a refusal of an application for parole or home leave, or the censorship of letters, or the continued segregation under Rule 43. The campaigns were usually conducted by making repeated applications to the governor, and to the Board of Visitors, to check on the progress of petitions, or to seek permission to write to MPs, the NCCL or to the European Commission on Human Rights. Some campaigns involved a prodigious amount of work. By 1973 it was clear also that some prisoners were sufficiently interested in escaping for at least the phantasy planning of escape attempts to become part of a viable mode of adaptation. That the modes of adaptation should change as the population and the circumstances of confinement changed, supports our contention that to understand the ways in which prisoners adapt to imprisonment one has to know a good deal about the context in which it occurs. Part of the convergence here between our findings and those of Cohen and Taylor may be explained by the fact that some of the same prisoners they described had actually been transferred from the Durham special wing to Albany, and others had come from similar situations elsewhere. We did not have enough information to relate modes of adaptation to the biographical characteristics of prisoners as we had done in 1969. However, it did seem to us, from what information we had, that the relationship between 'typical crime' and mode of adaptation suggested by Cohen and Taylor could not be sustained in Albany.

It was not, of course, only the avenues to certain modes of prisoner adaptation that were closed off in Albany. In much the same way some of the adaptations that had sustained various members of the uniformed staff in the past must have become less viable as the troubles escalated, and other forms of response must have seemed more attractive or even necessary.

Throughout the long build-up to a category-A establishment the prospects for *implementing Rule 1* had recognizably diminished, so much that a crisis of confidence had occurred even before the introduction of the standard category-A regime. Though this mode of adaptation still accounted for the biggest single group in our uniformed staff sample in 1969, the events that occurred subsequently can only have served to undermine it further. If members of the central management team were using metaphors of the electronic coffin and prisoners were smuggling letters to the Press about becoming vegetables, uniformed staff could scarcely be blamed for losing what faith they had in the notions of treatment, training and rehabilitation, especially once the staff training programme ground to a halt. Moreover, it would not be surprising if the sense of responsibility which had been welcomed by some hall staff, most notably those who felt they were *making a career,* turned rather sour in the face of a determined bid for power by prisoners. Indeed in such circumstances the orientation to learning the ropes of management may well have become little more than a grim struggle to hold the line, once it was recognized that responsible authority could be exercised only with the willing co-operation of prisoners.

Those members of staff whom we characterized as indulging their *secondary comforts* were always more concerned with such matters as the joys of living on the Isle of Wight or the comfort of their quarters than the facilities of the prison as such. While these extra-mural qualities may have become even more highly prized as the conditions inside the prison became more difficult, it is unlikely that they would be capable of sustaining the evaluation of Albany as the best prison to be in, as they had in the past. Even those experienced officers who were *marking time* may have been ruffled by the events developing in Albany. When they indicated to us that they were able to get on with the job in whatever prison they found themselves it was clear that their indifference was to the fashions in fancy methods of treatment and training. It does not seem likely that their indifference could have been maintained to quite the same degree when prisoners made a real challenge to their authority.

With such adaptations becoming more difficult we would have predicted that more and more officers would be forced into *uncertain withdrawal* or attracted into *negative detachment* as ways of getting by. Though we had no opportunity to replicate our earlier study of staff adaptations in the new situation at Albany, there was certainly some evidence, from the views expressed to us by officers in 1971 and 1972, that a process of this kind was at work. It should be no surprise at all, in these circumstances, if the ranks of the 'heavy mob' among the officers were somewhat swelled.

We may now turn to a consideration of what might have been done to prevent, or at least to contain, the worst effects of the dispersal policy in Albany. Perhaps the first thing to be said is that there remained some problems which in themselves were quite small but which gave some basis for legitimate complaints. The incentive earnings scheme had got off to a bad start because it was applied piecemeal, so that some prisoners benefited while others did not. When it was extended inequities remained because of difficulties in assessing non-production line, and especially non-industrial, work. Even quasi-production line work did not solve the incentives problem because there was little need for prisoners to spend money, and comparatively few things available in the canteen to spend it on. The tailor's shop became so unpopular that in 1970 a rule had to be introduced so that no one could be considered for a change of labour until he had completed six months in the shop. Throughout 1971 there were, on average, more than one in seven prisoners reporting sick daily, which may give some indication of the problems experienced at work. There were certainly more complaints over the incentive earnings scheme than over any other single issue. Industrial difficulties were not eased, as had been hoped, when the new woodmill was opened inside the security fence in January 1971. For the extractor fans broke down almost immediately leaving an atmosphere polluted by sawdust in the workshop. The woodmill was closed for months while the fans were being replaced so that the remaining shops had to bear the strain. Matters like these were beyond the control of the central management team in Albany. But they did provide fertile ground for the growth of disruptive activities which might otherwise have had more difficulty in taking root.

In March 1972, shortly before the St Patrick's Day incidents, we were able to repeat some of the interviews that we had carried out in 1969 with hall senior officers. The regime had not changed quite as much as we had expected, and it would be tedious to describe the details. Even though we were not able to interview in all halls it was clear that there remained minor variations in routine procedures from one hall to another, and from one shift to another, of the kind we discussed in chapter 7. In spite of all efforts to enforce the rulings on the appropriate clothes to be worn at meals – a problem which seemed to have been solved in 1969 – standards of dress still varied in 1972, and this was a recurring subject of debate at the principal officers' meeting. Where the staff in one hall, or on one shift, regularly interpreted rules more tolerantly or more strictly than their colleagues, then the differences were both capable of exploitation and likely to become the subject of resentment. There were indeed many complaints by prisoners that privileges freely allowed elsewhere in the prison were denied to them. Often these complaints arose out of misunderstandings of the regulations on the part of prisoners, but sometimes they reflected genuine differences of practice. The differences were not large and management had long been aware of the problem. It seems to us that some element of inconsistency is the inevitable price to be paid for running a reasonably relaxed regime. But the main reason that attempts to eradicate inconsistencies had failed was the differentiated nature of hall management and staffing.

The halls were nominally run by principal officers. But under the new duty hours introduced in February 1969 the four principal officers concerned were required to work on a shift basis. This meant that for the period he was on duty each PO had to supervise two halls, and thus could really be identified with neither. The management of the halls was thus effectively delegated for everyday purposes to senior officers, of whom there was one on each shift in each hall. Eight basic-grade staff were normally assigned to each hall per shift. In the early days of Albany some effort was made to keep six of them more or less permanently assigned to the same hall, and each officer was responsible for between four and eight prisoners as their 'case officer'. With the change to single-shift working for prisoners, the basis for allocating case officers also changed, so that four officers, two on each shift, were made jointly responsible for all the 24 prisoners on their landing. Under this system a prisoner might find that his 'case' was dealt with by all four officers instead of one. When the five-day week for staff, under the functional group working scheme, was finally introduced many officers had to be 'called back' after their normal duties elsewhere in the prison to maintain the new hall staffing rosters. For a time officers were even drafted in from Parkhurst on detached duties to make up the shortfall in Albany staff. In these circumstances continuity became virtually impossible. True, the case-officer system had by then become a dead letter: it was referred to in the past tense in Brian Howden's *Notes* and it received only a passing reference in the Albany handbook which was distributed to prisoners in 1971. But the lack of continuity led to other problems besides the impossibility of doing case work. Exploitable variations in methods of handling prisoners were more likely to occur, and staff knowledge of what was really happening in the halls became more fragmented. These problems were exacerbated by the fact that only the more senior officers could be assigned to security duties in the control room and elsewhere, leaving less experienced officers to work in the halls where most of the face-to-face contact actually took place.

It had long been recognized that the middle-management level was potentially the weakest link in the Albany chain of command. The use of principal officers as hall managers had been brought about because there were not enough assistant governors to fill these roles. The two assistant governors, it will be recalled, were incorporated into the structure with special responsibilities for staff training and resources, and for social training respectively. The setting up of the principal officers' meeting in October 1968 had represented the first step towards bringing consistency to the running of the halls. And for so long as principal officers spent the major part of their duty time in their own halls some progress appeared to be made. In his annual report for 1970 the governor pointed out: 'We have continued to use principal officers as hall managers and I am sure that this system is a good one.'

As the role of the prison changed, however, the division of functions between the two assistant governors made less and less sense, and Brian Howden pointed out to his successor the need for a third assistant governor. But he still confirmed his belief in the existing system of hall management: 'We regard the principal officer level of management as being most important because they run the prison in its everyday life.' In spite of these declarations of faith it is clear that he also entertained some doubts, especially after February 1969 when the principal officers began to work their new hours of duty. So much so that in the spring of 1969 the governor asked the principal officers' meeting whether a return to the old system of one principal officer on duty in each hall would not be desirable. The principal officers voted to wait and see. Some months later, shortly before our first period of field work ended, the governor raised the matter again. On this occasion opinion was equally divided for and against a reversion to the old style of management. It seemed to us that action would soon follow. But no action was taken, for when we returned to the prison in 1971 the debate was still going on. In December 1971 Mr Footer and his chief officer addressed the POM to express their concern that coverage in the halls by principal officers was unsatisfactory. The principal officers put forward proposals whereby they too would work the functional group shifts enabling each hall manager to spend all his duty hours in his own hall. This arrangement was put into effect in the new year. But by then Mr Footer had already prepared his annual report for 1971. He wrote: 'I am not satisfied that the management structure, with the principal officers as the hall managers, provides the stability or the continuity which is so essential to adequate control in the dispersal prison and to this end I have asked for an increase in the number of assistant governors to provide for one in each hall.' It was not until after the troubles of 1972 that headquarters responded. When the Home Secretary announced in May 1973 that as part of his review of the dispersal policy he had found it necessary to recommend an increase in the strength of management at dispersal prisons, the establishment of five assistant governors for Albany was assured. They duly arrived in post.

We find it hard to know what weight to attach to the weakness in hall management in accounting for the Albany troubles. The very existence of this structural defect meant that it was easier for prisoners to exploit situations, and the prolonged period when the responsibilities of principal officers were divided must have contributed, we think, to the transfer of power from staff to prisoners and the consequent lowering of staff morale. Had the hall principal officers been persuaded to return to their old system of working at the first attempt early in 1969, then it seems likely that a much firmer control could have been maintained. But such a development would not have prevented the troubles from arising in the first place.

The introduction of functional group working arose out of the national negotiations for a five-day week for prison officers, as we discussed in chapter 6. The necessity to employ the least experienced officers on the most difficult tasks in the halls derived partly from the requirement under functional group working that senior staff be assigned to security and control room duties, and partly from the pattern of recruitment to the service generally. Again these matters were not really under the control of the local management, but they greatly added to the problems of running the halls. By the end of 1971, the governor was able to report an improvement in the staffing situation, such that the manpower control team's recommendations were nearly met, bearing in mind that only four halls were then operating. He looked forward to the balance of staff needed arriving in 1972. But many of the new officers were posted to Albany fresh from the training school; and with little or no experience in handling prisoners they were expected to deal with some of the most difficult men in the system. After the August Bank Holiday riot in 1972 the chairman of the Board of Visitors wrote to the Home Secretary, urging him among other things to take steps 'to strengthen the staff by increasing the proportion of experienced officers'. In reply the Board was told that Albany was better off for experienced staff than most establishments: at that time 24 out of 143 basic-grade officers, or 16.8 per cent, had less than one year's service compared with an average of about 20 per cent for the remaining prisons in the system. We have no doubt that Albany was better off in this respect. But we do not think that a marginal improvement in the ratio of probationary staff from one in five to one in six adequately reflects the difference in scale of the problems of a dispersal prison when compared to the average institution run by Prison Department.

These inexperienced recruits received little or no in-service training when they arrived in Albany. When the prison opened, one of the assistant governors had been charged with responsibility for staff training and resources. It had never been easy to find time to fit in an adequate training programme. Once the functional group working scheme started, it became impossible to provide time except by calling officers back for training during rest days. Since many rest days were already used to cover basic duties within the prison, officers were reluctant to give up any that remained. In the early days training had been thought necessary to develop the case-work role of the officers. Now that new staff were being faced with prisoners much more experienced than themselves, the need was for training in everyday techniques of maintaining order and control. They learned, eventually, on the job – but at a price. In successive reports Gifford Footer commented on the need to change staff attitudes so that they would confront the 'stern realities of the dispersal policy' but without over-reacting to them. He was well aware of the difficulties facing staff trainers. But as the troubles deepened there was less and less time that could be made available for training. With officers working at full stretch, sickness rates began to rise and the pressures on remaining staff were increased as they tried to cover the gaps. Throughout much of 1971 and 1972 staff training programmes virtually ceased.

We suspect that most officers in Albany in 1971 and 1972 would have argued that the dispersal policy was wrong. But when discussing their particular problems in implementing the policy they tended to blame the local management for, in their view, failing to back them up. However, a few officers we spoke to listed a catalogue of contributory factors that they felt had led to the unhappy circumstances in which they found themselves. Most of the problems we have discussed, for example, were closely linked together in the minds of these men. Some of our informants were officers whom we had known well in the earlier days, and with whom we had developed relationships of considerable mutual respect. In a word, they felt that Albany was failing in its task as a dispersal prison because it lacked the right *tradition*. Some of them were quite bitter about the way in which they, and Albany, had been used: wrenched from one extreme to the other in the philosophy they were expected to follow and the inmates they were expected to contain in the space of a mere three or four years. Too many conflicting demands had been placed on Albany too soon, and too few resources in terms of men and training had been provided for it to do the job. A more established institution with a settled and established staff, they thought, would have been much better able to cope. We do not think these men were typical, but we do think they were right.

When all is said and done, however, the real causes of the troubles in Albany must be sought not just in the special circumstances of implementing the dispersal policy there, but in the inherent problems of the dispersal policy itself. The Radzinowicz sub-committee, in its advocacy of the dispersal method for dealing with the 'most difficult and dangerous prisoners' rather than the concentration method, thought that the majority of such men 'would be absorbed into the general population'. Where they were not absorbed, the use of Rule 43, to remove disruptive and subversive prisoners to the segregation unit, would provide a safeguard for the continuance of the 'liberal and constructive regime' which the sub-committee wished to see. As we have shown, Albany did disperse its difficult and dangerous prisoners among the general population – a general population that was bewildering in its variety. And it did maintain a liberal regime based on the almost complete freedom of association from unlock in the morning until lock-up at night. So many problems ensued, however, that even the heaviest reliance on the use of Rule 43 did not contain them. Indeed, it must be obvious that the measures that were eventually introduced in an attempt to solve the problems represented very severe inroads into, if not a complete reversal of, the two main elements in the dispersal policy: the principle of absorbing difficult prisoners, and the principle of maintaining a liberal regime.

The measures were not suddenly conceived. Communal dining in Albany had been regarded as a potentially dangerous situation even in the days when we first visited Albany. And the long periods of association in the halls had given both David Gould and Brian Howden cause for concern. The change to single-shift working had been promulgated, at least in part, to reduce the amount of aimless associated activity in the halls. Once further restrictions were introduced during the general lock-up of the prison in August 1972 it was but a short step to incorporating them as regular features of the routine. The liberality and constructiveness that had been Albany's hallmark, even as late as 1970, had gone.

Within three months of the arrival of category-A prisoners Brian Howden was considering ways of overcoming the pressures of hall life. In his annual report for 1970 he wrote: 'One solution would be to allocate men of a kind to a particular hall, where they would find life more bearable and congenial.' But he reflected that this might simply create difficulties of a different sort. By the end of 1971, however, when Gifford Footer presented his first report, it was clear that Albany could not cope with the essential features of dispersal. He wrote as follows about the extraordinary variety of people contained within the prison: 'Sentences range from 12 months to life, the ages range from 19 to 70, security categories from A to D, the widest range of social backgrounds is represented and every kind of offence.' It just did not make sense to hope that they would all mix happily, and he went on: 'The scattering of the hard-core subversives throughout the halls and workshops does seem to provide a maximum theatre for their operations.' Actually, of course, prisoners were not just assigned to halls indiscriminately, for Brian Howden had pointed out in his *Notes* that 'we try to consider individuals when placing them in halls'. But Albany had never had a very clear policy on the matter and something more systematic was required. Footer identified a group of about 25 young prisoners as a particularly difficult category to cope with: 'They tend to attach themselves to their more notorious seniors, bask in the reflected glory of their attachment and behave accordingly.' He informed headquarters that the psychology department had been considering ways in which the population might be redeployed so as to minimize the effect of the subversive element: that is, by separating and segregating different classes of prisoner. He looked forward to the opening of the fifth hall to facilitate such a reorganization. It was another fifteen months before the fifth hall came into operation and by then the Board of Visitors had added their voice to that of the governor. When the chairman of the Board wrote to the Home Secretary about inexperienced staff in September 1972, he also drew attention to the problem of dealing with difficult young prisoners as well as much more notorious criminals in the same setting, and called for a re-examination of the dispersal policy. In particular he pointed to the need to distinguish between prisoners who constituted a security risk and prisoners who constituted a threat to the stability of the regime. The Home Office acknowledged the distinction between troublemakers and escape risks in their reply, and pointed out that the complex and sensitive dispersal policy was already under review. In fact the riot over the August Bank Holiday led in any case to the introduction of a 'controlled' regime in D hall, midway between the main prison regime and the segregation unit. When the results of the Home Secretary's review were announced in the following May, such a separation of prisoners was officially sanctioned. Short-termers were held in B hall, long-termers in C and D halls, with the more difficult category-A and B prisoners and those serving very long sentences concentrated in D hall. The prison was quiet, but the spirit of the dispersal policy had gone.

Part IV

Conclusions

10   The end of an era

In this monograph we have traced the history of Albany from the time when it was described as a 'caravan in a meadow' to the time when it was made so secure that it was referred to as an 'electronic coffin'. We have tried to analyse the effects of the changing status of the prison, with its massive programme of upgrading the security precautions, on the administrative structure, the regime and the modes of adaptation among staff and prisoners. We hope now to bring together, as briefly as possible, some of the conclusions we think may be drawn from our work.

Research in prison

Perhaps we should begin by considering the implications for sociological research in prisons. We gave a number of undertakings about the way we would conduct ourselves and our work, and we have tried hard to live up to them. We were able to earn the co-operation and often the friendship of many members of staff and prisoners over a very long period, even though their previous experience of research had not always been good. We think that the approach which we described in chapter 2, of giving full information about what we were doing and why we were doing it, and of consulting our respondents at each stage of the enquiry, was largely responsible for the success of the fieldwork. We recommend such a direct approach to other would-be prison researchers, and we hope that we have done nothing to render their task more difficult.

But the acid test of the integrity of the research lies in the publications which flow from it. We are aware that our analysis of what happened in Albany, and our attempt to understand how and why it happened, have led us to make statements which will not always please the very people who made the research possible: Home Office officials, Albany staff and Albany prisoners. The lengthening interval between the completion of the fieldwork and the writing up has prevented us from getting as much feedback from our respondents as we would have liked. Such as we have obtained is discussed in a very brief postscript. Sometimes we have been frankly critical of government policy, of administrative decisions and of the attitudes and behaviours of staff and prisoners. It will be no help to our respondents to say that our remarks are not intended as personal attacks even though we believe that 'anyone in their position at the time' would probably have acted in much the same ways. Indeed, we have sought to render the activities of groups and individuals understandable in just those terms. But we cannot pretend that our criticisms are 'purely sociological' or 'scientifically neutral'. We have inevitably had to make selections in what we studied and reported, to draw out the implications of what we saw, and to reach conclusions from our analysis. The way we have done this obviously reflects our concern as ordinary citizens with the shape and nature of the penal system as much as it does our judgment of what was sociologically relevant. All we can say is that in our analysis we have felt constrained by our data, the 'facts' as we understood them from our respondents and our observations. We stand by our reasoning and by our judgments. But we hope that we have let our subjects speak sufficiently for themselves to allow those who do not share our perspectives to reach conclusions of their own. We believe that anyone who is at all concerned with the prison system, including the tens of thousands of staff and prisoners who at this moment are doing or spending their time within it, will have to come to terms with the account we have presented and its implications for policy.

Sociology of the prison
There seem to be at least three conclusions that emerge from the study which have an important bearing on the sociology of prisons.

First, our study shows that there is no simple way of understanding what makes a prison tick. The working of the regime in Albany could not have been grasped from a perusal of the policy decisions made by the Home Office alone; nor by an analysis of the objectives of the successive governors and the management structures which they set up to achieve them; nor by examining what staff and prisoners thought and did in the course of the everyday routine activities that made up life in the institution; nor by investigating how their actions were influenced by background variables; nor by a study of the aims and strategies of PROP and the POA. The reality is that making and unmaking a prison regime is a complex affair indeed. No doubt there is much that we have left out, but we are quite sure that to have neglected any of the levels of analysis we have just outlined would have been to miss something of importance in understanding the problems we set ourselves. Prison research must, we think, become harder to do – in the sense that there is so much to include – at the same time that it becomes easier – in the sense that at least we know better what to look for.

Second, our analysis of the way in which Albany prisoners evaluated the core regime and the strategies they adopted to cope with the problems of doing time there, suggests that prisoners adapt not just to the fact of imprisonment but also, in varying degrees, to the particular prison they are in. To understand the way in which prisoners do adapt requires more than a knowledge of their previous institutional history and their criminal careers and identifications outside prison, posited by Irwin. It requires also a good deal of contextual information about the circumstances in which prisoners serve their current sentence and how long they expect to be subject to those circumstances. The findings of Cohen and Taylor in the special security wing at Durham between 1967 and 1971, as well as our own findings in what was still primarily a category-C Albany in 1969, represent in our view rather special cases. Neither was exactly a run-of-the-mill establishment, by English or any other prison standards. But the fact that there appeared to be some convergence in the modes of prisoner adaptation in the two prisons as the regime and prisoners in Albany in 1971 and 1972 more closely came to resemble the regime and prisoners in Durham, suggests that there are also general principles involved. We might have extended our categories of adaptation, which we found in Albany to be associated with particular prisoner biographies, into a more general classificatory scheme. But we feel it would be premature to do so. Meanwhile there is everything to be said for exploring the modes of adaptation to be found in different types of establishment and with different groups of prisoners in a series of further researches.

That prisoners respond differently to different regimes has often been reported or at least implied in the prison sociology literature. And, of course, the assumption that prisoners will respond differently to different regimes has always been at the heart of the philosophy of treatment and training. However, we suspect that the differences in adaptation or response owe less to the ostensible aims of treatment programmes involved, and more to the opportunities for associated activity and the general facilities available in different prisons. These opportunities and facilities may be used in different ways from those intended. In a sense, in 1969, the officially preferred response to the Albany regime was the gleaning adaptation; yet only 8.7 per cent of our sample actually adapted in that fashion. None of the remaining modes of adaptation we described would have been approved by the management, although secondary comfort indulgence and doing one's own time, which between them accounted for 28.9 per cent of the sample, presented no threat to good order and involved no demands on the staff, so that they were probably welcomed at least unofficially. But that still leaves more than three-fifths of the prisoners adapting in other, less preferred ways as far as official or unofficial management thinking is concerned.

Third, it is not only prisoners who adapt to doing time in prisons: the staff have problems in spending their time there too. To be sure, the problems are less pressing on staff: the locks, bolts, bars, dogs and electronics are not to keep them in. But the problems of maintaining order day in and day out, among men who do not always accept the legitimacy of staff authority, are none the less real. We described some remarkable parallels between the ways in which uniformed staff and prisoners adapted. To prison officers the special qualities of the Albany regime were rightly perceived as special attributes of their own job specifications. While for some staff these attributes enabled them to think that they were doing a good and useful job by implementing Prison Rule 1 or by making a career, for others those same attributes presented special problems. Prison officers, perhaps more often than prisoners, liked to know where they stood; and we see nothing wrong with that. But to the extent that this brought them into conflict with managerial policy they felt obliged to take adaptations which were not mentioned in the recruitment literature. Just as some modes of adaptation available to prisoners were closed off as Albany assumed its dispersal role, so did some modes of adaptation become less attractive for staff. As the circumstances changed both staff and prisoners were more likely to respond in ways that did not meet with official approval. Once again the lesson we draw from this is that the responses of prison officers have to be seen in the context within which they occur, rather than as a global response to a prison career as such. In any case our analysis of the relationship between the biographical character-istics of staff and their preferred modes of adaptation suggest that the familiar stereotypes of prison officers as authoritarian per-sonalities, military martinets or sadistic perverts are not particular-ly helpful in understanding what happens in prisons. We hope that other researchers will be encouraged to explore further this badly neglected area of prison sociology.

Re-writing Prison Rule 1
So far as we are aware, this is the only study that has been able to examine at close range and in great detail the establishment and growth of a new prison virtually from the outset. But we think that the unfortunate experiences of Albany have also marked the end of an era in the English prison system. Hence our title. The era which in our view closed as Albany began to prepare for dispersal, was the era of the struggle to give meaning to Rule 1 of the Prison Rules:

> The purpose of the training and treatment of convicted prisoners shall be to encourage and assist them to lead a good and useful life.

The problems of implementing Rule 1 are much greater than is implied in Sir Alexander Paterson's famous paradox: 'It is impossible to train men for freedom in a condition of captivity', which has bedevilled the prison system ever since it was first uttered in 1932. Such a statement is nothing if it is not misleading. For it fails to apprehend the fact that it is in the nature of training that it takes place in one setting while preparing the recipient for another of which he has yet to gain experience. Society is full of examples of institutions, even involving considerable elements of captivity, from the kindergarten to the military academy, which have been established with just such ends in view. The difference is that in these institutions the training comes first, and the elements of captivity are only introduced to facilitate that training, rather than the other way around. Even so, there is no reason to suppose that one could not train a man for freedom in conditions of captivity if one *really* wanted to, providing of course that certain other conditions also obtained: namely, that the man concerned was assured of freedom at some time; that he wanted, or was at least willing, to be so trained; and that the trainers knew what the training involved and had the resources to carry it out.

But the truth is that prisons have never *really* been about training at all. They have always *really* been about, and continue to be about, captivity: that is, safe custody. And there is nothing on earth to be gained from pretending otherwise. At different times and in different degrees according to one or another of the parties involved, they have also, if often half-heartedly, been about punishment, deterrence, political suppression, moral reform, medical or psychiatric treatment, attitude or behavioural change, education, vocational training, industrial work, social welfare and rehabilitation. Usually prisons have entertained several of these additional objectives at the same time, and it is by no means impossible to imagine that someone could be found to make serious claim to each and every one of them within a single establishment. But what endures and what is common to them all is their custodial function for the duration of the sentence of the court; and therein lies their reason for existence. Unlike the kindergarten or the military academy, there can be few alumni of the prison who would wish to stay on to take advantage of the various programmes that might have been offered once their time is served.

The assumptions that prisons ought to be about treatment or training, and that prisoners, however much they may be incarcerated against their will, ought to want to receive it, have caused a great deal of difficulty for all involved in the prison service, not least because the actual meaning of the concepts of treatment and training – apart from a few specific programmes that have been introduced from time to time with varying degrees of success – have been left remarkably vague.

The brief given to Albany involved the implementation of Rule 1 through the development of social training and industrial training. While we hope that we have conveyed something of the prodigious energies that the successive governors and staff of Albany were able to inspire and harness in an attempt to achieve that end, we doubt that any reader who has followed us through this book could regard our account as a success story. It is difficult to say what might have happened to Albany had its future never been contaminated by the fate of Alvington. We have often been tempted to think that it might have succeeded if, for example, the first governor had not been moved on so soon, if a real attempt had been made to ensure that there were enough instructors available in post in time to make the two-shift system fully operational, if . . . But there are too many ifs. And we doubt whether even under the most propitious circumstances the prison would have succeeded in its original form.

The essential vacuity of the concept of social training was finally exposed at the traumatic central management meeting on 7 August 1968 (see chapter 6). No one then knew what 'tools' would enable them to do the job they had been given, and nothing we have heard since suggests that anyone has been able to come up with more effective answers. 'Industrial training' may have been easier to understand than 'social training', though whether there was any real training content to any of the industrial activities in Albany is more doubtful. When industrial training was supplemented by 'industrial production' after the two-shift system was abandoned, that was easier still to understand. But the fact is that people do not go to prison either for social training or industrial training. Most people are sent to prison because the courts think that they deserve punishment, or that society needs protection from their activities, or simply because the bench thinks that something has to be done with them but cannot think what else to do. Because prisons are sometimes thought of as humane places geared up for treatment and training, some judges and magistrates may find it easier to choose prison as an appropriate disposal for marginal cases. Sometimes, to be sure, the courts act ostensibly in the belief that some persons *do* need special 'treatment' or 'training' and send them to prison apparently in the belief that it will there be provided. If some firm and reliable diagnosis of the condition can in fact be made in such cases, and a known and effective treatment for it exists, then ordinarily we think that such treatment should be provided outside prison. Only if such persons *also* need, in the view of the courts, to be punished or to be kept away from society should they be sentenced to prison. We see no point whatever in the prison service claiming a more general 'treatment or training' role: no justification for designating half our adult prisons for men as 'training prisons'.

The frank recognition that prisons are custodial institutions and that treatment or training have little effective place within them should, we think, lead to a much more careful appraisal of who is to be sent there and why. We hope it might lead to a reduction in the use of imprisonment, and perhaps to a reduction in the size of the prison population and the size and number of prisons needed to contain it. But that there will remain a substantial prison system we regard as inevitable for the foreseeable future. And if it is not to be based on treatment and training, perhaps we should say something about what might replace Rule 1.

It is clear that the coefficient of security in English prisons has been raised dramatically in recent years. We say more about that later. But to say that prisons are more or less secure custodial institutions does not mean that they either should or need be merely 'human warehouses' (Cohen, 1974). Nor does it mean that staff must revert to a purely turnkey role while prisoners simply vegetate.

Our principal objections to the notions of treatment and training within the prison system are concerned with the implicit assumptions that it is somehow the absence of the relevant programme of treatment or training that has led to a person's delinquency or criminality in the first place; and that the provision of the relevant programme will somehow reduce the likelihood of a future occurrence. We suspect that no one in the system has ever really had much faith in such assumptions, and the white paper *People in Prison* gave voice to some disillusion about the way in which treatment had been conceived in the past. But the reformulation of the concept of treatment to embrace 'all that is done by or for the offender in custody', which is proposed in the white paper, simply strips the term of all intelligible meaning (Cmnd 4214, 1969, para. 32). In any case the white paper makes clear elsewhere that it remains one of the expressed aims of classification 'to attempt to identify [a prisoner's] needs and, if possible, the factors that may have led to his criminal behaviour as an essential to any attempt to deal with them while he is in custody' (para. 167); and of allocation to ensure that 'the great majority of convicted prisoners apart from those serving very short sentences . . . would be sent to training prisons with a regime suited to their needs' (paras 170 and 171). Many persons in the prison service live daily with the virtually impossible tasks of diagnosis and allocation, and of providing the supposed remedial programmes. Few have publicly challenged the nature of their task, and while the Prison Department has clearly moved somewhat away from these notions it has not yet relieved staff of their awesome burdens. The result has been an endless charade of data collection, categorization, and the development of 'treatment plans' which have done little more than to fill F 1150s, give prisoners scope for censoriousness, and give staff feelings of guilt, inadequacy or contempt.

Much that is unacceptable in these notions would disappear, we think, if the burden of diagnosis and allocation (for matters other than security and, as we shall argue later, good order and discipline) was removed from staff and handed over to the prisoners. Almost all of those whom the courts punish or isolate by sending to prison will one day be re-admitted to our society. If they think that their re-entry to 'normal' society will be facilitated, or merely that their time inside may be more easily served, by taking educational classes, learning a trade, joining Alcoholics Anonymous, or receiving psychotherapy, then, within reasonable limits, they should have the right to do so. We hold out no expectations that in prisoners taking such programmes the risk of future criminality would be reduced. Nor do we think that early release on parole should in any way be dependent upon the completion of programmes. For many prisoners we would hope that arrangements could be made to use facilities which are available in the free community. But the prison system should be responsible for ensuring that there is a reasonable range of facilities in each prison, and for operating flexible arrangements whereby prisoners could be transferred easily to other prisons of the same security class to take full advantage of what opportunities are available.

After one year of seeking to implement the concept of social training, the first governor of Albany had adopted a view not too dissimilar from our own. He argued that the prison should try to provide activities that would facilitate behaviour changing for those prisoners who were interested. We would only reserve judgment about the desirability, and indeed the efficacy, of any of these activities as behaviour changing devices. The governor also went further, however, in giving an active or prompting role to staff, whose task it was to engender 'therapeutic anxiety'. We think that where staff wished to develop a more positive role over and above security and control functions, then their energies might most practically and profitably be directed towards the task of maintaining and developing links between the prisoner and the community, perhaps under the guidance of the prison welfare officer. We would certainly like to see serious consideration given to the development of such a welfare assistant role for at least some prison staff, even though such proposals have not been well received in the past.

We discussed at some length how in Albany industrial production was seen as something that was compatible with the new emphasis on security. But we hold no brief for industrial prisons. It does not seem likely that prison industry in this country will provide an activity for the majority of prisoners that they could regard as meaningful, either in its intrinsic content or in its preparation for work after release. And the long-cherished hope of some criminologists that prisoners might one day contribute to their keep and the maintenance of their families seems to be as far off as ever. As it is we view with some alarm the possibility, however remote, that prison industry, based on a captive labour force paid at preposterously low rates, might become such an important investment that the prospect of closing down prisons in favour of alternative methods of dealing with offenders could become problematic on economic grounds. None the less we accept that there is a place for prison industry. If persons are consigned to custody they should not also lose the right to work.

We would not expect everyone to agree with our view of prisons, but there is good reason to believe that the Prison Department has increasingly adopted the view that prisons are just prisons, places of safe custody. Though the task of formally re-writing Rule 1 has not yet been undertaken it cannot long be delayed. We doubt that the notions of treatment and training will die easily, and we would not be surprised to see them retained for women and children. But we would be surprised if any new prisons are opened for adult males with a brief remotely approximating that which was given to Albany.

Prison administration
We think that there are many lessons to be learned from our study of the development of Albany Prison from the point of view of prison administration. Perhaps we should draw attention to some of them here, even though it is fair to say that Prison Department has in some respects already acted on some of them.

What we had to say in chapter 3 can scarcely be regarded as anything other than a massive indictment of the way in which the new prison was planned and commissioned. It is true that the opening was a rushed affair, brought about under political pressure to deal with the growth in the prison population. But Prison Department will ever be subject to pressures of one kind or another, and it is quite unrealistic to expect a new prison to materialize and be made to work without very much more careful planning than was evidenced at Albany. Quite apart from the extraordinary defects in the design of buildings, the lack of site preparation and the poor quality control of the actual construction, there were major deficiencies in the briefing, allocation and organization of staff. In the event these deficiencies seemed to contribute to the *esprit de corps* that marked Albany in its early days. But that, of course, could scarcely be relied upon and constitutes no argument against more rational planning in the future. Governors designate need to be brought into planning discussions at the earliest possible stage, *not* sent the minutes of such discussions two or three months before the opening. Members of the management team need to be appointed well in advance, and some of them should be brought together with the governor at least several months before the opening of the establishment to familiarize themselves with the site and buildings and to work through the details of the management structure. They should be able to call on assistance from headquarters as well as other members of the management group in an attempt to anticipate and deal with problems before they arise. All staff should be in post several weeks before the prisoners arrive, for training and discussions on the running of the establishment. There should be a carefully controlled intake of prisoners.

Judging from the published accounts of the opening of Blundeston in 1963, Albany enjoyed only the most slender of advantages in its commissioning. But when Coldingley was opened in 1969 considerable efforts were made to avoid the difficulties which had beset Albany. It seems unlikely that if the remaining prisons in the present building programme are brought into operation there will be a reversion to the slap-dash, makeshift procedures adopted in Albany. At any rate we hope not.

One advantage that Coldingley enjoyed over Albany was that as the first industrial prison in the country its brief was at least relatively unambiguous. The task of finding a management structure suitable to its objectives was therefore potentially soluble. Indeed the 'Folkestone Worksop' report of 1967 which we discussed in chapter 3 had offered a preliminary blue print for the organization of just such a prison. There were many problems to be sorted out in the event, but nothing like those which presented themselves at Albany. Albany prison was born out of its time. The delicate, undernourished twins of social and industrial training had been conceived in the bed of optimism left by the Prison Commission; and they were allowed to be born without regard to the rigours of bringing them up in the same household. Even before Albany opened, the hesitant findings of the 'Folkestone Worksop' report had indicated that quite different management structures were required for prisons organized around social training on the one hand and industrial training on the other. Yet Albany was expected to fashion its own structure, using principal and chief officers and deputy and assistant governors, as well as a range of specialist personnel, whose traditional roles had been cast from moulds which allowed them to overlap in their functions and responsibilities yet prevented them from fitting well together as a team. We do not know the basis on which the numbers of each grade of staff were allocated to Albany, though we assume it was decided on some rule of thumb which took account of size of prison and perceived difficulty in handling the inmates. The allocation was evidently *not* decided with a view to filling the job specifications of an appropriately derived organizational chart. Indeed the numbers of staff ever after constrained the kind of structures that could be devised. And Albany had to live with the consequences of that.

We hope that the third stage of the Prison Department's management review will be successful in stating clear objectives for prisons and in setting out guide-lines for management structures capable of achieving the objectives set. In particular we hope that something will be done to clarify the line responsibilities at chief officer, deputy governor, assistant governor and principal officer grades. We think that there are too many grades for the possible functions they could fulfil. We do not think it would be too difficult to devise an appropriate management structure for custodial institutions in which security and good order are seen as the primary tasks, and in which a well-defined range of industrial, educational, and other opportunities are provided in the facilitative way we have suggested. We also think it would be much easier to construct a welfare-assistant role for at least some prison officers than the ambiguous, anxiety-provoking role they have had in the past, where they were expected to look to the needs of training 'the whole man'.

We recognize that the decisions affecting Albany in the few years it has existed form a tangled web indeed. They cannot be regarded entirely independently. But we cannot refrain from commenting on the obvious fact that prisons do not take well to rapid or extensive change. Albany was required to change too much too fast. It never acquired a settled way of life, still less a tradition.

Among the many changes with which Albany had to cope were two 'planned' changes of governor: the first after less than 18 months, the second after a further 34 months. Since the plans for Albany changed so dramatically that it was soon to be quite a different prison from the one originally intended, the first change of governor may be at least understandable. But the second is not. Prison Department appears to take the view that no governor is indispensable, and that there is no place in a prison system for programmes that cannot be replicated by persons other than their originators. Such a view would be quite acceptable if the problems concerning organization and management in prisons had been solved. But they have not. It would be a tolerable view in institutions where even an unsatisfactory structure had been passed from one generation to the next over the years. But in Albany, where the management structure had been made problematic from the outset, such a view seems to us to be quite untenable.

Until the August Bank Holiday lock-in of 1972, the biggest change in the regime was the change-over to single-shift working for prisoners. As we discussed in chapter 6, the change was introduced to make way for the implementation of the standard category-A regime. The abandonment of two-shift working may or may not have been a necessary pre-condition for the operation of dispersal prisons. That the two-shift scheme should have been tried only in prisons which were subsequently to become dispersal prisons seems an unfortunate coincidence. We shall probably never know how category-A and Category-B prisoners would have responded to the system. Unfortunately, it is unlikely that we shall find out whether it could have operated successfully in any prison, because it has been labelled a failed experiment even though it was never really tested. The 'experiments' in Albany and Gartree cannot be evaluated because neither sufficient work nor sufficient instructors were ever provided for the system to operate fully. If experiments are to be evaluated then a real effort must be devoted to setting up the right conditions, if necessary by diverting resources even from hard-pressed areas elsewhere. There is no point in making experiments otherwise, unless, of course, it is just politically convenient to say that they have been tried and failed. We accept the difficulties associated with the scheme. But we do not think they are insuperable, and assuming that other difficulties with dispersing high-risk prisoners are overcome, we do not see why it could not be operated with any category of prisoner. It seems particularly suitable for prisons which also provide a wide range of alternative educational and other facilities. We would like to see further experiments take place.

The future of the dispersal policy

In chapter 9 we drew attention to the failure of the Press and the public, and initially at least the Home Office, to distinguish between prisoners liable to constitute a threat to security of the prison and prisoners liable to undermine the good order and discipline of the prison. We attributed the troubles in Albany in 1971 and 1972 largely to the implementation of the dispersal policy without adequate regard to this distinction. It is fitting that we should conclude this monograph, therefore, with some remarks on the future of that policy, which has hung like a spectre over Albany since 1968.

The dispersal policy cannot be considered sensibly in isolation from the policy which it replaced: the policy of concentration advocated by Mountbatten, towards which the Prison Department had been moving for several years. The Mountbatten report was concerned with the problem of keeping *prisoners* inside prisons and not with the problem of keeping *order* inside them. Accordingly the method for classifying prisoners suggested by Mountbatten, and subsequently officially adopted, took as its criterion the consequences of escape. Questions of good order and discipline were not directly raised. It is worth noting, however, that where internal order was mentioned it was linked to the security problem. Thus, 'symptoms of unrest' were said often to 'indicate the planning of an escape attempt' (Cmnd 3175, 1966, para. 322); and the only persons who were listed as needing to be prevented from taking advantage of a liberal and permissive regime were 'a few determined escapers' (para. 326).

The members of the Radzinowicz sub-committee were concerned with the regime for long-term prisoners in conditions of maximum security, a brief which embraced many other matters besides keeping such persons inside prison. In a misquotation of Mountbatten, but one that nevertheless effectively summarizes his views, the sub-committee seem to accept that category-A prisoners should be those 'whose escape would be highly dangerous to the public or the police, or the security of the State' (Advisory Council, 1968, para. 20). They list five operational reasons which might lead to a prisoner being so categorized; a record of planned escapes, probable commission of further very serious offences if unlawfully at large, probable use of firearms to resist recapture, risk of killing or injuring women or children while at large, and the possibility that escape of such notorious persons would lead to a national scandal and gravely damage the repute of the prison service. None of these reasons is concerned with the prisoner's behaviour in prison. The focus is rather on the likelihood and consequences of his getting out.

The Radzinowicz sub-committee was well aware, however, of the distinction between the risk of escapes and the threat to internal order. It dealt with the first under the heading 'security', and the second under the heading 'control'. Following an analysis of some of the characteristics of the 138 prisoners then assigned to category A which was carried out by D. J. West, the committee recognized that not all prisoners deemed to be escape risks also constituted risks to good order of the prisons. About one in 20 were spies, who were thought to behave well in prisons. Another three in 20 were convicted of serious sexual offences, often against children, and were thought to be more likely the subjects of abuse in prison rather than the perpetrators of it. However, most of the remainder, perhaps three-quarters of the total, were characterized as violent, professional criminals likely to cause problems of control inside prison. West's analysis was based on a study of records, and these indeed showed that no fewer than 24 had been found guilty of assaulting officers during their current sentence. But just how prisoners do react to prison, as we think our study has shown, depends on many things; and without further information we do not think it is justified simply to assume that all of the remainder actually did or would give trouble inside, however violent their records as professional criminals on the outside. No doubt many of them were capable of disrupting good order and discipline; but, if Albany is any guide, it seems unlikely that all of them would want to. And in any case many prisoners who do not get into category A because they constitute lesser risks to security, are equally capable of exercising a disruptive influence on the prison regime.

To be fair, the sub-committee acknowledged that threats to good order and discipline can come from prisoners not defined as security risks, and also that the bulk of prisoners in category A 'appear to differ in degree, rather than kind, from other violent recidivists serving long sentences' (para. 25). Indeed, in the same paragraph, the sub-committee stated that this fact 'had a considerable effect' on its recommendations. Unfortunately, in our view, it led the committee to the wrong conclusions. The Radzinowicz sub-committee simply assumed that the problem of 'the disruptive minority' was inevitable and something which could and should be dealt with on an *ad hoc* basis by the pre-emptive removal of 'subversive' prisoners – who need not be charged with disciplinary offences – to the segregation units under Rule 43 (paras 42 and 159-67, especially 166).

Few would deny that in deciding where to allocate a prisoner, and in deciding what regime might be suitable for him, careful attention should be paid to his security risk. This seems to involve an assessment of at least two dimensions, both of which were considered by both Mountbatten and Radzinowicz. The first is what might be termed escapability, and involves seeking answers to the questions how likely is a prisoner to try to make an escape, and how successful is he likely to be bearing in mind his resources outside prison? The second involves an assessment of how catastrophic the consequences of an escape are likely to be, for members of the public, the police, the prison service or the State. Presumably the consequences of some escapes may be thought to be so catastrophic that even a low likelihood of escape could not be tolerated. For others a much higher escape risk might be viewed less stringently, because even if successful the escape would result in consequences of minimal impact. The balance between these assessments, what might be called the *escape catastrophic quotient,* may well vary over time as a prisoner passes through his sentence, with obvious implications for re-allocation.

But we would also suggest that prisoners might be classified according to the problems of discipline and control which they raise, or are likely to raise, inside prison. On the basis of our analysis at Albany we think this would also involve at least two kinds of assessments. First would be the determination of a prisoner's subversive potential; that is, his willingness and ability to organize campaigns or activities aimed at subverting the authority of the staff, or undermining staff morale. Second would be an evaluation of a prisoner's stature as an enforcer: that is, his readiness and ability to act upon his own plans, or upon instructions from others, to intimidate or manipulate fellow prisoners. What might be called the *subversive enforcement quotient* would reflect the balance between these assessments. On the basis of what we learned at Albany we would expect that different prisoners would be rated highly as enforcers from those rated highly as potential subversives. The great majority of prisoners would be rated as having low subversive and low enforcement potential. We think that the policy implication of such a classification is simply that each category should be kept separate from the others.

Before we are taken to task by radical reformers, or by our professional colleagues, for prostituting the name of sociology in the interests of maintaining a docile and subservient prison population, we should say at once that we think our proposals would command the support of the great majority of prisoners we spoke to in Albany. Like their fellows in Trenton, they argued that one of their worst problems was living with other prisoners. Let us make clear what we have in mind. In advocating classification of prisoners according to subversive-enforcement potential, and the separation of those with subversive intent from those with enforcement ability and both of these from the rest of the population, we are *not* proposing anything more than that. We do not envisage that any of these prisoners need be kept in solitary confinement, or in special wings where the regime is comparable to those found in existing segregation units, still less anything approaching the infamous control units which have reappeared from time to time since the Home Secretary's announcement in May 1973 but fortunately have not had very much use. Prisoners would be able to mix freely with others in their category, but not with prisoners in other categories, who would live and work in separate areas. We see no reason why the same generally relaxed regime should not be applied for the benefit of all prisoners. In so far as gathering together a group of subversive prisoners may in itself be troublesome, however, we would propose that the extra difficulties be met by employing extra high staffing ratios, and using the most experienced officers, for these prisoners, without otherwise altering the regime. If the process of classification and separation were successful it should be possible to reduce staffing ratios elsewhere to compensate. Nothing we are suggesting here would further restrict the rights of prisoners: indeed we would expect there to be less use of Rule 43, for example, rather than more as a result. And the difficult problem of distinguishing between 'subversion' and 'genuine protest' would be less important because less consequential. In any case classification in terms of the subversive enforcement quotient could be subject to review by the Board of Visitors as is withdrawal under Rule 43 at present.

The principle of separation we are advocating is not new. It is as old as the classification process itself. But it is a principle that was eroded by the dispersal policy. Much of the aggro at Albany was generated by the failure to separate long-term from short-term prisoners, which had an unsettling effect on those who had to watch a procession of prisoners being released. Such a mixture of prisoners would have been unthinkable a few years earlier. If long- and short-termers had been kept apart in Albany from the outset, and if long-termers had been granted special privileges in recognition of their lengthy separation from society instead of being dealt with as though they were the same as any other prisoners, many would have settled down to gleaning, doing their own time, or indulging their secondary comforts. This is not to say that no trouble would have ensued, but that the motivation for subversive activity and the need for enforcers would have been greatly reduced. We do not pretend that the task of identifying prisoners with high subversive or enforcement potential is an easy one. But it is a task which is at present tackled in circumstances designed to create the greatest possible resentment: by removing suspected prisoners from relatively relaxed regimes to severely restricted ones under Rule 43. We think it far better to tackle the problem head on, as a routine matter of separation and without the punitive consequences of a restricted regime.

The principle of separation according to subversive enforcement potential can, of course, be carried out either within a policy of dispersal or within a policy of concentration for high-security-risk prisoners. We think it should be adopted whatever happens to the dispersal policy itself. Indeed, as we argued in chapter 9, something like it has already happened in Albany. Since 1973 prisoners there have been classified according to length of sentence and other criteria which cut across security ratings, and these have been used as a basis for allocating prisoners to halls. The prison appears to have been quieter since then, but the principle was introduced too late to safeguard the liberal regime which had formerly operated. It remains to be seen whether the facilities and privileges which had to be sacrificed can be restored. But since the notion of separation runs directly counter to the concept of dispersal, whereby advantages were supposed to accrue from the very mixing of difficult and dangerous prisoners with the general population, we would prefer to see that policy reversed.

In chapter 1 we noted that the Radzinowicz sub-committee opted for the dispersal of high-security-risk prisoners rather than their concentration, apparently on its assessment of the evidence of the 'sociology of the prison community' (para. 41). We pointed out there that the sub-committee did not present any well-documented evidence to substantiate their belief that dispersal represented the lesser of two evils. Instead they offered a series of hypotheses and conjectures. We doubt that there was any real evidence on the matter one way or another that could be regarded as unambiguous, or even directly relevant to the English situation. The evidence now available from the study of Albany suggests that the dispersal policy – at least in so far as that embodies the indiscriminate mixing not only of prisoners with a high escape catastrophe quotient but also prisoners with a high subversive enforcement quotient among prisoners who share none of these characteristics – can lead to just the kind of dangers which the sub-committee was warned about by so many of its witnesses.

In any case we believe that some of the disadvantages that the sub-committee thought would be more likely to occur under a policy of concentration have now been shown to occur under dispersal, and that some of the fears the sub-committee expressed about concentration were unfounded.

Thus, the committee argued that a prisoner sent to a prison such as Mountbatten envisaged would be publicly labelled as the most incorrigible and that it would be illogical to move him until it was felt that security precautions could be reduced for him. This would result in an excessively custodial, repressive and potentially explosive environment (para. 35). Of course it would be illogical to remove a prisoner from secure conditions if he was thought to remain a security risk; that would apply whether those secure conditions were provided in Mountbatten's Vectis or the several dispersal prisons as suggested by Radzinowicz. But we cannot understand why the sub-committee should use the phrase 'excessively custodial' in connection with high-security-risk prisoners. Any prison to which the highest-security-risk prisoners were sent which was not completely and effectively custodial would be an absurd contradiction in terms. When we returned to Albany in 1971 the paraphernalia of security were ever and obviously present: electronic locks operating on virtually all doors with a system of double gates at strategic points, a perimeter bounded by two high security fences topped with barbed wire and fringed with geophonic alarms, high-mast floodlights, television cameras, dog patrols and UHF radio communications. Only the underground corridors and anti-vehicle concrete blocks were missing from Mountbatten's plans for Vectis! We certainly found the atmosphere oppressive, and no one could have mistaken the custodial intent of Albany. As for repressive and potentially explosive environments, we do not know to what extent these would obtain under concentration. We do know that both have been found in the dispersal prisons. The cherished notion of a relaxed regime within a secure perimeter has been extremely difficult to apply in practice. When Albany was built, security, such as it was, was designed into the buildings themselves. The provision of an exceedingly secure perimeter did not preserve the relaxed regime. Not only were more and more restrictions introduced on the fraternization of prisoners within and between halls at meals and during association, but the very buildings themselves underwent a massive strengthening operation.

Where the phrase 'excessively custodial regime' does have some meaning is precisely in respect of those prisoners who are not deemed to be a security risk but who are still held in conditions of maximum security. In 1971, 117 of the 351 prisoners then held in Albany were classifed in category C – prisoners according to the Mounbatten definition who lack the resources and the will to make escape attempts – and two were classified as suitable for open conditions. Under a policy of concentration over a third of the population could and would have been held in conditions much more appropriate to their very low escape potential.

But these prisoners are not the only ones who may be kept in excessively custodial conditions under the dispersal policy. The dispersal system operates so that more prisoners, on real or spurious grounds, are defined as actually needing conditions of maximum security than would otherwise be the case. We never did understand the contention of the Radzinowicz sub-committee that by concentrating the most recalcitrant prisoners in a small maximum-security prison and leaving them there, the numbers of incorrigible prisoners in the rest of the system would thereby be increased (para. 41, and see our discussion in chapter 1). On the contrary, we believe the failure to separate some prisoners in Albany to have led to the recruitment of several men to the ranks of those with high subversive enforcement quotients. We can well imagine that the same has happened in other dispersal prisons. Though such men might 'legitimately' be regarded as trouble-makers, they had perhaps become so as a result of implementing the dispersal policy. In other circumstances they might have adapted to their imprisonment in one of the ways we described in chapter 9.

9. Moreover, as we argued in chapter 1, the fear expressed by the Radzinowicz sub-committee that officials would play safe by expanding the maximum-security classification to include prisoners who were not really dangerous (para. 30) has always seemed to us much more relevant to dispersal than to concentration. With only one or two really high-security establishments, very careful attention would have to be paid to the problem of classification. The merits of keeping existing prisoners there when other well-qualified candidates appeared would have to be scrupulously and regularly reviewed. With the multiplication of high-security establishments, as under the dispersal policy, there is little need for such careful evaluations of security status. Since some low-security-risk prisoners will be housed there anyway, does it really matter who else is lumped into the top-security categories besides those who constitute a danger to the public, the police or the State? And since the evaluation is to some degree a relative matter, in which any prisoner's status will be judged in relation to the rest of the population at the time, then as more people get pushed up into categories A and B so the less safe it seems to leave category-C and category-D prisoners in semi-secure and open conditions. Mountbatten reported that Home Office plans for a maximum-

security prison in 1966 provided for a mere 80 places, just 0.3 per cent of the adult male prison population. Mountbatten envisaged a prison catering for 120 prisoners, and considered that a second such prison might become necessary in due course (Cmnd 3175, 1966, para. 214). When the Radzinowicz sub-committee met in 1968 there were 138 prisoners in category A, though that number was already subject to review. The sub-committee felt that only a small proportion of the 3,000 or so long-term prisoners required conditions of maximum security, and that these could be housed in three or four dispersal prisons each designed to accommodate about 400 prisoners (paras 26 and 83). By the end of 1973, however, seven dispersal prisons had been brought into operation (at Wormwood Scrubs, Albany, Gartree, Hull, Long Lartin, Parkhurst and Wakefield), with the possibility of two others to be added to the list. Between them they accommodated, on average, 3,508 prisoners, some 13 per cent of the total adult male prison population, including prisoners not yet under sentence! In advocating a return to a policy of concentration for high-security-risk prisoners we do not wish to identify ourselves with the design advocated by Mountbatten for Vectis, which had obvious limitations on the kind of regime that could be operated. Fortunately it is not necessary to consider the design of a new maximum-security prison, nor to go to the expense of building one. We already have seven prisons of the requisite standards of security; and no doubt the costs of refashioning them, often out of the most unpromising material, has already exceeded what it would have cost to build even two prisons of the Vectis type at which the Radzinowicz sub-committee baulked. The cost of building Albany to its original specification, excluding staff quarters, was £1.2 millions. The cost of making all the security improvements brought into effect by October 1976 was £1.6 millions, excluding the electronic installations for night sanitation. The electronic installations had themselves cost another £300,000, and by 1976 these were scheduled for further modification at an estimated cost of £160,000 (Hansard, vol. 918, col. *523*). If the costs of modifying each of the remaining dispersal prisons were only half as much as those for Albany there would still have been ample funds for implementing the Mountbatten proposals. The problem with our maximum-security establishments is that we have too many of them and that they contain large numbers of prisoners who do not require these conditions.

The return to concentration could be achieved by changing the procedures for allocation of both prisoners and staff. Prisoners with a high escape catastrophe potential might be allocated to say two, or at the most three, of the existing dispersal prisons. Even allowing for the growth in life sentences we doubt that there can be many more than 500 prisoners in the system who could seriously be regarded as requiring conditions of top security. Accordingly we would envisage that these prisons would operate with substantially lower numbers of prisoners than the present dispersal equivalents, even though this would mean adding to overcrowding elsewhere. Allocation within each prison would ensure that prisoners with high subversive or enforcement potential would be kept separate from each other and from the rest of the population. Some remodelling of the prisons might be required to ensure adequate separation, and to provide for a spread of facilities and a relaxed regime for each group. Substantially higher staffing ratios would be required to maintain control while operating a regime based on a high degree of association within groups. Prisoners might be moved from one group to another, or from prison to prison, as circumstances changed. And, of course, if the escape catastrophe quotient changed then a prisoner would be transferred to conditions of lesser security elsewhere, but where the same principles of separation would apply. We do not think this proposal would eliminate troubles in the prisons. It might be necessary to retain segregation units, although we would be surprised if they had to be used as frequently as the one in Albany during 1972. Transfers to special cells in local prisons from time to time might well be enough to defuse potentially explosive situations, should they arise. We do think this proposal would substantially contain troubles, without introducing unnecessary restrictions, while allowing the great majority of prisoners to do their time in reasonable conditions of peace and safety. Above all, it would mean that a process of de-escalating the security provisions in the remaining dispersal prisons could be set in motion so that once again, in the words of Peterson (1961a), security would not be 'excessive having regard to the purpose for which the establishment is intended'.

Perhaps the new era – of humane but unambiguously custodial prisons in which the security precautions reasonably reflected the threat to the community by those incarcerated, and which provided opportunities for the prisoner to work, recreate and if he were at all interested to attend courses and programmes which he thought might be helpful – is not an inspiring one to behold. But we think that if it were brought about, the trials, tribulations and traumas suffered by the staff and inmates of Albany will not have been in vain.

Postscript

As we noted in chapter 2, we undertook to show a pre-publication draft to the governor or his nominated representative; to the local branch committee of the POA; to some prisoners; and to anybody else who could make a reasonable case for seeing it. We offered to discuss any points which were raised and to make necessary amendments only if we could be convinced that what we had written was inaccurate or misleading. We assured our respondents, some of whom were fearful of Home Office interference, that we would take the same approach to any points raised by officials. In this brief postscript we describe our attempt to carry out those undertakings.

We have not been as successful as we would have liked in generating a dialogue arising from the research, largely because of the passage of time between the end of our fieldwork and the completion of a first draft. During that interval, of course, we were engaged on comparative studies of prison regimes in other prisons. Once our draft was completed we sent copies to both surviving governors of Albany (Mr Footer had died during the preparation of the manuscript) and to representatives of the local branch of the POA as we had agreed. We also supplied copies to two members, or former members, of the central management team, to one of the former advisers on the Albany management structure from the Wakefield staff college, and to one other uniformed officer who asked to see the report. It was quite another matter trying to locate prisoners who had been in Albany during our study. Our own personal contacts had, by this time, effectively ceased; and when we approached the Home Office to seek their help we were told that it would be very difficult for us to honour our undertaking, and that Prison Department did not see how it could be done. When we persisted with our request, however, it was pointed out that even if some ex-Albany prisoners could be located we might find that neither Prison Department nor ourselves could regard them as sufficiently articulate and responsible to carry out the exercise required. Recognizing this as a potential problem, we suggested that the search might be confined to a list of ten prisoners known to us whom we regarded as suitable. In fact all ten had been released from their original sentences some time before our request was made, and so we made it clear that we would also consider any suggestions that the Department might make about alternatives. Some time after supplying this list we wrote to Prison Department to see what progress had been made, and were referred to another division which was said to be looking into the matter. We did not receive a reply to our next and last letter on the subject, but were later told unofficially that none of the prisoners we listed could be traced in the system and that the Department could suggest no alternative possibilities. We did not feel justified in attempting to locate these men outside the prison system. We did consider advertising for ex-Albany prisoners in the national Press but rejected the idea as being unlikely to yield effective results. Our effort to contact prisoners to enable them to comment on the draft was, therefore, regretfully abandoned. We would still be very pleased to hear from any ex-Albany prisoners who happen to read this monograph.

Most of our respondents, in our view, reacted to the manuscript in rather too kindly a fashion. It was not so much that there were no points of disagreement, for indeed there were several and it would have been surprising had that not been so. It was rather that they preferred to let what they accepted as constructive criticism stand, and the lessons to emerge, without attempting to assert what they felt would be their own personal views. As one of them put it: 'I have no desire to try to set the record right . . . all that means is making the record more comfortable to live with.'

But one point raised by a former member of the central management team is worth recording here. He commented as follows: 'The rehearsal of key events is inevitable but gives the impression of an inexorable build-up to an avalanche. Maybe this is just how it seemed and those of us less perceptive than others were unable to see it. But my recollection is not so much of an impending avalanche as of a series of blizzards which were not catastrophic in themselves and from which we tried to salvage as much as we could. Maybe what I'm really struggling to say is that the account makes painful reading!' We would largely agree with that view. We too saw each blizzard as a relatively isolated piece of bad weather; only when the avalanche actually came did it seem that the climate itself had changed. We have tried throughout our reporting to stick to our understanding of events as we recorded them at the time; but the very act of analysis and the provision of a narrative account in a situation of hindsight is bound to make things seem more ordered and interconnected than perhaps they were.

We should say something of the response to the research by the Home Office, if only because the nature of the relationship between academic researchers and government departments seems sometimes to be misunderstood. As we indicated in chapter 2, the research proposals were entirely our own, though funding for the study, apart from the salary of the principal investigator and the cost of office accommodation which were provided by the University of Southampton, came from the Home Office. In writing our report we made no attempt to impose self-censorship with the single exception of details relating to matters of the physical security of the prison. We sent a copy of the draft to the Home Office Research Unit, enclosing further copies for circulation within the Home Office, in accordance with what we believe to be normal practice. Seven months later we received a six-page memorandum from the Research Unit which brought together all the comments from the various interested departments in the Home Office. The covering letter simply stated that the comments were 'attached for your consideration when you amend the current draft'.

The comments provided by the Home Office included both general remarks and very detailed points. Broadly speaking, they fell into one of three categories: technical points concerning methodological aspects of the study, corrections as to detailed matters of fact or procedure, and differences of interpretation of events and policies described or discussed. While we did not agree with all the methodological points raised, most of them were helpful and in some instances we did take advantage of the redrafting to achieve greater clarity in the light of Home Office comments. In all instances where errors of fact or procedure were brought to our attention—for example, on the way staff were posted to Albany, on the statutory obligations placed on the medical officer, or on the status of the Albany prison hospital—we amended our text accordingly and were very glad to do so.

As might be expected, disagreements over the interpretation of events and policies were somewhat more numerous and problematic. Though we carefully considered each of the points put to us by the Home Office we finally decided, working on the principle that facts are sacred but criticism is free, to make no changes whatever. Several Home Office comments, for example, were directed at remarks we had made about the difficulties of providing professional, including medical, services within the prison context. It sometimes seemed to us that the burden of the Home Office comments here was not merely to put the prison medical service in a better light, but almost to place it effectively beyond criticism. We do not wish to suggest that there was any pressure placed upon us to redraft what we had said, for there was not. But in the event, and upon reflection, we decided to leave the text exactly as it was.

Perhaps the biggest differences between us and the Home Office, however, concerned the operation of the dispersal policy. Once again we made no changes in our text. But since it was suggested that we had been writing about a period when the dispersal policy was still being developed, and the Home Office comments may be seen as presenting current thinking on that policy, it is fitting to conclude with a brief review of the differences. The Home Office argued that the situation described at Albany represented an early phase of the evolution of the dispersal policy; that the strengthening of cells and guniting of the perimeter fence were part of a more 'general development of dispersal architecture'; and that it may be impossible to evaluate the policy objectively until a purpose-built prison is constructed. We need hardly say that we would disagree with that view. To suggest that a policy cannot be evaluated while it is still evolving is tantamount to saying that nothing can ever be evaluated in a changing world. Prison Department certainly did not apply the same logic even to the experimental situation involved in the two-shift system of industrial work for prisoners. And for the reason that we gave in our conclusions – namely, that we already have too many secure prisons – we earnestly hope that Prison Department is not seriously contemplating the construction of a purpose-built dispersal prison.

The Home Office pointed out that although we suggested that there may perhaps be no more than 500 prisoners actually requiring top-security conditions because of their escape catastrophe potential, no evidence was provided to indicate that this number is either realistic or finite. They further argued that the number of category-A and B men may be due simply to receptions of those types of prisoner rather than to the labelling activities of

Prison Department, and that in any case the present system allowed for the flexible review of cases and possible downgrading in security status. We were disappointed to find that the Home Office made no attempt to repair the lack of evidence by any demonstration as to how many more prisoners there are than we had suggested who do require top security. It could, of course, be the case that the numbers of category-A and B men may result simply from the pattern of receptions. But we would be surprised if the receptions of prisoners of those types had accelerated so much in the last decade to have so completely outstripped the pre-Mountbatten Home Office estimates, Mountbatten's own estimates, and even the Radzinowicz sub-committee's estimates as to the size of the problem. And we stand by our observation that the trouble with the dispersal policy is that the labelling process is more likely to occur precisely because there is less need to pay attention to the classification process than under a policy of concentration.

The Home Office explained that there are now no category-C men in Albany, and that the location of more than 100 such prisoners there during our study was but a transitional phase of the dispersal policy. We do not know quite how to interpret this, but two observations may be made. On the one hand, as we have already argued, it seems likely that with the expansion of top-security places in the dispersal prisons there would be a tendency to upgrade the security rating of all prisoners in the system. If this were the case the removal of the category-C men may itself be no more than a change of labels. On the other hand, assuming the change to be a genuine one and that 100 category-C men who might formerly have been lodged in Albany are now located elsewhere, one might ask whether the dispersal policy any longer has any meaning? For to disperse top-security-risk prisoners only amongst those who are next below them in degree of security risk is surely not what the Radzinowicz sub-committee and the Advisory Council had in mind.

Bibliography

Atchley, Robert C. and McCabe, M. Patrick (1968),'Socialization in
  correctional communities: a replication', *Amer. Sociol. Rev.*, vol. 33,
  no. 5, pp. 774-85.
Becker, Howard S. (1967), 'Whose side are we on?' *Social Problems,* vol.
  14, no. 3, pp. 234–47.
Blake, James (1970), *The Joint,* Dell, New York.
Bottoms, A. E. and McClintock, F.H. (1973), *Criminals Coming of Age,*
  Heinemann, London.
Burns, Tom and Stalker, G. M. (1961), *The Management of Innovation,*
  Tavistock, London.
Castell, F. (1968), 'Prisons – has the Home Office blundered', *Police,*
  October.
Christie, Nils (ed.) (1968), *Aspects of Social Control in Welfare States,*
  Scandinavian Studies in Criminology, vol. 2, Tavistock, London.
Clemmer, Donald (1940), *The Prison Community,* Holt, Rinehart &
  Winston, New York.
Cline, Hugh F. (1968), 'The determinants of normative patterns in
  correctional institutions', in Christie, N. (ed.), *Aspects of Social Control
  in Welfare States.*
Cloward, Richard A. *et al.* (1960), *Theoretical Studies in Social
  Organization of the Prison,* Social Science Research Council, New
  York.
Cohen, Stanley (1974),'Human warehouses: the future of our prisons',
  New Society, vol. 30, no. 632, pp. 407-11, 14 November.
Cohen, Stanley and Taylor, Laurie (1972), *Psychological Survival: the
  experience of long-term imprisonment,* Penguin, Harmondsworth.
Cohen, Stanley and Taylor, Laurie (1975), 'Prison research: a cautionary
  Tale', *New Society,* vol. 31, no 643, pp. 253-5, 30 January.
Cooper, M. H. and King, Roy D. (1965), 'Social and economic problems
  of prisoners' work', in *Sociological Review Monograph No. 9,
  Sociological Studies in the British Penal Services,* Keele.
Cressey, Donald R. (ed.) (1961), *The Prison: studies in institutional
  organization and change,* Holt, Rinehart & Winston, New York.
Cressey, Donald R. (1965), 'Prison organizations', in March, James G.
  (ed.) *Handbook of Organizations.*
Cross, Rupert (1971), *Punishment, Prison and the Public,* The Hamlyn
  Lectures, Twenty-third series, Stevens, London.
Emery, F. E. (1970), *Freedom and Justice Within Walls: the Bristol prison
  experiment,* Tavistock, London.
Fairweather, Leslie (1961), 'Prison architecture in England', *Brit, J.
  Criminol.,* vol 1, no. 4, pp. 339-61.

Fowler, Norman (1967), 'Hard times for the Home Secretary', *The Times,*
17 August.
Garabedian, Peter C. (1963), 'Social roles and processes of socialization
in the prison community', *Social Problems,* vol. 11, no 2, pp. 139-52.
Hall Williams, J. E. (1970), *The English Penal System in Transition,*
Butterworth, London.
Irwin, John (1970), *The Felon,* Prentice-Hall, Englewood Cliffs.
Irwin, John and Cressey, Donald R. (1962), 'Thieves, convicts and the
inmate culture', *Social Problems,* vol. 10, no. 2, pp.145-55.
Kassebaum, Gene G., Ward, David and Wilner, Daniel (1971), *Prison
Treatment and Parole Survival: an empirical assessment,* Wiley, New
York.
King, Roy D. (1972), 'An Analysis of Prison Regimes', Unpublished.
Report to the Home Office, University of Southampton.
King, Roy D. and Morgan, Rodney (1976), *A Taste of Prison: custodial
conditions for trial and remand prisoners,* Routledge & Kegan Paul,
London.
King, Roy D., Raynes, Norma V. and Tizard, Jack (1971), *Patterns of
Residential Care: sociological studies in institutions for handicapped
children,* Routledge & Kegan Paul, London.
Klare, Hugh J. (1964), 'The problem of remand in custody for diagnostic
purposes', in Lopez-Rey, M. and Germain, C. (eds) *Studies in Penology.
to the Memory of Sir Lionel Fox.*
Klare, Hugh J. (1968), 'Prisoners in maximum security', *New Society,* vol.
11, no. 288, pp. 494-5, 4 April.
Klare, Hugh J. (1975), 'Custodial alternatives', in McConville, S. (ed.)
*The Use of Imprisonment: essays in the changing state of English penal
policy.*
Lopez-Rey, M. and Germain, C. (eds) (1964), *Studies in Penology to the
Memory of Sir Lionel Fox,* Martinus Nijhoff, The Hague.
March, James G. (ed.) (1965), *Handbook of Organizations,* Rand
McNally, Chicago.
Mathiesen, Thomas (1965), *The Defences of the Weak: a sociological
study of a Norwegian correctional institution,* Tavistock, London.
Matza, David (1969), *Becoming Deviant,* Prentice-Hall, Englewood
Cliffs.
Mayhew, Henry and Binny, John (1862), *The Criminal Prisons of London
and Scenes of Prison Life,* Griffin, Bohn, London.
McConville, S. (ed.) (1975), *The Use of Imprisonment: essays in the
changing state of English penal policy,* Routledge & Kegan Paul,
London.
Moos, Rudolph (1968), 'Assessment of social climates of correctional
institutions', *J. of Res. in Crime and Del.,* vol. 5, pp. 174-88.
Morris, T. P. (1967), 'Research on the prison community', in *Collected
Studies in Criminological Research,* vol. 1, European Committee on
Crime Problems, Council of Europe, Strasbourg.
Morris, T. P. (1968), Notes on 'The regime for long-term prisoners in
conditions of maximum security', *Brit. J. Criminol.,* vol. 8, no. 3, pp.
312-14.

Morris, T. P., Morris, P. and Barer, Barbara (1963), *Pentonville: a sociological study of an English prison*, Routledge & Kegan Paul, London.

Mountbatten, Lord (1972), Interview with Dr Bolt, *Prison Officers' Magazine*, vol. 62, no. 8, pp. 86-87

Norman, Frank (1958), *Bang to Rights: an account of prison life*, Secker & Warburg, London.

Oversby, Clive and Hill, Richard (1970), *The Good Jail Guide*, Wolfe Publishing Limited, London.

Parker, Tony (1970), *The Frying Pan: a prison and its prisoners*, Hutchinson, London.

Peterson, A. W. (1961a), 'The prison building programme', *Brit. J. Criminol.*, vol. 1, no. 4, pp. 307-16.

Peterson, A. W. (1961b), 'The prison building programme: a postscript', *Brit. J. Criminol.*, vol. 1, no. 4, pp. 372-5.

Peterson, A. W. (1962), 'The next decade', *Prison Service Journal*, vol. I, no. 4, pp. 3-8.

Schrag, Clarence (1944), 'Social Types in a Prison Community', Unpublished MA Thesis, University of Washington.

Stanton, Alfred H. and Schwartz, Morris S. (1954), *The Mental Hospital: a study of institutional participation in psychiatric illness and treatment*, Basic Books, New York.

Street, David, Vinter, Robert D. and Perrow, Charles (1966), *Organization for Treatment*, Free Press, New York.

Sykes, Gresham M. (1958), *The Society of Captives: a study of a maximum-security prison*, Princeton University Press.

Taylor, I. (1968), Letter, *New Society*, vol. 11, no. 290, pp. 576.

Taylor, I., Walton, P. and Young, J. (1975), 'Critical criminology in Britain: review and prospects', in Taylor, Walton and Young (eds), *Critical Criminology*, Routledge & Kegan Paul, London.

Thomas, J. E. (1972), *The English Prison Officer since 1850: a study in conflict*, Routledge & Kegan Paul, London.

Thomas, J. E. (1974), 'Policy and administration in penal establishments', in Blom-Cooper, Louis (ed.), *Progress in Penal Reform*, Clarendon Press, Oxford.

Towndrow, E. A. (1964), 'Blundeston', *Prison Service Journal*, vol. IV, no. 13, pp. 40-4.

Weber, M. (1904), *The Methodology of the Social Sciences*, Eng. Trans., Shils, E. and Finch, H. A., Free Press, New York, 1949.

Wheeler, Stanton (1958), 'Social Organization in a Correctional Community', Unpublished PhD Thesis, University of Washington.

Wheeler, Stanton (1961), 'Socialization in correctional communities', *Amer. Sociol. Rev.*, vol. 26, pp. 697-712.

Official publications and reports

Advisory Council (1961), *Work for Prisoners*, Report of the Advisory Council on the Employment of Prisoners, HMSO.

Advisory Council (1964), *Organization of Work for Prisoners,* Report of the Advisory Council on the Employment of Prisoners, HMSO.

Advisory Council (1968), *The Regime for Long-term Prisoners in Conditions of Maximum Security,* Report of the Advisory Council on the Penal System (Radzinowicz Report), HMSO.

C.7702 (1895), *Report from the Departmental Committee on Prisons* (Gladstone Report).

Cd 6406 (1912), *Report of the Commissioners of Prisons and Directors of Convict Prisons.*

Cmnd 645 (1959), *Penal Practice in a Changing Society.*

Cmnd 1467 (1961), *Report of the Commissioners of Prisons for 1960.*

Cmnd 2296 (1966), *The War Against Crime.*

Cmnd 3175 (1966), *Report of the Inquiry into Prison Escapes and Security* (Mountbatten Report).

Cmnd 3774 (1968), *Report on the Work of the Prison Department for 1967.*

Cmnd 4186 (1969), *Report on the Work of the Prison Department for 1968.*

Cmnd 4214 (1969), *People in Prison in England and Wales.*

Cmnd 4486 (1970), *Report on the Work of the Prison Department for 1969.*

Cmnd 5037 (1972), *Report on the Work of the Prison Department for 1971.*

Cmnd 5375 (1973), *Report on the Work of the Prison Department for 1972.*

Cmnd 6148 (1975), *Report on the Work of the Prison Department for 1974.*

Cmnd 6523 (1976), *Report on the Work of the Prison Department for 1975.*

HMSO, 104 (1961), *Civil Estimates for 1961-62.*

HMSO, 125 (1963), *Civil Estimates for 1963-64.*

HMSO, 599, (1967), *Eleventh Report from the Estimates Committee Session 1966-67, Prisons, Borstals and Detention Centres.*

Home Office (1966), Unpublished report, 'The Scope for Management Services in Prisons'.

Home Office (1967), Unpublished report 'Structure of Responsibilities in Training Prisons' (Folkestone-Worksop Report).

Royal Commission (1967), Evidence submitted to the *Royal Commission on the Penal System in England and Wales 1964-66.*

S.I. No. 1073 (1949), *The Prison Rules.*

S.I. No. 388 (1964), *The Prison Rules.*

Index

A hall, 27, 72, 121, 123
  electronic systems, 26, 27, 73, 109,
    123, 171, 218–19, 276–7
  management of, 108–11
  regime in, 128–31, 159–61, 223,
    276–7
  staff and prisoner views of, 223–5
  use of, 108–9, 302
Adaptation to prison
  prisoner modes of, 213, 235–61, 331,
    333, 351; blowing your top, 257;
    campaigning, 256–7, 260, 317;
    doing your own bird, 237–8, 243,
    246, 249, 254–6, 258–9, 260, 310,
    314–16, 334, 348; effects of
    dispersal policy, 313–18, 334–5;
    finding your feet, 256, 271;
    gleaning, 237, 239, 246, 250–2,
    253, 256, 258–60, 269–70, 310, 313,
    315–7, 334, 348; jailing, 238–40,
    243, 246–50, 252, 253, 255, 256,
    258–60, 267, 310, 313–15;
    opportunism, 240, 252–4, 255,
    258–9, 270, 310, 313; problems of
    classification, 236, 238–41, 256;
    secondary comfort undulgence,
    244–6, 258–9, 265, 279, 310, 316,
    334, 348; uncertain negative
    retreat, 241–4, 247, 248, 249, 254,
    258–60, 264, 310, 313–14, 316
  staff modes of, 261–73, 331, 334–5;
    effects of dispersal policy, 318–19,
    334–5; implementing Rule 1,
    268–9, 270, 272, 318, 334; making a
    career, 269–70, 273, 318, 334;
    marking time, 228, 270–1, 273,
    318–19; negative detachment,
    265–8, 272, 319; secondary comfort
    indulgence, 264–5, 272, 318;
    uncertain withdrawal, 263–4, 272,
    319
Adjudications, 30, 31, 141, 224–5, 284,
  287–9, 294, 298, 300, 304
Administration block, 71
Administration of prisons
  changes in, 4–6, 9–10, 12, 22;

lessons for, 11–12, 82, 340–4
  see also Home Office, Prison
    Commission, Prison Department
Administration officer, 85–7
  in Albany, 91, 98, 101–2, 127, 153,
    155, 181, 200
Administrative staff, 55, 200–1, 232,
  261
Advisory Council on the Employment
  of Prisoners, 10, 80, 362, 363
Advisory Council on the Penal System,
  15, 16, 20, 21, 25, 345, 359, 363
After-care, 6
Aggro, 139, 242, 255, 268, 284, 291,
  313, 316, 348
Aims of prisons, 335–40
Alarms, 30, 120, 284, 304
Albany Argus, 164, 165, 181, 243
Albany barracks, 23–4, 70, 118
Albany file, 109, 112, 119, 129, 131, 166
Albany handbook, 321
Albany House, 72, 207, 268
  see also Officers' mess
Albany Prison
  aims, 76, 78
  adverse publicity, 30, 31, 281,
    288–305, 306–9
  building costs, 23–4, 70, 352
  commissioning of, 90–5, 341
  favourable publicity, 3, 26, 27, 29,
    68–9, 122–3, 187, 283
  opening of, 3, 25, 26, 67, 91
  planning and design, 23, 69, 70–5,
    245, 310, 341
Alcatraz Prison, 18
Alcoholics Anonymous, 214, 239, 339
Allocation of prisoners
  to case officers, 109, 166
  to halls, 104, 111, 302, 312, 325–6,
    339, 349, 353
  to labour, 83, 86, 87, 109–10, 339
  to prisons, 19, 302, 338–9
Alvington Prison, 16, 17, 20, 26, 52, 68,
  151, 337
  postponement and abandonment, 21,
    26–8

see also Maximum-security prison, Vectis Prison
Amenities and facilities, 235, 244–7, 250, 253–4, 258, 261, 265, 279
Applications, 129, 131–2, 137–8, 214, 256, 275, 317
  change of labour, 135–6, 215, 254, 319
Approved schools. 125, 194, 240, 311, 313
Architecture of prisons, 7–8, 70–1, 358
Arson, incidents at Albany, 29, 283
Assistant governors, 55, 81, 84–5, 87, 342
  in Albany, 91, 98, 101, 106, 126, 155, 158, 163, 199, 200; AG II for social training, 102–4, 105, 110–11, 113, 165, 176, 181, 321; AG II for staff resources, 102–4, 106, 107, 112, 158, 164, 176, 178, 180–1, 321, 323; contact with prisoners, 214; as hall managers, 322; review board, 113, 143, 166
Association, 35, 130, 132–3, 216–18, 221–2, 235, 242, 244, 262, 268, 309, 312, 353
  difficulties of, 134–5, 163, 262–3, 325
  limits on, 32, 284, 299–300, 303, 316, 325, 350
  room, 72, 216–17
Atchley, Robert C., 188, 360
Attica Prison, 228–9
Aylesbury Prison, 301

B hall, 109, 291, 292–3
  installation of electronics, 168
  management of, 109
  regime in, 131–3, 160, 219–20
  use of, 109, 303, 326–7
'Banging up', 123, 219, 242, 296, 299
Bank Holiday search and lock-in, 295–9, 323, 325, 343
Barer, Barbara, 362
Baroning, 141, 248
Bathing, 139, 216, 245, 316
Beatings, alleged, 257, 287–8
Becker, Howard S., 45, 360
Bela River Prison, 150
'Big men', 308, 316
Biggs, Ronald, escape of, 13, 25
Binny, John, 81, 361
Blake, George, escape of, 11, 13, 25
Blake, James, 227, 360
'Block, the', 257, 285, 291, 292
Blom-Cooper, Louis, 362
blowing your top *see* Adaptation to

prison (prisoner modes of)
Blundeston Prison, 7, 23, 70, 76, 90–5, 171, 244, 341
Board of Visitors, 224, 284, 302, 348
  adjudications and applications, 138, 287–9, 298, 304, 315, 317
  letter to Home Secretary, 323, 326
  mediation with POA, 299
  relations with research, 52–3, 62
Boredom, 163–4, 175
Borstal, 85, 226
  Albany likened to, 144, 274, 279–80
  boys, 49, 255
  prisoners' experience of, 125, 194, 240, 248, 259, 311, 313
  staff experience of, 202, 269, 272–3
Bottoms, A.E., 35, 36, 44, 48–51, 109, 360
Briefing meeting, 153–4
Brighton College of Education, 134
Bristol Prison, 34
  see also Research
British Institute of Management, 95
Brixton Prison, 292
Budgerigars, 134, 291
  burning of, 287
Building programme, 7–8, 21, 70, 341
Burns, Tom, 88, 360

C hall, 109–10
  regime in, 131–3, 160, 219–20
  used for long-term prisoners, 303, 327
Callaghan, James, 16, 27, 28
Calling back, 321, 323
Calling up, 276
Camp Hill Prison, 94, 142, 171, 292, 297
Campaigning, *see* Adaptation to prison (prisoner modes of)
Canteen, 72, 132, 182, 212
  clerk, 211
Canterbury Prison, 125
'Caravan in a meadow', 3, 67, 73, 172, 331
Cardiff Prison, 14, 297
Carnegie, Tom, 304
Carpentry
  shops, 118, 136, 180–1, 208–9, 211–12, 254, 275, 290, 319
  trades, 68, 76, 114, 118, 208
Carr, Robert, 31, 32, 302
Case officer system, *see* Case officers
Case officers, 108–9, 111–13, 129, 131, 187, 214–16, 316, 321
  codification of duties, 163, 166

difficulties of, 134, 166, 264, 321–2
prisoner views of, 164–5, 215, 242,
    244, 247, 251, 253
staff views of, 215–16, 264, 267, 272
Castell F., 16, 360
Category-A dispersal prison, Albany
    as, 28–9, 172, 283, 352
Category-A prisoners, 15, 16, 18, 21,
    345, 346;
  in Albany, 124, 172, 182, 194, 277,
    285, 310; absorption of, 167–8,
    312; adaptations of, 314–15;
    confinement in segregation unit,
    286; involvement in disturbances,
    308–9; preparation for reception
    of, 28–9, 166–7, 169–70, 173, 181,
    187, 222, 281, 283; separation of,
    303, 327; staff and prisoner views
    of, 278–80
regulations for visiting, 29, 282
Category-A regime, in Albany, 184,
    186, 204–25, 318, 343
Category-B prison, Albany as, 26, 28,
    73
Category-B prisoners
  in Albany, 28, 172, 194, 308, 310,
    314, 327; adaptations of, 315;
    preparation for reception of, 119,
    172, 278
Category-C prison
  Albany as, 29, 121, 122–45, 333
  regime in, 122, 128–45, 161–3
Category-C prisoners
  in Albany, 26, 28, 109, 124, 171–2,
    186, 193, 308, 310, 350–1;
    preparation for reception of,
    91–4, 119; removal from, 359
Category-D prisoners in Albany, 124,
    194, 310
Catering officer, 91, 287, 290–1
Cells
  described, 71–2
  strengthening of, 151, 167, 350, 358
  strong, 290
Central automatic control system
    (CACS), 74, 170–1
Central management meeting (CMM),
    25, 55, 92, 98, 167, 262
  7 August, 153, 163–4, 337
  28 August, 158
  functioning of, 98–101, 119, 153–7
  24 July, 151
Central management team, 25, 55,
    154–5, 169, 276–9, 286, 319, 355
  evaluations of Albany, 232, 261–2,
    318

Chapels, 72, 107, 170
Chaplain, 81, 87, 105–6, 126, 134, 155,
    176, 178, 200
  contact with prisoners, 214, 239, 251
Chelmsford Prison, 14–15, 297
Chief officers, 55, 60, 81, 342
  in Albany: chief I, 91, 98, 126, 137,
    144, 159, 160–1, 164, 199, 293, 322;
    role of, 101–3, 120, 141, 155;
    participation in research, 201, 263;
    chiefs II, 107, 126, 199, 200, 290;
    participation in research, 201, 263;
    roles of, 101–5, 108, 110–11, 155,
    176, 181
  role of, 84–5
'Chokey', 290
Christie, Nils, 34, 360
Chronological overview, 23–32
Church services, 133
Civil Estimates 1961–2, 23, 363
Civil Estimates 1963–4, 24, 363
Classification of prisoners, 6, 7, 338
  by security category, 11, 339, 344–6,
    350–2, 358–9
Classrooms, 72, 74, 107, 163
Cleaners, 127, 200, 210, 211
Clemmer, Donald, 34, 188, 360
Clerical staff, 55, 127, 200
Cline, Hugh F., 188, 360
Closed prisons, 7, 20, 202, 269
Cloward, Richard A., 34, 360
Cohen, Stanley, 13, 34–6, 44–8, 227–8,
    230, 238, 258–9, 314, 317, 333, 338,
    360
Coldingley Prison, 7, 21, 25, 89, 94–5,
    174, 341–2
  guiding group, 21, 94–5
  see also Industrial prison, 'Worksop'
Community contacts, 240–1, 245, 249,
    251, 253, 255–6, 258, 259, 260, 340
Computer, 168, 171, 287
Concentration policy, 16, 18–21, 27,
    344, 349–51, 359
  advantages of, 351–4
  costs, 20
  POA support for, 12, 284, 307
Confinement to cells, 287, 295–9
Confrontation
  between officers and governor, 31,
    32, 294–5, 298, 305
  between prisoners and staff, 30, 287,
    306, 316, 318–19
Conjugal visits, 15, 24–5
Contraband, 142, 212–13, 239–40,
    247–8, 252, 296–8
Control of prisoners, 9, 69, 188, 345, 353

pressures for consistency, 159, 189
staff anxieties about, 307, 314
Control units, 32, 302, 347
Cooper, M. H., 87, 117, 360
Corrective training, 6
County Press, 27, 68–9, 71, 122, 123
Cressey, Donald R., 34, 188, 237, 360, 361
Crime rates, increase in, 5, 6
Criminal Justice Act, 1948, 6
Cross, Rupert, 4, 5, 360
Current offences, 125, 194, 196–7, 311
Custodial orientation, 188–9
Cutting shop, 116–17, 209, 212

D hall, 109, 110, 291
controlled regime in, 300, 326
regime in, 131–3, 160, 219–20
use for long-term prisoners, 303, 327
Daily Express, 31, 294, 297, 308, 314
Daily Mail, 30, 288
Daily Mirror, 31, 297
Daily routine, 128–36, 175, 204–6
Daily Telegraph, 30, 288, 292, 307
Dangerous prisoners, 3, 8, 18–19
Dartmoor Prison, 8, 13, 23, 68, 194, 297
Death of prisoner, 32, 304
Demonstrations in Albany, 31, 290, 292–4, 297, 305–6
Department of industries and stores, 87
Deputy governor, 81, 86, 87
in Albany, 91, 98, 126, 199, 256, 262, 291; change of, 200, 274; in charge of prison, 151–2, 167, 285; role of, 101–3, 182
role of, 83–4, 342
Deputy governor's record party, 210, 245
Detention centres, 125, 194, 311, 313
Deterrence, 79, 336
Development of industries meeting, 119
Diagnostic centres, 7
Dining halls, 69, 129–32
abandonment of, 31, 299–300, 316
disturbances in, 30–1, 286, 290, 292, 295, 306
orderlies, 207, 210
use as games room, 164, 217
Director General, 22
Discipline offences, 141, 255, 257, 284, 286, 287–8, 298
reporting of, 294, 300–1
Discipline office, 85–6, 88, 178
Discipline staff, *see* Prison officers
Disorganized criminals, 238, 242, 249,

257, 258
Dispersal policy, 16, 18–21, 27
in Albany: effects of, 183–5, 309, 315, 349, 351; implementation of, 90, 125, 309–19, 344, 348; POA views on, 284, 288–9; staff views on, 324
compared with concentration, 349–52
costs of, 20, 352
effects of, 16–17, 20, 183–5, 348
future of, 344–54
Home Office defence of, 358–9
Home Office review of, 31, 32, 298, 301, 322, 336
inherent problems of, 325, 349–52, 359
working party on, 28, 167–8
undermining of, 32, 325–7, 349
Dispersal prisons, 21, 27, 32, 172, 175, 182, 350, 359
costs of, 352
future use of, 353
increase in numbers of, 302, 351, 352
upgrading security in, 302, 358
see also Gartree, Hull, Long Lartin, Parkhurst, Wakefield, Wormwood Scrubs
Disposal party, 210, 211
Disturbances in Albany, 31, 287, 290–1, 304, 320
distinguished from peaceful protests, 305–6
predicted, 279–80, 287
Dog handlers, 28, 127, 168, 171, 182, 278
Dog patrols, 9, 11, 28, 120–1, 168, 171, 187, 277–8, 280, 350
Doing time, 140, 161, 226–31, 237, 281, 353
Doing your own bird, *see* Adaptation to prison (prisoner modes of)
Dover Borstal, 25, 35, 36, 40, 48–51, 109
see also Research
Dress of prisoners, regulations relating to, 139–40, 144, 159, 160–1, 222, 247, 253, 320
Drug users, 237, 259
Du Cane, Sir Edmund, 4
Durham Prison, 34
guarding by troops, 20, 24
special security wing, 10, 15, 16, 35, 45, 230, 258–60, 317, 333
see also Research
Durham University, 35, 47

E hall, 110, 217, 292
  reconstruction of, 171
  re-wiring of, 32, 301–2
  temporary use during ELSA installation, 74, 109
  use as extension to segregation unit, 31, 298–300, 316
  use as induction unit, 303
Education classes, 6, 14, 132, 339
  attendance at, 217, 239, 251–2, 253, 257, 276
  curtailed, 299, 316
  difficulty of organizing, 134, 163
  resumed, 300
Education clerk, 211
Education department, 200
  effects of single shift working, 175, 178
'Electronic coffin', 3, 277, 281, 286, 304, 318, 331
Electronic devices, 9, 10, 24–6,73, 95, 123, 129–31, 168, 277, 286, 350
  see also Central automatic control system, ELSA system
ELSA system, 26–7, 73, 109, 123, 128, 187, 234
  control room, 26, 73–4, 128, 130
  costs, 352
  effect on A hall regime, 129–31, 276–7
  extension of, 168, 277
  interference with, 208, 277
  security implications, 74, 130, 168, 277
Emerson, R. W., 156
Emery, F. E., 34–6, 44–5, 48, 360
Employment exchange, 136
Engineers, 126, 200
Escape-catastrophe quotient, 346–8, 353
Escape list prisoners, 295
Escapes, 10, 11, 13, 25
  attempted, 345; in Albany, 141, 283, 294, 297–8, 305
  equipment for, 31, 294–5, 298, 301
  phantasies of, 260, 317
Estimates Committee
  criticism of Albany costs, 26, 70
  report of, 12, 15, 21, 26, 82, 363
  visit to Albany, 26, 27
European Commission on Human Rights, 317
European Conference of Directors of Criminological Institutes, 38, 42
Evening Standard, 27
Everthorpe Borstal, 7

Executive officers, 127, 200
Exercise, limits on, 299, 300
'Exigent day', 82, 97, 101–2

F 1150, 109, 112, 124, 194, 339
Face-to-face contact, 113, 219–20, 276–8, 321
'Fairies', 243, 257
Fairweather, Leslie, 7, 360
Farm foreman, 98, 127, 200
Fences, 26, 28, 71, 73, 120, 168–9, 170, 187, 277–8, 280, 350
Films, 134
Finch, H.A., 362
Finding your feet, see Adaptation to prison (prisoner modes of)
Firebombs, 30, 283, 305
Fires, 32, 289, 296–7, 304
Five-day week
  prisoners, 21, 174, 177, 180
  staff, 22, 116, 176, 180–1, 321, 323
Floodlights, 24, 67, 120, 170, 350
'Folkestone', 88–9, 103
'Folkestone-Worksop Report', 88–90, 94, 97, 174, 342, 363
Food
  complaints about, 290–2, 300
  refusal of, 30, 223, 287, 292
Footer, Gifford, 304, 312, 315, 325–6
  administrative style, 158, 322
  appointment as governor, 30, 284
  death of, 32, 305, 355
  relations with research, 281–2
  segregation unit policy, 285, 316
  summary of regime, 30–2
  see also Governors of Albany
Foreman of works, 81, 87, 91, 104, 126, 155, 169, 200, 262
Fowler, Norman, 13, 361
Fox, Sir Lionel, 6, 7, 23, 167, 361
Functional group working, 121, 181, 321–3

Gambling, 141, 164, 218, 248, 253, 312
Garabedian, Peter, 188, 250, 361
Gartree Prison, 7, 21, 90, 93, 174–5, 297, 306, 352
  similarity to Albany, 75, 80
  see also Two-shift working
Gate officers, duty hours, 128, 170
Gatehouse, 29, 71, 121, 170
General purposes committee, 217
Geophonic alarms, 29, 120, 170, 350
Germain, C., 361
Getting by
  prisoners, 226, 235–6

staff, 226, 261
Gladstone Report, 4, 5, 6, 79, 363
Gleaning *see* Adaptation to prison
(prisoner modes of)
Good Jail Guide, The, 281, 362
Good order and discipline, 5, 139, 224,
284, 289, 309, 339, 344–6
Gould, A. (David), 35, 114
administrative style, 76–9, 96–8, 124,
149, 150, 152, 163, 177, 186,
216, 250, 262, 325
appointment as governor, 25
appointment at headquarters, 27
commissioning the prison, 69–70, 75,
90, 92
departure from Albany, 122, 151–2,
200, 284
relations with research, 51–2, 55–6,
60, 281
segregation unit (Y hall) policy,
172–3
staff and prisoner perceptions of,
161, 271, 273–4
summary of regime, 25–7
see also Governors of Albany
Governor's journal, 113, 120, 138
Governor's orders, 83, 98, 100, 140
Governors of Albany
changes of, 27, 29–30, 32, 105, 142–3,
281, 284, 304, 343
contrasts of style, 156–7, 186
Footer, 289–95, 298; annual reports,
322, 324, 325–6
Gould, 3, 25, 27, 31, 35, 92–4, 126,
142, 339; aims of Albany, 76–9;
annual reports, 69–70, 74–5, 90,
92, 107–8; on training of prisoners,
106–8
Howden, 155, 158, 180, 199, 201,
225, 262, 278; annual reports, 169,
172, 314, 316, 325
problems of succession, 149–57
staff and prisoner views of, 273–4
see also Carnegie, Footer, Gould,
Howden
'Grasses', 243
Grendon Underwood Prison, 7
Guardian, 285, 293, 301, 305, 307
Gymnasium, 72, 170, 217
orderly, 211

Haircutting, 216
Hall Williams, J.E., 16, 361
Halls
cleaners, 211
management of, 103, 106, 108–11

difficulties of, 137–9, 182, 280, 320–1
office, 72
staffing, 55, 86, 109–10, 129
strengthening of, 170
Hansard, 28, 32, 302, 352
'Heavy mob', 257, 267–8, 272, 296
growth of, 319
High mast lighting, 29, 120, 170, 350
High-security prison, *see* Maximum
security prison
High-security-risk prisoners, 10, 19, 29,
186, 194, 278–80, 284, 287, 289, 294,
349–50, 359
distinguished from trouble-makers,
308–9, 326, 344–5
numbers of, 352–3, 358–9
see also Category-A prisoners,
Concentration policy, Dispersal
policy
Hill, Richard, 281, 362
Hindley Borstal, 7, 8
Hobbies rooms, 72, 74, 163
Home leave, 15, 107, 124, 166, 248,
296, 317
board, 86, 182, 227
Home Office, 5, 9, 16, 17, 26, 80, 167,
183–4, 229, 256, 282, 299, 326, 332,
344, 351
relations with POA, 176, 180, 284
relations with PROP, 31, 293, 306–7
relations with research, 35, 41, 50,
60, 62, 331, 355, 357–9
spokesman for, 30, 285–6, 307
and Treasury Working Party, 10, 12,
22, 70, 80
see also Prison Department
Home Office Research Unit, 53, 60,
357–8
Home Secretary, 11, 15, 16, 20, 27, 54,
138, 224, 284, 323, 326
review of dispersal policy, 31, 298,
301–2, 322, 347
Hospital
officers, 105, 128, 200
orderly, 211
Hostages, 32, 304–5
Hostels
board, 77, 86, 182
scheme, 13–14, 107
Howden, R.A.B. (Brian)
administrative style, 150–3, 155–6,
172, 223–4, 250, 321–2
appointment as governor, 27, 149,
200, 284
appointment at headquarters, 29,
284–5

implementation of dispersal policy,
312–13, 315–16, 321–2, 325–6
industrial policy, 174, 175, 179
relations with research, 150, 281
segregation unit policy, 172, 224,
285, 316
staff and prisoner perceptions of,
273–4
summary of regime, 27–9
working party on dispersal, 28, 167–8
see also Governors of Albany
Hull Prison, 21, 292, 352
Humane treatment, 69–70, 75–80, 353
Hunger strikes, 16, 138, 292
Hunt, Lord, 54
Hustlers, 237, 259

Implementing Rule 1, *see* Adaptation to
prison (staff modes of)
Incentive earnings, 9, 22, 26, 136, 175,
177, 178, 180, 186, 266, 276, 300, 319
Incorrigible prisoners, *see* Recalcirtant
prisoners
Induction
of prisoners, 104, 108–10, 165–6, 180,
214–15, 247
of staff, 91, 92–3, 98, 103
Industrial manager, 82, 86–7
in Albany, 98, 119, 127, 155, 176–81,
200
Industrial prison, 9, 21, 88, 340, 341
see also Coldingley, 'Worksop'
Industrial production, 155, 166–7,
173–85, 213, 250, 336–7, 340
Industrial staff, 55, 200–1
Industrial training, 80, 89–90, 101,
113–19, 342
decline of, 155, 173, 336–7
Inmate social system, *see* Inmate
subculture
Inmate subculture, 49, 237–8, 239–40,
241, 246–50, 253, 254–5, 256–7, 310
Inside gardens party, 210–11
Inside works party, 210–11
Inspections, 32, 303
Inspector General, 22
Institute of Criminology, Cambridge, 6,
36, 50
Institute of Education, London, 52
Intake of Prisoners, 91–4, 341
Intercom, 123, 130
Intimidation of prisoners, 347
in Albany, 29, 30, 283, 287,
291, 293–4, 308
Irwin, John, 34, 237–42, 249, 258–60,
333, 361

Isle of Wight, 3, 10, 11, 67, 196, 261,
264, 265, 272, 318

'Jail of fear', 3, 31, 297
Jailing, *see* Adaptation to prison
(prisoner modes of)
Jenkins, Roy, 11, 25
Job specification in Albany, 98, 101,
123–4, 159, 262, 334, 342
Joint, The, 227
Juvenile institutions, 189

Kassebaum, Gene G., 188, 361
King, Roy D., 52, 87, 117, 192, 220–1,
360, 361
Kirkham prison, 150
Kitchen, 133, 213
party, 206–7, 210–11
Klare, Hugh J., 13, 16, 361
'Knitting circle', 83, 98
'Knowing where you stand'
prisoners, 107, 140, 157, 161, 243,
254, 273, 334
staff, 107, 140, 157, 264, 267, 272,
274, 334
Kray gang, 30, 288

Labour allocation board, 86, 182
see also Allocation of prisoners
Labour control unit (LCU), 178, 180,
181, 276
Letters, 240–1, 259, 285
censorship of, 317
Leicester Prison, 10, 15
Library, 72
clerk, 210–11
curtailment of access, 299
Life sentence prisoners, 9, 24, 70, 125,
194–5, 227, 287, 291, 315, 353
Light textiles shop, 116–18, 135, 209,
212, 275
Liverpool Prison, 297
Local prisons, 7, 23, 35
prisoner experience of, 241, 253, 258,
313
staff experience of, 202, 265, 266,
269, 272, 279
strong cells in, 302, 353
Locking and unlocking, 218–20
see also ELSA system
Long Lartin Prison, 21, 25, 352
Long-term prisoners, 8–10, 20, 48, 68,
227, 346
in Albany, 23, 30, 125, 194–5, 285–6,
304, 310, 314; mixing with short-term
prisoners, 125, 137, 278–80, 315, 348;

privileges, 137, 312, 315, 348
regime for, 15, 16, 18, 20, 345;
authors' proposals, 347–8, 353;
see also Radzinowicz Report
Lopeź-Rey, M., 361

McCabe, Patrick M., 188, 360
McClintock, F.H., 35, 36, 44, 48–51,
109, 360
McConville, S., 361
'Mafia' groups, 30, 31, 288, 294, 307–9
Maidstone Prison, 38, 117, 297
Maintenance staff, 200
Making a career, *see* Adaptation to
prison (staff modes of)
Making out
prisoners, 226, 235–6, 244, 310
staff, 226, 261
Management consultants, 12, 22, 95
Management of prisons, 4–6, 8, 21,
69–70, 75–90
review of, 21–2, 342
Management services in prisons, report
on, 10, 12, 80, 363
Management structure
in Albany, 97–106, 331; effects of
industrial priority, 176, 181–2; *see
also* Central management, Middle
management
types of, 80–1, 88–90
Manpower control teams, 22, 303, 323
March, James G., 360, 361
Marking time, *see* Adaptation to prison
(staff modes of)
Martin, J.P., 51, 52
Mathiesen, Thomas, 34, 361
Matza, David, 45, 361
Mayhew, Henry, 81, 361
Maximum security conditions, 19, 21,
25
Maximum-security prison, 8, 10–11,
14–16, 18–20, 23–5, 70–2
see also Alvington, Dispersal prisons,
Special security wings, Vectis
Medical officer, 81, 85, 87, 98, 105–6,
126, 155, 176, 200, 225
contact with prisoners, 214–15, 239,
276
Mental hospitals, 188
Messing committee, 217
Middle management, 100, 106, 118
consolidation of, 157–63, 189
problems of, 138, 143, 182, 262,
320–1
see also Development of industries
meeting, Principal officers,

Progress meeting
Military, used at Durham prison, 20, 24
294
Military, used at Durham prison, 20,24
Ministry of Public Buildings and
Works, 20, 24, 27
Mitchell, Frank, abscondsion of, 13
Moos, Rudolph, 189, 361
Morgan, Rodney, 54, 192, 361
Morris, Pauline, 35–6, 38–44, 48–50,
55, 81, 124, 203, 218, 228–9, 271, 362
Morris, Terence, 16, 33–44, 48–50, 55,
81, 124, 188, 202–3, 218, 228–9, 267,
271, 361, 362
Mountbatten, Lord, 12–14, 23, 67, 70,
72, 82, 89, 172, 344, 346, 349, 351–2,
359, 362
appointment to enquire into escapes,
11, 17, 25
speech at York, 14, 15
visit to Albany, 25, 27, 73, 170
Mountbatten Report, 25, 363
authors' defence of, 13–14, 17–21
compared with Radzinowicz Report,
17–21
criticisms of, 12–13
effects of, 14
recommendations, 11–16, 68, 119
Movement of prisoners, restrictions on,
216–17
NADPAS, 81
National Council for Civil Liberties, 30,
285, 317
Needle trades, 68, 76, 114, 118
Negative detachment, *see* Adaptation to
prison (staff modes of)
New Hall Camp, 5–6
News, 29, 283
Night patrol, 98, 130, 304
Norman, Frank, 34, 362
'Norwich system', 35
Notes on Albany Prison, Some, 312,
315, 316, 321, 326
'Nutters', 243, 257

Observation centres, 7
Observation towers, 16
Officer trade assistants, 126, 200–1
Officers' mess, 72, 133, 213, 272
party, 206–7, 210, 211; prisoners'
attitudes towards, 207
Officer Training School, 203–4, 264
Open prisons, 5–7, 13, 202, 269
Opportunism, *see* Adaptation to prison
(prisoner modes of)
Organization and methods, 10, 12, 22,

70, 80, 90
Outside gardens party, 210
Outside working parties, 13, 14
Outside works party, 210–11
Oversby, Clive, 281, 362
Overtime, 8, 265, 272, 284, 303
  ban on, 294, 303
Oxford Prison, 125

PABX, 170
Padre's hour, 214
Pains of imprisonment, 236, 241
Parker, Tony, 34, 362
Parkhurst Prison, 21, 26, 91, 114, 141,
  171, 194, 297, 321, 352
  ex-prisoners in Albany, 26, 29, 93,
    125, 137–9
  hospital, 105, 124
  riot at, 29, 282, 286, 293, 306
  special security wing, 10, 15
'Parkhurst trial', 282, 286
Parole, 77, 107, 108, 166, 227, 317, 399
Parole Board, 53, 54, 198
Paterson, Alexander, 5, 7, 23, 167, 335
Pay
  of prison officers, 265, 284, 289, 295,
    303
  of prisoners, 208–11, 245, 340
  see also Incentive earnings
Penal Practice in a Changing Society,
  6–8, 10, 22, 76, 363
Pentonville Prison, 33, 81, 202–4, 218,
  228–9, 267, 292
  see also Research
People in Prison, 22, 53, 79, 338, 363
Perimeter defence force, 55, 120–1, 171
Perquisites, 207–13
Perrow, Charles, 189, 362
Personal possessions, 212–13
  radios, 130, 212
  unauthorized, 212–13, 218,
    239–40, 296–8
Personal responsibility, 216, 250, 262
Peterhead Prison, 297
Peterson, A.W., 7, 8, 71, 80, 353, 362
Petitions, 138, 256, 292, 317
Physical education, 163, 175, 178, 276
  instructor, 163
Picketing, 32, 297, 305
Political suppression, 336
Portsmouth News, 289
Positive science, 7
Pre-release, 165–6
Preventive detention, 6, 244
Principal officers, 55, 85, 91–3, 98,
  102–3, 106, 108, 126, 199, 200, 268,

272, 290, 342
  anxieties of, 111, 138, 143, 159, 163
  duty hours, 128, 182, 222, 320–2
  as hall managers, 109–11, 158, 160–3,
    166, 187, 321–2
  meeting, 111, 158–63, 222–3, 320–2
  review boards, 166
Principal psychologist, 93, 98,
  126, 200
  contact with prisoners, 215
  role of, 55, 102, 104, 110–11, 155, 158
Prison Commission, 4, 8–9, 23, 24, 35,
  45, 76, 80, 342
Prison Department, 68, 181, 303, 323
  criticisms of administration, 10,
    11–12, 82, 340–2
  headquarters and regional
    organization, 9, 10, 12, 22, 174
  high security risk prisoners, 309, 359
  industrial policy, 155, 167, 174–5,
    178, 180, 182, 358
  relations with PROP, 293, 307
  relations with research, 60, 64, 281,
    355–6
  security policy, 10, 12, 13, 14, 16, 24
  social training policy, 53, 78, 339–40
  see also Administration of prisons,
    Home Office
Prison governors, 226
  methods of administration, 5, 82–3
  role of, 12, 83
  see also Governors of Albany
Prison industries, 9, 10, 21, 22,
  85–7, 113
  see also Coldingley Prison, Industrial
    prison, Industrial production,
    Industrial training, 'Worksop'
Prison medical service, 358
Prison officers
  in Albany, 98, 108, 120–1, 126,
    199–200, 264, 268, 271–3, 281; duty
    hours, 128, 181; inexperience of,
    137, 202, 323; involvement in
    social training, 150; probation of,
    127, 202, 263–5, 271–2, 323;
    restraint of, 296, 304; see also Case
    officers
  arming of, 15–16
  career structure, 15
  role of, 80, 82, 85, 338–40; authors'
    proposals, 340, 343
Prison Officers' Association (POA) 12,
  16, 30–2, 80, 115–16, 120, 175, 181,
  184, 279, 283, 293, 333
  Albany branch, 29–30, 55, 60, 159,
    283–4, 294–5, 299, 355

general secretary, 288–9, 307–8
national executive, 31, 176, 180,
    294–5, 303
policy on discipline offences, 294, 301
Prison Officers' Magazine, 36
Prison population
    in Albany: 1968, 124–6; 1969, 193–9;
        1971, 310–12, 326
    growth of, 10, 13, 23
Prison regimes, *see* Regimes
Prison research, *see* Research
Prison Rules, The, 5, 363
    Rule 1, 5, 79, 82, 173, 177, 179,
        182–3, 188, 229, 268, 269, 270, 272;
        re-writing of, 335–40
    Rule 6, 5
    Rule 8, 138
    Rule 43, 32, 224–5; 'own protection',
        29, 141, 224, 283, 285, 291–2,
        308–9; 'subversives', 30, 130, 224,
        284–5, 287, 289, 293, 295, 298, 305,
        308, 316–17, 325, 346, 348
    Rule 45, 290
    Rule 47, 308
    Rule 50, 224
    Rule 51, 224
    Rule 52, 224
Prison service, changes in, 4–23
Prison Service Journal, 27, 123
Prisoners
    anxieties of, 107, 140, 241
    attitudes to Albany, 137–45, 161–2,
        232–5, 241–58
    sample: attitudes to prisoners, 236,
        243, 244; attitudes to staff, 229–30,
        242–3, 244, 251, 253;
        characteristics of, 193, 195–9,
        241–61 *passim*; contact with hall
        staff, 220–2; contact with
        treatment staff, 214–16, 239,
        251–2, 253; evaluation of Albany,
        232–5, 241–58; evaluation of core
        regime, 242–3, 250, 258, 333;
        evaluation of halls, 223–4;
        evaluation of jobs, 211–12;
        reactions to changes in Albany,
        273–80; selection of, 195
Prisoners' union, *see* Protection of the
    Rights of Prisoners
Prisonization, 188
Prisons board, 26, 177, 179, 183, 184
Probation and after-care service, 82
Professional thieves, 237–8, 255, 258,
    259, 314
Progress meeting, 118–19
Protection of the Rights of Prisoners

(PROP), 16, 30–1, 292–3, 294, 297,
    306–7, 333
Provocation
    by prisoners, 243, 288, 290, 304
    by staff, 31, 32, 288, 290, 296, 304;
        lack of, 218
Psychologists, 81, 85, 87
    in Albany, 98, 104, 126, 200; contact
        with prisoners, 132, 133, 214–15,
        239, 251
Psychology department, 86, 200,
    286, 326
    effects of single shift working, 175,
        178
Psychotherapist, 127, 200, 251
Punishment, 336, 337
    see also Adjudications
Punishment cells, 72, 224–5
    see also Segregation units, Y hall

Quarters, roads and yards
    party, 210
'Queers', 243
Quiet room, 72, 216–17

Radical Alternatives to Prison, 16, 285
Radzinowicz, Sir Leon, 15, 23, 50, 363
    letter to Home Secretary, 17, 20, 26
Radzinowicz Report, 21, 27, 28, 167–8,
    363
    authors' critique of, 17–21, 345–6,
        349–52
    compared with Mountbatten Report,
        17–21
    recommendations, 16, 89, 121, 151,
        171, 175, 184–5, 325
Radzinowicz sub-committee, 15–16, 17,
    25, 68, 359
    visit to Albany, 27
    see also Radzinowicz Report
Raynes, Norma V., 361
Recalcitrant prisoners, 10, 16, 18–19,
    351
Reception, 72, 214
Recidivists, 3, 7, 23, 25, 124, 194, 310,
    346
Record keeping, 86, 88, 112, 178
Recreational activities, 130–4, 163, 245,
    275
Reform, 79, 226, 336
Regimes
    in Albany, 206–25, 320, 331; core
        elements of, 216–24, 235, 262, 333;
        restricted, 31–2
    brutalizing, 4
    characterization of, 187–93

comparative study of, 53, 187, 281, 355
defined, 190
diversification of, 6, 53, 338
for long term prisoners, 15, 16, 18, 20, 25, 68, 184–5, 306, 325–6, 345, 347–9, 353; *see also* Radzinowicz Report
Prison Regimes Project, 53
psychotherapeutic, 7
Rehabilitation, 6, 13–14, 79, 150, 226, 286, 318, 336
Remand centres, 7, 202
Report of the Commissioners of Prisons for 1960, 23, 363
Report of the Commissioners of Prisons and Directors of Convict Prisons 1911–12, 4, 363
Report on the Work of Prison Department
1968, 14, 363
1969, 14, 363
1970, 22, 363
1972, 22, 363
1973, 22, 363
1975, 22, 363
1976, 21, 363
Research, 33–64
in Albany conduct of, 27, 51–63, 96–7, 122; funding, 52, 357; genesis of, 51–2; lessons from, 60, 62–3, 331–53; methods, 62–3, 186–93, 231, 235–6, 238–41, 261, 263, 282, 320; objectives, 51, 54, 56; reactions to, 332, 355–9; relations with prisoners, 58, 63, 222, 236, 257, 282, 331; relations with staff, 58, 63, 222, 263, 282, 324, 331; role of research workers, 52–5; undertakings given, 59–60, 331, 355; writing-up, 63–4, 281, 332, 355, 357–8
in Bristol Prison, 34–6, 44–5
in Dover Borstal, 35–6, 48–51
in Durham Prison, 34–6, 44, 45–8
in Pentonville Prison, 33, 35–44, 124, 202–4; funding, 35, 41; independence of, 35, 36; introduction of, 38–40; legacies of, 36–7, 56; lessons from, 35, 36, 38, 43–4, 55, 58, 62; relations with prisoners, 38, 40–2; relations with staff, 36–8, 40, 42–3
roles, 33, 36–63; classified, 36
Rewards and punishments, review of, 298, 302

Richardson gang, 141
Rights of prisoners, 306–7, 348
see also Protection of the Rights of Prisoners
Riots
at Albany, 31, 296–9, 326; predicted, 280, 287
at Parkhurst, 29, 282, 286, 293, 306
Risley Remand Centre, 7, 32, 304
Roof-top protests, 285, 297
Royal Commission on the Penal System, 6, 363
Ruggles-Brise, Sir Evelyn, 4
Rules, in Albany, 137–9
inconsistencies, 139, 263–6, 272, 320
interpretation of, 216, 222, 235, 242, 244, 247, 262, 296

Sabotage, 277
Safe custody, 70, 75, 79, 336, 338, 340
St Mary's Hospital, 256
St Patrick's Day disturbance, 290–1, 304, 320
Schrag, Clarence, 188, 362
Schwartz, Morris, S., 188, 362
Scope for Management Services in Prisons, The, 10, 12, 80, 363
Searching of prison, 31, 133, 283, 295–9, 305
Secondary comfort indulgence, *see* Adaptation to prison (prisoner modes of and staff modes of)
Security
in Albany; committee, 102, 182; control room, 27, 28, 74, 120–1, 168, 171, 304, 321; costs of, 352; excessive nature of, 171–2, 277–8, 350; meetings 170; prisoner views of, 142, 171–2, 277; security officer, 102, 119–20; staff views of, 277–9; upgrading of, 3, 25–32, 67, 119–21, 155, 166, 167–73, 250, 281, 302, 350; weaknesses of, 25, 72–3, 124, 142
coefficient of, 16, 20, 310, 338
developments in prison service, 8–23 *passim*, 25, 32, 71–3, 350–4
Segregation units, 16, 19, 32, 325, 346–7, 353
in Albany; alleged beatings in, 257, 289; construction, 28, 29, 168, 171–2; disturbances in, 30, 31, 287, 289, 290, 300–1; orderly, 211; regime, 172–3, 224–5, 326; strengthening of, 302; use of, 30–2, 168, 284–7, 289, 292, 298–300, 316
Senior officers, 92–3, 110, 127, 199,

200, 268, 272, 274,
responsibilities in halls, 182, 222,
  321–2
Sex offenders, 261, 317
Shils, E., 362
Short-term prisoners, 7, 125, 137,
  194–5, 338
  mixing with long-term prisoners, 125,
    137, 278–80, 315, 348
  separation from long-term prisoners,
    303
Sick bay, 105
Sick, reporting, 135, 214–15, 319
Single shift working, 28, 175, 181, 186,
  204, 299, 343
  effects of change-over, 175–6, 181–2,
    262, 275–6, 321–2
  4½ day week proposal, 178–9, 182–4
  working party, 175–81
Slopping out, 129, 131, 132, 218–19,
  295, 298
Social distance between staff and
  prisoners, 220–2, 229, 235, 267
Sociology of prisons, 18, 332–5, 349
Solitary confinement, 30, 285–6, 347
Soskice, Frank, 20, 24
Southampton University, 51, 52, 78,
  150
Southern Evening Echo, 289
Special security prison, *see* Maximum
  security prison
Special security wings, 10, 15, 21, 29,
  279, 282, 306, 315, 347
Specialist staff, *see* Treatment staff
Spending time, 228, 281, 334
Sports, 132–4, 217, 245
Square john, 238, 245, 257
Staff
  adaptations to prison, *see* Adaptation
    to prison (staff modes of)
  attitudes; to Albany, 142, 223–4,
    232–5, 262–73; to prisoners,
    229–30, 257, 263
  college, 10, 91, 355
  culture, 267–8
  establishments, 12, 22, 303, 341–2; in
    Albany, 232–5, 262–73; reactions
  morale, 122–4, 182, 186, 274, 279,
    294–5, 322, 347
  promotion, 201, 261, 270, 274
  quarters, 74–5, 265, 318
  ratios, 348, 353
  recruitment, 69–70, 80, 203, 284, 303,
    323
  relationships; with other staff, 176–7,
    263–4, 269, 271; with prisoners, 3,

29, 35, 125, 137, 216, 221–2, 235,
  262, 268, 283; deterioration of, 3,
  29, 30, 284
sample: characteristics of, 201–4,
  263–73 *passim*; evaluation of
  Albany, 232–5, 262–73; reactions
  to changes in Albany, 273–9;
  selection, 200–1
training, 8, 11, 83, 92–3, 98, 103–4,
  107, 111, 159, 203–4, 264; decline
  of, 300, 316, 318, 323–4
Stalker, G.M., 88, 360
Standard category-A regime, 184, 186,
  204–25, 318, 343
Stanton, Alfred H., 188, 362
State raised youths, 238, 240–1, 245,
  248, 251, 253, 258–9, 311–15
Steward, 81, 85
Stoke Heath Borstal, 7–8
Stonham, Lord, 3, 26, 67–8, 69, 115,
  117, 173, 179, 183
Storemen, 98, 127, 200, 211
Street, David, 34, 189, 362
Strike, by prisoners, 31, 293–4, 307
*Structure of Responsibilities in Training
  Prisons*, 81, 88, 363
  see also 'Folkestone-Worksop
    Report'
Subversive-enforcement quotient,
  347–8, 350, 353
Subversive officers, 301
Subversive prisoners, 30–2, 224, 260,
  284–7, 292–5, 298, 300–5, 308–9,
  316–17, 325–6, 346–8
  see also Prison Rules, Rule 43
Supervision of prisoners, 8, 9
  in Albany, 69, 74, 216–17, 235,
    242–3, 244, 247, 262, 268, 300, 310;
  difficulties of, 74, 133, 217, 262–3,
    265, 310
Supper, difficulties with, 133, 159–60,
  223
Swimming pool, 24–5
Swinfen Hall Prison, 301
Sykes, Gresham M., 34, 36, 188, 228,
  236, 362

Tailoring shop, 72, 116–17, 180, 208,
  211–12, 234, 247, 319
Tannoy, 130
Tattoos, 252
Tavistock Institute of Human
  Relations, 35, 45
Taylor, I., 13, 362
Taylor, Laurie, 13, 34–6, 44–8, 227–8,
  230, 238, 258–9, 314, 317, 333, 360

Teachers, 127, 134, 200
Television committees, 217
Televisual surveillance, 10, 24, 29, 120, 170, 277, 350
'Telex', 9, 22
Temporary officers, 126, 200
Tension, 32, 277, 283, 288, 291, 292, 304
  see also Aggro, Confrontations
Theft, among prisoners, 141, 213, 243, 248
'Therapeutic anxiety', 106–9, 143, 156, 163, 250, 266, 339
Therapeutic community, 188
Thief culture, 237
Thomas, J.E., 16, 362
Times, The, 16, 26, 93, 294, 295, 296, 297, 298, 307
Tizard, Jack, 361
'Top men', 255, 259, 266, 271, 314, 316–17
Top-security prison, *see* Maximum-security prison
Top-security prisoners, *see* High-security-risk prisoners
Towndrow, E.A., 90, 92, 98, 362
Trade staff, 55, 98, 126–7, 200–1
Tradition, lack of, 324, 343
Train robbers, 13, 24, 229
Training and 'fall-out' shop, 136, 209, 211–12
Training of prisoners, *see* Treatment and training of prisoners
Training prisons, 245, 249–51, 253, 258, 265, 269, 272–3, 313, 337–8
Transfer of prisoners, 19, 287, 291, 298, 317, 339, 353
Trawl notice, 80, 266
Treasury, 10, 12, 22, 24, 80
Treatment and training of prisoners
  compatability with industrial production, 89–90, 173–85 *passim*, 276, 342
  compatability with security, 14, 21
  demise in Albany, 155, 157–67, 187, 213, 336–7
  development in Albany, 3, 75–80, 106–19
  evolution within prison service, 5–6, 8–9
  future of, 335–40
  operation in Albany, 131–6, 143
  prisoner expectations, 226, 249, 286
  responsibility for, 101, 104, 150
  staff implementation, 264, 268–9, 286–7, 318

  see also Industrial training, Prison Rules, Rehabilitation, Rule 1
Treatment orientation, 188–9
Treatment staff, 48, 50, 87, 121, 200–1, 229
Trenching party, 210
Trenton Prison, 36, 228–9, 347
Two shift working
  in Albany: abandonment of, 173–85, 216, 250, 275, 337, 343; attitude of Prison Department, 117, 174–5, 182–5, 344, 358; compatability with treatment and training, 68, 80, 115, 173; operation of, 26, 114–19, 129–36, 187, 299; staff and prisoner attitudes, 135–6, 174, 275–6
  in Gartree, 27, 115, 174, 184–5, 344
  'unsuitability' for long-term prisoners, 27, 175, 184–5, 344
Tutor organizer, 81, 88, 98, 105–6, 126, 134, 155, 176, 200

UHF radios, 9, 120–1, 128, 171, 350
UN-WHO seminar, 7
Uncertain negative retreat, *see* Adaptation to prison (prisoner modes of)
Uncertain withdrawal, *see* Adaptation to prison (staff modes of)

Vectis Prison, 11, 15, 25, 26, 68, 72, 350, 352
  comparison with Albany, 172, 350
  see also Alvington Prison, Special security prison
Vehicle access, 25, 73, 170
Victimization, alleged, 286
Vinter, Robert D., 189, 362
Violence, 30, 141, 248, 287–90, 294, 304–5, 314
  see also Arson, Disturbances, Fires, Intimidation, 'Mafia', Subversive prisoners, Young 'toughs'
Visits, 240–1, 259, 275–6
  accommodation, 71
Vocational training, 114, 173, 336

Wakefield Prison, 21, 302, 352
Wall, at Albany, 277, 302, 358
Walton, P., 362
Wandsworth Prison, 14, 26, 141, 161, 172, 241, 243–5, 247, 266, 298, 313
  ex-prisoners in Albany, 26, 93, 125, 137, 144
War Against Crime, The, 6, 363

Ward, David, 361
Weber, Max, 49, 362
Welfare department, 74, 86, 104, 162
  effects of single-shift working, 175,
    178, 181–2, 262, 275–6
Welfare officers, 81, 85, 87, 93, 98, 126,
    200, 340
  attitudes to single-shift working, 262
  contact with prisoners, 132–3, 135,
    214–15, 239, 251, 253
  role of, 104–5
  senior, 93, 104–5, 127, 155, 177, 200,
    215
West, D.J., 345
Wheeler, Stanton, 34, 188, 229, 250,
    362
Whitley Council, 80
Williams, Robin, 54
Wilner, Daniel, 361
Wilson, Charles, escape of, 13, 25
Winchester, Prison, 125
Wives
  of prison officers, 32, 297, 305
  of prisoners, 32, 297, 304
Work
  parties, 114, 129, 206–7, 210–11, 213
  refusal to, 135, 290–2
  situation: prisoners, 207–12, 234;
    staff, 227–30, 234, 261–3, 265–6,
    272, 334
  shortages of, 117–18, 174

Work-to-rule, 31, 284, 294, 295, 299,
    304
Working-out, 77, 107
Works department, 75, 104, 169, 200
Workshops
  activities in, 173, 208–9
  carrying party, 210
  closure of, 117, 299, 319
  instructors, 119; civilian, 86, 119,
    127, 200–1, 305; officer, 86, 126,
    200–1; shortages of, 116–17, 174
  interruptions, 135, 175, 178, 180, 276
  pace of work, 135, 175, 208–9
  strengthening of, 170, 350
  see also Carpentry shops, Cutting
    shop, Light textiles shop, Tailoring
    shop, Training and 'fall-out' shop
'Worksop', 88–9, 101
  see also Coldingley Prison,
    Industrial Prison
Work-study, 9, 136, 177, 180, 186, 276
Wormwood Scrubs Prison, 11, 21, 25,
    194, 302, 352

Y hall, 72, 141, 224–5, 171
  board room, 154, 158
  see also Segregation units
York, 14, 15
Young, J., 362
Young 'toughs', 248, 294–5, 308, 314

For Product Safety Concerns and Information please contact our EU
representative GPSR@taylorandfrancis.com
Taylor & Francis Verlag GmbH, Kaufingerstraße 24, 80331 München, Germany

9 781032 562667